Britain, the Soviet Union ar

Also by Sir Curtis Keeble

BRITAIN AND THE SOVIET UNION, 1917–89
MACMILLAN AND THE SOVIET UNION
THE SOVIET STATE: The Domestic Roots of Soviet Foreign Policy (*editor*)

Britain, the Soviet Union and Russia

Sir Curtis Keeble

New Edition

This edition published in Great Britain 2000 by
MACMILLAN PRESS LTD
Houndmills, Basingstoke, Hampshire RG21 6XS and London
Companies and representatives throughout the world

A catalogue record for this book is available from the British Library.

ISBN 0-333-71956-5 hardcover
ISBN 0-333-71957-3 paperback

 This edition published in the United States of America 2000 by
ST. MARTIN'S PRESS, LLC,
Scholarly and Reference Division,
175 Fifth Avenue, New York, N.Y. 10010

ISBN 0-312-23134-2

Library of Congress Cataloging-in-Publication Data
Keeble, Curtis.
Britain, the Soviet Union, and Russia / Sir Curtis Keeble. — 2nd ed.
p. cm.
Rev. ed. of: Britain and the Soviet Union, 1917–1989. 1990.
Includes bibliographical references (p.) and index.
ISBN 0-312-23134-2 (cloth)
1. Great Britain—Foreign relations—Soviet Union. 2. Soviet Union—Foreign relations—Great Britain. 3. Great Britain—Foreign relations—20th century. 4. Great Britain—Foreign relations—Russia. 5. Russia—Foreign relations—Great Britain. I. Keeble, Curtis. Britain and the Soviet Union, 1917–1989. II. Title.
DA47.65 .K44   2000
327.41047—dc21   99–054885

© Sir Curtis Keeble 1990, 2000

First edition (*Britain and the Soviet Union, 1917–89*) 1990
Second edition (*Britain, the Soviet Union and Russia*) 2000

All rights reserved. No reproduction, copy or transmission of this publication may be made without written permission.

No paragraph of this publication may be reproduced, copied or transmitted save with written permission or in accordance with the provisions of the Copyright, Designs and Patents Act 1988, or under the terms of any licence permitting limited copying issued by the Copyright Licensing Agency, 90 Tottenham Court Road, London W1P 0LP.

Any person who does any unauthorised act in relation to this publication may be liable to criminal prosecution and civil claims for damages.

The author has asserted his right to be identified as the author of this work in accordance with the Copyright, Designs and Patents Act 1988.

This book is printed on paper suitable for recycling and made from fully managed and sustained forest sources.

10 9 8 7 6 5 4 3 2 1
09 08 07 06 05 04 03 02 01 00

Printed and bound in Great Britain by
Antony Rowe Ltd, Chippenham, Wiltshire

To Margaret and all our colleagues in the Moscow Embassy from 1978 to 1982

Contents

List of Plates	viii
List of Maps	ix
Preface	xi
Acknowledgements	xvi
Introduction: Britain and Imperial Russia	1
1 Response to Revolution	19
2 Intervention	30
3 Facing the Facts	67
4 Working Relations	84
5 Relations Broken and Resumed	102
6 The Approach to War	120
7 Alliance	159
8 Post-war Confrontation	206
9 The Khrushchev Years	237
10 Between the Europeans and the Superpowers	265
11 The End of Confrontation	302
12 A New Russia	321
Appendixes	
1 Chronology of Relations	349
2 The British, Soviet and Russian Leadership, 1917–99	360
3 British, Soviet and Russian Diplomatic Representatives, 1917–99	363
Notes	365
Index	384

List of Plates

1. The British landing in Vladivostok (1918)
2. Propaganda leaflet (1918–19)
3. Chicherin and Litvinov at Genoa (1922)
4. Election poster (1924)
5. Police raid Soviet Commercial Offices (May 1927)
6. Departure of the Soviet Chargé (1927)
7. Eden leaves for Moscow (1935)
8. Stalin, Molotov and Ribbentrop celebrate signature of Non-Aggression Treaty (August 1939)
9. Stalin, Truman and Churchill at Potsdam (1945)
10. A Russian girl sniper in London (1942)
11. Hurricanes at Murmansk (January 1942)
12. A Ministry of Information wartime poster
13. Eden, Bidault and Dulles prepare for the Berlin Conference (1954)
14. Eden, Bulganin and Khrushchev signing the official communiqué at the Foreign Office (April 1956)
15. Soviet forces in Hungary (November 1956)
16. Macmillan, Selwyn Lloyd, Khrushchev and Gromyko in Moscow (February 1959)
17. Curtis Keeble and his wife in the Moscow Embassy
18. Curtis Keeble's farewell to Moscow (1982)
19. Geoffrey Howe and Eduard Shevardnadze signing the Memorandum of Understanding in Moscow (1987)
20. Mrs Thatcher and Mikhail Gorbachev in the Kremlin
21. The new British Embassy in Moscow
22. President Yeltsin and Queen Elizabeth II
23. President Putin of Russia meets Tony Blair

List of Maps

1 Russia and neighbouring states after 1991   xvii
2 From Brest-Litovsk to Stalingrad   35
3 The Polish–Soviet frontier   76
4 European battlefronts, January–May 1945   192

Preface

This book was first written in the dying days of the Soviet Union under the title *Britain and the Soviet Union 1917–89*. Its purpose was to analyse the policies which successive British Governments pursued towards the former Soviet Union and to argue that the accession of Mikhail Gorbachev offered the possibility of replacing a relationship based on confrontation of doctrine and armed might with one based more on the search for areas of common interest. Subsequent events established the validity of that argument but proved false two of the assumptions which, in common with many observers of the Soviet scene, I had made. In my last despatch from Moscow in 1982 I wrote that the Soviet Union needed something closer to revolution than to reform. When I came to write the book, I found it hard to believe that this would happen. I assumed that, although we might be witnessing the terminal stage of old-style Soviet socialism and of the Soviet imperial structure in Eastern Europe, the Soviet Union would remain in being and the Communist Party would continue for some years more to control its government. Now, the years of Soviet power fall back into the long, anguished history of the suffering Russian people a new Russian Federation struggles to establish a new identity, and an infirm Boris Yeltsin makes way for a new President, it is appropriate to take stock again.

For the greater part of the twentieth century the relationship between the Soviet Union and the Western democracies coloured, even if it did not determine, the whole structure of international relations. It raised issues which plagued the statesmen of the Western democracies for seven decades. In the conduct of British foreign policy, it had a unique quality and a unique potential for good or ill. Mishandled, it could have brought nuclear catastrophe. In the event, despite all the muddle, all the doubts and all the controversy, there emerged in the West a consistency of purpose which eventually brought the years of confrontation to a peaceful end.

In the years between the two world wars, the new Soviet state was the unknown factor. Lloyd George did his best to draw her into the community of nations, but those who governed Britain throughout most of the 1920s and 1930s preferred not to deal with her. When, too late, they tried to deal, they found their prejudice confirmed by experience.

Among the British people, some of us viewed her with hope, some with apprehension, some with detestation, some with scorn, most with perplexity and many with the sadness which comes at the sight of the corruption of brave ideals. Some few chose treason. All had their reasons, for the Soviet state could show many faces. Might a more determined effort to establish a sound relationship in those years have lessened the suffering which Europe had to bear? The answer will never be certain. It is hard to accept that the effort should not have been made. It is harder to believe that it could have succeeded.

My own first contact with the reality of Soviet power came as the wartime alliance was disintegrating into the post-war confrontation. Experience in the repatriation of British and Soviet prisoners of war revealed in stark clarity those qualities of the Russian character and the Soviet system which, in peace and in war, made the conduct of relations such a frustrating task. I came to grips with the reality of the Iron Curtain in West Berlin in the early 1950s and in East Berlin twenty years later, but when I was appointed to Moscow in 1978 it was in a spirit of some optimism about the future course of British–Soviet relations. I was in fact to experience the full cycle as we moved from that false dawn of detente into the chill of the Scharansky and Orlov trials, the invasion of Afghanistan, the Western counter-measures and the Polish crisis. Throughout that period, as through the decades which preceded it, the West was confronted with essentially the same dilemma. The Soviet Union proclaimed a doctrine which required the eventual collapse of society as it was structured in the Western democracies and it implemented policies which in many respects were designed to achieve that result. Within its own borders it pursued practices which were abhorrent to Western standards of individual liberty. Outside them it demonstrated a readiness to use military force and political subversion to sustain and extend its imperial frontier. The 'evil empire' epithet evoked a certain resonance in the West and a Soviet response which, if less memorable, was no more amiable. Yet the realities of superpower weaponry required that both the Soviet Union and the Western powers should contain their conflict at a level which excluded the risk of armed conflict between them and the realities of national interest indicated a greater need for cooperation than for confrontation. So it was unsurprising that our relationship should have been characterised by a continual oscillation. Each swing represented a change in the balance between the search for a basis of mutual interest, be it only the basic interest of self-preservation, and the profound conflict of ideology and power. Its course ran through many of the critical episodes of twentieth-century European history, episodes where it was identifiable and relevant, but only occasionally dominant. By the end of the 1970s there was still much of the old tension between the West and the Soviet Union and at the same time a recognition of the need for restraint in the deployment of national power. What was missing was still the qualitative change which would permit the construction of the sounder and more durable relationship which had eluded generations of Western statesmen.

It was the accession to power of Mikhail Gorbachev which offered the prospect of that qualitative change. After the internal stagnation and external confrontation which had marked the rule of Brezhnev and his two short-lived successors, there followed years of swift and exhilarating change as the basis was laid for the development of free societies in Eastern Europe and within the Soviet Union until, in 1991, British diplomacy was able to begin the task of constructing a new relationship with a new Russia. Now, as the new century opens and the Russian people endure the privations of a crude and corrupt version of market capitalism, they are not alone in questioning the wisdom of the Western advisers who urged them into it.

Soviet theorists used to claim that the October Revolution brought with it a wholly new concept of foreign policy based on the worldwide struggle between socialism and capitalism. Yet the legacy of Russia's imperial past could not be wholly thrown off. Nor can those who are shaping the course of the new Russian Federation ignore the legacy of the Soviet years. It is present in the millions of Russians who, happy to escape the tyranny of the KGB, still yearn for the comfortable certainties of the barrack hut which was the old Soviet state. It is present in the restless armed forces, hungry, humiliated, resentful and despondent. It is present in the rusting nuclear arsenal. It is present in a vocal body of Communist and nationalist politicians. It is present in a generation of collective farm managers and factory foremen. It is present in the determination of once suppressed states in Central and Eastern Europe to align themselves with the West and in the complexity of relations with former Soviet Republics from Latvia to Kazakhstan. Like the massive stone blocks of some ancient ruined temple, like the fallen statues of fallen Soviet leaders, the building blocks of Soviet Communism are strewn across the plains and forests of Russia. Beneath them lie the ancient instincts, the lasting interests, the physical resources and the human qualities of the peoples of Russia.

The men and women who have the task of building the new Russia have borrowed Western designs, just as the Italian architects of the

Kremlin did in the sixteenth century. What they are building is new, but it is being built by Russians, using unfamiliar new tools to shape old materials. It will be a new architecture, but it will be as Russian as Ivan the Great's Kremlin. The rigid structures of the Soviet state have been torn down. For all the flaws in the materials, all the intractability of the problems, all the sketchiness of the plans, the Russian people had – perhaps still have – the opportunity, if the vision, the will and skill are there, to carry through a project comparable in scope to the construction of the United States. But they build on poor foundations and as one surveys the sorry muddle of today's Russia, the dream may seem fanciful. What emerges may be neither magnificent nor monstrous but, whatever it is, it will, for better or worse, form a significant element in the pattern of international relations of the twenty-first century.

The study of Russia herself is for others to undertake. What I have tried to do, as one whose career has been devoted to the untidy and often equivocal profession of diplomacy, who can lay no claim to being a historian, and who has become ever more aware of the gaps in his knowledge is to plot the course of a unique segment of British diplomacy. The British relationship with the former Soviet Union still constitutes the main body of the present edition. I have slightly expanded the very brief consideration of the British relationship with Tsarist Russia and have carried the study forward to look into the conduct of relations with the Russian Federation. These sections, however, constitute no more than a preamble and a postscript to the main theme. I have continued to rely essentially on the British documents, including those recently released, and I am conscious that a Russian observer might see a different picture. Now that more Soviet documents are available that, perhaps, is a deficiency which others may be inspired to fill.

The construction of a new Russia and its integration into a new structure of relationships presents the West with a set of problems, some new, others rooted in the past, all presenting themselves in a new form and calling for a new response. In 1989 I wrote that there were periods in history when the pressures of interest, ideology, precedent and power shaped a mould which no effort of political will could break, but that, with the arrival of Gorbachev, we had reached one of the rare moments of flux. Ten years on, the melt has not yet hardened. Today, as in 1989, the imagination to perceive opportunities has to be matched by consistent, realistic and constructive statesmanship to exploit them over a very long haul. Our response to the travails of the new Russia may be the more effective if it is based on an understanding of the course which we have travelled. If nothing more, this study may, I hope, serve to remind the reader of what was achieved by the patient diplomacy of earlier years and to underline the need to develop an effective diplomacy for the very different and more complex circumstances of the future.

January 2000   CURTIS KEEBLE

Acknowledgements

In its origin, this book owes much to the stimulus which I received from the late David Watt and Hugh Seton-Watson. The analysis of the official records would not have been possible without the work of earlier scholars, whose detailed studies of various periods are referred to, with grateful acknowledgement, in the Notes.

In preparing the first edition I was much helped by the late Sir Frank Roberts, who gave me the benefit of his unrivalled personal experience in the conduct of relations with the Soviet Union from the 1930s onwards; by Lord Callaghan who very kindly gave me his comments on Chapter 10; by Sir Michael Howard, Dr Stephen White, Dr Alex Pravda and Robin Edmonds, as well as by the Royal United Services Institute. In preparing this revised edition, I owe a particular debt of gratitude to Dr Margot Light and to Sir Patrick Reilly. I have also received much help from my former colleagues in the Foreign and Commonwealth Office and would single out in particular the Historians and the staff of the Library, including their Map Service. In the tracing of various documents I have been very grateful to the staff of the Public Record Office and the Librarians of the School of Slavonic and East European Studies and the Royal Institute of International Affairs.

Crown Copyright material is reproduced with the permission of the Controller of the Stationery Office.

To my wife goes a special word of thanks for the all the years of support without which this project could never have been realised. To Keith Povey I am indebted for swift, meticulous and professional copy-editing and to Maurice and Anne Tinniswood for their generous help with proof-reading. For the errors and inadequacies the responsibility remains mine.

C. K.

Map 1 Russia and neighbouring states (post-1991)

Introduction: Britain and Imperial Russia

Throughout much of the pre-Soviet period, four main elements combined, sometimes in harmony, sometimes in conflict, to set the pattern of Britain's relationship with Imperial Russia: on the positive side a potential community of interest in respect of the control of Continental Europe and in mutually profitable trade and investment; and on the negative side a deepening hostility flowing from conflicting imperial ambitions combined with a mutual antipathy reflecting British detestation of the Russian system of government and Russian fear of contagion by British constitutional democracy. All four elements remained identifiable after 1917, albeit in changed form, but distorted in their effect by the dominant Marxist–Leninist doctrine of pre-ordained, irreconcilable confrontation. Now that the collapse of the Soviet system has removed that doctrinal overlay, it is possible to envisage a more 'normally' fluctuating relationship. But does 'normal' mean anything in this context? Is there a 'normality' to fall back on?

The legacy of history

In diplomacy one cannot start with a clean sheet. No matter how radical the change of course – and they do not come much more radical than 1917 and 1991 – there is likely to be a potent but ill-defined legacy of historical legend, territorial friction, political prejudice, personal friendships and antipathies, stereotypes and preconceptions, commercial and financial interests and long-cherished grievances. Equally difficult to define are the underlying and enduring national characteristics of two peoples. Much has been written about the Russian mind, but much of what has been written is little more than anecdotal in character. There are national characteristics and they do not change with every change of regime. But international relations are not determined by some national genetic pattern and, even if they were, the scope for mutation in response to environmental change would be so great as to mask the direct evolutionary line. So it has been with the evolution from the foreign policy of Imperial Russia to that of the Soviet Union and from the Soviet Union to the Russian Federation. Nevertheless, the legacy is there. It is real. And it merits recall. What follows is an attempt not so much to condense into a few pages the history of Anglo–Russian relations from 1079 to 1917, but rather to illuminate with a few flashes of colour from earlier centuries a background – in which familiar features can be discerned – to the long, sad Soviet era and the brief, crowded post-Soviet years.

Writing in 1943, Sir J. Marriott offered an analysis of British–Russian relations which lacked nothing in the crispness of its cliches: 'Englishmen do not easily understand foreigners; still less do foreigners understand Englishmen. This is especially true of Englishmen and Russians. Nor is this remarkable. Russia is not, and has never been a member of the European family.'[1] One may smile, but many would no doubt echo his sentiments. They recur in one form or another over the centuries. Nor are they unique to the British and the Russians. President de Gaulle could as easily have said the same about the British as he vetoed their application to join the European Economic Community in 1963. But Marriott, looking back to the Napoleonic wars and writing at a time when Britain and Russia were, for the second time in a quarter of a century, partners in a brief and troubled alliance against Germany, might with more justification have seen a certain parallelism in the equivocal relationship of both to Continental Europe. Neither saw its destiny in purely European terms. Neither could afford to ignore Europe. Both had suffered grievously when Europe was dominated by a hostile power.

In 1980 a member of the KGB, anxious to find a point of common interest by persuading me of the long-standing links between Britain and Russia, took as his point of departure the fact that after the Norman invasion of Britain King Harold's family had sought refuge in Russia – or, in contemporary terms, Ukraine – and that in 1079 his daughter had married the prince Vladimir Monomakh. Limited though his story was in its relevance to the conduct of relations with the Soviet Union, it certainly caught my interest. Equally picturesque, although not much more relevant, are some of the other much-cited episodes which, over the centuries, have lodged in the crevices of history. It seems mandatory for every account of British–Russian relations to begin with the London merchants forming the Muscovy Company in 1551 and with Richard Chancellor's arrival in Moscow two years later, after the failure of his attempt to find a route to the Far East through the northern oceans. He found 'such men for hard living as are not under the sun', but was well received by Ivan IV, and began a process which soon brought a commercial agreement between the Tsar and Elizabeth I. Ivan would have extended it to a comprehensive alliance and there were those who believed he had contemplated marriage. Had it happened, their progeny might indeed have made Europe tremble. But Elizabeth was content with the trading relationship. The experience of her first envoys to Moscow was such that in August 1590 she addressed to Tsar Fyodor, Ivan's feeble-minded son, a communication which evoked a heartfelt echo from more than one of my predecessors in Soviet Moscow. Its force still shines clearly through its tortured grammar:

> The entertainment that our Highness's Ambassadors and messengers receive of Your Majesty is not agreeable to our princely quality, and not such as we show unto your Ambassadors and messengers of what quality soever they be of, which refer to their own reports. Yea, we are credibly informed that Your Majesty maketh more estimation of other princes of meaner quality; heathens, Tartars, Turks etc. receive better exceptance than ours in all respects ... These gross injuries, whether it were tolerable by you if we should show the least of them towards Your Majesty; and the like were never offered of no prince towards us, not of our greatest enemies, and although they are hardly to be digested of any princely nature, yet have we not been desirous of revenge or breach of brotherly amity.[2]

Brotherly amity maybe, but Elizabeth had no desire for a wide-ranging alliance with Russia. Trade was to remain the core of the relationship and it is not wholly fanciful to trace a thread running from the Elizabethan adventurers to Lloyd George's trade agreement of 1921, by which Britain became the first among the wartime Allies to open relations with Soviet Russia and from there to Harold Wilson's repeated efforts to expand bilateral trading links. Or, for that matter, from Peter the Great's study of Dutch and British shipbuilding techniques in 1697–8 to the continuing effort of the Soviet and Russian intelligence services to acquire industrial intelligence, most notoriously through the nuclear espionage of the 1940s. It was a Scot who put the clock tower on the entrance to the Kremlin, a Welshman who began the

4 *Britain, the Soviet Union and Russia*

metallurgical industry of the Don basin and British financial advisers who joined the international teams helping to reconstruct the Russian economy after the collapse of the Soviet Union. Examples enough can be cited but, impressive though they are, trade with Russia has rarely met the expectations of either party and the record is littered with as many disputes and failures as agreements and successes.

In the field of political relations, it was not until Peter the Great opened Russia's window to the West, aroused concern at the possible scope of his Baltic ambitions, flirted with the Jacobites and moved into the Caspian region that Britain began to have cause to take serious note of Russia. Then, under his daughter, the Tsarina Elizabeth and under Catherine the Great, Russia began to become a significant factor in the shifting pattern of alliances as the European powers struggled for supremacy. To trace the course of those struggles and their implications for British–Russian relations would be to range far beyond the proper scope of this book. As the two nations developed and as they built up their empires, the one by sea from the Western border of Europe and the other by land to the East, it became progressively harder for them to ignore one another. At some of the turning points of European history they found themselves in alliance, but there were long periods of low-level friction, mutual distaste and occasional hostility.

For all the complexity of the sources of conflict, they fell into two broad, albeit overlapping groups, those deriving from the conflict of imperial ambitions beyond Europe and those where the security of one party or the other was directly affected by the shifting balance of power within continental Europe. Palmerston listed Russia with France and the United States as one of the three powers capable of challenging Britain's naval supremacy. In fact neither country presented a direct and inescapable threat to the home territory of the other, but for much of the time Russia could afford to treat Britain with indifference, whereas in British eyes Russia loomed rather larger as an actual or potential threat to British interests. As Britain approached the zenith of imperial power, Russia was uniquely placed both to threaten her lines of communication by sea and to tilt the balance for or against her in Europe. The diplomatic relationship with Russia was therefore not so much a strategic confrontation as constant tactical manoeuvring. For all that Palmerston enjoyed moving Britain up to the brink in opposition to Russia's expansion, he was still able at one point to declare: 'Russia gives the world quite as much security for the preservation of peace as England'[3] and to align Britain for a time with Russia rather than with France. In St Petersburg he was seen as a committed foe, but his doctrine of 'no eternal allies, no perpetual enemies' certainly applied to his conduct of relations with Russia.

Imperial Russia could in fact be seen as a threat or an ally to Britain in so far as her policy might facilitate or hinder the domination of continental Europe by a hostile power. Napoleon brought Britain and Russia into conflict before they came into a victorious alliance, but any natural coincidence or conflict of interest was usually temporary and in Britain's only war with Russia she had France as an ally. More continuously and more directly, Russia's southward thrust was seen as a potential threat to Britain's Indian Empire. As the Ottoman Empire decayed, these factors, sometimes separately, sometimes in combination, led British governments to support the independence of the countries of South Eastern Europe; to oppose Russia's drive to secure access to the Mediterranean; and to clash with her over Persia and Afghanistan. They brought the Crimean War and they brought other crises close to war.

Disraeli was right to warn against 'an invasian of Russia rashly and thoughtlessly decided upon' and to point to the risk of a 'lingering, fruitless and inglorious war' in the Crimea, a warning which might with advantage have been heeded by those who planned the 1918 intervention.[4] There were situations in which conflicting national interests could bring recourse to a military or naval solution, but so far apart were the two countries in terms of geography and so different in military potential that, *pace* some nineteenth-century novelists and twentieth-century generals, armed conquest was never an option for either acting alone. (Paradoxically, the twentieth-century logic of deterrence meant that while nuclear weaponry made conquest a theoretical option, the consequences of its use served not only to exclude this option but also to inhibit the more limited forms of direct military conflict which in earlier times had been regarded as acceptable.)

In terms of foreign policy, it had, in the early decades of the nineteenth century, been France which, naturally enough, was perceived as Britain's most dangerous potential enemy. Russia, by contrast, was a powerful rogue element with the capacity to sustain or to disturb the stability which was Britain's primary requirement in Europe, but not a direct threat. However, as the signs of Tsarist imperialist expansion multiplied, it became easy, against a background of mutual dislike, to fit them into a pattern not dissimilar to that of President Reagan's 'evil empire'. To see, as some have done, the 'Great Game' and the 'Cold War' as different names for the same phenomenon is to misunderstand the latter. Nevertheless, it is easy to trace a direct line from many of the conflicts of the nineteenth century to the later conflicts with Soviet imperialism and to extrapolate from British concern with the balance of power in nineteenth-century Europe to the British and German attempts to woo Russia in 1939. It might have been Churchill, but it was actually Gladstone, who argued: 'The best resistance to be offered to Russia is by the strength and freedom of those countries that will have to resist her ... There is no barrier like the breast of free men.'[5] It was Curzon, not Brzezinsky, who wrote [6] that the concession to Russia of a port on the Persian Gulf by any other power would be 'a wanton interruption of the status quo and an intentional provocation to war'. When, in 1979, the Soviet Union used its army in a vain attempt to hold Afghanistan within the imperial grasp, the ghost of Curzon might have exhorted Margaret Thatcher to read the warning contained in his 1885 analysis.[7] As for Poland, throughout the centuries, from the first partition to the Polish–Soviet war of 1920, the 1939 partition with Nazi Germany, the Solidarity crisis and martial law of the early 1980s and the extension of NATO to Poland, the Polish–Russian relationship has been a continuing element in British–Russian relations. Serbia still echoes down the years.

Russophobia and Russophilia

In the conduct of relations with Russia the British political leaders of the nineteenth century were much influenced by a growing Russophobic mood in public opinion. (The designation of Russophobe was appropriate enough for the cold warriors of that day. There were also Russophiles, but many of those so described differed from the Russophobes only in so far as they recognised that the threat of Russia could be contained better by negotiation than by conflict.) There were periods when Russophobia rose to a high pitch of excitement, partly jingoistic – 'We've got the ships, we've got the men, we've got the money too' – but partly a genuine reflection of abhorrence at Russia's internal system, an abhorrence not dissimilar to that aroused by the Gulag Archipelago. It was not only such cranks as David Urquhart, with his denunciation of Palmerston as a Russian spy, who were involved. The Russophobes could for a time count Disraeli and Queen Victoria among their ranks as they looked with suspicion at Gladstone's involvement with Olga Novikova, wife of a member of the Russian General Staff but, firm though Victoria was in opposition to Russian expansion, she took care of her family ties with the Imperial house and no less than four of the Tsars were her guests. In 1853 she lamented to the King of the Belgians: 'The Russians accuse us of being too French and the French of being too Russian.'[8] The British antipathy to the whole structure of Russian society had deep roots. Some of the Russian aristocracy certainly cherished their links with Western Europe and there was some growth of cultural understanding as the British came to respect the great nineteenth-century Russian writers, but to many British the Tsarist regime symbolised all that was most hateful in a stifling, secretive and intolerant autocracy ruling over an ignorant, drunken, brutal peasantry and pursuing an expansionist foreign policy. As the *Edinburgh Review* put it in 1839, Russia was 'active in every court in Europe, aiding and abetting the cause of despotism'. Half a century later, Alexander III, not the best but by no means the worst of the Tsars, was regarded as not so much the contemporary of Queen Victoria, whom he described memorably as a 'gossiping old hag', but rather of Isabella of Castile. For its part Russia saw Britain's belief in constitutional democracy in the first half of the nineteenth century as a dangerously destabilising radicalism. As the century drew towards a close, Curzon summed up the classic controversy in the dedication to his book *Russia in Central Asia*: 'To the great army of Russophobes who mislead others and Russophiles whom others mislead I dedicate this book which will be found equally disrespectful to the ignoble terrors of the one and the perverse complacency of the others.'[9]

The mood of 1900

There are those who contend that in the twenty years before the First World War it was Russia, not Germany, which was seen as the most significant long-term threat to British interests and that a driving force – perhaps the driving force – in British diplomacy was the effort to reach an accommodation with Russia.[10] This may be to overstate the significance of the British–Russian relationship, but there is no doubt that the British Government made the effort; that they found a response; and that they were successful. The public mood of 1900 was one of simmering irritability. The press was complaining, in terms which were to be repeated throughout the Soviet era, about the secretiveness of the Russian Government:

> The purpose of the Government is determined by the will of the Sovereign. If mistakes are made they are not allowed to be disclosed. No explanations are given or asked for. No criticisms are allowed.

8 *Britain, the Soviet Union and Russia*

The press find it prudent to support the Government ... At the same time, when Russian journalists are given a free hand in attacking other Governments, and more particularly this country, the Russian Foreign Office is always ready to declare that it does not interfere with the Russian Press.[11]

At the start of the century Britain was, however, more concerned with South Africa than with Russia and it was fortunate that Russia resisted the Kaiser's attempt to induce her to take advantage of that preoccupation. With it out of the way, a new focus of British interest was the extent to which, with the completion of the Trans-Siberian railway, the Tsar had turned his eyes eastwards. The Russian press was warning that Britain had to accept the 'irreversibly accomplished fact' of Russia's position in the Far East and must not 'truckle to the incorrigible Russophobes'.[12] It was by a narrow margin that the Russo–Japanese War failed to produce a major British–Russian conflict. Minor incidents at sea added to the tension, but prudence prevailed and even the Dogger Bank incident in 1904, when the Russian Baltic fleet, on its way to annihilation by Japan, fired on British trawlers in the North Sea, was resolved by payment of compensation. The 1905 Revolution then gave reason to hope that constitutional reform might begin to take root in Russia and at the same time external events were bringing a change of mood. With Russia chastened by defeat in the East and Britain beginning to be concerned by the growing power of Germany, both countries could see grounds for some accommodation. The immediate outcome was the conclusion in 1907 of an Anglo–Russian Convention which stabilised the conflicting interests in Central Asia, notably Tibet, Afghanistan and Persia. As Prince of Wales, the future King Edward VII had attended the wedding of the Tsarevich in 1866 and had returned in 1881 for the funeral of Alexander II. In the summer of 1908 he became the first reigning British sovereign to visit Russia, when he travelled in the Royal Yacht *Victoria and Albert* to meet Nicholas II at Reval, appointed him an Admiral of the Fleet in the British Navy and accepted an equivalent appointment in the Russian Navy. Despite violent left-wing opposition in Britain and an article by Ramsay MacDonald denouncing this 'hobnobbing with a blood-stained creature', the visit helped to support the Government's desire for a better relationship and was followed in 1909 by a return visit by the Tsar.

With the improving political relationship, the British set out to rediscover a strange and fascinating country. Between 1900 and 1914 there was quite a flow of books on Russia, translations of Chekhov and Tolstoy, little descriptive volumes oddly reminiscent of the sixteenth-century works of Chancellor and his contemporaries, and a new edition of Mackenzie Wallace's massive *Russia*. Typical of the period was a book by R. J.Barrett, the editor of *The Financier and Bullionist*, who made his own voyage of discovery in 1907 and published the results in *Russia's New Era*. His words were capable of being echoed eighty years later: 'The mists of prejudice are clearing off' he wrote, 'and old estrangement seems an evil dream'. He found a country in its growing pains, but one which was 'bound to be a world's wonder'. A year or so later, Stephen Graham wrote of Russia awaiting the British 'with all the freshness and allurement of newly discovered country'. The mood of the Russophiles was well summed up by the *Russian Year Book*, published in London in 1911:

> There are no two powers in the world and there have been no other two in history more distinct in character, less conflicting in interest, or more naturally adapted for mutual agreement and support than are Britain and Russia. Of these vast sovereignties, one is essentially a maritime empire and the other a continental dominion. The former is commercial and rich in capital, the latter is agricultural, with immense potential resources still undeveloped. Whether regarded from the political or the economic standpoint, these powers are not competitive, but complementary; and experience shows that as the two empires, by their fundamental conditions are marked out for friendship and not for antagonism, the two races in their private relations, so far from finding difficulty in getting on well with each other, are as sympathetic in tendency as they are contrasted in temperament.

It was a far cry from Asquith's description of the two countries as being 'catalogued as nations which are natural foes'.[13]

Sir George Buchanan must have felt something of this new enthusiasm in 1910 when he arrived in St Petersburg to take up his appointment as His Britannic Majesty's Ambassador to the Emperor Nicholas II. At 64 he was at the peak of his diplomatic career. Tall and distinguished in appearance, an excellent linguist, but not a Russian speaker, he combined courtesy and firmness in a measure which commanded respect both in St Petersburg and in London as he strove to promote British interests in Russia, while seeking to understand and to interpret to London the travail through which that country was passing.

He had gained experience of the problems of Central and Eastern Europe during service in Vienna and Sofia, but had then been sent to The Hague and had remarked to King Edward VII that he was afraid he might sleep away the remaining years of his career as a kind of diplomatic Rip van Winkle. 'Something is sure to turn up', said the King. On appointing him to St Petersburg, the Foreign Secretary, Sir Edward Grey wrote: 'The place is one of great importance, as, though our relations with the Russian Government are happily cordial, there are questions which present difficulties for both Governments, which require constant tact and skill on the part of the Ambassador at St. Petersburg.'[14]

Buchanan's enthusiasm was tempered by the caution of the experienced professional. In British political circles, the resentment at Russian pressure on Persia was still combined with abhorrence of Tsarist repression and recollections of the repeated and vicious anti-Jewish pogroms. In one of Buchanan's first despatches he wrote of the two countries as 'friends over whom still hung the shadow of past differences and misunderstanding' and who 'had not yet cast aside the mutual suspicions with which they had for more than half a century regarded the trend of each other's policy'.[15] The friction over Persia continued during the early years of his appointment and was not wholly allayed by a visit which M. Sazonov, the Tsar's Foreign Minister, paid to Balmoral. In 1912, when an impressive British delegation representing Parliament, the Church, the Army, the Navy and the press, visited St Petersburg, it evoked the comment from the Russian side that 'for the first time the two great powers stand side by side on a footing of political equality'.[16] Nevertheless, in a generally complimentary leader on the tercentenary of the Romanovs, *The Times* of 6 March 1913 could still speculate on whether the European sense of order or the 'wild Asiatic instinct for the spasmodic and monstrous' would prevail in Russia, and when, in early 1914, Tsar Nicholas spoke of his desire for 'a closer bond of union between England and Russia, such as an alliance of a purely defensive character',[17] there was no response. Buchanan summed up the issue succinctly: 'What really barred the way to an Anglo–Russian alliance was the fact that it would not have been sanctioned by public opinion in England.'[18]

The commercial relationship

In its commercial relationship with Russia at the beginning of the twentieth century, Britain was struggling against the growing power of the German traders. Prior to Buchanan's appointment, the British share of Russia's trade had been declining. There had been an influx of British capital into Russia in the years after the Crimean War and British mercantile interests had for a time predominated over German, but by 1913 Russian imports from Britain, at 170 million roubles (£17 million), were not much more than a quarter of the value of imports from Germany. There was a resident British community of some 7000 in Russia, about a third of them in St Petersburg. Many were engaged as technical experts running the textile mills owned by firms such as Coates in the region around St Petersburg and Moscow. Others were in the grain and flax trade, the metallurgical and mining industry, some were in banking, and a doughty regiment of British nannies, governesses and tutors was engaged in the upbringing of the Russian nobility. The fine street fronting the Neva close to the Imperial Palace, where the British merchants had traditionally resided, was known as the English Embankment and names of British manufacturers of farming equipment such as Howard and Ransome were household words in Russian agriculture. For the most part, however, the British commercial community seem to have lost the dynamism of their predecessors and to have become a somewhat conservative and unenterprising group, losing ground to more thrusting German competitors. By 1913 the British flag still covered 35 per cent of all shipping entering Russian ports, but here too the British share was declining. The total British capital investment in Russia was estimated in 1910 at £38 million, only just over 1 per cent of total British overseas investment.[19] About a quarter of this was in state bonds and the remainder in trade and industry. It was, however, increasing rapidly. The new oil industry was causing considerable interest and it was said that the naphtha area of Maikop had attracted 200 million roubles (£20 million) from Britain in the two years 1909 and 1910. An estimate of £60 million or so for the value of private British investment in Russia at the time of the Revolution may be not far from the mark.[20]

The Russian émigrés in London

In the early years of the century there was a Russian community of some 4000 or 5000 in London, among them a group of political exiles. It was from London in the 1850s that Alexander Herzen had championed the cause of Russian reform and it was in the Herzen Circle room in the Communist Club at 107 Charlotte Street that the exiles met. In 1912, on his way to join them, a young man, Ivan Maisky, stepped off the boat at Dover. He recounts[21] how, travelling third class, he was required to produce the sum of £5 in order to satisfy His Majesty's Government that he would not be a burden upon British resources. Sadly, his total resources amounted to £3.15s (£3.75). He was threatened with immediate deportation, but succeeded in securing entry as a political refugee. Maisky settled in London and became a leading member of a group which included Maxim Maximovich Litvinov, already settled for some years in London and married to an English girl. On the outbreak of war in 1914, they were joined by a member of a Russian aristocratic family, of Italian origin, Georgii Vasilievich Chicherin, who had thrown up his post in the Tsarist Foreign Ministry in order to join the revolutionary socialist movement and had lived since 1905 in Germany and France. The Russian émigrés were on good terms with the leaders of the British Labour and trade union movement although, as Maisky was later to write, 'their peace of mind, their complete indifference to theory and their profound belief in evolutionary progress through the medium of Parliament' made them totally different from the Russian socialists.

Litvinov, Chicherin and Maisky were to play an important role in British–Soviet relations during the whole period of the inter-war years. Litvinov became Lenin's first representative in London immediately after the Revolution and then deputy to Chicherin as Commissar for Foreign Affairs, succeeding him in 1930 and holding the office until May 1939. Maisky, the refugee of 1912, was to return as a diplomat and to be expelled in 1927, before finally being conveyed by State Coach to Buckingham Palace to present his credentials to King George V as Soviet Ambassador in London. Thus, throughout these early, crucial years, Soviet foreign policy was in the hands of men who knew England well, spoke the language and even, despite the fact that both Litvinov and Chicherin had experienced periods in British gaols, had a certain respect for the country, if little sympathy with its political leaders. In at least one respect the familiarity was reciprocal. The British security authorities had, by the time of the Revolution, long been aware of the linkage between the new rulers of Russia and the network of conspiratorial activity which, although less significant in Britain than elsewhere in Europe, had contributed to the unease which was threatening the comfortable certainties of Edwardian England.

Alliance in the war with Germany

In the summer of 1914, with the improving Anglo–Russian relationship still in its early stages, there was much to be done in terms of the political and the commercial relationship, but Sir George Buchanan could look back with some satisfaction at the progress made during the first few years of his stewardship. Then, having rejected the suggestion of an Anglo–Russian alliance, the British Government nevertheless found itself, as a consequence of the existing Franco–Russian alliance, committed alongside Imperial Russia in the war against Germany, a commitment which was formalised in 1915 by the Treaty of London, precluding either party from negotiating a separate peace. Four years later, Imperial Russia had been swept away and British forces were engaged in operations on Russian soil in an undeclared war against the successor government of their former ally. The origins of the Bolshevik Revolution and the extent to which it was precipitated by the strains of the war with Germany have been exhaustively treated elsewhere. What is relevant in this context is the way in which the existence of the wartime alliance and the dominant influence of military considerations upon British foreign policy determined the British reaction to the Revolution and conditioned British policy towards the Soviet Government in its early years.

The extravagant hopes placed on the Russian 'steamroller' were short-lived, but as the war in the West dragged on, it became increasingly apparent to the British Government that the prospect of ultimate victory depended to a significant extent upon the maintenance of an Eastern front which would continue to tie down substantial enemy forces. Some 80 German and Austrian divisions were engaged on that front in a war in which it was estimated that Russia had lost three and a half million in dead and wounded two million prisoners. Had it been open to the Germans to deploy even half these forces in the West at an early stage in the war, it is questionable whether the Allied front in France would have held. As it was, defeated at Tannenberg, the Russian army continued the struggle into 1917 at a level which prevented the bulk of the German forces from being withdrawn. In an attempt to shore up the Russian forces, the British Government gave substantial support in the form of supplies and finance. British wartime loans to the Russian Government amounted to £562 million,[22] of which some £74 million was in respect of supplies from the United States. But things were going badly. There was growing concern in London about the demoralisation of the Russian forces and the growth of German influence in Russia. In October 1916 Buchanan reported to the Foreign Office: 'Never since the war began have I felt so depressed about the situation here, more especially with regard to the future of Anglo–Russian relations.'[23] The whole country was in mourning and

Britain was blamed for the colossal losses which Russia was sustaining in a war from which it seemed she had nothing to gain. The situation went from bad to worse and in January 1917 the Ambassador had a memorable final interview with the Tsar. After warning him bluntly of the incompetence and worse of his ministers and of the revolutionary talk in Petrograd (as the city had by then been renamed), he concluded: 'You have, Sir, come to the parting of two ways, and you have now to choose between two paths. The one will lead you to victory and a glorious peace – the other to revolution and disaster.'[24] The warning was not heeded. It was, in any case, already too late to save the Tsar.

It might not, however, be too late to save the Russian army. In Britain, David Lloyd George had for some time been deeply concerned that the Russian front might collapse because of the desperate shortage of ammunition, and when he became Prime Minister one of his first acts was to despatch Lord Milner to Petrograd in February 1917 for an inter-Allied conference designed to improve the supply of munitions to the Russian forces as well as the efficiency of the forces themselves. In consequence, upwards of 2 million tons of military stores had been delivered through Murmansk, Archangel and Vladivostok.[25] The Allied supply bases and the military links associated with their establishment were to become a major factor in the intervention in 1918. As yet, however, although revolution was foreseen, its nature and its consequences were not.

The revolution of March 1917

A month after Buchanan's warning, revolution had come and the Tsar had abdicated. There were those at the time who held Buchanan responsible for having played a part in instigating the Revolution. He had seen and indeed warned the Tsar of the need for change, but it should, in his view, be change by evolution, not by revolution. What is of interest is not so much Buchanan's personal role, but rather this illustration of the authority which, in the Petrograd of 1917, attached to the opinions of the British Ambassador concerning the internal development of Russia. It reflected in part the personality of Buchanan, but in greater measure the power which he represented and against which the Bolshevik leaders were before long to be engaged.[26]

The British Government wasted no time in coming to terms with the situation created by the March (old style February) Revolution. It was more than ever necessary to try to instil into the new Russian Government the will to continue the war, and at its meeting on

21 March the War Cabinet approved a draft by the Prime Minister of a resolution to be passed by the House of Commons:

That this House sends the Duma its fraternal greetings and tenders to the Russian people its heartfelt congratulations on the establishment among them of free institutions, in full confidence that they will lead not only to the rapid and happy progress of the Russian nation, but to the prosecution in close alliance with the constitutional governments of Western Europe and with renewed steadfastness and vigour of the war against the stronghold of autocratic militarism which threatens the liberty of Europe.[27]

The Ambassador was instructed that he had authority to recognise the Provisional Government, but must obtain guarantees that they would carry out the engagements of their predecessor. It was a swift and sound response, inspired by the hope that a constitutional Government in Russia might, with British support, prove a stronger ally than the crumbling, inefficient autocracy of the hesitant Nicholas and his German-born Tsarina. As for the Tsar, despite the affection which King George V had for his cousin, both the King and his Ministers were in some doubt as to whether it was expedient for the Imperial family to take up residence in Britain, even if he were permitted to leave Russia.[28] The reluctant offer of asylum subsequently – and fruitlessly – conveyed by Buchanan indicated that if they were to come to Britain the Russian Government must be responsible for their maintenance.

In British left-wing circles the new regime in Russia was welcomed with particular enthusiasm. A great rally was held in the Albert Hall and, helped by a Committee with Maisky as its Chairman, Litvinov as Secretary and Chicherin as a member, the émigrés began a return to Russia. By the time Litvinov's turn came, events had moved on and he was forced to unpack his trunks. In June a United Socialist Council, including MacDonald and Snowden, called for the setting up in Britain of councils of workers and soldiers in order 'to do for this country what the Revolution had accomplished in Russia'. By contrast, between March and November, the references to Russia in the minutes of the War Cabinet were few, brief and gloomy. By May the Chief of the Imperial General Staff was already putting forward a paper on the 'possible effect of Russia's secession from the war'.[29] Ministers considered 'that the success or failure of the Allies in this war depends to a great extent on what Russia is going to do'.[30] They wondered whether they should replace Buchanan by someone whose standing would not be affected by a previous close relationship to the Imperial Government. It was thought that Mr Arthur Henderson, the Labour leader, might command the respect of Kerensky's Government, but having paid a long visit to Petrograd, Henderson advised that Buchanan should be left at his post. The right-wing press, in particular the *Morning Post*, waged a bitter campaign against the Provisional Government. The Prime Minister offered words of encouragement and another 58 000 tons of shipping for supplies to Russia. In Petrograd, it seemed to Buchanan for a moment that the Government might have regained its grip by the decision to put down the Bolsheviks in July. Buchanan's daughter records[31] how one of Kerensky's officers came to the Embassy on 18 July, to be received by the Ambassador, clad in a greatcoat over his pyjamas, and to warn him that the Embassy would be in the direct line of fire as the troops ejected the Bolsheviks from the Peter and Paul fortress. With the Siamese cat packed safely into its travelling basket, the Ambassador and his family watched the successful attack from the drawing room window. But the moment of success was brief. Kerensky took over the leadership from Prince Lvov, but as summer moved into autumn, there could be little doubt that his hold was slipping away. The abortive Kornilov *coup d'état*, ending in the arrest by Kerensky of his Commander-in-Chief, accelerated the disintegration, but did nothing to weaken the subsequent determination of the British Military Attaché in Petrograd, General Knox, to support the anti-Bolshevik military leaders. Knox was to play a not insignificant role in the later conduct of British policy.

For Lloyd George, 1917 had been a bad year. As Kerensky came to power, the U-boats had savaged British shipping to such effect that disaster seemed imminent. The introduction of the convoy system had made a dramatic improvement, but a British Prime Minister could spare little time for the internal politics of Russia as 400 000 British and Canadian soldiers were being killed or wounded, floundering through the mud of Passchendaele in an ill-conceived offensive. By October, the British forces under Allenby were moving into Palestine, but the Italian front was in danger of collapse. One thing only mattered so far as Russia was concerned – that by some means she should be kept in the war, if only until the weight of American men and equipment could begin to turn the scales in the West.

On the afternoon of 7 November 1917 the Ambassador stepped out onto the Palace Embankment, a few hundred yards from the Imperial Winter Palace. Now, after three years of war the city was virtually in the hands of the Bolsheviks and the cruiser *Aurora*, which had arrived from Kronstadt to support them, was moored opposite the Embassy. The Prime Minister, Kerensky, had left the capital in a vain attempt to muster army support. Sir George's stroll was uneventful and he noted only a few soldiers near the bridges. He returned to the Embassy and shortly afterwards heard the *Aurora's* gun signal the attack on the Winter Palace, where Kerensky's ministers, guarded only by some cadets and a company of the women's battalion, were awaiting the end. It came that night. The garrison surrendered and the Ministers were marched off to imprisonment. The Ambassador was not surprised. He had already reported that Kerensky might have to make way for a Bolshevik Government. Even if this happened, however, he did not think that things could be much worse than they were at present. In any case, 'such a Government would not be of long duration and before long would provoke counter-revolution'. Now it had happened. He sent his telegram reporting the events of the day. 'Order prevails', he concluded, 'at present all quiet'.[32]

1
Response to Revolution

The problem facing the War Cabinet

Britain was approaching the fourth dreary winter of an apparently interminable war when, on 9 November 1917, the news of the Bolshevik Revolution broke in the morning newspapers. Under the heading 'Anarchy in Petrograd', *The Times* carried a full report of the proclamation by the Revolutionary Military Committee announcing the fall of the Government and the transfer of power to the Soviets. In a leading article, headed 'Russia's critical hour', it remarked that the latest events would hardly surprise those who had watched events in Petrograd: 'Russia, free for an instant, has found herself bound afresh.'

In the Prime Minister's absence, the Conservative Bonar Law, Chancellor of the Exchequer, was in the chair at the meeting of the War Cabinet that morning. The main item on the agenda was the progress of the German offensive in Italy, which was causing considerable concern. Arthur Balfour, the Foreign Secretary, had, however, received Sir George Buchanan's telegrams reporting the Revolution. The Cabinet minutes record only that he read them to his colleagues.[1] They moved to the next item of the agenda. The process of adjusting British foreign policy to the Bolshevik Revolution had now to begin.

The next four years were to see a remarkable, but in retrospect understandable, sequence of conflicting policies as Britain struggled to make up its mind whether it wanted to try to work with the Bolsheviks or to break their power. Two great figures of British twentieth-century politics, David Lloyd George and Winston Churchill, were to contest the issue, and the political, military and economic realities were to decide it in Lloyd George's favour. In these early years, as the Bolshevik power was established in the old Imperial Russia and as its first external impact was felt, many of the problems which were to recur throughout the twentieth century were encountered and the seeds of subsequent disputes were sown. They were years crowded with events, years not only of strategic policy but also of extraordinary incident, years in which at one point British motor torpedo boats sank a large part of the Russian Baltic fleet, at another gas was used against the Bolshevik forces, and at yet another a British commander, without reference to London, established a Government for North-West Russia. They saw the creation of legends, which still live, about British complicity in the murder of the Baku commissars and the Lockhart plot against the Soviet Government. Although the history of the period has been much researched and documented, it tends for most of us to fall into that historical limbo, beyond the range of personal recollection but not yet into that of familiar history. It cannot be retold here in all its complexity. This Chapter and Chapter 2 will, however, trace the main steps by which the British Government, acting sometimes independently, sometimes in concert with and sometimes in opposition to their wartime Allies, sought first to establish an unofficial relationship with the Bolsheviks while simultaneously supporting the anti-Bolshevik forces in Russia; were led into an escalating but never wholehearted military intervention designed initially to further the conduct of the war against Germany and later to overthrow Bolshevik power; deployed tiny British forces thousands of miles apart, from Archangel and Murmansk in the North, to Vladivostok in the East and the Caucasus/Caspian in the South; withdrew them as the White forces crumbled; strove to reshape their policy as the Poles advanced to Kiev and the Russians to the gates of Warsaw; and finally became the first of the wartime Allies to give *de facto* recognition to the Soviet Government.

In his memoirs Lloyd George wrote: 'The problem with which the British Government and indeed the Allies as a whole were faced, was a purely military one. We were not concerned with the internal political troubles of Russia as such.'[2] Was the description wholly honest? The evidence of the Cabinet minutes is clear that at the outset the pursuit of the war against Germany was indeed the one issue which mattered. It was in terms of relevance to the war that the Government determined policy towards Russia. So far as Russian internal policy was concerned, it would be naive to suggest that the Government could have been indifferent as to the nature of the new regime. The fall of the Tsar had caused little regret and the Provisional Government had, as we have seen, commanded a wide measure of sympathy from all but the extreme right of the British political spectrum. The sympathy had waned as Kerensky's inability to control the march of events became apparent, but the Bolsheviks seemed to have nothing to recommend them. Their political philosophy was a challenge to the whole social and economic structure represented by the British Government and their methods were an affront to all constitutional democrats, whether of the right or the left. Marxist doctrine had its echoes in Britain, but Lenin's Government was regarded as no more than a disagreeable and probably transient stage in the political evolution of Russia. There can scarcely have been one of those gathered around the Cabinet table on the morning of 9 November who did not wish to see the Bolsheviks fall. Nevertheless, irrespective of their personal opinions on the nature of a Bolshevik Government, most of the members of the War Cabinet did not see it as their business to interfere. What they had first to do was to form a judgment on two aspects of the problem:

(a) Would the Bolsheviks be able to retain their hold on power and establish themselves as the Government of the whole of the former Imperial Russia?
(b) What would be the effect of a Bolshevik Government in Russia on the prosecution of the war against Germany?

According to their judgement on these questions, Ministers had to decide whether there was any action which the British Government and its Allies could take in order to redress the potential damage to their collective military effort against Germany.

On the first point, there was no good reason for Ministers to dissent from Buchanan's advice that Lenin's Government would not be of long duration. For the moment, they controlled the central civil power and probably the principal military power of the state, but their grasp appeared localised and tenuous. The quality and strength of the opposition to them was unproven, but its existence was beyond doubt. The Bolsheviks might in time consolidate their authority, but to predict that they would do so would at this stage have required a remarkable prescience. With no substantial case, on the facts available, for immediate recognition either of the Bolsheviks or of any other group, there was everything to be said for waiting to see how matters would develop and meanwhile keeping all options open.

The military implications of the Revolution

On the military effect of the Revolution, there was less room for doubt. The disintegration of the Russian army was already far gone and it was doubtful whether Kerensky's Government would have been capable of continuing the war for very much longer. Nevertheless, a million or more German and Austrian troops were still engaged on the Eastern front. Many of these were substandard, but General Haig's estimate[3] was that there were perhaps 32 divisions which were fit to take part in severe fighting on the Western front, where both sides, pausing after the bloody struggle of October 1917, were preparing for the coming year. In the West, the scales, for the moment, seemed evenly balanced. The German submarines had been checked and with America now in the war, the Allies could hope that the flow of men and material across the Atlantic would build up to a point which might make victory possible in 1919. They would need to conduct a spring offensive in 1918, but it seemed premature to hope for victory in that year. For Germany, on the other hand, 1918 offered possibly the last chance of a decisive offensive which would defeat the Allied forces in France and win the war before the combined pressure of the Allied blockade and the American reinforcements turned the tide. The one factor which might assure the success of such an offensive would be the victorious conclusion of the war in the East, permitting not only the transfer to the West of the German forces engaged there, but also the addition of Russian grain and raw materials as a blockade-free reinforcement to the economic resources of the Central Powers. It was very much a matter of time. Could the Eastern front be held open for another twelve months?

The Allies had done, and were still doing, all they could to sustain the Russian forces by supplying arms and other military supplies as well as raw materials. These supplies would, however, be of no avail unless the men in the field, their commanders and their Government had the will to continue the fight. By the time the Revolution took place, the army was already disintegrating fast and the prospects were thoroughly bad. Immediately upon assuming power, Lenin read a proclamation to the peoples and governments of all the nations at war. He proposed immediate peace without annexations and without indemnities, with a three month armistice as a first step, and called upon the workers of England, France and Germany to join the struggle for peace and the liberation of the exploited working masses. To the British Government, it seemed that, if the Bolshevik Government were firmly established, the prospect of keeping a Russian army in the field against Germany was slender indeed. Without that army, defeat in the West seemed not inconceivable and stalemate quite probable.

For a time, Lloyd George and his ministers clung to the hope that perhaps Buchanan might be right and the Bolsheviks would be overthrown. By 12 November *The Times* was reporting that Kerensky had gathered forces to retake the capital and its leader writer opined that Lenin's reign was apparently drawing to a close. Soon, however, it was clear – and confirmed by a telegram from the Military Attaché in Petrograd – that there was no prospect of Kerensky regaining power. Moreover, the Bolsheviks were quickly extending their control over the country and, within a week, held not only Petrograd and Moscow, but many provincial centres. It was clear, too, that they were resolved to end the war against Germany.

As the Bolshevik power grew, so the issues with which the British Government was confronted were sharpened. Buchanan received an 'insolent communication' from Trotsky threatening to negotiate a separate peace and, in default of recognition, to appeal to the peoples as against their Governments. The Ambassador recommended that Russia should be freed from her obligation under the Treaty of London and left to take her own decisions on continuing the war or negotiating for peace. He was authorised to issue a lengthy statement to the effect that 'the Allies ... are ready as soon as a stable government has been constituted that is recognised by the Russian people as a whole, to examine with that Government the aims of the war and the possible conditions of a just and durable peace'.[4] It was, however, soon clear in London that there was no realistic prospect of preventing separate Russo–German peace negotiations. But if the Bolsheviks were determined to make peace, could the terms be influenced in such a way as to minimise the loss to the Allied cause? If the Bolshevik grip were still not total, could those Russian commanders who were known to be hostile to the Bolsheviks be induced, by the grant of money and supplies, to continue the fight? These were the questions which were in the minds of British Ministers as they sought to work out policy in a series of Cabinet Meetings and Allied Conferences during November and December of 1917.

The policy of deliberate drift

It is necessary to set the decisions which British ministers reached in regard to Russia against the background of contemporary British opinion. In Parliament, Lloyd George commanded a substantial majority, but it was a Coalition majority, in which the Conservatives were by far the largest element. The Coalition existed for the pursuit of the war against Germany and in Parliament as in the country the war dominated all other issues. To the great body of Conservative backbenchers, dealings with Bolsheviks who were about to betray their Allies were tantamount to treason. On the left, the first warnings of Labour and Trade Union troubles were perceptible, but there was little sympathy for the Bolsheviks. They were denounced in the *Herald* for their terrorism, fanaticism and violence as well as for being false to their own internationalist creed in contemplating a separate peace without explicit assurances for Belgium, Serbia and Romania.[5] Nowhere was there a significant body of opinion which would have welcomed early recognition of Lenin's Government.

Against this background, ministers confronted the basic choice which was to remain for many years, in one way or another, before Western Governments. It was set out in Minute 13 of War Cabinet 294 on 7 December:

> It was suggested that the many questions arising out of the state of affairs in Russia would be easier of settlement if the policy of the Allies was more clearly defined. It was open to the Allies:
> (a) to recognize the Bolsheviks and make the best arrangements possible with them
> or (b) to refuse to recognize them and to take open and energetic steps against them.

It was easy enough to phrase the choice in these terms, but another matter to make the decision. Arthur Balfour, the Foreign Secretary, was certainly not the man to rush into a hasty decision. Describing a later stage of the debate over Russian policy, Lloyd George was to say of him that he 'as usual saw very clearly the arguments on both sides and felt that whichever way we decided there would be a strong case. He was therefore on the whole indifferent and prepared to support either course, but with a natural disinclination for energetic action on either side.'[6] After discussion with Lloyd George, Balfour put to the War Cabinet a memorandum recommending a 'wait and see' policy.[7] The British Government, he argued, had not concerned itself with the composition of the Russian Government during the Tsar's reign and it need not do so now. The Bolsheviks were fanatics, 'dangerous dreamers ... who would genuinely like to put into practice the wild theories that have been germinating so long in the shadow of the Russian autocracy'. But their aspirations – and, for that matter, those of other political parties – were a matter of concern only so far as they bore on the conflict with the Central Powers. For the remainder of the war, Bolsheviks were going to fight neither Germany nor anyone else, but even if Russia could not fight, she would not be easily overrun. If she could not be kept in the war, then the purpose of policy should be to ensure that she was as helpful to Britain and as harmful to the enemy as possible. No policy would be more certainly fatal than to give the Russians a motive for welcoming German officials and German soldiers as friends and deliverers. Balfour did not call for recognition, but expressed his entire dissent from the view of those who had suggested that the Bolsheviks could only be regarded as avowed enemies. 'I am clearly of opinion', he wrote, 'that it is to our advantage to avoid as long as possible an open breach with this crazy system. If this be drifting, then I am a drifter by deliberate policy.'

Support for the Cossacks and Ukrainians

In opposition to the policy of Balfour and Lloyd George were those who were not only convinced of the essential hostility of the Bolsheviks, but also saw in the anti-Bolshevik forces a means of holding open the Eastern front. If the result of supporting these forces were the overthrow of the Bolsheviks, so much the better. But the primary objective was the pursuit of the war against Germany. At this stage, Winston Churchill played little part in the debate. His energies were fully occupied with his responsibilities as Minister of Munitions. Oddly enough, it seems to have been Lord Robert Cecil who provided something of a focus for the interventionist group. Cecil, who is remembered today as the father of the League of Nations, combined the responsibilities of Minister for the Blockade with those of Under Secretary in the Foreign Office and, in Balfour's absence, he was frequently able to nudge policy in the direction of intervention. Political decisions might be deferred, but the war had to be fought. So, with military considerations paramount, the essential policy choice was gradually preempted and the first steps were taken which were to lead inexorably to armed intervention by Britain and her Allies. Even before the members of the War Cabinet considered Balfour's memorandum, they had decided, in the absence of the Prime Minister and the Foreign Secretary, that Buchanan should be told that the policy of the British Government was to support 'any responsible body in Russia that would actively oppose the maximalist movement and at the same time to give money freely and within reason to such bodies as were prepared to help the Allied cause'.[8] At that stage, the most promising anti-Bolshevik leader seemed to be Kaledin, the leader of the Cossacks. Buchanan understood the situation and warned that the Cossack and Ukrainian movements were concerned with the internal political situation, not with the continuation of the war against Germany. He was, however, authorised to make available 'to Cossacks or Ukrainians any funds necessary by any means you think desirable'.[9]

Anglo-French coordination

The interventionists in the British Government derived further support from the need to coordinate policy with Britain's allies. In practice, at the end of 1917, Allied policy was Anglo–French policy and Clemenceau was in no mood for such nonsense as recognition of a Bolshevik Government. On the British side, the task of working out a joint policy was entrusted to Lord Robert Cecil, Lord Milner, Secretary of State for War, and General Macdonogh, Director of Military Intelligence. The group visited Paris and it would have been scarcely suprising if their visit had produced a clearly interventionist policy. It did, indeed result in the conclusion on 23 December 1917 of an Anglo–French Convention,[10] dividing southern Russia into British and French 'zones of influence' for the purpose of support to the anti-Bolshevik forces. But the policy document which emerged,[11] in the form of a British draft approved by Clemenceau, very fairly represented the division of view in the War Cabinet and left the British Government with the option of backing either side, both sides or neither. Each country would 'get into relations' with the Bolsheviks through unofficial agents. It would be made clear 'that any idea that we favour a counter-revolution is a profound mistake', but at the same time the two Governments would 'keep in touch as far as we can with the Ukraine, the Cossacks, Finland, Siberia and the Caucasus etc.'

An unofficial link with the Bolsheviks

While Lloyd George and his colleagues were struggling to define policy, events in Russia were taking their course. Buchanan, with no valid accreditation to the new regime, was trying to maintain the Embassy, but his health was failing and in November he had already been forced to ask for permission to return home. As it happened – and rather to the relief of the Foreign Secretary – he was able to stay on for a little longer, but, with no prospect of early recognition of the Bolshevik Government, his position was becoming increasingly anomalous. It is risky, but not impossible and sometimes very useful, for an Embassy to maintain some form of contact with various warring factions in a country torn by civil war, but Buchanan could not himself have conducted relations between the British Government and the Bolsheviks without breaching the agreed policy of non-recognition. Consequently, implementing the decision to establish unofficial contacts, the Prime Minister appointed a young British consular officer, Robert Bruce Lockhart, to carry out this task.

Few of Her Majesty's Ambassadors to the Soviet Union had the opportunity to establish such a close relationship with a member of the Soviet leadership as was open to Lockhart with Trotsky during the first half of 1918. The son of a Scottish schoolmaster, boasting proudly that there was no drop of English blood in his veins, Lockhart was a remarkable mixture of strength and insecurity, best summed up in his own autobiography, in which he speaks of his ineradicable romanticism and says that 'the strongest impulse of the moment has governed all my actions'.[12] In 1912, at the age of 24, after a brief and disastrous attempt to become a rubber planter in Malaya, Lockhart had joined the Consular Service and had been appointed Vice-Consul in Moscow. He remained there until September 1917, by which time, enjoying to the full all that Russian society had to offer, he had acquired a deep feeling for the country and its people. His qualities matched those of many Russians and his circle of friends was as wide as it was varied. At the beginning of 1917, he met Milner in Petrograd and then took responsibility for Milner during his visit to Moscow. It is clear that they got on well and when, in 1917, Lockhart was abruptly removed from Moscow after an over-public attachment to a Russian lady, Milner did not forget him. It was Milner to whom, three months later, in London, he repeated his arguments about the need to establish contact with the Bolsheviks, it was Milner who introduced him to Lloyd George and it was Milner who briefed him before his departure to the very new Russia of January 1918. In many respects he was uniquely well qualified for the appointment, but the qualities which fitted him for it did little to help him to secure respect for his views in Whitehall. He certainly felt that this lack of understanding between the man at the centre and the man on the spot, a common lament of diplomatists, was a significant contributory factor in the eventual failure of his mission. In truth, however, it was a mission doomed from the beginning.

Lockhart's brief, received orally from Milner, was to do as much harm to the Germans as possible, to put a spoke in the wheels of the separate peace negotiations, to stiffen by whatever means he could the Bolshevik resistance to German demands and to gather all the information he could as to the real nature and strength of the Bolshevik movement.[13] He travelled to Bergen by the cruiser which was to bring the Ambassador home and eventually reached Petrograd on 29 January, bearing with him a letter from Maxim Litvinov to Trotsky commending Lockhart as 'a thoroughly honest man who understands our position and sympathises with us'.[14]

Almost simultaneously with Bruce Lockhart's appointment, Trotsky had appointed Litvinov as the Bolsheviks' unofficial representative in London. Working for a time under the pseudonym of Maxim Harrison and married to an English girl, Ivy Low, Litvinov had already acted as representative of the Bolshevik party in the International Socialist Bureau, in which capacity he had come to the attention of the British security authorities. Through the intermediary of a Foreign Office official, Rex (later Sir Reginald) Leeper, Litvinov and Lockhart had met in London shortly before Lockhart's departure and the introduction to Trotsky was written out in the Lyons Tea Shop where they met. In the same letter, Litvinov mentioned that the question of his own recognition was not yet settled, but that he was making the acquaintance of the representatives of the Labour movement and had issued an 'appeal to the English working-men in all the Socialist papers'.

Thus, by the end of 1917, the pressure of events was bringing the first period of 'wait and see' to an end and the elements which were to determine the early years of the Anglo–Soviet relationship were falling into place. On 31 December the War Cabinet decided[15] that 'executive action with regard to South Russia', in other words the organisation of support for the anti-Bolshevik forces, should be concerted by a Committee sitting in the Foreign Office under Cecil's chairmanship and with War Office and Treasury representation. The flow of British military supplies had been cut off, but there were still large dumps at Vladivostok and smaller ones at Archangel. A naval force, comprising the battleship *Glory* and eight trawler–minesweepers under Admiral Kemp still lay at Murmansk.[16] The links with the Russian army, forged during the wartime alliance, were still maintained by British officers and served as a basis for relations with the anti-Bolshevik forces. Meanwhile, the Bolsheviks were pressing ahead with negotiations for a separate peace and on the same day that the Russia Committee was established in the Foreign Office the German negotiators arrived in

Petrograd. In all but name, the war between Russia and Germany was over and it seemed that unless the anti-Bolshevik forces could be turned against the Germans, the German High Command would be able, by the spring, to concentrate the whole of its forces for the final offensive in the West. To make matters worse, the Bolsheviks were maintaining a propaganda of world revolution and in London Litvinov was already active enough to alarm a significant part of the British establishment, if not to make much impact on the Labour movement.

2
Intervention

The need to choose

The contradictions inherent in the situation at the end of 1917 had now to work themselves out.[1]

> I have pointed out to the Foreign Office that we shall have to choose between coming to some working arrangement with the Bolvsheviks or breaking with them altogether. ... He [Trotsky] and Lenin are out to overthrow all the so-called imperialistic governments, but it is against Great Britain rather than against Germany that their main offensive will be directed. The situation is quite hopeless, as the Bolsheviks have monopolized all the energies and organizing power of the nation.[2]

This entry in Buchanan's diary was written just before his final departure for London, early in the New Year of 1918. The mission which had started with such promise was ending in failure and the Ambassador had good reason to be in a gloomy mood. A young British officer who stayed behind in Petrograd was equally gloomy. He summed up the scene in a blunt letter to London:

> Attitude to British bad. We are considered quitters and weak kneed. This is because the English out here, chiefly business men, have chucked up the sponge and bolted, while the Germans have been trying hard to get what the English have left. Other Englishmen, not only civilians, have lost their tempers, cursed Russia and departed. The attitude of the British Government in recognising no one, helping no one, wishing to help no one is only making us

unpopular with everyone. The silly perpetual attacks on the Bolsheviks in the English press – Lenin is a German agent, etc. etc. – mislead people at home and infuriate the Bolsheviks here. It's too childish. The French are worse. But the Yanks are playing more astutely.[3]

When Buchanan returned to London, he was accompanied by his Military Attaché, General Knox, who was subsequently to figure prominently as an advocate of British intervention and as British military representative in Siberia. The Counsellor of the Embassy, Francis Lindley, was left as Chargé d'Affaires in Petrograd, with the task of maintaining the rump of an Embassy accredited to a vanished regime, and matters were complicated when, at the end of January, Lockhart arrived to take up his unofficial mission to the Bolsheviks. Balfour's policy of deliberate drifting was achieving little and there were many pressures on the British Government to come off the fence and commit itself for or against the Bolsheviks. For the time being, however, Lloyd George and his colleagues had no option but to pursue a policy based on the realities of political power in Russia as they saw them. Unfortunately, not only was reliable information hard to come by, but the politico–military map was changing day by day as the various parties staked out their positions. Poland, Finland, Estonia, Latvia and Ukraine – all formerly within the Russian Empire or subordinate to it – had declared their independence. Armenia, Georgia, Azerbaidjan and Daghestan had proclaimed a Federal Republic of Transcaucasia and Bessarabia had formed an independent Moldavian Republic. The Bolshevik forces had already launched their offensive against Ukraine, only to be forced to withdraw by the Germans, and there was bloody fighting against the Cossacks. In the East, all was confusion. Stranded in the apparently disintegrating Russian Empire was a body of Czechoslovak troops, variously estimated at between 45 000 and 70 000, whom the Czechoslovak National Council, with the strong support of the French Government, was seeking to evacuate to the West as an organised military body. The only substantial organised military force in the country was that of Germany, and Lenin had not yet made peace with them. It was by no means clear that the Bolsheviks would survive, but there was no other single body which offered a convincing alternative central government. The British Government's policy was therefore to try, without recognising the Bolsheviks, to establish some kind of working relationship with them while at the same time continuing to support any groups which seemed to have the potential to act as a focus for resistance to the Germany army.

On 19 January, the Bolsheviks took a step which went far towards disillusioning their supporters abroad and reinforcing the hatred of their enemies. Faced with a newly elected Constituent Assembly in which they held only 175 out of the 707 seats, they had to choose between observance of the normal standards of constitutional democracy and the maintenance of their hold on power. The choice was easy. The Assembly was forcibly dissolved. If there had been hesitations on the part of the British Government about the kind of men they were dealing with, this might have removed them. Certainly it helped to turn Buchanan into an ardent supporter of intervention, a course which he advocated in a series of speeches in Britain during 1918.

In Petrograd Lindley, with no illusions about the Bolsheviks, nevertheless recommended recognition on the ground that 'It will be necessary for us to humour them by getting into closer touch if we desire to remain here'.[4] This produced from Balfour a lengthy reply, explaining that 'Wherever any *de facto* administration is set up, we have the right to establish informal relations with it, without prejudice to the informal relations we may choose to cultivate with organisations beyond its effective jurisdiction.' In other words, the British Government would deal with anyone who held power in a particular area. As for the Bolsheviks, although they neither could nor would fight the Germans, this was apparently true of every party in Russia. So, the Foreign Secretary concluded, very much as he had done consistently since the Revolution: 'Delay seems desirable, if only because it will give time for the situation to develop in South Russia and elsewhere.'[5]

Lockhart and Trotsky

It was on this equivocal basis that Lockhart had to begin the task of establishing a relationship with the Bolshevik leaders. He found Trotsky bitter against the English, yet he was able to report to Balfour that some cooperation might be possible. The price would, however, be the abandonment of support for the anti-Bolshevik forces. It was the classic price demanded by revolutionaries throughout the ages as soon as they begin to grasp power. It placed the British Government in the classic dilemma. Should they abandon traditionally more friendly groups in favour of those whose aims were in many respects hostile to their own and whose hold on power was, as yet, far from being established throughout the country they purported to rule? Balfour was not a man to gamble and he was certainly not going to 'abandon our friends and allies in those parts of Russia where Bolshevism cannot be regarded as the *de facto* government'.[6] When Lockhart next saw Trotsky on 23 February, Trotsky's mood was worse: 'While you are here trying to throw dust in my eyes, your countrymen and the French have been intriguing against us with the Ukrainians, who have already sold themselves to the Germans. Your Government is working for Japanese intervention in Siberia.'[7]

There was much substance to Trotsky's complaint. The British Government had placed high hopes on Ukraine. As early as the beginning of January they had informed the French Government that they considered official recognition of the Ukrainian Government desirable, but there is a certain irony in the fact that, two weeks before Lockhart's second interview with Trotsky, the Prime Minister had commented in Cabinet that 'It had turned out that the Ukrainians whom we had regarded as our friends had failed us'.[8] A project to stimulate Japanese intervention in Siberia had been under discussion since the previous December, when the Allied Military Representatives at Versailles had submitted Joint Note No. 5 recommending the opening of a direct line of communications to friendly groups in Russia through Vladivostok and the trans-Siberian railway. It was in fact only two days after the interview with Trotsky that the War Cabinet decided to seek the concurrence of the US Government in such a project.[9] By the time it came to fruition the war with Germany was virtually over. At the beginning of 1918, however, the Allies were desperate to find any means they could of preventing Germany from exploiting her victory over the Russian armies.

Germany drives home her victory

In the chaos which was Russia, only the German army, it seemed, had the ability and the will to achieve dominance. It was poised to resume the offensive against an enemy, its view of whom is illustrated by the note by General Hoffman on 17 February: 'The whole of Russia is no more than a vast heap of maggots – a squalid, swarming mass.'[10] Yet, although the Germans had the military power available inside Russia, it was by no means easy for them to determine how best to deploy it. They were stretched to the limit. Their top priority was the conduct of the war in the West and the maximum reinforcements were needed from the Russian front in order to mount a major land offensive in France in March 1918. Both sides knew that this attack had to come, and both were preparing for it. The Germans had already withdrawn 35 divisions for this purpose during the winter of 1917–18.[11] At the same time, there was a desperate need for both Germany and Austria to obtain Russian supplies, if they were to break the economic strangulation of the Allied blockade. Lloyd George in his memoirs quotes evidence given before the German Reichstag Committee after the war by General von Kuhl, who cited a report to Ludendorff in December 1917, stating 'the state of our food supplies of breadstuffs and provisions makes it a matter of extreme urgency to give first place to the possibility of bringing corn from Russia'.[12] The Austrian situation was even more desperate. Corn from Ukraine was essential if collapse and revolution were to be averted. It would suit Germany to acquire her supplies by agreement with Russia, if this were possible but, if it were not, then she would have to press on and take them. In any case, a resumed offensive would stand a good chance of inducing an unstable Bolshevik Government, struggling to avoid its own total collapse, to concede all Germany needed. Not surprisingly, the Germans decided to use negotiation and force in combination. They needed a final decision within a matter of weeks in order that their full force might be concentrated against the Allies in France. Otherwise they faced the prospect of defeat.

Brest-Litovsk

On 10 February Trotsky, faced at Brest-Litovsk with German demands which he saw as unacceptable, attempted the ingenious manoeuvre of 'no war – no peace': 'We are going out of the war, but we feel ourselves compelled to refuse to sign the peace treaty.'[13] Against a desperate German High Command it produced the predictable result. The German advance was resumed and it appeared that Petrograd itself would shortly fall. So, after a historic debate in the Central Committee at which Lenin, with a threat of resignation, secured approval for immediate acceptance of still harsher German peace terms, the Treaty of Brest-Litovsk was signed on 3 March. The leader of the Bolshevik negotiators in the final stages, Grigori Sokolnikov, was later to become the first Soviet Ambassador to the Court of St James. By the Treaty, Russia surrendered territory containing about a third of her population and a third of her industrial potential. The margin of time was slim. The German offensive in France opened on 21 March (Map 2).

Intervention 35

Map 2 From Brest-Litovsk to Stalingrad

German policy in relation to the Western and Eastern fronts had been well coordinated, both militarily and economically. With the first-line fighting divisions concentrated on the Western front, the Treaty of Brest-Litovsk eliminated the Russian front and at the same time provided the potential for a substantial increase in economic resources, vital for the prosecution of the war and of major importance for the subsequent enhancement of Germany's power, whether the war ended in victory or stalemate. In fact, the military gain was not enough to secure victory in the March offensive and Germany and Austria lacked the strength to continue the fight long enough to realise the potential economic gain. This, however, was not apparent to the Allied Governments at the time. What they could see was a possible major alteration of the strategic balance and they reacted accordingly, trying, by any means they could devise, to prevent Germany from reaping the gains of Brest-Litovsk.

The plan for allied intervention

In these circumstances, some form of military intervention by the Allies began to seem both important and urgent. This was in fact the point at which the war against Germany was about to swing decisively in their favour, but in the context of British–Soviet relations, it was the point at which Balfour's policy of drift was effectively, although not explicity abandoned and at which the British Government, still uncertain of both its objectives and its methods, set out with its Allies on the course of direct military operations in Russia. We have seen how, as early as December 1917, the plan for a Japanese landing at Vladivostok had been recommended by the Allied Military Representatives. At an Allied Diplomatic Conference held in London on 16 March it was decided to send to the US Government a despatch prepared by Balfour asking for active American support for Japanese intervention through Siberia. 'What Germany desires', he wrote, 'is that Russia should be impotent during the War, subservient after it, and in the meanwhile should supply food and raw material to the Central Powers.' Russia could not help herself, so she must be helped by her friends. Only Japan had the necessary manpower and Siberia was for her the most accessible route. Lloyd George claims that he was dubious as to the wisdom of this step, but gave way under strong pressure by France for immediate Japanese intervention.[14] At the same time, however, he left Lockhart to continue the search for a basis of cooperation with Trotksy's new armies.

The German offensive in France demanded the complete attention of the War Cabinet and for a week Russia disappeared from the agenda. By the end of the month, however, it was back again, with attention focused by a paper by Lord Curzon.[15] What worried Curzon was the fact that, faced with conflicting advice, the Government seemed to be courting disaster by continuing with the pursuit of mutually incompatible policies, seeking simultaneously to deal with the Bolsheviks and to fight them. 'While great events are happening in France', he wrote, 'we seem to be in some danger of losing sight of what is going to happen in Russia.' On the one hand he saw Lockhart as 'acting in the closest collaboration with Trotsky and repeating to us daily with increasing passion the Trotsky formulas: Creation of a new Russian revolutionary army; Allied assistance in this undertaking; no Allied or Japanese intervention in Vladivostok; no Allied or British intervention at Murmansk or Archangel'. As against this, there was, he said, no Russian army and 'the majority of our advisers tell us that the hope to create a new state or a new army out of the shattered debris of Bolshevism is a fantastic dream'. General Poole was advising occupation of Murmansk and Archangel and opinion even among Russians was veering in the direction of Japanese intervention in Siberia. 'Ought not we to decide between the two policies?', he concluded. 'To believe in one while we pursue the other or to believe in neither but to pursue both seems equally to lead to destruction.'

Cecil came in quickly in support, arguing[16] that 'on the whole, since the outbreak of the Bolshevik Revolution, almost every step taken by the Bolshevik Government has been precisely that which would have been desired by the German General Staff'. He did not recommend actually obstructing the construction of Trotsky's army, but 'we should take all other steps we can to secure Russia from German penetration, quite irrespective of anything Trotsky may be doing or saying that he is doing'.

So it was that the War Cabinet moved to a policy of armed intervention in Russia, with the principal effort to be made by the Japanese moving westwards along the trans-Siberian railway in order to link up with the Czech forces in Central Siberia. British, American and Japanese naval vessels had for some time been lying off Vladivostok and concern over the safety of the supply dumps was growing. The town itself was not controlled by the Bolsheviks, but their influence was growing and early in April small detachments of Japanese and British marines were landed to maintain order and protect the supply dumps. On their withdrawal, the Bolsheviks took over, only to be ejected two months later. Various factions were fighting for local control in Siberia at this time and the pattern of conflict was further complicated by Japanese support for a peculiarly unsavoury ex-Cossack adventurer, Semenov, who had indeed, for a time, enjoyed British support.

In April, when the Czech forces were far to the West on the trans-Siberian railway, the British Government still hoped that large-scale intervention might take place without the opposition of the Bolshevik Government, and Lockhart was instructed that his main task was to secure their concurrence. The scheme, as he was to put it to Trotsky, was set out in a telegram from Balfour dated 13 April.[17] The Bolshevik administration should try to raise an efficient national army, organise guerrilla warfare against the Germans and prevent supplies from reaching them: they should invite Allied military and naval assistance at Murmansk if the railway was threatened and, in any case, through Vladivostok; the Allies should bind themselves to evacuate all Russian territory at the end of the war and, while in Russia, should take no part in political or economic controversy. The whole Allied object would be to free Russian soil from the enemy and to restore Russia's independence. 'There was', said Balfour, 'little use in making the attempt to persuade the Japanese to accept the plan if Troksky refused to play his part'; but in that event Japan might intervene on her own, with all the disadvantages and few of the advantages, so far as Russia was concerned, of the British plan. This was indeed a risk, since Japan's interest in establishing herself on Russia's Pacific Coast could be met without in any way serving the British interest in relation to the war against Germany.

A stream of diplomatic communications passed between London, Washington and Tokyo as the British Government sought American support for the planned Siberian operation. It became increasingly clear that President Wilson profoundly disliked the proposed scheme and the British Government, losing patience, took the first step towards intervention with action at Murmansk and then at Archangel. At Murmansk, there was a certain coincidence of interest between the British, who needed to prevent the port falling under German control, and the local Soviet, who faced a Finnish threat. For a brief initial period their cooperation even had the blessing of Trotsky. At Archangel, the situation was rather different. In April, an armed ice-breaker and two supply ships were sent, followed quickly by a cruiser, and it was decided that, although the captain should not prevent by force the removal of the Allied stores, he should be given wide discretionary powers to deal with any situation without reference back to the Admiralty. At the beginning of May, a Committee of Milner, General Smuts, the First Sea Lord and the Chief of the Imperial General Staff (CIGS) met to consider action 'to organise military resistance to the enemy in Russia while correspondence with America and Japan is proceeding'. It was recommended that General Poole should take charge of military affairs in Russia, with his initial base in Murmansk and a small office in London 'to assist him in organising the Czechoslovaks and other forces of intervention from Archangel and Murmansk'. The Committee expressed the opinion that 'undue weight had been placed in our recent correspondence on the desirability of an invitation for intervention from the Bolshevik Government'.[18] The War Cabinet approved the report and also decided to send a reinforcement of 350 Royal Marines to Murmansk. Thus, by a series of separate decisions, the British Government had moved close to the point at which British forces were to be committed to military operations in Russia in opposition to the Bolshevik Government.

Support for the anti-Bolshevik forces

In following the gradual development of British policy during this period, it must be remembered that, from the earliest stage after the Revolution, the British Government, like the French, had been trying by various means to prop up the assorted groups within Russia which were opposed to the Bolsheviks and which, it was hoped, might hold open the front against Germany. The tale of intrigue is too long and too complex to recite here. Not much of it appears in the minutes of the War Cabinet and this is in itself significant. The experience of more recent times has shown how hard it is for those who interfere in other countries' revolutions to understand the objectives of the various factions and how much harder still to determine the use to which arms and money will be put once they are in local hands. It was inevitable that, once broad ministerial approval for support to the anti-Bolshevik forces had been given and funding authorised, the Cabinet would lose effective control, with operational decisions falling to assorted agents on the spot and their controlling Departments in London. It was precisely in the operational detail that the potential for disaster lay. Support for the anti-Bolshevik groups was, both before direct military intervention and subsequently, the means by which the British Government's agents, including Lockhart, were implementing a major part of the Government's policy. It was this activity, more than the formal statements of the Government's desire not to interfere in the Russian political scene, which constituted the effective policy and which impressed itself upon the Bolshevik leadership. It was this activity, too, which created implicit obligations to continue support to the White forces after the end of the war with Germany, thus involving the Allies in the prolongation of the Russian Civil War and converting the intervention from an operation directed at the defeat of Germany to one directed at the defeat of the Bolsheviks. Althought the support to the anti-Bolshevik groups was, in part, covert, much had to be done openly. Throughout Russia, British and Allied representatives were being besieged by all those who saw in the defeat of the Bolsheviks their only hope for the future of themselves and their country. In London a running battle was waged between the Foreign Office and the Treasury over the supply of funds for a variety of ill-fated schemes advanced by plausible claimants upon British beneficence; and it was with remarkably innocent faith that the British Government's representatives were authorised to advance significant sums in sterling to those who claimed to be able to provide roubles to the anti-Bolshevik forces. It may suffice to quote a minute by the Russian Department of the Foreign Office in reply to a letter from the Treasury dated 11 November 1918, seeking the recovery of funds advanced for the purpose of obtaining water-marked currency paper and printing ink for notes to be printed in Tiflis for the Trans-Caucasus Confederacy: 'As far as we can discover, neither the paper nor the Government for which it was supplied is still in existence'. Not all those who were dependent upon British support disappeared so quickly and the disentangling of the British Government's inherited obligations was to prove a major element in later policy.

The conflict of professional advice

During the critical period leading to armed intervention in Russia without the consent of the Bolshevik Government and without the full support of the US Government, the British Government was handicapped by sharply conflicting assessments from its professional advisers. The whole problem was considered primarily in military terms and it was natural that the views of the Government's military advisers should carry special weight. Prominent among the advocates of intervention was the former Military Attaché in Petrograd, General Knox.[19] Knox's views were supported by the CIGS and counted for much in the consideration of the question by the War Cabinet, but their bias was probably recognised, at least by Balfour, who said of him on a later occasion that he was 'not a reactionary as the term was understood by members of the Cabinet', but 'there was no doubt that he was anti-Bolshevik, while a man of his strength of character, knowledge and ability was bound sooner or later to play a political part'.[20] Knox was bitterly hostile to Lockhart and so too was the Director of Military Intelligence, General MacDonogh, who argued at one point that General Poole, as the military representative in Russia, should be given authority for all questions, whether political, military or financial, and that Lockhart, if he were to be retained at all, should have only a consultative function. Balfour, however, minuted that he saw 'great objection to a military mission controlling our whole policy, even in Russia'.[21] He seems to have had some sympathy with Lockhart, but others in the Foreign Office certainly did not. Lockhart's telegrams sorely tried their patience and drove the Under-Secretary, Sir R. Graham, to minute, 'With every desire to make allowances for Mr Lockhart, the tone of his telegrams can only be described as intolerable'. The conflict of professional advice must have aggravated the problems of the War Cabinet. A glimpse of the conflict emerges from the remark by the CIGS in the War Cabinet that General Poole was just leaving for Russia and was 'quite sanguine as to raising a large army' to which the Prime Minister replied that Mr. Lindley was also going and apparently had no belief that anything could be done at all in Russia. The response to the Milner report suggests, however, that by May the divergence of views among ministers had been reduced. Even the Prime Minister was arguing that Britain should if necessary proceed without the United States and Japan, on the ground that the Germans were withdrawing troops from the Russian front, the British army was bearing the brunt of the fighting in France and no material American contribution had yet arrived.[22]

It was at this point, two months after Brest-Litovsk, that a new note of urgency was introduced by the appointment of a German Ambassador, von Mirbach, in Moscow. The situation was promptly assessed by Lockhart, who had accompanied the Bolshevik leadership when they moved from Petrograd to Moscow. On 23 May he reported that there had been a marked change in the situation in Russia so far as Germany was concerned. The Germans had announced that their military operations had been completed; that they had no intention of occupying Petrograd or Moscow and that they were anxious to cooperate economically with the Russian Government. Lockhart went on to argue that the changed situation in Russia left the British

Government with two alternative courses: to recognise the Bolsheviks and conclude an economic treaty with them, accompanied by a provision that they would accept Allied intervention in the event of any further German aggression; or to undertake large-scale Allied intervention, preferably with Bolshevik consent but, failing that, without it.[23] He came down in favour of the latter, but warned that no substantial assistance could be expected from pro-Allied forces in the early stage. A few days later, he telegraphed again, urging that, with Bolshevik power decreasing, the Allies could expect neither an invitation, nor consent to intervention, but that they would never have a more favourable moment for it. From the Consul in Petrograd came a recommendation that nothing but armed force could protect British interests and that Archangel and Murmansk should be occupied with a division at each.

Lockhart had for some time harangued London with a series of telegrams and it was noted with irritation in the Foreign Office that he had now recognised what others had seen two months earlier. His ever-changing recommendations brought a telegram from Balfour which bears traces of having been personally drafted and which testifies to the problems the Government faced in dealing with the differing counsels of their advisers and the differing interests of their Allies.[24] Having assured Lockhart that his work was not unappreciated and that he had not in any way lost the Government's confidence, Balfour continued:

> Your telegrams during the last five months have faithfully reflected the variation in opinion produced and no doubt justified by the constantly changing aspects of the present transitional period of Russian history. You have at different times advised against Allied intervention in any form; against it by Japanese alone; against it with Japanese assistance; against it at Vladivostok; in favour of it at Murmansk; in favour of it with an invitation; in favour of it without an invitation since it was really desired by the Bolsheviks; in favour of it without an invitation, whether the Bolsheviks desired it or not.

Balfour then set out, with a patience which in the circumstances was remarkable, the problems of the alliance, the contradictory reports and the differing conclusions, with Britain, France and Italy thinking the dangers of intervention less than its advantages, America taking the contrary view and Japan unwilling to do anything on a great scale without an invitation. 'The only thing on which everybody agrees is that without the active participation of America nothing effective can be accomplished through Siberia and active participation of America has so far been refused.' The Bolshevists were behaving as the tools, willing or unwilling, of the Central Powers and no other party seemed able to do anything against them. So, Balfour concluded, 'We can do no more than press our views on the Administration at Washington and hope that by the time the necessity of intervention is universally admitted and common action becomes ... possible it may not prove too late'.

It is not difficult to see how, at this point in mid-1918, six months after the Revolution, there should have been a broad measure of agreement in Britain among the members of the War Cabinet and their professional advisers on the need for some means of preventing Germany from securing the full fruits of her military victory over Russia. The Bolshevik power was by no means assured and it was not wholly impossible that Germany might have secured a degree of control over Russia's economic resources which, if it could not have brought victory in the West, might at least have brought a stalemate from which Germany could have withdrawn to renew her strength. What is more remarkable – and for this a measure of responsibility must rest with the government's military and political advisers – is the faith which was placed in the ability of the Allies to prevent such an outcome by means of an operation which, to have had any chance of success, would have required the deployment of forces far in excess of anything which could realistically have been expected. What was envisaged was in effect an attempt to reconstitute Russian national resistance to the German forces by means of landings of relatively small Allied contingents at three points separated by several thousand miles of exceptionally difficult terrain. As a scheme, it bordered on the fantastic. The case for it could only be sustained by the political judgement that, once Allied landings in force had taken place, the Russian people would rise in welcome and overthrow the Bolsheviks. Exactly this point had been made when the idea was mooted in January. At that time Balfour, commenting on the proposal for intervention put up by the Interdepartmental Russia Committee, declined to offer any opinion on its practicability, commenting only that it had been devised by important members of the War Office and the Foreign Office and deserved careful consideration by the War Cabinet. General Macdonogh, the Director of Military Intelligence, was asked for his assessment and wrote a most cautious letter to Balfour on 27 January, pointing out that a statement of the feasibility of the scheme from the military point of view would be a purely theoretical exercise, since 'the question is entirely dependent on the attitude of the Russians which is a political rather than a military matter'.[25]

Five months of discussion and the absence of any alternative plan had left Ministers so wedded to the scheme that by June they were prepared to close their eyes to its inherent impracticability and to abandon all reserve. Cecil was arguing in Cabinet that without intervention in Siberia there was no prospect of a successful conclusion to the war. His view was embodied in a formal memorandum in which it was stated that unless Allied intervention in Siberia was undertaken forthwith 'we have no chance of being ultimately victorious and shall incur serious risk of defeat in the meantime'. British and French reserves would have been exhausted by June 1919 and the Germans might then obtain a decision in their favour in the West. In any case, 'No military decision in the Allies' favour can ever be expected as a result of operations on the Western front alone. Only by immediate Allied intervention would it be possible to prevent the complete absorption of Russia by the Central Powers which would imply world domination by Germany.'[26]

Concern about trade prospects

Although, by the summer of 1918, the British Government was concerned primarily with the preparation for armed intervention in Russia, it did not wholly ignore the need for some more constructive longer-term policy. The British financial interest in Russia was substantial, in respect not only of the direct financial assistance given for the pursuit of the war, but also of British industrial and mining investments which it was hoped to recover. These issues were, for many years, to play a dominant part in the British–Soviet relationship and they were first considered in June 1918, when the War Cabinet took a joint memorandum[27] by the Foreign Office and the Department of Overseas Trade on the question of future economic relations with Russia. It was decided to send a mission of officials and businessmen to explore the situation and recommend how best to develop trade. The mission left, with no very high expectations, on the same ship which was taking Lindley back to Russia as British Commissioner with the intervention forces in the North. By the time they reached Moscow the Allied landings were only a few days off. It was, as Lockhart said, a Gilbertian situation, and it illustrated very clearly the way in which up to the last moment the British Government sought to hedge its bets. But it was the last such attempt for a long time.

The decision to intervene

The final stage of the preparation for intervention began on 28 June, when the Imperial War Cabinet approved a formal resolution: 'The British Imperial War Cabinet ... having carefully considered the military situation and prospects of the Allies in all theatres of war have come to the conclusion that immediate Allied armed intervention and armed assistance to Russia is imperatively necessary.' The Government appealed to President Wilson to accept this policy, but the American reply was firm. The proposed military intervention 'would add to the present sad confusion in Russia rather than cure it, injure her rather than help her and would be of no advantage in prosecution of our main design, to win the war against Germany'. The United States therefore could not take part in such intervention or sanction it in principle. What the US Government would do was to assist in the consolidation of the Czechoslovak forces and in the guarding of military stores. The President also made clear, however, that he was not seeking to set limits to action by America's associates.

Allied landing at Vladivostok –

This statement, unsatisfactory as it was from the British point of view, left the Allies free to go ahead – and they did so. Not surprisingly, each envisaged a substantially different operation. Britain still cherished the objective of establishing an independent Government in Siberia, linking up with the force moving south from Archangel and providing a base for support of anti-Bolshevik forces in southern Russia. Japan wanted to establish its own power in Russia's Pacific provinces. France, having been consistently the most hostile of the Allies towards the Bolsheviks, sought to control the Siberian operation, but made little material contribution to it and wanted mainly to secure the transfer of the Czech forces to the Western front. The United States, instinctively disliking the whole operation, was determined not to move beyond the limited initial objective of facilitating the evacuation of the Czechs. Such were the circumstances in which on 3 August 1918, with the war against Germany almost won, a battalion of the Middlesex Regiment landed in Vladivostok, to be followed by 70 000 Japanese, 8000 Americans and contingents from France, Canada and Italy, as well as a second British battalion.

and at Archangel –

While urging on President Wilson the case for intervention in Siberia, the British Government had to decide whether to exploit its toehold at Murmansk and mount a major operation from Archangel. When the War Cabinet considered this aspect of the Russian problem in June[28] the CIGS said that the occupation of the two towns would require two and a half divisions of infantry alone. He was inclined to abandon the Murman coast unless the operation there were backed up by intervention through Siberia. The Prime Minister, however, argued that, even if the Siberian operation could not be implemented, Archangel and Murmansk would be invaluable as inlets to Russia and it was essential to maintain the British position 'if such could be achieved without the expenditure of large forces'. So the build-up of forces went ahead and with Lindley as his political adviser, Poole took the Anglo–French landing party into Archangel on 2 August, a day before the first British battalion landed in Vladivostok.

– and in the Caucasus

The principal point of friction prior to the Revolution had been the southward thrust of the Russians in Afghanistan and Persia, the border zone between the Russian and Indian Empires. In 1918 the old friction was revived in two new forms. On the one hand, Bolshevik propaganda directed at the Muslim world carried the threat of insurrection against British rule. On the other, the collapse of Russian resistance to the German armies raised the risk that German–Turkish imperialism might replace Russian imperialism in Central Asia. German–Turkish domination of the Caucasus might lead in the short term to control of the Baku oil fields and possibly, in the longer term, to a threat to the border areas of the Indian Empire. In these circumstances, it seemed to the strategists in London that control of the Caucasus should be an important element in British policy and in January 1918 Major-General Dunsterville was appointed as British Representative at Tiflis in Georgia, where he sought to mobilise opposition to Turkish and German encroachment. After considerable hesitation in London, he was eventually given permission to take a force of two battalions to Baku and was invited by the local anti-Bolshevik authorities to help in the defence of the city. The first battalion arrived on 4 August. The timing owed much to chance and little to plan. It is, however, of interest to note that these three operations, Archangel, Vladivostok and Baku, began effectively on 2, 3, and 4 August.

The full irony of the timing is best illustrated by the passage in Lloyd George's *War Memoirs* in which he notes how on 8 August the Anglo–French offensive on the Western front had convinced both General Ludendorff and the Kaiser that the war had been lost. 'We are at the limits of our endurance. The War must be brought to an end', the Kaiser had written.[29] Had the operations in Russia been in fact rather than in theory part of a concerted drive from East and West to break the power of Germany, they might have had a certain logic. They were, however, conceived against a different and earlier strategic assessment and implemented with no clear or agreed purpose. The sector of the Eastern front which was to prove important in precipitating the final collapse of the Austrian and German forces was the southern, Salonika sector, not the Russian and certainly not the Siberian. So it was that by August 1918, just three months before the end of the war with Germany, Britain embarked on operations in Russia which had minimal relevance to the outcome of the war, but which were to dominate the Anglo–Soviet relationship in its immediate post-war phase.

'We are coming as friends'

On 9 August 1918, with the commencement of the phase of active intervention, the British representatives in Murmansk, Archangel and Vladivostok were instructed to issue a 'Declaration by the British Government to the Peoples of Russia':

> We are coming as friends to help you to save yourselves from dismemberment and destruction at the hands of Germany ... We wish solemnly to assure you that while our troops are entering Russia to assist you in your struggle against Germany we shall not retain one foot of your territory ... Our one desire is to see Russia strong and free and then to retire and watch the Russian people work out its destinies in accordance with the freely expressed wishes of the people.[30]

The declaration, of a type which is not unfamiliar in situations of 'liberation', may well have been issued in good faith, but it would have required a remarkable degree of trust on the part of the Bolshevik leadership to accept it at face value. The British Government were now committed to a policy, the logic of which was that the claim by the Bolsheviks to constitute the central Government of Russia was not merely unrecognised, but was directly challenged. Either the Bolshevik power had to be broken, or the intervention had to fail. This was the dilemma which the War Cabinet had long perceived and long sought to avoid. Although the breaking of Bolshevik power would have been by no means unwelcome to the majority of the Cabinet, it had not been the direct objective of their policy. Even in August not all members of the Government would have accepted that it was a necessary implication and there was no clear concept as to the preferred alternative to Bolshevik power. The question whether a state of war existed between Britain and Russia was one which did not particularly trouble the British Government so long as the operations in Russia were seen as part of the war against Germany. After the end of the German war the problem was to become rather more acute, especially in relation to the continuation of the blockade. The conclusion then was that although, in practice, war was being waged, it could not be declared as such against a body, the Bolsheviks, who were not recognised as the Government of Russia.

So far as the Bolsheviks themselves were concerned, there was some uncertainty as to whether a state of war existed, but little doubt as to Allied intentions. Lockhart reported[31] that immediately after the first landings Lenin had emphatically declared at an official and public meeting of the Soviet that a state of war existed between the Allied powers and the Russian Republic. However, in the face of a *démarche* by the Allied representatives, Chicherin replied that it was a 'state of defence rather than one of war' and that his Government wished 'to continue relations with the Allied powers as they had done with Germany under analogous circumstances'. In its official history of Soviet Foreign Policy, the Soviet Government presented the August intervention as a step in the implementation of a policy of armed invasion and civil war which had already been decided on by the end of 1917.[32] It was, however, scarcely surprising that the Soviet Union should have sought to depict the Allied intervention in the blackest light. In August 1918 it would have been hard for a Bolshevik Government, itself born of conspiracy and skilled in the arbitrary and violent use of power, to avoid the interpretation, incorrect though it was, that Allied policy since the Revolution had been directed continuously, by whatever means were available, to the overthrow of Bolshevik power.

In the period prior to August, the attempt by the Allies to organise anti-Bolshevik forces into an effective opposition to German domination of Russia had been relatively ineffective. The threat to the Bolshevik hold on the country was, however, under constant threat from various sources, some financed by one or other of the Allies, others quite independent of any Allied support and all pursuing their own ambitions. The summer of 1918 was a period of particular tension. On 4 July came the open denunciation of Lenin by the Socialist Revolutionary Spiridinova at the Fifth All-Russian Congress, followed on 6 July by the murder of the German Ambassador von Mirbach and the seizure by Socialist Revolutionaries under Boris Savinkov of Yaroslavl, only 125 miles from Moscow. Savinkov had links with French agents but was also probably receiving finance from the British agent Sidney Reilly. The Czech forces which were to be the main element in the Siberian intervention were gaining the upper hand well before the main Allied landings and on 16 July, as they outflanked the city of Ekaterinburg, the Tsar and his family were murdered.

Then, on 30 August, a Socialist Revolutionary shot and killed Uritsky, the head of the Petrograd branch of the CHEKA. This predecessor of the OGPU and KGB, its acronym standing for the All-Russian Extraordinary Commission for Fighting Counter-Revolution and Sabotage, had at its head the Polish Communist Dzerzhinski and its central office in Lubyanka Street in Moscow. Throughout the succeeding decades it was to symbolise for Soviet citizens and for foreign observers the processes of espionage, repression and terror by which the Soviet leadership sought to sustain their personal power and the revolutionary purity of the Soviet state.

On the day of Uritsky's murder Lenin was severely injured by two bullets fired by Fanny Kaplan in Moscow. Lenin himself called this the most critical period of the Revolution and it must have seemed equally possible both to him and to the Allied Governments that the Bolshevik experiment was on the point of failure. The effect of these events was significant in both the short and long term, not only for the development of Soviet Russia, but for the British–Russian relationship.

The 'Lockhart plot'

The landings at Archangel and Vladivostok effectively meant the end of Lockhart's mission. The immediate Bolshevik response was the arrest of British and French residents of Moscow, including members of the Consular staff. Although most were quickly released, they were not permitted to leave the country. On 9 August, the British Consul-General, Oliver Wardrop, handed over the responsibility for the care of the British community to the Netherlands Embassy. Negotiations for permission for the British to leave Russia in exchange for permission for Litvinov and his staff to leave London were continuing when the murder of Uritsky was followed by the storming of the former British

Embassy by agents of the CHEKA and the murder of the Naval Attaché, Captain Cromie, who shot two of the intruders before himself being killed. In Moscow, Lockhart was arrested immediately after the attack on Lenin, and although briefly released, was re-arrested on 4 September. The official Soviet legend was created that 'the most dangerous of the anti-Soviet conspiracies was the Lockhart plot'[33] aimed at physically exterminating leaders of the party and the Soviet Government, first and foremost Lenin.

With British forces operating on Russian soil and the British Government, with Lockhart as their agent, actively supporting military operations by groups in various parts of Russia, the allegation is not entirely surprising. Lockhart was certainly in contact with various anti-Bolshevik groups and was providing finance for the forces which Alexeyev, the former Commander-in-Chief, was gathering in southern Russia. The British intelligence authorities were operating through agents such as Paul Dukes, Sidney Reilly and George Hill in a mixture of operations, some directed against the Germans and others against the Bolsheviks. Cromie's activities against the Germans had, according to Lindley, brought him 'more or less into cooperation' with anti-Bolsheviks. Reilly was closely involved with Savinkov and was attempting to suborn the Kremlin guards in preparation for a coup d'état against Lenin's Government. The overthrow of that Government was certainly not the direct objective of British policy and, with the archives closed, there is no evidence of the extent to which Reilly's activities, although doubtless known to Lockhart, had been approved by Balfour. Nor is there a known link between Fanny Kaplan and the British agents. A telegram from Balfour indicating his concern that Lockhart should not be placed in a compromising position may be interpreted either way. In the absence of any convincing evidence, it may well be that Lockhart's personal complicity in the plots to overthrow Lenin and his Government was minimal, but the personal accounts of Hill and others[34] indicate the varied operations of the British intelligence services in Russia at that time.

The end of unofficial relations

The negotiations for an exchange of Lockhart and other British subjects against Russians in Britain had been in train for some time when the news of Cromie's death was received. In an attempt to secure some extra leverage, the War Cabinet decided to arrest Litvinov and instructed the Foreign Secretary to threaten reprisals against Lenin,

Trotsky and other Bolshevik leaders if the lives of British subjects were not safeguarded.[35] Balfour's message stated that the members of the Soviet Government would be held individually responsible for any further acts of violence and that the Government would 'make every endeavour to secure that they shall be treated as outlaws by the Governments of all civilized nations and that no place of refuge shall be left to them'. After difficult negotiations, agreement was reached and Lockhart arrived back in London on 19 October. On his return, he wrote a report on his mission.[36] The Bolsheviks, he wrote, had been in power for exactly a year, their power was stronger and more consolidated than at any previous period and they possessed one fundamental attribute of any real Government, the physical power to enforce their decrees. He saw Bolshevism as such a danger that it had to be crushed. It was no use relying on anti-Bolshevik forces in Russia to do this. What was needed was Allied intervention on 'a proper scale', with an Allied force of 50 000 driving north from the Black Sea to Moscow and at least as many moving through Siberia. 'Very interesting, but I fear the conclusion is impracticable', minuted Lord Robert Cecil. Lockhart went off to Scotland on half pay. Having abandoned a reluctant and half-hearted attempt to establish some kind of relationship with the Bolsheviks, the British Government was now committed to an equally reluctant and half-hearted military intervention.

Among the British public, the murder of the Tsar did not of itself cause a great public reaction, but the murder of Cromie, the campaign of terror which followed the attack on Lenin and the accumulating reports of Bolshevik atrocities did much to harden opinion. On the other side of the political divide, the bulk of the British Labour movement had no love for the Bolsheviks, but throughout the spring and summer, as talk of the impending Allied operations grew, opposition to intervention had begun to build up. Litvinov had been doing his best to encourage pro-Bolshevik sentiment among the British workers and had been under close observation by the security authorities, who provided the Cabinet with regular reports on subversive activities. As early as 9 March 1918 the *Herald* was writing of the 'peril from the East' and saying to 'our comrades' in Russia: 'We share your shame and your indignation. The blow struck at your heart strikes at our heart too.' Cecil was described as 'the most reckless militarist now in office in Europe' and when the main landings took place the *Herald* registered its protest: 'Great Britain and her allies are at war with the Bolshevik Government of Russia ... British Labour dare not stand by without protest'. Douglas Young, the Consul in Archangel, who had long realised the inconsistency of his Government's policy, returned to Britain in the autumn of 1918 and wrote an article 'Britain and Russia' for the *Herald*, expressing his hatred of Bolshevism, but his anger that 'the British Government played a dirty and double game with the Soviet Government in Russia'.[37] At this stage, with the war against Germany still the dominant factor in public opinion, the Government had little need for concern but, with its ending, the political background to British policy was to undergo a significant change.

Intervention – the fantasy and the reality

The first news of the Allied military operations was encouraging. The CIGS put a paper to the Cabinet in September[38] reporting that control of the trans-Siberian railway from Vladivostok to the Volga had been secured, that the Czech forces ought to be able to link up with Poole's forces driving south from Archangel and together they could then join the anti-Bolshevik forces under General Alexeyev between the Don and Volga, thus opening up by the spring of 1919 a new Eastern front against Germany. For generals who had deployed men by the million to gain ground by the yard in France, it must have been exhilarating to plan on their maps these grand designs across thousands of miles of Russia. It was far from certain that the Bolsheviks would be able to consolidate their power and there were moments in the early autumn of 1918 and again in the autumn of 1919 when it looked as though the fantasy had a chance of realisation. Fantasy it was, both political and military, but it was to be another year and a half before the Bolshevik power was finally established. Politically, the Japanese Government wanted only to hold the Pacific Coast and they made it clear that they had no desire to move east of Lake Baikal, at which point they were still some 2000 miles from the Volga. Politically, the American objective of helping the Czechs was realised by the opening of the railway which would make possible their evacuation through Vladivostok, and President Wilson had never proposed to become involved in a campaign to control Russia. Politically, the anti-Bolshevik forces lacked the will to create a system which might have commanded the mass of popular support. Militarily, the British would soon have to dig in for the Arctic winter on the Archangel front, the Czechs had all they could do to sustain their existing position and the Allied lines of communication within Russia would have become increasingly vulnerable to guerrilla attack. So long as the war in France continued, Britain could not find the forces or the transport for major operations in Russia and, with the ending of the war, it would be a political impossibility to embark on another major campaign. Perhaps most important of all, the various Russian groups supported by the Allies were continuing in pursuit of their separate and sometimes conflicting objectives, for the most part unable to comprehend the change in the mood of Russia and unable to capture that popular enthusiasm which alone might have justified and secured their victory. Lloyd George consistently took the line that the anti-Bolshevik forces deserved the chance to show whether they could win that support, but that if they could not, no Allied support would save them. He soon had to recognise that the latter was the case.

It was not long before the War Cabinet began to doubt whether the Volga line could be held. They still hoped that the Americans might yet be persuaded of the need to do so: 'If we were now to ask the Czechs to withdraw to the East of the Urals, that would be to cut off from Alexeyev and those with him their last hope of Allied assistance.'[39] Meanwhile, the political attempt to consolidate an anti-Bolshevik Government in Siberia and to raise a Russian force was pursued. The Government appointed Sir Charles Eliot, Vice-Chancellor of Hong Kong University, as High Commissioner for Siberia. A Siberian Provisional Government was functioning at Omsk and it was thought that, if the link with Alexeyev in the South could be made, there might be a possibility of developing a provisional Russian Government under military leadership.

It was at this point, just two months after the commitment to intervention that, with a rapidity which took the Allies wholly by surprise, the war with Germany ended and Britain faced the prospect that she would be left with forces on Russian soil in pursuit of an unsustainable and irrelevant policy. The forces committed to the intervention were by then approximately as follows:[40]

Siberia: 70 000 Japanese; 8000 Americans; 4000 Canadians; 2000 British; 1500 Italian; 1000 French, in addition to a Czech force estimated at between 45 000 and 70 000.
Murmansk and Archangel: A total of 13 000, mainly British, but also including contingents from France, Italy, Canada and the United States.
The Caspian: 5000 British.

For the most part, the British forces had not at this time been involved in major actions against the Bolsheviks. In Murmansk, they were able to establish a satisfactory relationship with the local Bolshevik administration, but at the price of a breach between the latter and Moscow. At Archangel, where the local Soviet was loyal to Moscow, Poole had to organise a coup and dispose of the existing administration before establishing one favourable to the Allied occupation. Having done so, his attitude to the inhabitants was that of a commander holding conquered territory.[41] Probing southwards from the two ports, the British forces had been engaged in minor but sharp operations designed to hold off the Bolsheviks and extend the bridgehead. In Vladivostok, by the time the main landing was made, the town was held by an administration which was not subject to orders from Moscow. The British troops moved westwards down the railway to Omsk but, with the remarkable exception of a naval gun team, made little contact with the Bolsheviks. In the South, Dunsterville was working in cooperation with the Socialist Revolutionary administration which had replaced the Bolsheviks in Baku and was forced to withdraw after a bitter engagement not with the Bolsheviks but with the Turks. On the other side of the Caspian at Ashkhabad, Major-General Malleson was also cooperating with a Socialist Revolutionary and Menshevik administration. His small British–Indian force fought off the Bolsheviks and established a small flotilla on the Caspian. It was Malleson's Socialist Revolutionary allies who gave rise to one of the legends of the intervention when, without his concurrence, they shot the 26 Bolshevik Commissars who had left Baku after the Socialist Revolutionary takeover.

The British officers, operating with minuscule forces in a vast and war-torn country, had little option but to make such arrangements as they could with the factions controlling the areas in which they operated. The commitments they made were in line with the general tenor of British policy and, indeed, necessary if the intervention were to succeed. With a political direction from London which could, at best, be described as fitful, the consequence was, however, a casual accretion of formal and informal obligations, lacking either political or military coherence and, in sum, constituting a significant complicating factor in subsequent British policy.

Post-war policy

The ending of the war with Germany compelled the Cabinet to rethink its whole military policy in Russia. Cecil saw the dilemma. He made it plain in Cabinet that 'he hated the idea of abandoning to Bolshevik fury all those who had helped us, but he quite saw that it might end badly if we tried to destroy Bolshevism by means of military interference'.[42]

Not for the first nor for the last time, ministers succeeded in diagnosing the problem correctly, before embarking on the wrong course. The War Cabinet met on 14 November to consider the recommendations of a meeting in the Foreign Office at which the Foreign Secretary, Cecil and Milner, together with Foreign Office officials and the Directors of Military and Naval Intelligence and Operations considered the whole field of policy in Russia. The British Government could not, said the Foreign Secretary, 'embark on an anti-Bolshevik crusade in Russia' despite the contrary advice from advisers on the spot who were 'obsessed with the external and visible violence of Bolshevism'. Cecil agreed. So did the Prime Minister, but everyone then agreed with Milner that east of the Don and the Volga, where anti-Bolshevik Governments were in existence, they should be supported. Specifically, the War Cabinet approved the recommendations[43] that the 'border states of Western Russia from the Baltic to the Black Sea' should be recognised; British forces should remain in occupation of Murmansk and Archangel; the Omsk Directorate in Siberia should be recognised as a *de facto* Government; the Siberian expedition should be maintained; the Baku–Batum railway should be held; Denikin, who had taken command in southern Russia after the death of Alexeyev, should be given all possible assistance in military material; so, also, should the Baltic states when they had Governments ready to receive and utilise it; the British sphere of 'influence' defined in the Anglo–French agreement of 1917 should be extended to cover the country between the Don and the Volga; and consideration should be given to taking over Krasnovodsk on the eastern shore of the Caspian. At the same meeting, the Prime Minister for the first time expressed his concern about the need to ensure that the 'great inflammable industrial population' of Britain understood what Bolshevism meant in practice, and measures to this end were put in hand. So, in the moment of victory, the members of the War Cabinet reaffirmed, with no apparent dissent, a policy which, originally conceived as part of the war with Germany, was now in practice a policy for the internal reconstruction of Russia.

It was a policy which would have to be carried through against a very different background. With the ending of the war, the victorious Allies were to gather in Paris at the beginning of 1919 for the Peace Conference and were to concern themselves effectively with the postwar structure of Europe. What was to be the position of Russia, their ally for most of the war? There was no longer an Allied Russian

Government to sit with them at the table. The Allies were not formally at war with Russia, but their armed forces were engaged in conflict with the Bolsheviks and there was no other group which could claim effectively to control the territory of Russia. The boundaries of post-war Europe could not be settled without any settlement of the boundary of Russia. Independent, quasi-independent and would-be independent states had been carved or were in the process of being carved out of the territory of Imperial Russia. The Treaty of Brest-Litovsk was denounced on 13 November and all was in flux. It might fairly be said that the future of Russia was the business of the Russians. But what was Russia? Who were the Russians? How were they to decide their future?

Lloyd George and Churchill

By the time the Peace Conference assembled, Lloyd George's power had been substantially enhanced by the overwhelming Coalition victory in the December election. With the formation of the post-war Government, Winston Churchill was to move from his post of Minister of Munitions to become Secretary of State for War, an appointment which Lloyd George had seen as concerned with the readjustment of the army to the peace. As Churchill described it, he, having been responsible for no commitment in relation to Russia – and, indeed he had not – 'became an heir to the pledges and tragedies' of the situation.[44] His policy was: 'Contract your commitments; select your obligations; and make a success of those to which you are able to adhere.' In practice, however, Churchill was to become the principal advocate of policies designed to secure the military overthrow of the 'nameless beast' of Bolshevik Government. Time and again he was to urge upon the War Cabinet the need for a clear policy, which he believed should be a policy of active intervention, in relation to Russia. Lloyd George recognised clearly the force of opinion against Bolshevism. In *The Truth About the Peace Treaties* he describes how there was 'throughout the Allied countries, especially amongst the proppertied classes, an implacable hatred, born of real fear, of Bolshevism'. There could, he said, be no doubt 'that the great majority of the inhabitants of Western Europe and America would have liked to see Bolshevism crushed, but no one was prepared to undertake the task'. He recognised, too, the inherent contradictions of the existing policy, but whereas Churchill drew the conclusion that a concerted effort was needed to overthrow the Bolsheviks, Lloyd George sought not always consistently, to end the intervention and bring Russia back into the community of nations. 'We could', he wrote, 'prolong the Civil War, perhaps for years until Russia had become a continent of desolation stretching from Central Europe to the Eastern shores of Asia, but we could not achieve any solution by force and certainly not a final or satisfactory solution.'[45]

The great debate began at the meeting of the Imperial War Cabinet on the last day of 1918,[46] when Churchill sought to swing his colleagues in favour of decisive collective intervention, while Lloyd George made it clear that he was opposed to intervention in any shape and argued that the one sure way of establishing the power of Bolshevism in Russia was to attempt to suppress it with foreign troops. In accepting Lloyd George's arguments, the Cabinet nevertheless registered provisos about the need to continue material help to the anti-Bolshevik forces and to support, without military intervention, those who might be threatened by external Bolshevik aggression. The continuing debate can be traced though the Cabinet minutes and documents of 1919 and 1920. Lloyd George commented[47] that Churchill 'threw the whole of his dynamic energy and genius into organising an armed intervention against Russia'. It is legitimate to wonder whether, had it not been for the pressure of Churchill, Lloyd George's policy might have prevailed more quickly and a constructive relationship with Russia been established much earlier. It is equally legitimate to wonder whether, had Churchill's advice been followed, the actions which at various times brought Kolchak from Vladivostok to the Volga, Denikin to within 250 miles of Moscow, Yudenich to the gates of Petrograd and the Poles to Kiev might have brought about the fall of the Soviet Government. The truth is, however, that the great debate was of more symbolic than practical significance and was largely irrelevant to what actually happened in Russia.

British policy continued to be inspired in the peace very much as it had been in the war – and indeed very much as it has been in the decades which have followed – by an attempt to grapple with the practical day-to-day realities rather than by the adoption of one or another grand design. Policy had to be developed within the limits imposed by the physical impossibility of immediate withdrawal of the forces in Russia and the practical difficulty of any significant reinforcement; the war weariness of the British people; the financial burden of continued intervention; the balance of political opinion, with the strident anti-Bolshevism of Lord Northcliffe and the main body of the Conservative Party confronting the growing force of left-wing sentiment; the discord among the former Allies; and the failure of the anti-Bolshevik forces in

Russia to recognise the new mood of the Russian people. The war in Russia was politically and militarily unwinnable with the forces which could be committed to it. Yet simply to walk away from the problem was an option which no member of the Government would have advocated. So Russia worked out her own future while Britain, moving by fits and starts over a period of eighteen months, gradually withdrew first her own forces and then her support for the anti-Bolshevik forces, having sought first to break and then to come to terms with the reality of the power of the first Soviet Government.

Bolshevik peace overtures

The first practical trial of strength between those who were more inclined to fight the Bolsheviks and those who were inclined to do a deal with them came when feelers were put out by the Bolsheviks for an armistice between the Russian and British forces and the opening of peace discussions. Chicherin himself spoke of 'buying ourselves out as we did in Brest'[48] and it is reasonable to conclude that the initiative was serious, although any agreement might well have proved as ephemeral as the Brest treaty. What is important for the assessment of British policy is that War Cabinet decided[49] to follow up the first approach. President Wilson approved. The French Government were then consulted and in the face of their strong opposition no action was taken.

Prinkipo

With the opening of the Peace Conference, the policy-making process was further complicated by the need for the Prime Minister and Balfour to spend much time in Paris, leaving Curzon in temporary charge of the Foreign Office until he finally took it over in 1919. Neither in London nor in Paris could effective British policy be made. In the Conference, Lloyd George tried to secure agreement that the Allies should deal with the Soviet Government as well as with the various anti-Bolshevik authorities located in Paris. Once again, in the face of French refusal 'to make any pact with this criminal regime' he failed, but it was possible to secure agreement to a proposal that the various parties in Russia should cease military action and meet the Allies on Prinkipo Island in the Sea of Marmara. To the considerable satisfaction of the French Government, the initiative failed because the Bolshevik acceptance, although embodying substantial concessions, was qualified by a refusal to cease military operations and was met by a flat rejection by the other parties.

At Churchill's request the War Cabinet considered policy once again.[50] The Bolsheviks, he said, were getting stronger every day. If we were going to withdraw, it should be at once. If we were going to intervene, we should send larger forces. He foresaw the menace of an eventual alliance between Germany, Japan and a Bolshevik Russia and was for intervention. 'A million men?' queried the Prime Minister. The Cabinet decided to commission a paper on the various options. Two days later Churchill went in Lloyd George's place to the Peace Conference, argued the case for disposing of the Prinkipo proposal if the Bolsheviks would not agree to cease military operations, and put forward a 'Proposal for a Committee of the Associated Powers to examine the possibilities of Allied Military Intervention in Russia'. Lloyd George, concerned that Churchill was 'planning a war against the Bolsheviks', telegraphed, agreeing to the disposal of Prinkipo, but begging Churchill 'not to commit this country to what would be a purely mad enterprise out of hatred of Bolshevik principles'.[51] So both the plan for discussions and the plan for concerted intervention were abandoned, the Russian Civil War took its course and the Western frontier of Russia remained to be settled. An Anglo–Russian bilateral agreement would probably not have been attainable in the current state of British opinion and the Prinkipo initiative could scarcely have resulted in agreement between the Bolsheviks and their opponents within Russia. That struggle could only be resolved by force. What Prinkipo might have done was, however, to have facilitated the process of withdrawal from intervention. As it was, with the movement towards a more stable relationship, whether on a bilateral or a multilateral basis, frustrated, the British Government was left with its policy of half-hearted intervention, exhorted to belligerence by France and to withdrawal by the United States, while Japan pursued her own interests in Siberia, and Germany was, for a brief period, in no position to undertake any independent action.

Withdrawal of British troops

So far as the direct involvement of British fighting units was concerned, the decisions of principle were taken quickly by the British Government. On 4 March 1919 the War Cabinet decided to withdraw from North Russia[52] and on 6 March the decision was taken to withdraw from the Caucasus and the Caspian.[53] The withdrawal from the

North was not accomplished before a volunteer relief brigade had been recruited and, the better to cover the evacuation, had carried out a substantial drive southwards from Archangel. In the South, an attempt to transfer responsibility for the Caucasus to Italy ended in a fiasco but, with the withdrawal of the two battalions from Siberia, the only British fighting unit left in Russia by the autumn of 1919 was a battalion which remained at Batum until the Turkish peace settlement in 1920. Thus, the decision to withdraw the limited British ground forces which had been deployed in Russia between the summer of 1918 and the autumn of 1919 was taken without their having been engaged in substantial hostilities against the Bolsheviks and without their direct operations having had any significant effect upon the outcome of the Civil War. Before the withdrawal could become effective, however, the fortunes of the anti-Bolshevik forces were to change dramatically.

Continued support for the White forces

Far from implying the end of the British involvement in the Civil War, the decision to withdraw marked the beginning of a more serious phase. There was some force in the argument which the British Government had espoused shortly after the Revolution, that the Russian state had disintegrated and that, in the absence of an effective central Government, other powers were fully entitled to deal with such autonomous bodies as had established themselves in parts of it. Where, as in the case of Poland and Finland, the Bolsheviks themselves accepted the creation of new independent states, the doctrine was unexceptionable, even if the application of it was anything but simple. Beyond this, however, the complexities escalated with the differing situation of the Baltic States, whose independence would in due course be recognised; the Caucasian states of Georgia, Armenia and Azerbaidjan which had a good case but could not sustain it against the Bolshevik armies; and regions such as Siberia, Ukraine and White Russia which could not have been severed from the control of Moscow without reducing Russia to something like the principality which confronted the Tartars in the fifteenth century. Moreover, among the anti-Bolshevik commanders were some who sought primarily local objectives and others whose aim was to establish a new Imperial Russia within its pre-Revolutionary borders. Thus it was that, ignoring President Wilson's advice not to meddle in other people's revolutions, the British Government was led into a post-war stage of intervention in which its political and financial commitment was substantial and its power to

Intervention 61

control events minimal. Confronted by the need to determine whether British interests would be better served by the disintegration of Imperial Russia or by the establishment of a strong non-Bolshevik central Government, the British Government was divided, but the pressure of anti-Bolshevik opinion in Britain had its effect in prolonging and extending the moral and material support which was given to the forces of Kolchak in Siberia, Alexeyev, Denikin and Wrangel in succession in the South and Yudenich in the North. Their story is the story of the Russian Civil War and this is not the place to retell it. What we must note here is the tangle into which the British Government was led by the decision not to abandon those whom it had regarded as its friends in Russia. The support to the anti-Bolshevik forces was continued not only out of a sense of loyalty, but in response to the widespread hope in Parliament and in a substantial sector of public opinion that those forces would prevail and that in consequence the Government of Russia would pass into the hands of men who would not seek to overthrow the whole structure of European society.

Lloyd George was faced in April 1919 with a Parliamentary revolt occasioned primarily by concern about reparations, but also by worries among the Conservatives about his apparently over-accommodating attitude to the Bolsheviks. In a statement clearly designed to appease right-wing criticism, he took the opportunity to repudiate not only the idea of recognition of the Bolsheviks, but even the enquiries which the American diplomat William Bullitt had made, after discussion with British officials, as to possible terms for the ending of hostilities in Russia and the establishment of normal relations and which had elicited a specific and not unpromising Soviet response. The Prime Minister described military intervention as 'the greatest act of stupidity that any Government could possibly commit', but at the same time justified continued material support for the anti-Bolshevik forces on the ground that it would have been thoroughly unworthy to say to those who had tried to reconstruct the Eastern front, 'Thank you; we are exceedingly obliged to you. You have served our purpose. We need you no longer. Now let the Bolshevists cut your throats.'[54] Describing his handling of the debate Lloyd George wrote subsequently:[55] 'To the majority of British citizens Bolshevism was a hideous and a terrifying monster. The action of the British Government in attempting to deal with it was represented as tendering a friendly hand to murder whilst it was reeking with the blood of its victims.'

It was against this background that the British assistance to the anti-Bolshevik forces was maintained and indeed increased. It took the form not only of supplies of equipment, but also of military and political missions, whose task was to maintain political liaison with the Russian generals and their embryo Governments, to administer the supply of equipment and to assist in the training of those who were to use it. During the spring and summer of 1919 Major General Ironside and later General Rawlinson were in North Russia, with Foreign Office political advisers; Major-General Knox, the former Military Attaché in Petrograd, was with Kolchak in Siberia where Sir Charles Eliot was High Commissioner; Major-General Holman was in the South with Denikin; Major-General Thomson commanded the two British divisions which had not yet been withdrawn from the Caucasus; and Lieutenant-General Gough with a civilian British Commissioner was with Yudenich in the Baltic provinces.

It was with no great enthusiasm that Lloyd George agreed to the continuation of supplies to the anti-Bolshevik generals, but suddenly, in May 1919, it seemed that they were on the verge of success and that, with the German war over, the fantasy of the previous year was about to be realised. Kolchak and the Czechs advanced west of the Urals, almost to the Volga and a junction with Ironside's forces moving south from Archangel did not seem out of the question. In the South, Denikin had begun the advance which was to carry him to within 250 miles of Moscow. In Paris and London Ministers began to think of the nature of the Government which, after the victory, would succeed the Bolsheviks. A note to Kolchak was despatched on 27 May over the signatures of the French, British, Italian, American and Japanese heads of Government, specifying conditions for the establishment of a democratic Russia with independence for Finland and Poland and autonomy for Estonia, Latvia, Lithuania and the Caucasian and Trans-Caspian territories. If Kolchak and his associates gave satisfactory guarantees on these points, they would be assisted with 'munitions, supplies and food to establish themselves as the Government of all Russia'. A satisfactory reply was received and on 12 June the heads of Government confirmed their willingness to extend to Kolchak and his associates the promised support. As Churchill commented:[56] 'The moment chosen by the Supreme Council for their declaration was almost exactly the moment when that declaration was certainly too late.'

The blockade of Russia

The summer of 1919, when the British Government had already decided to withdraw its operational forces from Russia and to continue only with the supply of material, proved to be the high point of the intervention. It was a high point in the advances made by the anti-Bolshevik forces; in the degree of political recognition accorded to them; and in the direct involvement of British forces in their operations. It was at this stage that the British Government was forced to consider whether it was now at war with the Bolsheviks. The issue was precipitated not by the operations on land, but by the attempt of the Allied Heads of Government to agree upon a policy for the continuation, after the signature of the peace treaty with Germany, of the blockade of Russia. The blockade was administered by units of the British fleet in the Baltic. President Wilson was adamant that, if there was no state of war with Russia, there was no legal justification for a blockade of Russia. The British Cabinet decided on 4 July[57] that 'a state of war did exist between Britain and Bolshevik Russia' and in consequence British naval forces were authorised to engage the enemy. The blockade, although enforced by the British navy, was, however, a matter for collective decision by the Allies. It was Balfour who drafted the telegram for the other Heads of Government to send to President Wilson on the justification for the blockade. In true Balfourian style, it neatly evaded the question:

> Russia during this period of transition is not a state, but a collection of *de facto* governments at war with each other ... The Allied and Associated powers are not in a state of belligerency with Russia, but it is quite true to say that they are involved in military operations with one of these *de facto* governments and are supplying arms and ammunition to the others ... It may not be right to describe this condition of things as war, but it cannot be right to consider it as peace.[58]

It was not until the autumn that a compromise was agreed upon among the Allies and the German Government and the neutrals were asked to operate an embargo on commercial and financial transactions with Russia.

Changing fortunes in the Civil War

On land, events had moved with remarkable swiftness and the Cabinet was left struggling to adapt its policies to the changing fortunes of the various parties in the Civil War. The proclaimed decision of the Allied Governments to assist Kolchak to establish a Government for the whole of Russia stimulated a Bolshevik offensive which met with such success that within two months Curzon had written Kolchak off as a lost cause.[59] At the beginning of July, as Kolchak was retreating, Denikin launched his major offensive from the South, sweeping towards Moscow on a front of 1000 miles. Abandoning Kolchak, the Cabinet decided[60] to concentrate British assistance on the southern theatre, bringing home the two battalions from Siberia and giving all the available resources to Denikin. Among the equipment supplied to him had been tanks and aircraft. It made sense that the British mission should contain officers and men capable of instructing the Russians in the use of this equipment, but the Cabinet can scarcely have envisaged that these instructors should themselves take the British tanks and aircraft into action against the Bolsheviks. As it was, their operations played a significant part in Denikin's swift advance. Orel, 250 miles from Moscow, was reached early in October, Moscow itself seemed within his grasp and it was necessary for the War Office to intervene to prevent the bombing of the capital by British aircraft.

Even before Denikin began his advance from the South, Yudenich was gathering an army in the Baltic provinces and seeking Finnish support for an attack on Petrograd. The British Government and the Allies collectively, while indicating their readiness to concur in a Finnish attack, refused to take responsibility for it. Consequently, the Finns held back and there ensued a ludicrous incident in which General Gough's assistant, Brigadier-General Marsh, acting on Gough's instructions, with the support of Pirie-Gordon, the Acting British High Commissioner and of French and American representatives, but in the absence of both Gough and Yudenich, virtually ordered the members of Yudenich's Political Council to constitute themselves as the North West Russian Government for the Provinces of Pskov, Novgorod and Petrograd. Not until it was all done were the War Office and the Foreign Office informed. A bewildered Balfour was left to report belatedly to the Supreme Allied Council in Paris on 20 August, with the comment that the representatives of the three countries 'seemed to have been engaged in fostering a *coup d'état* without consulting their own Governments'.[61] Gough was reprimanded and recalled, but the attack on Petrograd was launched without Finnish assistance. On 18 August British motor torpedo boats, supported by British aircraft, sank two Russian battleships, a destroyer and a submarine depot ship. Yudenich penetrated into the suburbs of Petrograd, but his victories were ephemeral and by November his army and his Government had ceased to exist. In the Archangel sector, where the British Government had decided in March to withdraw its forces, the summer of 1919 saw some of the fiercest fighting as the two relief brigades, enlisted to support the evacuation, were used for offensive operations against the Bolsheviks in the course of which the British forces used gas, albeit without any great effect,[62] before their final withdrawal in the autumn. The autumn also saw the withdrawal of the British forces from the Caucasus.

The last, flickering hopes that the Bolsheviks might be displaced as the Government of Russia came in the autumn, when, at the height of Denikin's success, Kolchak launched a counter-offensive in Siberia and there came renewed pressure for formal recognition. The British Government had reason to be grateful for Curzon's scepticism, when he minuted on 19 October:[63] 'We seem to be swinging round rather rapidly.' A fortnight earlier he had been reading the predictions by the head of the Russian Department, J. D. Gregory, of the failure of Kolchak and the impending collapse of Denikin. Now, he found Gregory 'advocating ... the hasty despatch of Commissioners right and left so as to catch the rays of the rising sun'. Gregory, in reply, argued the need to adapt to any change in the situation 'with no matter what rapidity it upsets previous calculations', but Curzon fortunately saved the British Government from yet another humiliating muddle by deciding to wait. He did not need to wait long. By the beginning of 1920 the British Government was considering how to organise the evacuation to the Crimea of the remnants of Denikin's forces; on 6 February 1920 Kolchak was executed by the Bolsheviks in Irkutsk; in March the post of High Commissioner in Siberia was abolished. The Caucasus was closer to Curzon's heart and as the Bolshevik forces moved southwards and eastwards in the wake of Denikin's retreating army, Oliver Wardrop, formerly Consul-General in Moscow and now British High Commissioner for Transcaucasia, urged the need for support. On 10 January 1920, at Curzon's recommendation, the Allied Foreign Ministers decided upon immediate *de facto* recognition of Georgia and Azerbaidjan, leaving Armenia's future for consideration in the context of the peace treaty with Turkey. Fortunately Curzon was dissuaded from the idea of reintroducing the two British divisions which had just been withdrawn and thus the creation of a new area of British military involvement against the Bolsheviks was avoided.

The British Government, which had been eager to introduce Japanese forces into Siberia, showed rather more caution in responding to suggestions that Finnish forces should be used in order to capture Petrograd and rejected the use of Bulgarian forces to prop up Denikin. Plans for the use of various foreign forces had been a feature of the

Civil War and had originated, above all, in France. Lloyd George recounts how, early in 1919, Marshal Foch 'outlined a scheme for a vast attack on the Soviet Union by Finns, Esthonians, Letts, Lithuanians, Poles, Czechs, Russians – in fact all the peoples that lie along the fringe of Russia – all under Allied direction' with Poland as its base and Polish forces as its spearhead.[64] Later, when Yudenich's offensive against Petrograd was hanging in the balance, serious consideration was given to the use of German troops in his support. In a speech in April,[65] Churchill had aired the idea, much to Lloyd George's alarm, that Germany might find 'a way of atonement' through the fight against Bolshevism and he gave more specific expression to this idea in a Cabinet memorandum written in September[66] in which, while pointing to the potential danger of a future German–Russian combination, he was inclined at least to use the German forces in the Baltic States to sustain Yudenich, if not to join him in the attack on Petrograd. The Foreign Office view was clear, 'It would be better that Petrograd should not be captured at all than that it should be captured by the Germans' and nothing came of the idea. More serious however, was the resurrection, in that autumn of 1919, of Foch's scheme for an assault based on Poland. Preoccupied with fighting on three fronts – against Kolchak in Siberia, Yudenich in the Baltic and Denikin in the South – the Bolsheviks were at that time in no position to wage war against Poland. The new Polish Government took advantage of the situation to establish a hold on territory well to the East of that to which they had clear ethnographical claim and on 14 September the Allied Council considered a proposal by Paderewski, the Polish premier, to provide half a million men to march on Moscow at a cost to the Allied Governments of £600 000 a day. The minutes record that, 'In response to an enquiry by M. Paderewksi, M. Clemenceau explained that the Council did not desire that the Poles should march on Moscow'.[67] The British Government did, however, seek, without success, Polish cooperation with Denikin's forces. The Polish–Soviet War was to break with full fury in the following year, and to become a significant factor in Anglo–Soviet relations. Before that, however, the British Government, reluctantly accepting the failure of the intervention, had begun, under Lloyd George's personal stimulus, the reversal of policy which was to make Britain, hitherto the most active, albeit not the most vehement, participant in the policy of intervention, the leader in the movement to establish relations with the Soviet Union. It was the first of those major oscillations which were to characterise the relationship throughout the next seventy years.

3
Facing the Facts[1]

A new relationship – the first move

The Lord Mayor's Banquet provides the traditional occasion for a major speech by the Prime Minister. On Saturday 8 November 1919, for the first time since the end of the war, the dignitaries of the City of London, the Ambassadors to the Court of St James, the judges, the clergy and members of the Government, gathered in the full splendour of the victorious citadel of free enterprise to listen to David Lloyd George. *The Times*, reporting the speech on the Monday, said 'Few utterances more serious in effect or involving issues wider than their bearing upon the welfare of the Empire have ever been made by a British Prime Minister in the historic Guildhall.' What the Prime Minister had done was to give the first indication of the change of policy in relation to Russia. His words were carefully chosen: Britain could not afford to continue the intervention and he was glad that the troops were out of the Russian quicksand. He hoped that the time was not distant when the Prinkipo attempt might be renewed and 'when the winter gives time for all sections there to reflect and to reconsider the situation, an opportunity may offer itself for the Great Powers of the world to promote peace and concord in that great country'.[2]

Cautious though the Prime Minister's language was, his intentions were far-reaching. Intervention had failed. If the power of the Bolsheviks could not be broken, then its reality must be accepted. The time had come to turn back to the path first hesitantly trodden with the Lockhart mission, the Prinkipo proposal and the attempt to respond to Chicherin's peace overtures. A stable relationship had to be established with the new Russia, but now the route to it was to lie through the resumption of trade. The responsibilities of international statesmanship and the requirements of British interest coincided.

The steps by which, in the course of just over a year, Lloyd George secured the conclusion of the Anglo–Soviet Trade Agreement of 1921 and thus made Britain the first of the wartime Allies to accord *de facto* recognition to the Soviet Government are one of the more fascinating episodes of diplomatic history.[3] The British Government had simultaneously to construct a totally new relationship with the Soviet leadership; to liquidate the remains of the intervention policy by jettisoning those anti-Bolshevik forces which it had hitherto supported; and, with the outbreak of a bitter Polish–Soviet war, to grapple with one of the perennial problems of Russia's relationship with the West. Discussions which had been presented as a limited negotiation with representatives of the Russian cooperatives on a possible exchange of goods rapidly became the first attempt by a Western government to confront the central issue of the relationship with Soviet Russia: was the Soviet Government determined to establish itself as the driving force behind a process of doctrinally determined revolutionary change throughout the world, or was it prepared to renounce this role and establish relations on a basis of mutual interest? The issue was to be confronted in these terms. It was to be put bluntly to the Soviet leadership. But it was not to be resolved.

The Prime Minister had never been happy with the policy of intervention. By the autumn of 1919, the disastrous effect of the war on Britain's finances had not yet fully impressed itself on the public and it was to be nearly another two years before the 'Geddes axe' was to fall on government expenditure. Already, however, it was abundantly clear that the demobilisation of the wartime army, the war weariness of those who were still serving, the burden of debt and the growing financial stringency left neither the military nor the financial resources for continued intervention. The mounting pressure of the Labour party and the trade unions for a change of course was shifting the balance in the direction Lloyd George wanted, but politically, both in Britain itself and in relation to France, his room for manoeuvre was limited. In the summer of 1919, in protest at the offensive operations being undertaken by the British relief brigade in Archangel, the Labour party at its annual conference had passed a resolution denouncing intervention and instructing the National Executive to consult the Parliamentary Committee of the Trades Union Congress 'with the view to effective action being taken to enforce these demands by the unreserved use of their political and industrial power'.[4] The threat of strike action was not implemented, but the mood of the left was clear and the Government recognised it when taking the final decision on British withdrawal.[5] On the right, however, there was still no disposition to have dealings with the Bolsheviks and Lloyd George's Guildhall speech was met with fury. The CIGS commented in a private letter: 'Our PM seems to have thrown a Prinkipo fly into the turtle soup with the result that the City Fathers vomited up the whole dish.'[6] *The Times* quoted a French press reference to 'capitulation to the Bolsheviks', demanded no 'bartering with Bolshevism' and, denouncing the Prime Minister's 'irresponsible improvisations', sought to reassure its French friends that 'fortunately his voice is not the voice of Britain'. In reply to a barrage of Parliamentary questions, Bonar Law explained that what the Prime Minister had expressed was 'simply a hope that there may be some method of arranging peace in Russia'. The Prime Minister himself made a statement two days later, pointing out that in the past twelve months some £100 million had been spent or sanctioned in support of the anti-Bolshevik forces. New obligations could not be contemplated. A settlement of the Russian problem was essential, but it would have to be discussed by the Allied and Associated powers and there would be no new British policy without full discussion in the House.

Then, quietly and deviously, Lloyd George went ahead. His Foreign Secretary, Curzon, was at this time preoccupied with the fate of the Caucasus. In the lower reaches of the Foreign Office Lloyd George would certainly have found support. Mr Harvey, later as Sir Oliver Harvey to serve as Ambassador in Paris, had written a paper[7] some months earlier, arguing the case for an early negotiation on the grounds that the bulk of the Russian people accepted the Bolshevik Government and that Lenin's Government might as well be left to justify itself in the light of its works. The sooner Britain negotiated, the better the terms would be. At that time the Cabinet had, however, committed itself to further support for Denikin. Harvey's paper never reached Curzon. So, when the time for a change of course came, Lloyd George relied upon his own staff, Hankey and Kerr, and in particular E. F. Wise, an official of the Ministry of Food and principal British representative on the Supreme Economic Council, who was later to become a Labour MP and economic adviser to the Soviet cooperative trading organisation. It was Wise who proposed that this organisation, Tsentrosoyuz, should be used to provide a non-governmental cover for the resumption of trade.[8]

The Allies are consulted

Lloyd George's Guildhall speech had been badly received in Washington, but Clemenceau was by this time weary of the muddle of intervention, concerned about Germany and anxious simply to put a barbed wire fence around Russia. He made little difficulty over the idea of some non-political commercial exchanges and thus, after a brief discussion on 16 January 1920, the Supreme Council put out an announcement that it would 'permit the exchange of goods on the basis of reciprocity between the Russian people and the Allied and neutral countries'. Clemenceau, on behalf of the Supreme Council, informed the American Government, explaining that the attempt to overthrow the Bolshevik regime by anti-Bolshevik forces supported by the Allies had failed; Russian food was needed in the West and the reorganisation of trade would be the best means of destroying the 'extremist forms of Bolshevism' in Russia; it was not proposed to recognise the Bolsheviks or permit their representatives to enter Allied countries; there would be a policy of non-intervention within Russia, but support for neighbouring states, including Georgia, Azerbaidjan and Armenia, if their independence were threatened.[9]

At a subsequent conference in London, Lloyd George secured Allied agreement on the broad lines of his new policy and the Allied Governments made a formal statement[10] to the effect that:

(i) They would not advise 'the communities which border on the frontier of Soviet Russia and whose independence or *de facto* autonomy they have recognized ... to continue a war which may be injurious to their own interests'. If, however, Soviet Russia were to attack them inside their own legitimate frontiers, the Allies would give them every possible support.
(ii) They would not enter into diplomatic relations with the Soviet Government 'until the Bolshevist horrors have come to an end and the Government of Moscow is ready to conform its methods and diplomatic conduct to those of all civilised governments'.
(iii) Subject to this, commerce between Russia and Europe would be 'encouraged to the utmost degree possible'.
(iv) The Council of the League of Nations should be invited to send a fact-finding mission to Russia.

So there began, at British initiative, the process of establishing relations with Soviet Russia, but for the present, in deference to right-wing opinion, it could not be described as such. The great debate was not over. Nor, in Russia, was the fighting. There can be a peculiar viciousness to civil war and the reports coming out of Russia lost nothing in the telling. There was terror on both sides and, with the collapse of administration, its direct effects were aggravated by malnutrition and disease. Returning British residents like the Reverend F. W. North, the Anglican Chaplain from Moscow, argued that trade would merely prolong Russia's agony. Against them a group of the Government's former military and civilian advisers in Russia addressed a memorial to the Prime Minister arguing for peace, pointing out the risk of growing German influence in Russia and claiming that the non-Bolshevik Governments in Siberia and the South had not proved superior in humanity to the Bolsheviks, while in energy, union and resource they were inferior. Their view of the ability of the Bolsheviks was shared by the CIGS who, in a letter of September 1919, had noted that with the single exception of Denikin, there was no doubt that Lenin and Trotsky and those around them were far the abler men.[11]

In the public campaign against any accommodation with the Bolsheviks, Churchill spoke of 'the ghost of the Russian bear padding across the immense field of snow', sitting outside the Peace Conference in silent reproach, disturbing Afghanistan, distracting Persia and creating agitation and unrest in India. On the day after the decision to re-open trade had been taken, he debated with his colleagues Curzon's proposal to send troops to the defence of Georgia and Azerbaidjan. His own policy, said Churchill, was what it had been throughout 1919: 'Have a definite policy of making war on the Bolsheviks with every available resource and by every possible means.' But, if this could not be done,

> then do not let us blind ourselves to facts which we have to face; and do not let us, in a pitiful effort to conceal those facts from our own minds or from the public at large for a few months longer, fling a few handfuls of British soldiers and sailors into positions from which it may be impossible to extricate them and where their poor lives will only be another unavailing sacrifice to the prolonged indecision of the Allies.[12]

By this time, there was no will among British ministers to embark upon another half-hearted military campaign in Russia, and although the CIGS hated Lloyd George's politics he was determined to avoid the strain of new commitments on Britain's overstretched forces. Curzon's proposal stood no real chance and it was only a few months before the Caucasian states, whose governments had so recently been recognised by the Allies – *de jure* in the case of Georgia – were forcefully taken over by the Bolsheviks. It took but a little time before the whole thrust of British policy was turned towards the liquidation of the British commitment in South Russia in order to reach an accommodation with the Bolsheviks.

The Polish–Soviet war

The first effective negotiations between the British and Soviet Governments had begun in the autumn of 1919 when, after an exchange of radio messages between Curzon and Chicherin, the Labour MP James O'Grady was appointed to negotiate with Litvinov on neutral ground in Copenhagen, for an agreement on the exchange of prisoners. The agreement,[13] which was concluded on 12 February 1920, was less than watertight in its drafting and was to give rise to substantial difficulties in implementation.

Concurrently with the signature of this agreement, preliminary discussions on trade were begun. Before they could be developed into substantive negotiations, the British Government were to encounter major problems in relation to Poland and to the White forces in South Russia, where Wrangel had taken over the command from Denikin. The new Polish Government, purporting to liberate a quasi-independent Ukraine, sought to take advantage of the chaos of Russia and push forwards its own eastern frontier. In January 1920, Lloyd George had made it clear to the Polish Foreign Minister that the British Government was not prepared to encourage Poland to make war on the Bolsheviks and would not support Poland against a Soviet attempt to regain areas which were indisputably Russian. Britain would, however, assist Poland if a sincere attempt to make peace on fair terms were rejected and Poland were attacked.

While Polish–Soviet negotiations dragged on through the spring of 1920, Lloyd George was busy, setting up the arrangements for trade talks. Then, in April 1920, the Polish forces launched a major offensive which, by 7 May, was to bring the capture of Kiev. Curzon had already decided upon a policy of non-intervention,[14] but a minor domestic crisis erupted when British dockers, having consulted Ernest Bevin, refused to load guns and ammunition consigned to Poland. Bonar Law put the Government's case in Parliament, stating that neither the British Government nor the British people had the will to throw British forces into the dispute and the Poles should be left to work as they thought best. With Poland on the offensive, non-intervention looked an easy option, but within a few months, Soviet forces were to be at the gates of Warsaw and there was to be talk of a new European war in defence of Poland. That, however, was for the future. For the present, Curzon's preoccupation was with the attempt to arrange terms for the honourable surrender of the remnants of the anti-Bolshevik forces under Wrangel and thus to eliminate without discredit to the British Government the last remnant of the intervention. Lloyd George's was to push on with the trade negotiations.

The trade negotiations begin

The prize of a trade agreement with Britain, the world's leading financial and commercial power and the main supporter of the intervention, meant a great deal to the Soviet Government. They quickly brushed aside the existing, non-Bolshevik, London representatives of the cooperatives and nominated a delegation led by Litvinov, with Leonid Krasin as his deputy. Krasin, an electrical engineer and previously manager of the Siemens plant in Russia, had been responsible for the supply of equipment for the new Red Army and was now Commissar for Foreign Trade. The negotiations were quite clearly now to become formal and inter-Governmental. In order to sustain something of the appearance of conducting purely discussions about commercial exchanges, with no political recognition, Lloyd George refused to permit Litvinov to enter Britain and, with the agreement of the Allies, the delegation led by Krasin were received for the discussion of 'general questions arising out of the resumption of trade', while Litvinov, still nominally their leader, remained in Copenhagen.

Rather than prejudice the opening of discussions, the Soviet Government accepted not only the exclusion of Litvinov from Britain, but also a requirement that the members of the Delegation should give a formal undertaking, orally from Krasin and in writing from the others, not to interfere in British politics or internal affairs and not to speak to the press without the approval of the British Government. They knew that, whatever the British Prime Minister might say in order to appease his critics in Britain and in France, they now had the opportunity to achieve both the substance and the form of recognition. Curzon, too, had his political objectives. He set them out in a paper for the Cabinet.[15] He wanted, and his Cabinet colleagues agreed, to deal with those cases 'in which the Bolsheviks are either openly at war with peoples or States in whom we are concerned, or are engaged in propaganda, plots and alliances directed against British interests or the British Empire in the East'. He was particularly concerned about Soviet pressure on Afghanistan. He also wanted to secure the effective implementation of the February agreement on the exchange of prisoners. The Cabinet decided to seek a 'comprehensive agreement' on these matters, including the curbing of Communist propaganda in Britain and, if possible, some understanding on debts to British creditors. Soviet 'propaganda' was for many years to be a source of concern to British Governments and some misunderstanding may have been caused by the tendency to use the term to cover the whole apparatus of Soviet ideological penetration and subversion. The foundation of the Comintern (the Third International) in 1919 as the vehicle through which the Russian communists would stimulate and control the further world-wide spread of revolution symbolised this threat. The Comintern's relative ineffectiveness, stemming largely from Lenin's insistence upon rigid adherence to Moscow doctrine, did little to lessen the concern of the British Government at the steady flow of reports of its aims and activities, if not successes. The search for formal safeguards was a feature of British–Soviet relations in the 1920s, culminating in the Arcos raid and the breach of relations. So far as trade was concerned, it was hoped that there might be an exchange of British goods for Russian gold, but a major objective was to secure a resumption of Russian supplies of food and raw materials to Europe. In view of the wide-ranging British objectives, the French Government were invited to join the talks, but refused.

The first meeting of the British and Soviet negotiators in 10 Downing Street on 31 May 1920 marked, in a very real sense, the beginning of the attempt to establish an effective and durable working relationship between the Soviet Union and the Western democracies. *The Times* did not mince its words about the reception of Krasin, 'this representative of a blood-stained despot', or about Lloyd George's policies, which had been 'kept from the public eye when he has been afraid that in their nakedness they would revolt the public conscience'.[16] The two sides set out the obstacles which they saw to the conclusion of a trade agreement. These, in effect, were their political objectives. For the Soviet side they were the ending of the state of *de facto* hostilities and, in particular, the Polish war, the formal lifting of the blockade, the legal protection of Soviet assets and the exchange of trade representatives with certain diplomatic privileges. For the British side, they were the problems of the comprehensive agreement on Bolshevik penetration which the Cabinet had agreed to seek.

The White forces in Russia were now jettisoned. On receiving the news of a new offensive by Wrangel on 6 June, Curzon decided that in good faith towards the Soviet Government the British mission to Wrangel must be withdrawn and all assistance terminated. That position was firmly held. An attempt to negotiate on behalf of Wrangel was abandoned and when, some five months later, the Soviet forces broke through into the Crimea, the British Government, despite an appeal from King George V on behalf of the women and children, refused any help, even with the evacuation.

Progress in the trade negotiations was, in some respects, by later standards, surprisingly quick. Chicherin, the Soviet Foreign Minister, was prepared to contemplate a deal under which his Government would give far-reaching guarantees as to its foreign policy, including undertakings as to its participation in 'hostile activities'. Such guarantees could, however, only be given in the context of a broader settlement, preferably a general peace conference, in which similar guarantees would have to be given by the powers which had made war on Russia. As for the question of debts, these could be considered only on the basis of an agreement recognising the Soviet claims arising from the intervention. This, however, went beyond anything which Lloyd George could accept. He needed his guarantees as the price for a trade agreement and he needed an assurance on debt repayment without qualification. When Krasin held firm, he suspended the negotiations with a memorandum dated 30 June 1919, asking for 'categorical replies, yes or no' to the statement of conditions on which the British Government was willing to enter into a trade agreement. Abrupt in form, the memorandum nevertheless made a concession to the Soviet objective by proposing 'what is tantamount to a general armistice, as the condition of the resumption of trade relations, in the hope that this armistice may lead ere long to a general peace'.[17]

A new threat of war

There was in fact at this point incentive enough for the Soviet side to conclude a deal, but before that could happen the Polish–Soviet war was to take an alarming turn. With the capture of Kiev, the Polish forces had badly overstretched themselves. A Soviet counter-attack met with swift and dramatic success and it seemed possible that Poland might be overrun.

Map 3 The Polish–Soviet frontier

Lloyd George was meeting the French and Italian Prime Ministers at Spa in July of 1920 in order to discuss the growing problems of the application of the Treaty of Versailles to Germany. While he was there, the Polish crisis erupted and he was faced with the task of reconciling three elements of the Russian problem: a telegram from Chicherin accepting the principles of the British memorandum on the trade agreement; an appeal by Poland for assistance in the war against Russia; and a perceived growing threat in terms of the German–Soviet relationship. Here were critical elements which were to recur throughout the years, as the British–Soviet relationship developed. In 1920 it was Britain which was in a position to exert a dominant influence over the outcome and it was Lloyd George who effectively controlled not only British, but also Allied policy. He could not, however, afford to quarrel too openly with France – despite his strong inclination to do so – and France was vehement, if not always practical, in support of Poland. A wireless message was therefore sent to the Soviet Government on 11 July with the Allied proposals. Poland was to sign an immediate armistice and withdraw to the line which the Supreme Council had fixed on 8 December 1919 and which became known as the Curzon line (see Map 3). The Soviet forces should stand 50 kilometres to the east of this line and there should then be a conference in London to make peace between Russia and the states on her Western borders. The British Government would neither assist Poland 'for any purpose hostile to Russia' or itself take any action hostile to Russia, but if the Russians were to refuse an armistice and take action against Poland on Polish territory, the British Government and its Allies would 'feel bound to assist the Polish nation to defend its existence with all the means at their disposal'.[18] Qualified though the commitment to Poland was, the CIGS was later to note in his diary: 'He [Lloyd George] is thinking of declaring war on the Bolsheviks, having thrown away every card in the pack.'[19] Britain might indeed have been drawn into the defence of Polish independence against Russia in 1920 and, as in 1939, would have had no means of giving direct and effective aid.

By the time Poland was ready to sue for an armistice, the Red Army had swept beyond the Curzon line in an advance which by mid-August was to bring it to the suburbs of Warsaw. Lloyd George was trapped. He had told Parliament[20] that 'if the Russian army still marches on, we shall have to give such assistance as is in our power to the Polish Government', but he knew, and the Cabinet was unanimous, that there was no question of committing British troops to the fight. He needed direct discussions with Russia. The Soviet Government rejected the London proposal for a conference in the form in which Lloyd George had put it forward, but agreed that a Soviet delegation should come to London 'not merely to conclude the trade agreement between Russia and the Allied Governments [sic] but also to discuss preliminary arrangements for the proposed peace conference'.[21] Krasin thus returned to London, accompanied by a member of the Politburo, Kamenev, with credentials 'to enter into negotiations with the British Government and also with the Governments of its Allies for the complete restoration of peaceful relations between the above mentioned countries and to sign to this effect a peace treaty as well as any other political and economic agreement'.

There was probably at this point more community of interest between Lloyd George and the Russians than may have appeared. For Lenin and his colleagues, a comprehensive settlement, recognising *de jure* Soviet Russia, ending foreign support for the remnants of the White armies and establishing Russia's western border was a prize worth gaining. If, at the same time, the Red Army could force a Communist Government upon Poland, so much the better. The Soviet tactic was therefore simultaneously to negotiate in London and fight in Poland. For Lloyd George, Poland was an embarrassment which he could not wholly shake off, but he was determined not to see British troops committed to another operation against Russia. In Russia itself, he wanted to avoid any new obligation to support the remnants of the White forces under Wrangel. Above all, he wanted to come to terms with the effective new rulers of Russia. Soviet and British interests might be reconciled, but the Soviet ideological offensive, backed by the Red Army, came close to frustrating Lloyd George's efforts.

In the summer of 1920, with its internal power nearly established and its armies pouring westwards, the Soviet leadership was inspired by the dream of carrying the revolution southwards into Muslim Central Asia, westwards into Poland and Germany and ultimately into Britain and France. Curzon had to watch, impotent, as the Caucasian republics fell to the Red Army. Pushing into Persia, a small Soviet force ejected the British garrison from Enzeli on the Caspian and with the withdrawal from Batum on the Black Sea, Curzon's first line of defence had gone. His anxiety to prevent the incursion of Soviet power into Afghanistan was the greater. But it was in Europe that the crisis broke. As the Soviet negotiators returned to Downing Street and the Soviet leadership proclaimed its respect for Polish independence, a Provisional Revolutionary Soviet was formed in occupied Poland and armistice terms were drafted, requiring the drastic reduction of the Polish army and the arming of Polish workers under the supervision of Russian, Polish and Norwegian trade unions. Recognising that British opinion would not have tolerated a settlement designed so blatantly to force a Communist Government upon Poland, Kamenev put to Lloyd George terms for a Polish armistice which, while referring to a Citizens' Militia, obscured the reference to the arming of the Polish workers. The British authorities were able to break the Soviet Delegation's cypher and consequently had available the text of most of the messages exchanged between the Delegation in London and Chicherin in Moscow.[22] Deciphering took some time, however, and although the British Government were doubtful about the accuracy of the terms communicated to them by Kamenev, they decided on 10 August to send them to the Poles, commenting that if these terms were offered and if Poland refused them the British Government could not assume the responsibility of taking hostile action against Russia. In the event, Kamenev's manoeuvre was pointless, since the terms actually offered contained the requirement he had concealed and were seen by an angry French Prime Minister as leaving Poland 'entirely at the mercy of the Bolsheviks'. Lloyd George had warned that if Russia was 'out to challenge the institutions upon which the liberties of Europe and civilisation depend, we shall meet in the gate'.[23] He made clear that no Allied troops would be sent to Poland, but plans for a resumption of the blockade of Russia and other naval measures in the Baltic and Black Sea were prepared. *The Times* was calling for the 'same unanimity and same courage with which we faced the crisis of 1914', and there was widespread public alarm at the prospect of war with Russia.

The Labour Party and Russia

The threat of conflict with Russia over Poland brought a political crisis in Britain. In 1920, interest began to develop as to the nature of the society which the Bolsheviks were creating. One of the first of the pilgrims to Moscow was George Lansbury, editor of the *Herald* who, on his return, wrote of the Bolsheviks 'striving to build a new Jerusalem'. Shortly after Lansbury came a Joint Labour Party/TUC Delegation whose report, a relatively sober and balanced piece of work, praised the achievements of the Bolsheviks, but was sharply critical of their methods. At the same time Bertrand Russell was making his own visit, which was to result in the publication of *Bolshevism: Practice and Theory*, a work in which, with a sharper eye than he was sometimes to use in his later years, he wrote of the 'elaborate dogmas and inspired scriptures' of this movement inspired by violence and conflict and drew an analogy between Bolshevik power in Russia and the British Raj in India.

While the British Labour movement was trying to understand Russia and prevent British intervention, Lenin and his colleagues were doing their best to exploit industrial unrest and direct the course of revolutionary Communism in Britain. Their efforts resulted in almost complete failure at the hands of the great mass of the British Labour movement. With the founding on 1 August 1920 of the British National Communist Party and its explicit subservience to the doctrinal control of Lenin, exercised both directly and through the Moscow-based Third International, there was no room for compromise with the

Labour Party. The Communist attempt to secure affiliation was rebuffed under the influence of men like Shinwell who spoke of the 'rigid cast-iron discipline imposed by Moscow', the miners' leader Hodges, who denounced the 'intellectual slaves of Moscow' and Ramsay MacDonald who warned against those who came holding out their right hand while concealing in their left the dagger which they would stick in the Labour Party's back. The struggle for the body and the soul of the British Labour movement was a not insignificant element in the tangled history of international Communism and, when the Communists lost, the International Labour Office was to write: 'London and Moscow are henceforth two antagonistic forces struggling for the supremacy over the working masses: the two poles round which the Socialist forces will crystallise.'[24] The early struggle was to have its significance not only at the time, but later, when Labour in power was to show itself fully alive to the reality of Soviet power and the techniques used in its deployment.

Conscious though the Labour Party was of the Bolshevik threat to its own independence, it was in no mood to tolerate military action against Russia in a war with Poland for which Poland was by no means blameless. The Report of the Labour Party/TUC Delegation coincided with the high point of anti-interventionist fervour during the Soviet–Polish war. A Council of Action was formed by the Labour Party and the Trades Union Council with the objective of deploying 'the whole industrial power of the organised workers' to prevent war with Russia, and Ernest Bevin led a delegation to speak to the Prime Minister. The anti-interventionist mood of the main mass of British Labour certainly had its effect on the Government. Ramsay MacDonald exaggerated when he wrote later of Labour's action saving Britain from war over Poland, but the Cabinet minutes of the period contain repeated references to the strength of public feeling against intervention and in a conference with the French Prime Minister at Lympne on 8–9 August, Lloyd George justified his caution by making the point that the working classes were frankly hostile to intervention. Certainly the Labour Party's position must have strengthened Lloyd George's resolve to press on with the task of constructing an inter-governmental relationship with Soviet Russia.

The expulsion of Kamenev

Warsaw was saved by a successful Polish counter-offensive, but at this point Lloyd George's search for an agreement was almost frustrated by the determination of the Soviet leadership to use Kamanev and Krasin to promote the Bolshevik cause in Britain. As a condition of the opening of the trade negotiation, the Soviet delegation had undertaken not to interfere in the British political scene. It became apparent to British ministers, as a result of their interception of Soviet communications, that the delegation were ignoring this undertaking. Not only had Kamenev deceived the British Government over the terms offered to Poland, but the delegation were in close contact with the Council of Action in an effort to influence government policy over Poland and were also providing finance to the *Herald*. Litvinov, in a telegram sent from Copenhagen to Chicherin in Moscow, commented that: 'In Russian matters it acts as if it were our organ.'[25] The Cabinet considered the evidence[26] and concluded that the conduct of Kamenev and Krasin was 'not compatible with the conditions under which their mission had been permitted to proceed to England'. Action was deferred until the situation in Poland was clearer, but as the Poles advanced eastwards, ministers received an intercepted telegram from Lenin telling Kamenev that, with an early Soviet victory over the Poles unlikely, the delegation should regard as its 'chief task' the spread of agitation among the British masses.[27] A Conference of Ministers chaired by Bonar Law on 2 September agreed that the delegation had been engaged in 'propaganda aimed at undermining the present economic organisation of society' and that they should be asked to leave.[28] This was possibly the make-or-break point in the negotiations. Those who were urging the expulsion of the delegation saw the possibility of frustrating a line of policy by Lloyd George which they believed to be fundamentally against the national interest. Lloyd George, for his part, was determined that his whole strategy of establishing relations with Soviet Russia through the medium of a trade agreement should not be jeopardised. Fortunately, Kamenev had already come to the conclusion that there was little point in his remaining in London. It was therefore possible for Lloyd George to make the gesture of accusing Kamenev of a 'gross breach of faith' and requiring him to leave, but continuing the negotiations with Krasin. In dealing with Kamenev, Lloyd George spoke in terms which can have left little doubt that his telegrams had been intercepted. A valuable source of intelligence may thus have been compromised, although subsequent intercepts continued to play a part in the determination of British policy. Such was the Soviet Government's interest in securing the trade agreement that Krasin was left to complete the negotiations.

Conclusion of the trade agreement

With the success of the Polish counter-offensive and the conclusion of a Polish–Soviet agreement under which the Polish frontier was established well to the east of the Curzon line, a major source of Anglo–Soviet tension was, for the moment, removed. Three other major problems remained:

(i) The release of British prisoners, some of whom, despite the O'Grady–Litvinov agreement, were still held.
(ii) The need for an assurance about recognition of outstanding Russian debts.
(iii) The requirement for an ending of Soviet activity directed against British interests and, in particular, against the British position in India.

On 1 November, after the Government had restrained the Admiral commanding the British Mediterranean fleet from bombarding Odessa by sea and air, agreement was reached on the release of the remaining prisoners. This left the two remaining British points of principle to be argued out in a hard-fought Cabinet meeting on 17–18 November.[29] Lloyd George made it plain that he was no longer prepared to defer to the feelings of his more intransigent colleagues, above all Curzon, who argued against giving up the trump card of the trade agreement while British interests and the British Empire were 'exposed without mitigation to the ceaseless and deadly assaults on the part of the Bolshevik Government and its agents'.[30] This group demanded an end to hostile activity before conclusion of an agreement. Lloyd George knew he could not get this. He could require the inclusion of guarantees of this type – for what they might be worth – in an agreement, but to require that they should be honoured in advance was, he knew, unrealistic and, as Curzon knew equally well, tantamount to saying that there would be no agreement. Meanwhile the depression would grow deeper and unemployment would mount. Lloyd George won,[31] but against the votes of Austen Chamberlain, Chancellor of the Exchequer, Curzon, Foreign Secretary, Churchill, Secretary of State for War, and of the Colonial Secretary and the First Lord of the Admiralty. Significantly, Montagu who held the responsibility for India, was not among those who dissented. Thus the decision to conclude the trade agreement was taken. The remaining negotiations lasted until 16 March 1921. On that date Krasin and Horne, President of the Board of

Trade, concluded the formal agreement under which 'pending the conclusion of a formal general peace treaty', the two countries agreed broadly to most-favoured-nation (MFN) treatment of trade and shipping, together with consequential arrangements including the appointment of 'official agents'. The two parties were to refrain from 'hostile action or undertakings' and 'official propaganda against each other's institutions'. The Soviet Government undertook to refrain from hostile action against British interests, especially in India and Afghanistan and the British Government gave a similar undertaking in respect of 'countries which formed part of the former Russian Empire, and which have now become independent'. A separate joint declaration left the claims of both parties and their nationals to be dealt with in the context of a general Peace Treaty and in a side letter Horne spelt out in detail the British complaints about Soviet actions designed 'to secure facilities for attacks through Afghanistan against the peace of India'.[32]

It had taken Lloyd George about a year and a half from the Guildhall speech to signature of the agreement. The attempt to break Soviet power had ended in what Ramsay MacDonald described as 'nothing but absolute, nothing but complete, nothing but unmitigated failure'.[33] Was it realistic to suppose that it could now be tamed? Certainly, the road was now open to move from a limited trade agreement to a comprehensive settlement. Defending the agreement in Parliament,[34] Lloyd George spoke of the 'gentlemanly process of instruction' of the Soviet leaders, a process which would result in their conversion and would put an end to their 'wild schemes'. But to hope for such an evolution was to ignore the political realities in both countries. The signature of the agreement helped to establish Soviet power, but it did nothing to moderate Soviet ideology. Nor did it end the political debate in Britain. The divisions ran deep – divisions within the Cabinet, in Parliament and in the country. *The Times* reminded Curzon of his warning that *de facto* recognition would be used by the Soviet Government 'to spread the tentacles of their poisonous influence throughout the world'.[35] The distrust of Soviet intentions was profound. It was to dominate the course of relations during the two critical decades which saw the destruction of the Europe of Versailles.

4
Working Relations

With the signature of the Trade Agreement, the British Government recognised that the Bolsheviks were in control of Russia. The attempt to break their power, never pursued with conviction or determination, was over. It remained to be seen whether cooperation was possible.

Symbolically, the change of course was dramatic. The problems, however, remained largely unchanged. The two Governments had recognised 'in principle' their liability to compensate private individuals in respect of goods or services supplied and had declared that their own claims and those of their nationals should be 'equitably dealt with' in a general peace treaty. They had agreed to refrain from hostile action or propaganda against one another. Whether these mutual assurances would have any effect would be determined as the practical working relationship developed. With no basis of mutual confidence, the debts were to remain largely unpaid and the hostility unassuaged. Yet, after twenty years, mutual interest was briefly to override ideology and when British and Soviet forces were next to encounter one another it was as allies, not as enemies.

In presenting the Trade Agreement to Parliament[1] the Prime Minister was at pains to point out that it was 'purely a trading agreement', not a treaty of peace and that all claims against the Soviet Government were reserved for settlement in the context of an eventual general agreement. Meanwhile, 'you cannot rule out half Europe and a vast territory in Asia by ringing down the fire curtain and saying that until it has burnt itself out you will never send another commercial traveller there'. Clearly, however, he was much impressed by the New Economic Policy (NEP) under which Lenin was permitting the resumption of some private commercial activity in Russia. 'We are simply converting them', he said. The Soviet leaders were men of great ability and they would realise that to achieve prosperity they would have to 'put an end to their wild schemes'.

Here, in its most optimistic form, was enunciated a line of thought which was to characterise one side of the debate about policy towards Soviet Russia for as long as the Soviet Union existed: maximise the practical day-to-day contacts and gradually the objectionable features of Communist doctrine will be abandoned. The history of the British–Soviet relationship in the 1920s and 1930s is the history of a tussle between those who accepted this and those who held the contrary thesis: that the price of acceptance into the international community must be the acceptance of British commercial principles and the abandonment of policies contrary to British interests; that the principles and the practice of a Communist Soviet Union were manifestly incompatible with this; that it was indeed essentially hostile to British interests and that there should therefore be no dealing with it. There was, of course, a broad spectrum of opinion ranging from the uncompromising hostility of the 'diehards' at one extreme to the unquestioning support for Soviet policy of the British Communists at the other. In the middle, in all parties, were those who, though their estimates of the nature of the Soviet regime differed widely, recognised the need to accept it as a fact of international life and to come to the best terms possible with it.

From 1945 to 1985, British policy was for the most part based in the middle ground. In the 1920s and 1930s, it tended to oscillate between the extremes, the oscillations coinciding broadly, but by no means precisely, with the ascendancy of the Labour and Conservative Parties, respectively. It was not that in the pre-war years the bulk of the Labour Party were violently pro-Soviet and the bulk of the Conservative Party violently anti-Soviet. Even *The Times*, at the height of the outcry over the Zinoviev Letter, pointed out that Ramsay MacDonald and his ministers hated the Communists and had excluded them from the party. Within the Conservative Party the 'diehards' were a vocal and powerful minority, but still a minority. The oscillations in fact resulted from the triggering effect of changes in the political balance which enabled the stronger elements of opinion on either side of the divide to acquire a temporary ascendancy. Thus the pursuit of a consistent policy was totally frustrated and successive British Governments gradually frittered away the leading position which in 1921 Britain enjoyed in the formation of Western policy towards the Soviet Union. This chapter will trace the course, the causes and the consequences of these oscillations of policy in the years between 1921 and 1930.

The official British agent in Moscow

With his Russian policy established, Lloyd George found his attention required by more pressing developments at home. Unemployment was rising, a miners' strike threatened public disorder and the situation in Ireland was critical. For a time, Russia disappeared from the Cabinet agenda. It was now for the officials and the traders to turn the provisions of the Trade Agreement into reality. Trade prospects were poor, but nevertheless British industry was taking up the threads. There were plans for the supply of railway equipment, the oil companies had their eyes on the Russian fields and those who had invested in Tsarist Russia were looking for compensation or for the return of physical assets. Early in August 1921 Mr R. M. (later Sir Robert) Hodgson arrived in Moscow as Official British Agent. He found the country already beginning to suffer from famine, the city in a sorry state and the officials more ready to promise assistance than to provide it. It was, he reported, as yet too early to decide how far his treatment was dictated by an intention to obstruct and how far by ineptitude and incompetence.[2]

Hodgson was not left to concentrate on commercial matters for very long. Within weeks of his arrival, he was confronted with the unresolved problem of Russian political activity against British interests. Curzon was not one to give up easily. He had wanted to require evidence of Soviet good intentions before conclusion of the Trade Agreement. Having failed to carry the Cabinet with him in requiring this, he was determined to ensure that the undertakings embodied in the agreement would be put into effect. Information was carefully collected from various sources, including intercepted communications and intelligence reports. No hard evidence of subversive activity in Britain itself could be obtained, but there were clear signs of continued pressure against British interests in Central Asia. An Interdepartmental Committee on 'The Bolshevik menace to the British Empire' was established. On the basis of its labours and of a detailed indictment prepared by the Government of India, Hodgson was instructed to hand to Chicherin a note setting out the evidence and complaining in strong terms about Soviet breaches of the assurance embodied in the Trade Agreement.[3] Soviet policy was illustrated by a report made by Stalin from the Eastern Secretariat of the Third International, setting out a 'general guiding purpose' of 'exerting pressure upon the capitalist powers of Western Europe through their colonies' and arguing that 'the problems connected with the class struggle in the West will be incomparably easier of solution if the external power of France and England can be undermined'. Lenin was quoted as telling the congress of the Third International that they should 'carefully prepare the revolution in capitalist states'. These policy statements were then supported by specific allegations relating in particular to India, Persia, Turkey and Afghanistan.

The Soviet response, while protesting a desire to 'promote friendly and sincere relations' with the British Government, was to describe the allegations as a 'mass of forgeries and inventions' and to prefer counter-charges against the British Government in respect of assistance to the remnants of the White armies. Curzon had the source of his information carefully checked, found most of it proven to be accurate, noted on the file that, although he did not feel completely satisfied, the report was 'on the whole reassuring', flatly rejected the Soviet denial, but left matters at that and brought the exchange to an end. Some of Curzon's evidence had been obtained by the theft of documents from the office of the Chief of the Political Section of the Soviet Mission in Berlin. One immediate result of its production – and apparent confirmation of its authenticity – was the despatch of a circular to all Soviet missions about the need to tighten security and the dismissal of fifteen members of the Berlin staff.[4] Whether the exchange had any effect on Soviet policy is more difficult to say. It does, however, seem that there may have been some modification, for the time being, of the Soviet drive for power and influence in Central Asia. Soviet Russia at that time had few friends. France remained bitterly hostile and, although the Soviet leadership saw Britain too as seeking the eventual downfall of their regime, they believed and commented publicly that it was with Britain that they could best make progress.[5] It was in their nature then, as it has been subsequently, to reject any accusation of breach of an agreement as a total fabrication, but it may be that, knowing that Curzon's charges were not unfounded, fearing cancellation of the trade agreement, and suffering in any case from a desperate shortage of funds, they concluded that some temporary change of emphasis would be prudent. The incident, in itself, was insignificant, but as a foretaste of Soviet policy, not uninteresting. There was subsequently to be considerable room for the Soviet leadership to adjust the scale of activity in the Third World in accordance with the requirements of the superpower relationship and the availability of finance. The security of the Soviet state remained an absolute, but the expansionist ideological drive, was then, as indeed later, variable in its application.

Famine in Russia

Concern with Soviet penetration into Central Asia remained a dominant influence on Curzon's policy, but for a time it had to give way to the considerations of economic policy. Three years after the end of the war, Europe was already in a bad way. France was pressing for drastic action to secure payment of German reparations, but it was plain that Germany was near to the end of her resources. In Britain, the economy was depressed and unemployment was mounting. Russia was stricken by drought and by a famine which, disastrous even by Russian standards, was aggravated by the effect of the Civil War and the Bolshevik requisitioning of food reserves. It is not easy for a Western observer to understand the scale of suffering in Russia at that time. The bald figure of 5 million famine deaths reflected a reality of misery, pillage, murder and, it was said, even cannibalism, against which the formal processes of intergovernmental diplomacy had an almost grotesque unreality. An international relief effort was mounted, but the British Government was not alone in refusing to finance the purchase of grain unless the Soviet Government would recognise its liability for existing debts and provide security for any new credit. The burden of relief was therefore taken up by voluntary agencies and, on a massive scale, by the United States.

In Western Europe, the unenforceability of the Treaty of Versailles was becoming ever more apparent. Tension between France and Germany was rising and, as it did, the Franco–British relationship came under increasing strain. It was in such a situation that Lloyd George conjured up the vision of an international economic conference in which Russia might be restored as a full member of the world community at the price of acknowledging at least a scaled-down debt obligation. He saw the re-opening of full relations with Russia as offering a stimulus to economic revival and affording commercial opportunities to foreign traders and investors which might enable Germany to procure the resources to service her reparation debt. Thus, in turn, some of the tension might be taken out of the Anglo–French relationship and, at a stroke, the political and economic scene in Europe could be transformed. To it all, Russia was to be the key.

The Genoa and Hague conferences

It was at a meeting with M. Briand at the beginning of January 1922 that Lloyd George, having discussed the problems of German reparations and European security, proposed that Britain and France should march together for the economic and financial reconstruction of Europe. He proposed the summoning of an economic conference including all the countries of Europe. 'Russia?', asked Briand. 'Yes, Russia', replied Lloyd George.[6]

So it came about that on 10 April 1922, at the Palazzo San Giorgio in Genoa, the Soviet representatives, Chicherin, Litvinov, Krasin and Joffe took their seats at, in Lloyd George's words, 'the greatest gathering of European nations which has ever assembled in this continent'. Right-wing opinion in Britain shared none of Lloyd George's dream. In the words of *The Times*:[7]

> The Bolshevists ... whose aim is the destruction of the present social order, who in subterranean conclaves have for years thought out their plans and methods and elaborated their scheme of action – are now, by the fatuous condescension of the leaders of Europe, placed in a position where they can display their consummate conspiratorial abilities to the full.

The basis of the Conference had been set out in a resolution proposed by Lloyd George, adopted by the Supreme Allied Council at Cannes[8] and sent with a letter of invitation to the Soviet Government. The terms of the resolution covered political guarantees such as refraining from aggression against neighbours and from 'propaganda subversive of order and the established political system', as well as commercial and financial guarantees on matters such as recognition of debts and compensation for confiscated property. They were clearly directed at Russia and designed, as Lloyd George put it, to 'make it quite clear to Russia that we can only trade with her if she recognises the honourable obligations which every civilised country imposes upon itself'. It was indicated that acceptance of the resolution would be a prerequisite for recognition of the Soviet Government. At the opening of the Conference, Lloyd George said that the participants met on terms of equality, but only on acceptance of the equal conditions defined in the invitation. Chicherin, in reply, remarked that, while accepting the Cannes principles, the Russian delegation reserved the right to put forward supplementary articles and amendments. He then proposed that the conference should deal not only with economic reconstruction, but also with disarmament and that it should lead to a universal congress at which workers' organisations should also be represented. Thus, at the very outset, was raised another of the perennial themes of East–West relations. As Lloyd George replied: 'Before you get disarmament, you must have understanding ... when you have got the understanding and the goodwill, when Russia and all the other powers have understood each other and go home in a spirit of friendship, then disarmament comes.'

Rapallo

The Genoa Conference totally failed to achieve Lloyd George's grand design.[9] The Cannes resolution had been overambitious in seeking to secure Soviet recognition of the inherited debt liability and comprehensive safeguards for Western European private interests in Russia. The formal proceedings were consequently concerned very largely with the questions of debt and compensation. The war credits advanced by the British Government to the Russian Government in the period from the outbreak of war to the October Revolution were now estimated at about £650 million. Private claims amounted to between £300 and £350 million, of which about £30 million was accounted for by investment in industry and manufacturing and about £180 million in respect of mining and oil investment. The latter figure was believed by the Foreign Office to be 'considerably inflated' and is not easy to reconcile with the pre-war figures of British investment.[10] The Government had little expectation of being able to recover any of the war credits, but found difficulty in compromising over private debt, the more so as the French Government, whose citizens had more substantial private investments in Russia, was intransigent. So no agreement was reached.

In reality, the seeds of failure were planted deeper than this. Lloyd George had gone as far as he could in the prevailing political climate to reach an accommodation. Not only French intransigence, but also his own parliamentary position, made it essential for him to insist upon guarantees going beyond anything which Russia was likely to accept. Between Germany and Russia there was what he later called 'a community of misfortune, a community of debasement'. The equality of participants was no more than nominal. Lenin might have expressed himself rather differently from the leader writer of *The Times*, but he shared the latter's view of the opening for Soviet manoeuvre and had instructed the Soviet Delegation to play on the disunity in the 'bourgeois countries'.[11] He scarcely needed to do so. Less than a week after the opening of the Conference, the German Government, concerned that the former wartime Allies might come to an arrangement which would disadvantage them, slipped out to the Soviet Delegation's headquarters in a hotel close to Rapallo and signed a treaty, the terms of which had been negotiated by German and Soviet Delegations in Berlin, prior to the conference, but to which at that point the German Government had hesitated to commit themselves. Now, to the contemptuous satisfaction of the Soviet delegates they did so, agreeing to a mutual waiver of claims, MFN treatment for trade and full diplomatic representation. It was a major political success for Soviet Russia. For Germany, it was a first step towards regaining that primacy in the Russian market which she had enjoyed before 1914. It was, said Lloyd George 'an act of base treachery and perfidy'. By any standards it was a remarkable act. The fear of German exploitation of Russia's resources had long haunted British Governments. It had taken shape with the signature of the Treaty of Brest-Litovsk and had been a major factor behind the policy of military intervention. With Brest-Litovsk swept away by the defeat of Germany, it had taken less than four years for the old fear to be realised again in a new form. The shadow cast forward to the Nazi–Soviet Agreement of 1939 was already discernible. Lloyd George saw it. Warning Parliament of the grave potential if nations such as these, treated as pariahs, were driven to despair, he argued that some arrangement with Russia was necessary in the interest of the peace of the world. But while Rapallo demonstrated the validity of Lloyd George's policy towards Russia, it left little of his grand design for Genoa.

The Conference toiled on after Rapallo. The Soviet Delegation still had an incentive to secure full recognition from the remainder of Europe, but the price was too high. The Allied request for acknowledgement of debts was met with a Soviet demand for £5000 million compensation in respect of losses sustained during the intervention and although concessions were made by both sides, the gap was unbridgeable. The end result was agreement to establish separate non-Russian and Russian Commissions to meet at The Hague with the object of settling the questions of debts, private property and credits. A 'pact of peace' between the Russian Government, plus its allies, and the other participants provided that, in order to restore confidence, all parties should abstain from aggression and subversive propaganda for a period of four months. On his return to London, Lloyd George defended his policy 'that abhorrence of the principles and conduct of a Government should not preclude relations with it which would enable you to deal with the people under its sway'. His defence of the ideal which inspired Genoa was firm. Whether the process would ultimately succeed, he would not say.[12]

The Conference at The Hague was very different in character from that at Genoa. Three non-Russian Commissions, dealing respectively with debts, private property and credits met separately to prepare their own positions and then met the Russian Delegation at intervals over a period of three weeks in June and July of 1922. Some information was exchanged, but the Allies would not commit themselves to new credits without Russian acknowledgement of existing debts and either return of nationalised property or compensation. On this crucial nexus neither side would move. Litvinov made a last-minute offer to refer to his Government a formula under which debts would be acknowledged and the right to effective compensation for nationalised property admitted, with the amount left for agreement between the Russian Government and the individuals concerned. There was, however, no reason to expect that even this qualified formula would be accepted in Moscow and the Conference broke up with no more than an Allied comment that such a declaration would 'help to create a favourable atmosphere for any further negotiations' and, if loyally carried out, would 'contribute to the restoration of confidence'.

The end of the Conference at The Hague may be seen as marking the end of the initiative begun by Lloyd George, with his Guildhall speech of 1919, to bring Soviet Russia back into the community of nations. Although, in its broadest sense, the initiative had been frustrated, it had not been wholly fruitless. Much had changed over the three years. Soviet Russia was still not recognised *de jure* by any of the Western powers other than Germany, but the British trade agreement had set a precedent which others were following and none could pretend that power over most of what had once been Imperial Russia did not now lie with the Bolsheviks. Without foreign credits, Russia would have to make her way by her own efforts, but Lenin, now close to death, could be well pleased. He was to make one final, personal intervention in the course of Anglo–Soviet relations.

The Urquhart agreement

The Litvinov formula had envisaged negotiation between the Soviet Government and the former owners of nationalised property. For some time, negotiations had been conducted with Leslie Urquhart, Chairman of Russo–Asiatic Consolidated Limited and President of the Committee for British Industrial Interests in Russia. After the breakdown of the Hague Conference, these negotiations had been continued and agreement had been reached in respect of a claim by Russo–Asiatic for £56 million, representing about a quarter of the total British claims in respect of nationalised property. Although acting privately, Urquhart was seen by the Russians as a representative of the British Government and there can be little doubt that the agreement with him was a political gesture, designed to influence Britain to move further towards full diplomatic recognition. Immediately after signature, however, the British Government sought to exclude Russia from participation in the Lausanne Conference dealing with Near Eastern questions and, in particular, the question of access to the Black Sea through the Dardanelles and Bosphorus. It was a foolish move, reflecting Curzon's intense distaste for any dealing with the Russians, and it could not be sustained. The French Government was at this time beginning to realise that Lloyd George's more flexible policy had begun to give Britain an advantage in the Russian market. M. Herriot, as Mayor of Lyons, visited Russia to promote French commercial interests and with some skill and subtlety French policy moved in the direction of reconciliation with Russia at precisely the moment when British policy was being turned by Curzon in the opposite direction. As a result of French and Italian pressure, Russia was invited to Lausanne but, meanwhile, Curzon's gesture of ill-will had been enough to induce Lenin to intervene personally and prevent ratification of an agreement with Urquhart which he described as 'bondage and plunder'. Formally the rejection was based on the 'absence of friendly, stable and settled relations' and Litvinov explained that it was a response to the 'new and negative' British policy towards Russia. He may have been merely scoring a point in respect of an agreement which, in any case, he saw as going too far in conceding the return of property to pre-war foreign owners. It is, however, very probable that it was Lenin's political assessment which turned the scale.

A new and negative policy

By the autumn of 1922, the Welsh wizard's spell was broken. A wartime Liberal Prime Minister remaining in office in the peacetime years by courtesy of a Conservative Parliamentary majority was bound to be vulnerable. Lloyd George held on too long, pursuing an ill-advised and nearly disastrous policy of support to Greece in the Greco–Turkish war. The failure of Genoa was only a minor factor in his inevitable fall. In October he gave up the office of Prime Minister to Bonar Law and British policy towards Russia entered a new cycle of development. Now was the time for Curzon to take the handling of relations with Russia out of the hands of Downing Street, move it across the road to the Foreign Office and set in train the dismantlement of Lloyd George's policy. Within a matter of months, British policy was to swing between the two extremes which were long to characterise it. From the Genoa policy of bringing Russia into the world community and gradually influencing her development, it had turned through 180 degrees to the policy of excluding her until she demonstrated acceptance of Western standards.

The Lausanne Conference itself was marked by a continuation of the bitter clash between Curzon and the Soviet representatives, primarily as a result of Curzon's determination to keep the Straits open to passage by warships and the Soviet determination to close the Black Sea to all but littoral states. The change of tone in British policy could scarcely be mistaken in Moscow. Chicherin commented to Curzon that the new British Government seemed much more hostile to Russia than its predecessor had been. He asked about British intentions. Curzon, replying with total frankness, went over the long list of complaints about Soviet action against British interests in Asia, which had formed the substance of the note communicated by Hodgson the previous year. He recognised that 'permanent estrangement was an international loss', but 'until there was an absolute desistence from this pestilent activity, there could be no real reconciliation'.

The mood of the Foreign Office at the time is well illustrated by a memorandum prepared by O'Malley for Curzon to circulate to his colleagues in April 1923 on 'The Policy of the Russian Soviet Government, March 1921–December 1922'.[13] It argued that, had matters been left in the hands of the Foreign Office, the Russian Government 'uncourted and isolated at Moscow ... might have been induced gradually to commit itself to a further step on the road to a saner policy'. As it was, the invitation to Genoa had merely 'ministered to the unfounded belief that Russia was at least as necessary to Europe as Europe was to Russia'. There was no intrinsic value in a 'paper agreement' with the Soviet Government, the Pact of Peace was 'a verbal undertaking without any kind of sanction to refrain from hostilities which no power had ever contemplated' and the firmness which led to the failure of the negotiations at The Hague would contribute more to the re-establishment of relations with Russia than any agreement at Genoa could have done. Turning to the future, O'Malley pointed out that 'armed intervention, direct and indirect, was tried and failed and considerations of public opinion and finance obviously render reversion to it impracticable'. The only practical choices were to renew Lloyd George's advances to the Russians, to break off relations, or to 'adhere to the cautious and negative policy which has been pursued during the last five months'. The last course was favoured: 'Where, as in Russia, there are so many imponderable factors, inaction is desirable for its own sake.' There should be 'so much intercourse with Russia as is necessary to dissipate the impression of a "blockade", but no more'. Curzon was at first inclined to endorse O'Malley's paper, but by the time it had been printed for circulation, his opinion had hardened still further.

The Curzon ultimatum

Under a new constitution, enacted at the end of 1922, Soviet Russia had become the Union of Soviet Socialist Republics, a change which the Foreign Office refused for some time to acknowledge. Concurrently with the later stages of Lausanne, Curzon returned to the attack with the newly renamed state on the theme of bilateral British–Soviet relations. Tension had been rising in connection with three matters:

(i) British opinion was much exercised over the treatment of the churches by the Soviet authorities and matters had come to a head over the execution of a priest. A sharp exchange of notes took place, in which the Soviet Government denounced attempts to interfere in the internal affairs of their country and pointed to the action taken to sustain British rule in Ireland, India and Egypt.
(ii) A dispute over the extent of Russian territorial waters, which antedated the October Revolution, had flared up again and British trawlers had now been arrested.
(iii) A British subject, Mr Davison, had been executed and another, Mrs Harding, imprisoned on charges of espionage during the Civil War.

In addition, Curzon was pursuing his allegations of hostile Soviet action in Persia, Afghanistan and India. In May 1923, sharpening O'Malley's policy recommendations, he brought all these matters together in a step which 60 years later was still recollected with some bitterness in Moscow. Hodgson was instructed to deliver a note requiring an undertaking by the Soviet Government to comply fully and unconditionally with British requests for the withdrawal of their notes regarding the trial of priests; the release of trawlers and crews, compensation and an assurance of non-interference in future outside the three-mile limit; compensation in the case of Mr Davison and Mrs Harding;

and the 'disowning and recall' of the Soviet representatives in Persia, Afghanistan and India. In respect of Soviet activities in Central Asia, the note was founded on intercepted communications, but it was agreed by ministers that this source should not be disclosed to Parliament. Hodgson was instructed to state that in the absence of full and unconditional compliance within ten days, the British Government would recognise that the Soviet Government 'do not wish the existing relations between the two Governments to be maintained' and that, albeit with much regret, the 'experiment' would be terminated and the British Government would consider itself free from the obligations of the Trade Agreement.

At the time the ultimatum was issued, Bonar Law was ill and Curzon presided over the Cabinet. As the storm of left-wing protest rose, Bonar Law died. Curzon had confidently expected to succeed him and the choice of Stanley Baldwin, in his place, was a profound blow to this brilliant, sick and embittered Foreign Secretary. There could scarcely have been a greater contrast in political motivation between his intellectual pursuit of an old-style imperialism and Baldwin's pragmatic pursuit of commercial and industrial interest. The problem of relations with the Soviet Union was dealt with as a matter of urgency at a meeting of ministers held even before Baldwin had formally assumed office. It was agreed that full satisfaction should be required and Curzon was fortunate in that it was obtained. The offending Soviet notes were withdrawn, compensation in the Davison and Harding cases was promised, a convention permitting fishing in the area outside the three-mile limit was offered, together with compensation for the arrest of the trawlers. Only in respect of the withdrawal of its representatives in Central Asia did the Soviet Government demur, proposing instead a detailed bilateral discussion. The representative in Kabul was, however, replaced. *The Times* was able on 14 June to congratulate Curzon on the 'refreshing vigour' of his handling of a 'tyranny more bloodthirsty than that of any Tsar' and the Cabinet was able to record a 'highly successful issue' to the dispute.[14] The Soviet reaction had demonstrated the key position which Britain held in the conduct of relations with a Soviet Government which was still ostracised by the great body of international opinion.

With the withdrawal of the ultimatum there was a certain revival of interest in the possibility of trade with Russia, and a delegation of businessmen, led by Mr F. L. Baldwin, a cousin of the Prime Minister, visited Russia. On his return, Baldwin said he was 'infinitely more hopeful'. The delegation had found a Soviet Government tackling its financial problems with 'extraordinary ability' and a people who, although shabby, did not seem poverty-stricken. *The Times* might denounce the travellers for their 'rosy views, not to say illusions', but Lenin's NEP, permitting a limited return to free enterprise, had made a certain impression on British opinion. The need for markets for British industry was desperate and, even if prospects in Russia were limited, the mood of the country was turning towards a more positive policy.

Full recognition

Stanley Baldwin's first tenure of office as Prime Minister was brief. The election of December 1923 brought Labour to power for the first time, with Ramsay MacDonald as Prime Minister, dependent upon Liberal support. The Labour and Liberal parties were both committed to the principle of full recognition of the Soviet Union and there was strong pressure from the left wing of the Labour Party and the trade unions for the pledge to be swiftly implemented. MacDonald himself had little time for revolutionaries. There was no bond of sympathy between him and the Bolsheviks, whom he saw as historical curiosities, 'socialists in crinolines', impediments on the road to a practical modern socialism, based on parliamentary democracy. However, the pressure from his own party was made the greater by the imminence of an agreement on the establishment of relations between the Soviet Union and Italy and, a mere ten days after taking office, MacDonald instructed Hodgson in Moscow to inform the Soviet Government that they were recognised 'as the *de jure* rulers of those territories of the old Russian Empire which accept their authority'. (With this phrase the British Government tacitly disposed of its *de jure* recognition of the independence of Georgia.) There was, however, a warning that 'genuinely friendly relations cannot be said to be completely established so long as either party has reason to suspect the other of carrying on propaganda against its interests and directed to the overthrow of its institutions'. Negotiations were proposed on all outstanding issues. King George V was not disposed to forget or forgive the fact that his cousin Nicholas, with his wife and children, had been murdered, their bodies dismembered and burned by the Bolsheviks. In deference to his unwillingness to receive a Soviet Ambassador, Hodgson was given the diplomatic rank of Chargé d'Affaires and it was stated that a Soviet Chargé d'Affaires would be welcome in London. As Hodgson reported,[15] Soviet opinion was not unanimous in welcoming an event which brought Russia once more into the ambit of Western civilisation, but the Soviet

Union had now emerged from the struggle as a world power and the party had every reason to be satisfied. Ominously, he added: 'The more recalcitrant may find consolation in Zinoviev's assurances [at the Thirteenth Party Congress] that the Labour Government in England is after all ephemeral and marks but a milestone on the road which leads to the inevitable world revolution.' So the Soviet Government notified its formal acceptance and Rakovsky, who – after the unique experience of being accepted, rejected and then again accepted by the British Government – had succeeded Krasin as Soviet Agent in London, was given diplomatic status.

The Draft Treaties of 1924

The Anglo–Soviet Conference began on 14 April 1924. Progress in the negotiation of a comprehensive bilateral treaty relationship was swift, but the difficulties were substantial. The political balance of Parliament might have changed, but the problems had not. The Soviet Union, having attained at no cost the objective of recognition, wanted to follow it by securing a commitment to a substantial British credit without a parallel commitment to the full satisfaction of British claims. Nevertheless, by August 1924 agreement had been reached on the text of a General Treaty and a Treaty of Commerce and Navigation. Both were signed as drafts by a less than wholly enthusiastic Ramsay MacDonald and were to become effective only upon ratification. The Commercial Treaty established mutual MFN treatment. The General Treaty dealt with formal matters concerning earlier treaties, established fishing rights on a satisfactory basis, provided that claims in respect of debts and nationalised property should be assessed by a Commission of three persons from each side and established that, when this commission had completed its work, a third treaty should set the amount of compensation, finalise the settlement of property claims and determine the amount and conditions of a loan to be guaranteed by the British Government. Governmental claims and counter-claims were effectively put into cold storage and the Treaty, lacking a definitive commitment on the extent of compensation or the amount of a loan, was in essence little more than an agreement to agree. Its supporters could claim that it committed the Soviet Government to the principle of compensation and that it secured useful fishing rights; and that the grant of full recognition was inevitable. Its critics could argue that the British Government had sacrificed its principles, undertaken to finance its avowed enemy and gained nothing of substance in return. The

Conservative press and politicians were vociferous in their denunciation and even Lloyd George, who had worked so passionately to establish relations, thought it 'a thoroughly unbusinesslike agreement, a thoroughly grotesque agreement'.[16]

The Zinoviev Letter

Without Liberal support, Ramsay MacDonald could not have secured ratification of the treaties and failure would probably have brought the fall of the Labour Government, when Parliament reassembled after the summer recess. As it happened, however, the election of October 1924 was precipitated by a different issue, an allegation that MacDonald, under pressure from the left wing, had persuaded the Attorney-General to drop proceedings under the Incitement to Mutiny Act against J. R. Campbell, the editor of the *Workers' Weekly*. From this point on, the question of Communist subversion was on the election agenda. It was, however, to take a more dramatic form with the publication of the 'Zinoviev Letter'.

While the treaty negotiations were in train, the Foreign Office had received from the Home Office copies of two letters allegedly sent by Zinoviev as President of the Comintern to the British Communist Party, urging direct action in support of the Soviet Delegation. MacDonald decided that until there was evidence of some action, no steps could usefully be taken on the letters. Then, in the last week of the election campaign, the Foreign Office received from the Intelligence Service a copy of a third letter from Zinoviev dealing with the treaty and also instructing the party on the formation of cells in the army which might be 'in the event of an outbreak of actual strife, the brain of the military organisation of the Party'. This last and most dramatic document was copied also to the *Daily Mail* and it is difficult to resist the clear implication that this action was taken – whether by an émigré organisation or by a Conservative Party supporter – with electoral considerations in view. Prior to publication by the *Daily Mail*, MacDonald had agreed that, provided he could be sure the document was authentic, a formal complaint should be made to the Soviet Chargé d'Affaires. He asked for a draft to be prepared 'to see how it looks'. A draft complaining of Soviet 'violation of specific and solemn undertakings' was sent to him while he was out of London. He amended it, but did not specifically authorise its despatch and that most meticulous of public servants, Sir Eyre Crowe, having been confined to bed for two days, failed to notice that the letter had not been initialled. It was therefore sent. Crowe's oversight may not have made much difference to the Government's fortunes, since had no action been taken, the Government would doubtless have been attacked for attempting to conceal the document. Despatch of the note did, however, mean that the authenticity of the letter was apparently accepted by the Government. Crowe subsequently minuted that it had been obtained from an absolutely trustworthy agent in Russia and its receipt confirmed by an independent source in Britain. He admitted, however: 'We have no photograph of the document and, as it is only a copy of the original, it would be useless if we had.'[17]

The whole incident was the subject of detailed investigation.[18] The Soviet Government maintained that the letter was a forgery and it may well have been. A Committee of Inquiry constituted by MacDonald before he left Downing Street found it 'impossible on the evidence before them to come to a positive conclusion' as to the letter's authenticity. It was well known that forged Soviet documents were being circulated by various White Russian sources. The frustration of the British–Soviet treaties must have been a major objective for the émigrés and the timing was singularly appropriate for their purpose. The letter itself shows features, some technical and others substantive, which make it seem improbable that it did in fact emanate from Zinoviev. Against this, it must be said that, whether or not the letter was genuine, the Comintern's objective was to spread the revolution and Britain was a major target. The Soviet Government had consistently sought to dissociate itself from the Comintern and to argue that it could not be held responsible for the 'private' activities of those leading personalities who linked the three elements in the control of Soviet foreign policy: the Politburo, as the central organ of party control of the Soviet state; the Government – and in particular the People's Commissar for Foreign Affairs – who were responsible for the conduct of relations with foreign Governments; and the Comintern, through which the party sought to promote the world revolutionary process. The disclaimers had a hollow ring. The letter itself was well enough in harmony with a speech by Zinoviev at the Thirteenth Party Congress. The willingness of the Soviet Government to use its resources for the destabilisation of capitalist society and the destruction of British imperial power could not be effectively gainsaid. Thus, behind all the synthetic furore of the election was a real and continuing issue of British policy. Was it right to establish closer relations with a state under the total control of a party whose objective was the world-wide triumph of an alien and hostile ideology?

The 1924 election had already been polarised in gross caricatures of this substantial issue. Labour was portrayed as the friend of revolutionaries. One Conservative election poster showed a brigand-like figure grasping a pile of coins, with the caption: 'It's your money he wants.' Another: 'You cannot trust him or his rag. Put your trust in Britain's flag.'

The political significance of the Zinoviev Letter, inserted into this campaign, was obvious. The fact that a protest had been sent to the Soviet Chargé d'Affaires implied that the Government accepted its genuineness. If the treaties had not been dead before, they certainly were now. On polling day, four days later, Labour still managed to increase its share of the vote, but lost 40 of its 191 seats. The Liberals were extinguished as a major party, falling from 159 to 40 and the new Parliament was dominated by a massive Conservative majority. One can only speculate whether, had it not been for the letter, the result would have been substantially different. Certainly it would be reasonable to assume that the rightward drift would have been smaller, but it may well be that MacDonald was doomed from the time he went to the polls. Whatever its effect on the outcome of the election, the Zinoviev Letter must have contributed to the polarisation of British opinion and thus have influenced substantially for the worse the chance of securing a stable and rational policy towards the Soviet Union. Those who believed the letter to be genuine were reinforced in their hatred of Bolshevist international conspiracy. Those who believed it to be a forgery were reinforced in their conviction that the enemies of Soviet Russia would go to any lengths to frustrate an accord. For the next phase of the relationship, it was the former who were to regain the ascendancy.

5
Relations Broken and Resumed

Austen Chamberlain: 'As distant as possible'

Stanley Baldwin's tenure of office in 1923 had been brief. So, too, was his absence from it. In November 1924 he returned to Downing Street, fortified by a majority of more than 200 over the combined strength of Labour and the Liberals. Curzon, with only a few months to live, accepted the office of Lord President of the Council and the Foreign Office went to Austen Chamberlain. Chamberlain was to execute the policies which again brought Britain's policy towards Russia full circle. Within a period of a little more than three years, the relationship which had so recently been formalised was to be severed. The years between the autumn of 1924 and the winter of 1926 were the last period in which Britain still held a clear priority over any other power in her ability to set the pattern of relations with Russia. They were years in which the Diehards of the Conservative Party were to gain the ascendancy and in which the Government, by the progressive reduction of British–Soviet contacts, was to sap its own ability to influence the course of events. Austen Chamberlain was no 'drifter' in the mould of Balfour, but it is perhaps legitimate to see a certain parallel between the way in which each, under the pressure of intractable circumstances, allowed the effective control of events to pass to the proponents of a more actively anti-Bolshevik policy. As Balfour's drift led to the policy of intervention, so did Chamberlain's policy of 'wait and watch' end with the severance of relations.

The circumstances of the 1924 election had been such that policy towards Russia was bound to take priority on the agenda of the new Cabinet. A Committee of Enquiry under the Chairmanship of the Foreign Secretary reached the unanimous conclusion that the Zinoviev

Letter was genuine[1] and it took the Government little time to decide not to recommend MacDonald's two Treaties to Parliament. Austen Chamberlain told the House that there was 'not a shadow of doubt as to the authenticity of the document' and that normal diplomatic relations were not appropriate without respect for the 'courtesies and conventions of international life', but for the time being, policy should be to 'wait and watch'.[2] Hodgson in Mocow was instructed – much as I was in the different circumstances of 1980 – that he should not be more than 'correct' in his relations with the Soviet authorities.[3] A Soviet overture for the resumption of negotiations was rebuffed, the Diehards, led by Joynson-Hicks, the Home Secretary, Birkenhead, Secretary of State for India and Churchill, stumped the country on the theme of the 'Red menace', and in one of those inter-departmental tussles which can do much to shape the course of governmental policy, Joynson-Hicks established the supremacy of the Home Office over the Foreign Office in the handling of matters concerned with Bolshevik 'propaganda'.

The first substantial foreign policy issue concerning Russia arose when the Diehards made allegations of Bolshevik instigation of disorders in Peking the basis of a call for more resolute policies to prevent the erosion of British influence in the Far East. Austen Chamberlain resisted the pressure for a breach of relations. His philosophy was set out in a memorandum written after a discussion in Geneva, where he was attending the Council of the League of Nations:[4]

> It would be very inexpedient to provoke a controversy with the Soviet Government if it can be avoided ... . The less attention we pay to them the more anxious they will be to come to terms with us. If we make them the subject of our denunciations, they feel that we are afraid of them and they are pleased, but when we ignore them entirely they are afraid because it shows that we have no need of them and nothing to fear from them and that we can afford to leave them out of account.

This was the policy which he then enunciated in Cabinet, concluding that:

> The proper course was to keep a watchful eye on their proceedings, to reserve liberty to take any action that might be deemed necessary when sufficient evidence of their misdeeds was forthcoming; to keep the formal relations as distant as possible; but in the meantime not

to yield to the demand in some quarters for an early breaking off of relations.[5]

Commenting on Chamberlain's policy, Chicherin remarked that the Foreign Secretary was wrong in thinking that if he looked the other way long enough the Soviet Union would come asking to be looked at and talked to.

Locarno

Although policy towards the Soviet Union had been a central element in the election campaign and had preoccupied the new Cabinet for a short time, it quickly fell back to the periphery of ministerial concern. The year 1925 was one when the Dawes scheme seemed at last to have removed the problem of German reparations and when Austen Chamberlain secured his triumph with the Treaty of Locarno. Britain, France, Germany, the Netherlands and Belgium were united around a package of agreements, central to which were guarantees of the Franco–German and Belgo–German frontiers. At last, it seemed, there might be a basis for peace and prosperity in Western Europe. Franco–Polish and Franco–Czech treaties formed part of the package, but there was no place for the Soviet Union in the Locarno scheme of things. All that the British Government desired was that it should not be a disruptive influence. Excluded, the Soviet leadership saw more potential menace than reassurance in Locarno and Chicherin spoke of Britain as playing the chief part in the effort to form a united front against the Soviet Union.[6] The suspicion that Britain and France would arrange relations with Germany at the Soviet Union's expense was to poison the British–Soviet relationship throughout much of the inter-war period.

Stalin could still speak of the growth of a revolutionary movement in Britain 'under the banner of friendship in Russia',[7] but with no prospect of a positive development in the British Government's policy the Soviet Union began to concentrate its diplomatic efforts upon Germany and France. In April 1926 a Soviet–German Treaty of Neutrality and Friendship was concluded, bringing the potential threat of Rapallo a step closer to realisation. At the same time, it seemed to the Foreign Office that, despite his public position, Stalin might be moving away from ideological communism to a more pragmatic concern with Russian national interest. If this were so, the threat of revolutionary infection in Britain would be reduced and the classical threat of German–Russian rapprochement enhanced. There was therefore a case for questioning whether a more active British–Soviet relationship might not prove more profitable. Even a group of Conservative MPs who visited Russia in April 1926 were favourably impressed and there was a suggestion that Chicherin was ready to resume negotiations. Hodgson, his views reinforced by five years' experience of post-revolution Moscow,[8] argued the case for a resumption, and preliminary work on a new treaty was put in hand by Chamberlain. It was at this point that domestic policy gained the upper hand. The General Strike broke out and work on the new treaty was soon abandoned.

The General Strike

Zinoviev had for some time been actively pursuing his attempt to link the British and Soviet trade unions and to exploit this linkage as a basis for eventual revolutionary action. An Anglo–Soviet Conference of trade unionists was held and a Joint Advisory Council formed, but the victory of the moderates, among them Ernest Bevin, in the 1925 election to the General Council of the Trades Union Congress was a severe setback to Soviet hopes. At the Home Office, Joynson-Hicks was pursuing his campaign against Communist subversion and in the autumn of 1925 the whole leadership of the British Communist Party was arrested. Neither the Comintern, nor, even less, the Soviet Government, could reasonably have been held to have any direct responsibility for instigating the strike and when it was announced on 1 May 1926, the structure for the exercise of Soviet influence over its course was in poor shape.[9] Financial aid, by way of 'fraternal assistance' from the Russian trade unions was immediately offered, but a first instalment of £26 427 was returned by the TUC General Council, who recognised only too clearly how they would be compromised by acceptance. A second instalment of £100 000 was blocked by emergency regulations introduced by the Government. The damage was, however, done. It took the Diehards another year to secure the severance of relations, but from the time of the General Strike they had the upper hand.

The 'Diehard' campaign

Joynson-Hicks launched his major attack at a Cabinet meeting on 16 June 1926, at which the minutes record complete unanimity that in view of the 'malignant hostility to the British Empire in the Soviet

Government repeatedly announced by its leaders and acted upon in all parts of the world and on every opportunity', a breach of relations would be fully justified. Nevertheless, a majority still believed that the immediate political advantage might be outweighed by the practical disadvantages and that 'the moment was not opportune for a rupture'.[10] From Moscow, Hodgson had for some time been pointing to the 'eternal contradictions' which mark Soviet policy – on the one hand a 'revolutionary dogmatism demands that every interest be subordinated to the one object of world revolution'; on the other the 'practical exigencies, the waning of revolutionary ardour, indifference to outside things as material prosperity within the country increases and inevitable erosion of the party monolith'.[11] His views were reflected in a Foreign Office memorandum[12] which may have substantially influenced the majority view. It set out the argument for maintaining relations in terms which were to recur throughout the course of British–Soviet relations. Distinguishing the Soviet Government's interest in satisfying the practical needs of the Russian people from the interest of 'the pure revolutionary and disturber of the order and welfare of other countries', it argued for the 'ultimate power of sanity'. Contact with the outside world, it claimed, would bring home to the rulers of Russia 'the obstacles which the revolutionary side of their work puts in the way of their practical efforts to improve the welfare of their country'. Moreover, the Foreign Office argued, Russia was almost as invulnerable economically as she was militarily. She could support with ease a rupture of trade relations, which would not only damage British trading interests, but would also lead to an increase of antagonism and an intensification of propaganda. For the time being, the Foreign Office prevailed and the Cabinet's policy was endorsed by Parliament. The House of Commons accepted the Foreign Secretary's argument that to break relations would be to introduce a 'new and disturbing issue' into both domestic and European politics.[13] The Government, had, however, published a Blue Book[14] containing documents seized when the communist leaders were arrested and this, in the words of *The Times*, showed a 'constant and systematic promotion by institutions in Moscow of a movement directed to the ruin of British trade, the overthrow of the British Constitution and the destruction of the British Empire'. The Diehards then stepped up their campaign in the country. Hicks spoke of conduct 'such as no civilized nation in the world would have been guilty of'; Churchill, speaking as Chancellor of the Exchequer at a dinner given by the Lord Mayor, castigated the 'representatives of a hateful and subhuman barbarism'[15] and on 15 July a mass meeting on the theme of 'Clear out the Reds' was held in the Albert Hall.

Krasin returned to London as Chargé d'Affaires and began the task of restoring relations, but the current of opinion was against him and when, on 24 November 1926, he died, the Cabinet decided to oppose the appointment of a successor. The Diehards succeeded in bringing the issue back to Cabinet in February 1927[16] and by this time, with further trouble in China, the opposition to them was crumbling. The minutes record: 'The view generally accepted by the Cabinet after considerable discussion was that, given the state of public opinion in this country, if the present policy of the Russian Soviet Government was continued, a breach of relations within the next few months was almost inevitable.' Again, however, Austen Chamberlain was able, with Baldwin's support, to avoid the immediate breach.

Gregory, in charge of the Russian Department, had circulated a memorandum on the case for and against a breach of relations. 'The ejection of the Bolsheviks from this country would be a thoroughly pleasurable proceeding, but it would be rather the satisfaction of an emotion than an act of useful diplomacy.' British Ambassadors in the European capitals were consulted and showed no great enthusiasm for a breach. Sir Ronald Lindsay in Berlin, for instance, argued that 'we are at a new kind of war with Russia and … within the limitations that its peculiar character imposes on us we must wage it so as to injure Russia wherever we can', but to expel the Soviet Mission would be to 'blind ourselves' and would represent 'a very long step indeed towards converting the present peculiar struggle into an armed conflict of the old fashioned sort'.[17] The argument which carried the day was probably that British–Soviet relations could not be considered in isolation. Despite Locarno, Europe was in an uneasy state, with tension over the continued Allied occupation of the Rhineland and doubt over the durability of the Franco–German understanding. In such a situation, Austen Chamberlain might not be disposed to seek an improved relationship with the Soviet Union, but was concerned that a formal breach might prove an additional cause of instability.

Taking account of his concern, ministers agreed to confine immediate action to the despatch of a Note demanding that the Soviet Government should refrain from interference with purely British concerns and should abstain from hostile action or propaganda against British subjects. The Note, delivered to the Soviet Chargé d'Affaires in London on 23 February 1927 complained of 'grievous outrages and injuries to British interests' and stated that the continuation of such acts would sooner or later render inevitable abrogation of the Trade Agreement 'and even the severance of ordinary diplomatic relations'. It was supported by quotations from Soviet speeches and articles, some referring to 'English imperialism egging on its faithful hirelings' against the Soviet Union, others urging support for the English miners and the Chinese revolutionaries as sectors of major importance in the world revolutionary process. It complained of a 'grossly insulting and mendacious cartoon' in *Izvestia* of 29 December 1926, showing Chamberlain applauding the execution of Lithuanian Communists, but while clearly demonstrating Soviet hostility, it cited no hard evidence of improper Soviet activities in Britain.[18] It was therefore scarcely surprising that the Soviet reply should expose the lack of hard evidence; draw attention to speeches by Birkenhead about the 'band of murderers and robbers' in Moscow and by Winston Churchill about the 'dark conspirators of the Moscow Kremlin'; profess the Soviet Government's desire to establish completely normal relations; and stress that a breach would be on the full responsibility of the British Government.

The whole issue of relations with the Soviet Union was debated in the House of Commons on 3 March 1927.[19] The tenor may be judged by the speech of Sir Robert Horne, the signatory of the 1921 Trade Agreement, who confessed 'that everything I hoped for has failed to materialise and everything in which I believed has proved a failure'. Still, however, the Foreign Secretary said that the Government would give the Soviet Government 'one more opportunity to conform ... to the ordinary comity of nations and abstain from the effort to promote world revolution and from all interference in our internal affairs'.

The Arcos Raid and the breach of relations

The Diehards must have realised that it would now take only one piece of evidence to push Austen Chamberlain over the edge. In May Joynson-Hicks mounted his final and successful blow for the severance of relations. The occasion for it was a report that a confidential War Office document, a training pamphlet, had been seen by a British employee in the office of Arcos, the organisation of Soviet Cooperatives which had been the first vehicle for Lloyd George's trade negotiations and which shared offices with the Soviet Trade Delegation. Among the advisers to Arcos was E. F. Wise, Lloyd George's principal adviser on relations with the Soviet Union during the critical period from 1919, through the Genoa Conference and up to the conclusion of the Trade Agreement. Arcos enjoyed no diplomatic immunity. Chamberlain could scarcely have refused – and did not refuse – Joynson-Hicks' request for his concurrence in a police raid on its office. The Trade Delegation as such also had no immunity, but the Head of the Delegation, in his capacity as Official Agent, had. In executing the raid, the police made no distinction between the offices of Arcos and those of the Delegation, except that the safes of the Head of the Delegation were marked 'To be preserved for decision'. It seems probable that Chamberlain did not at first realise that the search would cover an office which was arguably immune from search and Joynson-Hicks, determined to push the search to the maximum, may have been less than frank about its precise extent. In the event, the Government decided to rest on the claim that it was difficult, with two offices in the one building, to say where one began and the other ended and that, in any case, the raid was justified by the abuse of privileges by the Russians themselves, in conducting activities contrary to the terms of the 1921 Agreement.

The documents seized were in fact barely adequate to sustain such a charge. The mood of the Cabinet had, however, passed a point of no return and on 23 May 1927,[20] with Chamberlain now favouring a breach, the Cabinet decided that the Agreement should be terminated, the Soviet diplomatic mission expelled and the British diplomatic mission withdrawn from Moscow. The Arcos staff, except for those who had been engaged in 'illicit interference in internal affairs' would be allowed to remain and trade would continue as it did in the case of countries such as the United States which had no formal agreement with the Soviet Union.

In putting the Government's case to Parliament, Joynson-Hicks relied largely on evidence, including intercepted communications, from sources other than the Arcos raid and spoke of 'one of the most complete and one of the most nefarious spy systems that it has ever been my lot to meet'.[21] Accordingly, on 26 May 1927, the Soviet Government were informed that because the police examination had 'conclusively proved that both military espionage and subversive activities against the British Empire were directed and carried out from 49, Moorgate', the British Government regarded themselves as free from the obligations of the 1921 Trade Agreement and the existing relations between the two Governments were suspended. The German Government took over the protection of Soviet interests in Britain and the Norwegian Government that of British interests in the Soviet Union. As Winston Churchill put it: 'We have proclaimed them [the

Soviet representatives] treacherous, incorrigible and unfit for civilised intercourse.'[22]

It was widely believed at the time that the British Government's action was the prelude to a more active offensive against the Soviet Union and possibly to war. In the Soviet Union, the whole country was said to be 'plunged into a state of nervous tension', with moderates regretting the break and blaming party zealots for it, the subterranean organisations 'peeping like rabbits from their holes' and the security authorities setting out to 'exterminate the agents and spies of the British Government'.[23] Russians who had been employed by the British Mission were arrested on charges of espionage and sentenced to exile. A number of other people were shot as a result of unfounded allegations of espionage on behalf of Sir Robert Hodgson.[24] There was considerable concern in Germany, where the suspension of relations was seen as an inevitable stage in the age-long struggle, not between Communism and capitalism, but between Russia and England. Stalin wrote on 28 July: 'The English Government has entered firmly and decisively on the road of organising war against the USSR'[25] and Austen Chamberlain found it necessary to reassure Stresemann that no further action by Britain against Russia was contemplated. In doing so, he also expressed the view that there was no real danger of Communism in England and that while the Soviet leadership regarded Conservatives as their natural enemies they looked upon the more moderate Labour leaders as traitors. Nor, in his view, was there any likelihood of a new revolution in Russia. Thus, over a period of six years a full cycle in the development of Anglo–Soviet relations had been run. For the moment, British policy was at a dead point, with neither the means nor the will to develop it in either a positive or a negative direction. So it was to remain for the two years which were left of Baldwin's second premiership.

From the summer of 1927 to the summer of 1929 there was no movement in relations but, despite the absence of official contact, there was a moving incident when in August 1928 the Soviet navy handed over with full naval honours the coffins of sailors drowned when the British submarine L55 had been sunk while taking part in operations against the Bolsheviks in June 1919.[26] The British Government professed its intention to encourage the development of a normal trading relationship but, in the absence of any formal links, the volume of British exports to the Soviet Union fell from over £11 million in 1927 to less than £5 million in 1928 and it was made clear to a group of British industrialists who visited Moscow that there could be no significant expansion without a resumption of diplomatic relations. Concern about the economic situation was undermining the political base of Baldwin's Government and in June 1929 the end came with a disastrous defeat at the polls. A Low cartoon portrayed Baldwin and his ministers waiting in vain for the arrival of another Zinoviev Letter to save them, but on this occasion the Russian issue was not a substantial factor in the election. It was on domestic policy that the Government was defeated.[27]

The resumption of relations

A Foreign Office memorandum written in 1931 pointed out that one of the unfortunate legacies of the war was that Anglo–Soviet relations had become a subject of the most acute political controversy in Britain: 'From being a pre-war enigma, Russia has become a post-war obsession. So long as one section of opinion, even if a small one, hitches its wagon to the Soviet star, and another longs for nothing so much as the star's eclipse, the task of reducing Anglo–Soviet relations to normal remains hopeless.'[28] When the second Labour Government took office under Ramsay MacDonald, nothing in the realities which underlay the British–Soviet relationship had changed since 1927, but the mood was swinging in favour of a resumption of relations and industry was adding its voice. The party was, in any event, committed to resumption and as soon as the Government took office the process was begun. In place of Austen Chamberlain as Foreign Secretary was Arthur Henderson who, as a member of Lloyd George's wartime coalition, had been considered as a replacement for Buchanan as Ambassador in Petrograd in the immediate aftermath of the February Revolution and had seen at first hand the conditions there. MacDonald and Henderson were not by temperament disposed to rush matters but there was pressure from the left of the Labour Party for early action. Henderson's negotiating position was correspondingly weakened and the Soviet Government, no doubt sensing this, made it plain that they would not accept the prior negotiation of guarantees as a prerequisite for the resumption of relations. The first step, in 1921, had been the exchange of Trade Representatives and the second in 1924 had raised the representation to the diplomatic level with the appointment of Chargés d'Affaires. Now it was agreed that, subject to Parliamentary approval, Ambassadors should be exchanged and that, immediately thereafter, negotiations should be instituted on the following questions:

(1) Definition of the attitude of both Governments towards the treaties of 1924.
(2) Commercial treaty and allied questions.
(3) Claims and counter-claims, intergovernmental and private; debts, claims arising out of intervention and otherwise, and financial questions connected with such claims and counter-claims.
(4) Fisheries.
(5) The application of previous treaties and conventions.[29]

The House of Commons approved the resumption on this basis, but there was no bipartisan support. The Conservatives voted solidly against the resumption and in the House of Lords they succeeded in obtaining a resolution that diplomatic recognition of the Soviet Government was at the moment undesirable. It was thus against a background of continuing British political controversy that Sir Esmond Ovey presented his credentials on 21 December 1929 as the first British Ambassador to the Soviet Union. He was a career diplomat who had joined the Service in 1903, by 1925 had risen to be HM Representative in Mexico City and was about to leave for Rio de Janeiro when he was told to proceed instead to Moscow. There he found, despite the 'distinct impression of a lack of paint', a clean hotel and a 'state of dilapidation not greater than that which distinguishes many of the smaller towns and outskirts of larger towns in North America'. Simultaneously Griigorii Yakovlevich Brilliant, now known as Grigorii Sokolnikov, a commander of Bolshevik armies during the Civil War, presented his credentials to the Prince of Wales on appointment as Ambassador to the Court of St James. As their first official act, the Ambassadors confirmed the entry into force of the mutual pledge with regard to propaganda which had been in the unratified General Treaty of 1924. The parties affirmed:

> their desire and intention to live in peace and amity with each other, scrupulously to respect the undoubted right of a State to order its own life within its own jurisdiction in its own way, to refrain and restrain all persons and organisations under their direct or indirect control, including organisations in receipt of financial assistance from them, from any act, overt or covert liable in any way whatsoever to endanger the tranquillity or prosperity of any part of the territory of the British Empire or the Union of Soviet Socialist Republics, or intended to embitter the relations of the British Empire or the Union with their neighbours or any other countries.

Against the background of this renewed pledge, the negotiation of the substantive agreements was taken up between the Foreign Secretary and the Soviet Ambassador. Some progress was made. A temporary commercial agreement of April 1930 provided broadly for mutual MFN treatment, together with certain special features such as the grant of national treatment to British vessels in Soviet ports. A protocol to the agreement provided for the elimination of political discrimination, with particular reference to legislative or administrative action on commercial matters. The British Government saw this as a means of preventing political discrimination by Soviet purchasing agencies and the Soviet Government saw it as a means of preventing British political discrimination in the grant of export credit guarantees. The Soviet Trade Representative and his two deputies were accorded diplomatic privileges and immunities and the immunity attached also to the Delegation's offices. The Trade Agreement was followed by a temporary fisheries agreement concluded in May 1930 which gave British fishermen the right to fish up to the three-mile limit of Soviet waters.

In respect of the two long-standing issues of claims and propaganda no progress was made. The British Government put forward once again a claim in respect of intergovernmental debt (now amounting to £902 million) which it had no real hope of recovering, plus a somewhat exaggerated figure of £262million for private debt. In earlier negotiations the Soviet Union had had some incentive to reach a settlement, in that the grant of export credits was made conditional upon it. Now, however, they had secured the credits without making any concession on claims and could afford to prolong the negotiations indefinitely. On propaganda, it soon became apparent that the reiteration of the 1924 pledge was unlikely to have any practical significance. On January 1930 the *Daily Worker* came into existence, featuring in its first issue a message from the Executive Committee of the Communist International hailing it as the champion of the proletariat in the class struggle against the Labour Government. Growing concern over the activities of Soviet agents caused the Government to set up a special committee in the summer of 1930. On five occasions representations were made to the Soviet Ambassador until eventually the Foreign Office concluded that this course was not only useless, but progressively more undignified.

Denunciation of the 1930 Trade Agreement

The years of Ramsay MacDonald's second Government were years of economic crisis in which unemployment in Britain rose from just over

1 million to nearly 3 million. In such a situation foreign trade was vitally important and, as the crisis deepened, there was disappointment in the Government at the relatively slow growth in exports to the Soviet Union. At the same time, from the Conservatives, came growing agitation, supported by the press, on the dumping of Soviet wheat and timber, the use of forced labour for export production and religious persecution. A leading part was taken by Joynson-Hicks, Home Secretary at the time of the Arcos Raid and now, as Lord Brentford, Chairman of the Trade Defence League, designed to bring home to the people of Britain and of other nations the threat that the Soviet Union would use economic policy as a road to world revolution and to urge the need for a united front against the common enemy, Communism. Stanley Baldwin took up the cry and called for tariff protection, if necessary at the price of once more denouncing the trade agreement with Russia. The pressure had its effect. In early 1931 the Foreign Secretary reminded the Soviet Ambassador that the volume of trade was not yet back to the level of 1925–7 and that, in such a situation, 'the main argument in support of normal Anglo–Russian relations lost most of its value'.[30] The economic crisis brought the collapse of the Labour Government and when the National Government, formed in August 1931, was returned later that year with a massive, Conservative-dominated majority, the relationship with the Soviet Union came under threat once again.

With Ramsay MacDonald as Prime Minister, power was nevertheless very much in the hands of Stanley Baldwin as Lord President of the Council and leader of the Conservative Party, but it was the Liberal lawyer, Sir John Simon who, as Foreign Secretary, was to preside over the next critical stage in relations. In February 1932 he warned the Soviet Chargé d'Affaires that the adverse balance of trade was such that the British Government 'could not continue to acquiesce indefinitely' and would be forced to consider steps – which he did not define – to remedy the situation. That action was not long delayed and it initiated a new period of tension. The immediate cause for action was the introduction of Imperial Preference as a result of the Ottawa Conference in the summer of 1932. On 1 October 1932, in accordance with commitments entered into at Ottawa, and in order to leave itself free to take such action as might be deemed necessary against Soviet goods, the British Government gave formal six-months notice of termination of the 1930 temporary trade agreement with the Soviet Union. It was in these inauspicious circumstances that Ivan Maisky, the penniless refugee of the pre-Revolutionary era, arrived, proclaiming a policy of 'common sense', to succeed Sokolnikov as Soviet Ambassador in London.

The termination of the 1930 agreement was not, in itself, a matter of great moment. It was seen by the Government as a necessary consequence of Ottawa rather than as a major move in British–Soviet relations. The depth of the economic crisis was such that almost any measure to improve matters could have been justified. It mattered little that Soviet exports were largely irrelevant to the troubles of the West. The trade agreement with the Soviet Union had been a disappointment in its direct results. There had been no satisfaction of the British financial claims and the resumption of diplomatic relations had done nothing to reduce the continuing aggravation of the ideological offensive of the Comintern. The United States, France, Canada and other countries had all introduced discriminatory measures against Soviet exports and there was Canadian pressure for protection against Soviet exports of grain and timber. The British Government gave the required period of notice and in the House of Commons Mr Baldwin indicated the Government's readiness to negotiate a new agreement if they could secure a better proportion of Soviet orders and also the right to stop imports damaging to domestic industry.[31] The Soviet reaction was one more of sorrow than of anger. Litvinov, who had succeeded Chicherin as Foreign Minister in 1930, was pessimistic about the prospect for future negotiations, but his experience of the course of British policy since 1917 could scarcely leave much room for optimism. An anti-British campaign was briefly worked up in the Soviet press, but surprisingly a sharp complaint by Sir Robert Vansittart brought an apology from the editor of *Izvestiya* which was duly communicated by Maisky and accepted by Sir John Simon and the Prime Minister. Negotiations for a new commercial treaty were opened on 15 December 1932. The British Government might well have congratulated themselves that the process of terminating the agreement had been satisfactorily concluded and it is interesting that Gromyko and Ponomarev, in their history of Soviet foreign policy, made no mention of it. By an odd chain of circumstances, however, this may have marked a turning point in Britain's ability to influence Soviet policy.

This was the point at which the policies of the major powers were beginning once again to turn upon a German hinge and at which a certain reassessment of the pattern of Soviet foreign relations was perceptible. In July 1931 Litvinov spoke to the British Ambassador of his concern about the possible emergence of 'some form of Fascist Government' in Germany. The Japanese invasion of Manchuria in

September 1931 revived all the old Russian fears of the threat from the East and gave added force to the Soviet Union's search for security. On 25 July 1932 a Soviet non-aggression treaty with Poland opened the way for conclusion of a similar treaty with France in November of that year. The major tests of the will to resist Japanese, Italian and German aggression lay in the future, but already the pattern of diplomatic relationships which was to condition the response of the other powers was beginning to form. It may be that the search for collective security could never have succeeded, but it was unfortunate that, at the very time of Hitler's accession to power, Britain faced a new crisis in her relationship with the Soviet Union.

The Metropolitan–Vickers trial

In January 1933 Adolf Hitler became Chancellor of Germany and Europe began the swiftly accelerating course to war. In the spring and summer of 1933, it was not, however, the menace of Hitler which dominated the British–Soviet relationship, but the show trial in Moscow of six British engineers employed by the Metropolitan–Vickers company. The company had a long tradition of business with Russia, particularly in respect of heavy electrical generating plant and related equipment. They were responsible not only for supply, but also for installation and servicing of equipment and they consequently maintained, under the direction of a small team of British engineers, a group of British and Russian technicians dealing with plant in various parts of the Soviet Union. On 12 March 1933 Soviet security police raided the company's premises near Moscow. Six British and twenty Russian staff were arrested on varying charges of military and economic espionage, bribery and wrecking of plant.

It is probably the case, as Lord Strang has suggested,[32] that the trials were not conceived primarily as an act of foreign policy. More probably, they derived from the difficulties in the capital equipment programme under the five-year plan. On the very day the British engineers were arrested, it had been announced that thirty-five officials had been shot for counter-revolutionary activity and sabotage affecting agricultural production. It must have been tempting to seek at least one foreign scapegoat, easy to proceed from the failure of imported plant to the allegation of sabotage by the installer and easy to proceed from the normal collection of information to the allegation of espionage. Metropolitan–Vickers were vulnerable because of the scale of their activities, the close association between British and Russian staff and, finally, because of the bad state of British–Soviet relations after the cancellation of the commercial treaty.

British ministers were satisfied that the charges were effectively without foundation and the stage was set for a trial of strength between the two Governments.[33] Baldwin stated in Parliament on 15 March that the Government was convinced that there could be 'no justification for the charge on which the arrests were made' and warned of 'unfortunate consequences to Anglo–Soviet relations'.[34] Vansittart saw Maisky who, after a year as Soviet Ambassador, must have been finding London somewhat chillier than he had found it as a refugee some twenty years earlier. Maisky was told that unless the prisoners were released, there would be a 'rooted and growing disinclination to proceed with commercial negotiations'. The public Soviet response, not surprisingly, was a statement that no pressure and no threats would induce the Soviet Government to suspend or mitigate its laws with regard to British subjects. On 20 March[35] the British Government announced that negotiations for a commercial treaty were being suspended and in Moscow Sir Esmond Ovey informed Litvinov that a reference to the possible prohibition of Soviet imports was omitted only in view of indications that immediate release was still possible. On the advice of Vansittart, the Cabinet decided against threatening a second breach of diplomatic relations, but when it became clear that the trial would take place, a Bill was introduced giving the Government power to prohibit imports from the Soviet Union and after a bitter exchange with Litvinov, Ovey was instructed on 29 March to return for consultation, leaving Strang as Chargé d'Affaires. In view of the indictment of both espionage and sabotage, Sir John Simon made a further formal parliamentary statement to the effect that none of the accused had ever been employed directly or indirectly in connection with any branch of the Intelligence Service and that neither they nor the company had ever supplied any information to any such branch. After a trial marked by the classic features of Soviet show trials, five of the accused were convicted, two being sentenced to terms of imprisonment and the others to expulsion. (The two principal accused, Thornton and MacDonald, subsequently described at a meeting with Foreign Office officials the methods which had been employed to secure a confession by the former and a guilty plea by the latter. No physical violence had been employed or threatened but, by exploiting the feeling of helplessness on the part of the accused and by accumulating scraps of information, in themselves innocent enough, the interrogators had brought Thornton to the point at which 'he would have signed his own death warrant'. MacDonald's guilty plea was secured by the threat that if he persisted in pleading not guilty his Russian housekeeper would be made to give evidence and that this would 'make things much worse' for all concerned.) The embargo on Soviet imports was proclaimed on 19 April, to take effect form 26 April. On 20 April the Soviet Government responded with an embargo on British goods and measures against British shipping to remain in force for the whole period of the British embargo.

The crisis in relations was resolved almost as swiftly as it had erupted. It quickly became clear that the Soviet Government, having insisted upon their sovereign right to bring the Metro–Vickers employees to trial, were anxious to conclude the incident. In June, Litvinov visited London for the abortive World Economic Conference and in the course of two private meetings with Simon, it was agreed that there should be simultaneous release of the prisoners, cancellation of the embargoes and announcement of the resumption of negotiations for a new trade agreement.

More interesting than the fact of the Metro–Vickers settlement was the political assessment which made it possible. Ramsay MacDonald subsequently complained that Vansittart had pushed him into a wrong decision in applying the embargo and, indeed, it may well have been an over-reaction. Yet, in practice, the over-reaction may have served to make the Soviet Government realise the danger which it ran in needlessly antagonising British opinion at the very time when the constant threat from Japan to the Eastern frontier was being matched by the growing threat from Germany to the West. From Moscow, Strang reported that Stalin had expressed to a colleague his annoyance at having been brought to sanction the arrest and trial 'without having been warned by those whose duty it was to know of the risk of serious repercussions on world opinion and on Anglo–Soviet relations'. The report could not be confirmed, but it seems inherently likely that in a potentially dangerous situation, the Soviet leadership was disinclined to aggravate still further an essentially hostile Britain. This certainly was the tenor of comment made to Strang in Moscow after the affair was over.[36] In an analysis of Soviet foreign policy[37] he argued that the imperialist policy of Japan and the seizure of power by Hitler had played a decisive part in reorienting Soviet foreign policy. Britain which, in Soviet eyes, had now replaced France as the instigator of anti-Soviet movements in Europe, was seen as a less open, but not less dangerous enemy than Germany and Japan, seeking to turn German interest to the East and to cripple the Soviet economy. In this situation, Strang saw Soviet policy as essentially defensive, playing upon imperialist antagonisms, seeking equally to avoid a reconciliation which would permit the imperialists to join forces against the Soviet Union and a general war which might involve the Soviet Union and jeopardise the revolution. Litvinov's 'policy of peace' was, in his view, at that time, genuine. A temporary sacrifice of prestige or interests could be accepted by a state 'whose governors are, it seems, confident that its area, its population, its natural resources, its system of government and its programme of planned economic development will in the long run render it all-powerful and that the principles upon which it is founded are fated to capture the world'.

The analysis was perceptive in terms both of the immediate future and of the policies leading to the outbreak of war six years later. The German and Japanese threat provided a motive for a Soviet–British rapprochement and there could be a coincidence of interest, but the deeper contradictions remained. The long-term revolutionary objectives of the Soviet Union might not be a direct threat to British society, but they did little for mutual confidence, while on the Soviet side the suspicion persisted that an inherently hostile, capitalist Britain would seek to protect her own security by turning German expansion eastwards. Neither concern was wholly justified, but neither was without foundation. The story of the next six years is the story of the triumph of mutual mistrust.

6
The Approach to War

In Chapters 3–5 we have followed the development of the political relationship between Britain and the Soviet Union from the ending of military intervention by Lloyd George in 1919; through the negotiation of the 1921 Trade Agreement and the failure of the attempt to work out a multilateral settlement at Genoa and The Hague; Curzon's ultimatum of 1923; the establishment of diplomatic relations by Ramsay MacDonald and the signature by him of the two Anglo–Soviet treaties in 1924; the rejection of the 1924 treaties by Baldwin in the same year; the abrogation of the 1921 Trade Agreement and the breach of relations by Baldwin in 1927; the re-establishment of full relations, with the appointment of Ambassadors and the negotiation of a new Trade Agreement by MacDonald in 1929–30; and finally the notice of termination of the 1930 Agreement by Baldwin in 1932, followed by the Metro–Vickers crisis. Two years of confused politico–military action against the Bolsheviks were followed by fourteen years in which successive British Governments oscillated between attempts to establish a practical working relationship with the new Soviet state and attempts to banish it from the international community. Neither course could be said to have been marked by any significant measure of success. Now, as the potential of a rearmed and aggressive Germany began to be perceived, the stage was being set afresh. Would the script be rewritten? Before we trace the stages through which, over a period of eight years, successive Conservative or Conservative-dominated Governments moved from ostracism of the Soviet Union, close to open conflict and then to full military alliance, it may be helpful to stand back from the day-to-day unfolding of policy in order to look at the political and social climate within which it was being formulated.

The mood of the 1930s

It was in the 1930s that the great schism in British attitudes towards the Soviet Union was at its most evident. The thinness of the official documentation contrasts vividly with the outpouring of comment from other sources. In 1932 a young Conservative politician, Harold Macmillan, spent several weeks travelling with a friend in the Soviet Union. Later, in *Winds of Change*, he was to write of the impulse behind that visit:

> While the capitalist world seemed, to many observers, in decay if not in mortal agony, the Bolsheviks had apparently consolidated their power and stability. In the early years of my political life, Bolshevism was regarded in Britain with feelings ranging between contempt and fear. But by 1932 many British people were beginning to wonder whether, after all, the regime which had imposed itself over a vast part of the world's territory might not be worth careful and, if possible objective, study.[1]

Macmillan must have typified many of his generation. Born at the zenith of Victorian Britain's imperial power, he had served in the Grenadier Guards throughout the 1914–18 war, had seen the promise won by the suffering of those years squandered in the political bickering and economic bankruptcy of the 1920s. Now, with economic depression at home and the rising menace of the dictators abroad, he needed to assess where he stood and take new bearings. In his book, he reprinted many of the letters which he wrote home to his mother from Russia. It was 'a kind of looking-glass world, where everything was the opposite of what one would expect'. Like many who were to make a similar journey then – or, indeed, later – he found a proud and kindly people in the grip of a rigid political system whose practice bore little comparison with the grandiloquent proclamation of its ideals. Like many, he breathed more freely as he crossed the Soviet border on his way home. A quarter of a century later, he was to be the first British Prime Minister to visit the Soviet Union in peacetime.

Macmillan represented a broad cross-section of opinion – lying between the zealots of right and left – prepared to examine seriously and impartially the great Russian experiment, on the whole more saddened than encouraged by what they saw, but certainly not disposed to ignore the new Soviet state as a factor in the march of European politics. To his right the impulse of protection against the contamination of Communist ideology and the competition of Russian imports motivated a significant sector of the Conservative party. Little that they had heard of the first decade of Soviet Communism had modified their abhorrence at its practical consequences and, as the 1920s ended, the world heard the first reports of the great forced collectivisation, the deportations, the cattle slaughtered by the peasants and peasants by the militia, as the country dwellers of Russia were hammered into the Stalinist mould. On the left, Sidney and Beatrice Webb were producing the second edition of their great work, *Soviet Communism. A New Civilisation?* and, unworried by the Stalinist excesses, removing the question mark. The Society for Cultural Relations with the USSR, with J. M. Keynes and H. G. Wells as its first two Vice-Presidents, was serving as a focus for the support of men like the 'Red Dean' of Canterbury, Hewlett Johnson, who was to describe Soviet Communism as 'majestic in range, practical in detail, scientific in form, Christian in spirit ... a programme which thinks not in terms of a privileged class, but in terms of each individual soul' and whose book, *The Socialist Sixth of The World*, was to go through twenty-one impressions between 1939 and 1945. The 1930s have, with some justice, been called the 'Pink Decade'. So they were for an important and influential body of intellectual and political opinion. So, too, they were for a young man, Donald Maclean, at 19 in his second year at Cambridge when Macmillan went on his Russian tour. Many in that decade trod the path to Moscow. The governmental relationship was, however, another matter altogether.

When Macmillan first visited Moscow, no minister in any British Government since the Revolution had set foot in the Soviet Union. Ramsay MacDonald was still Prime Minister, but now, as nominal head of a National Government, a broken politician and a spent man. In his two brief periods of effective power in 1924 and 1929–30 he had committed the country to the establishment of a full relationship with the Soviet Union, but had lacked the political power to carry the relationship into effect. Although still respected by Baldwin for his grasp of foreign policy, there is little sign that, after 1931, he sought to exercise any great influence on the handling of relations with Russia. In all but name, Stanley Baldwin was in charge of His Majesty's Government and he was only too happy to leave matters to the Foreign Secretary, Sir John Simon.

Baldwin was not as negligent of foreign policy as he has sometimes been presented, but it was never of consuming interest to him and, in the realm of foreign policy nothing was more alien to him than the Soviet Union and its political system. It was alien to his roots in the kindly landscape of Worcestershire, to his instinct for a capitalism based upon responsible industrial partnership between the employer and his employees, individually and collectively and, above all, to his concept of a democracy based on respect for the individual citizen. 'The Christian state', Baldwin once said, at an Empire Rally of Youth, 'proclaims human personality to be supreme. The servile state denies this. Every compromise with the infinite value of the human soul leads straight back to savagery and the jungle.'[2] Baldwin's experience of dealing with the Russians was lengthy, but never very close. He had been President of the Board of Trade immediately after the signature of the 1921 Trade Agreement and played his part in the preparation for Genoa, where he is recorded as siding with Churchill. Coming into office after the Zinoviev Letter, he had presided over the demolition of the relationship in the years from 1924 to 1929 and was scarcely likely now to rekindle it with much fervour.

There was not in his Russian policy the cold hostility of Curzon, the crusading spirit of Churchill or the bludgeon of Joynson-Hicks, but rather an antipathetic indifference, perhaps best summed up by his comment, as the Nazi menace developed: 'If there is any fighting in Europe to be done I should like to see the Bolsheviks and the Nazis doing it ... If he [Hitler] moves East, I shall not break my heart'.[3] In Simon, Baldwin had a Foreign Secretary who was seen by some as an avowed hater of the Soviet Union and all its works. The record scarcely bears this out. The picture which emerges is much more that of a shy, aloof man, a good legal brain confronting dispassionately the problems of the British–Soviet relationship when they forced themselves upon him, but with little political impulse to shape the course of events.

Thus it was that for several critical years the conduct of British policy towards the Soviet Union lacked any positive ministerial lead. Eden, with a stronger personal involvement and a greater sense of the political relevance of the Soviet Union, might have had a substantial impact on the course of policy, but with the accession of Neville Chamberlain, the control of foreign policy moved back across Downing Street into the hands of the Prime Minister. The indifference of Baldwin was gone and the antipathy towards the Soviet Union was heightened.

At the time of Macmillan's visit, the Ambassador in Moscow was still Sir Esmond Ovey. The Counsellor was William Strang. Strang, the son of a Scottish farmer, brought up in Essex, educated at the local village school, followed by grammar school and a scholarship to London

University, entered the Diplomatic Service from the Army through the special examination held in 1919. He first comes into the story of British–Soviet relations when, as a junior member of the Northern Department of the Foreign Office, he was the only one to notice that MacDonald had not initialed the celebrated note on the Zinoviev Letter. His service in Moscow was marked by the trial of the Metropolitan–Vickers engineers. As Counsellor, he was left in charge of the Embassy when Ovey was recalled and the experience convinced him of the need to deal firmly with the Soviet Government. He wrote critically of the subjectivity of those like the Webbs 'who would not see what was plain' before their eyes, and remarked upon the way in which foreign opinion in Moscow had welcomed the British embargo as evidence that 'some government had at last taken resolute and decisive action against the arbitrary tyranny of the OGPU and that foreigners in the Soviet Union had acquired additional security thereby'.[4] In a despatch to the Foreign Office, sent during the trial, he warned against the trap of Soviet peace proposals and the continued goal of world revolutions: 'The present Soviet policy of the "breathing-space", of the peaceful co-existence of the two systems, should not blind us to the ultimate and still living revolutionary purpose of the first proletarian state.'[5] Strang, himself, was, however, no doctrinaire Bolshevik-hater, but rather one of the many who, looking impartially at the performance of the Soviet Government, could not ignore the menace either of its ideology or of its policies. A few years later it was he who was sent back from the Foreign Office to join the Ambassador for the abortive negotiations for a British–French–Soviet agreement in the summer of 1939.

At the time of the Metro–Vickers trial Strang's superior as Permanent Under Secretary in the Foreign Office was Robert Vansittart. Vansittart, who was more conscious of the German threat than most of his generation, may for that reason have been more charitably disposed to the Soviet Union. Certainly in a memorandum to Sir John Simon he described his own views as 'consistently less drastic' than Strang's,[6] although the Secretary of State professed himself unable to find the difference. Vansittart himself was to figure significantly in the course of dealings with the Soviet Union only in his initiation of a series of lengthy conversations with the Soviet Ambassador, Maisky, in the summer of 1934. Maisky recalled the 'highly constructive spirit' of those discussions.[7] For Vansittart himself,[8] it was a matter of regret that 'Russia and Britain were alike exposed to German designs and could never get together', but he had little doubt where the blame lay. 'The mental confusion of the Communists was as deep as their duplicity. Collaboration was basically impossible with people who would not willingly achieve their ends in peace.' Recalling an accusation by Winston Churchill of having a rigid mind, he commented that in respect of Communism, Deutschtum and homosexuality he was ready to be called illiberal. Maisky claims that Vansittart turned against the Soviet Union after the war through alarm at the growth of Soviet power. There is little reason to doubt that his natural antagonism was deeply rooted, but as a good public servant he did what he could to create with the Soviet Union in the mid-1930s the kind of relationship which might have formed the basis of collective security against Hitler.

In Moscow, from 1930 until he was succeeded by Molotov in May 1939, the People's Commissar for Foreign Affairs was Maxim Litvinov. Having lived in London since the early years of the century, married to an Englishwoman and responsible for Soviet foreign policy under Chicherin in the 1920s, he was as well equipped as any member of the Soviet leadership to formulate a constructive policy towards Great Britain if, in the judgement of the Soviet leadership, the interest of the Soviet state and its Communist Party should point in this direction. His tenure of office was to be marked by a significant reorientation of Soviet foreign policy, the establishment of relations with the United States, membership of the League of Nations and, above all, the search for collective security. As People's Commissar for Foreign Affairs, Litvinov's power base was slender. With success, he might have enhanced it, though it must be questionable whether he would ever have enjoyed the full confidence of Stalin. But speculation is irrelevant. He was to fail and in the summer of 1939 his policies were to be jettisoned with their architect.

An encouraging start

The closing months of 1933 saw the realignment of Soviet foreign policy beginning to take shape. At the end of October Lord Chilston arrived as HM Ambassador in Moscow, some six months after the recall of his predecessor. Litvinov had just returned in triumph from Washington, having secured American recognition of the Soviet Government and Chilston was much impressed with Soviet success in asserting itself as 'one of the greatest factors of world politics'. He saw a country setting out to make itself the most powerful state in the world, but thoughts of world revolution had given place to 'complete consolidation of communistic rule in this Empire'. Above all the Soviet Union needed peace and security: 'Peace is sought and will be ensured at all costs except in the event of an attack from outside.'[9] In Ankara, Sir Percy Loraine was explaining patiently to the Turkish Foreign Minister that 'a very large proportion of opinion in England held the view that the whole political system and creed of Soviet Russia was the work of Satan'. He nevertheless suggested gently that it might on the whole be better 'to give the Russians a seat at the dining-table, rather than have them poisoning the soup in the kitchen'. Simon was not greatly impressed by the potential for relations with the Soviet Union. But then it was not in Simon's nature to be greatly impressed by anything. He saw advantage in the Soviet desire at the moment to maintain the status quo, and noted their undoubted desire for better relations with Britain, but he was not convinced of the permanence of their sentiments and he was disinclined to hurry on a rapprochement. The Soviet Government could be left to make the running but it was 'all to the good that they and we should work, if not together as yet, at least on parallel lines'.[10]

The next few months saw a significant development in relations, with the signature on 16 February 1934 of a new Temporary Commercial Agreement establishing the principle of mutual MFN treatment between the two countries; an agreement which, despite its temporary character, was to govern the trading relationship for the next forty years. Although largely overtaken as a result of the Common Commercial Policy (CCP) of the European Union, it was still valid in 1999. On the Soviet side, the hope was expressed that the commercial agreement might serve as the starting point for the improvement of Anglo–Soviet relations as a whole.

The beginning of collective security

Soviet foreign policy was in fact at a turning point. With growing awareness of the menace of Germany and Japan, the Soviet leadership was seeking a less confrontational relationship with Britain and France. The leading role, for a time, was to fall to France rather than to Britain. The signal was the visit of M. Herriot to Moscow in August 1933, when it is probable that the first mention was made by the Russians of a possible Franco–Soviet alliance. This went too far for the French and instead they mooted a collective mutual assistance pact between Russia, Poland, Czechoslovakia and Germany, backed by a French guarantee to the Soviet Union and by a Soviet commitment to underwrite the Locarno structure. At Soviet insistence, the concept was enlarged to include the Baltic states. The French, for their part, made it plain that Soviet membership of the League of Nations was a prerequisite. So the concept of an Eastern Pact for the Guarantee of Mutual Security, the 'Eastern Locarno', was born. On Christmas Day 1933 Stalin indicated in a press interview that membership of the League of Nations might become possible and early in 1934 soundings were taken to this effect. After some hesitation, the British Government decided not merely to acquiesce in Soviet membership, but to join France in lobbying for it and also, after a Franco–British ministerial conference, to support the Eastern Locarno, on the clear understanding that Britain herself would not enter into any new regional commitment. In the foreign affairs debate in Parliament on 13 July 1934, the Foreign Secretary stated that the Government would 'welcome Russia warmly' to the League. He welcomed also the proposal for an 'Eastern Locarno' and, although Britain would not join in the pact, it undertook to commend it to the other Governments concerned. Here, in the words of Winston Churchill, was 'the reassociation of Soviet Russia with the Western European system ... an historic event'.[11]

British–Soviet relations at this point were interestingly poised. On 3, 12 and 18 July, concurrently with the parliamentary debate, Vansittart and Maisky had a series of private discussions[12] after which Vansittart wrote to Chilston in Moscow, instructing him to put the basic issue of the British–Soviet relationship to Litvinov.[13] The Soviet press, Vansittart said, used about Britain language which they would never use about the French, the Italians or the Americans. (In this, he had some justification. The Soviet press had spoken of Britain taking the 'leading role for the preparation of war against the USSR'.)[14] He continued: 'The Soviet Government cannot have it both ways and they must now choose between a policy of real friendship with us in all respects and the policy they have been pursuing hitherto, for they must realise that the public here is not yet convinced of their friendly intentions.'

For a time, relations did indeed improve. The attempt to organise an Eastern Locarno made little progress, but on 18 September 1934 the Soviet Union was duly elected to membership of the League of Nations, with a permanent seat on the Council and Litvinov commented that he was 'particularly gratified' at the improvement in British–Soviet relations.[15] He wasted little time in putting his concern about the Hitler regime bluntly to Eden: 'So long as the Hitler regime existed in Germany, there could be no real security for Europe.'[16] His proposals for the future of the League and the Disarmament Conference roused little interest in the West and it is reasonable to doubt whether, at this point, his doctrine of collective security commanded significant support among the leadership in Moscow. Nevertheless, the Soviet Union was now beginning to be seen as a factor in the European political scene. Policy had moved a long way since the abrogation of the trade agreement and the crisis over the Metro–Vickers trial. It was summed up by Sir Robert Vansittart in a memorandum of 21 February 1935.[17] The Soviet Government, he said, considered that they had only two enemies of real political importance, Japan and Germany, and, rightly or wrongly, they feared an attack by either or both. Consequently, they had become supporters of the status quo, had concluded pacts of non-aggression with all their European neighbours, had worked for rapprochement with France and Britain and had joined the League of Nations. 'It can hardly be maintained', he continued, 'that the attitude of the Soviet Government is not of great importance to us. We have gained much, both directly and indirectly, from the recent change in that attitude; and we stand to lose heavily if it is changed in the reverse direction.' The direct gains were increased trade, the cessation of Soviet pressure on Afghanistan, some consideration for British interests elsewhere in Asia and a diminution in anti-British propaganda. Indirectly Britain had gained by the general realisation in Europe that the Soviet Union was seeking the friendship of powers opposed to a change in the status quo.

So far as the Soviet Union was concerned, the immediate test of Western readiness for a new relationship was the Eastern Locarno. A pact of this nature, bolstered if possible by a direct Franco–Soviet alliance – and indirectly by the Franco–British link – was for them the key to British and French readiness to oppose a possible German move eastwards. Without it, they saw any increase in Western European security and, in particular, any easing of the British–French relationship with Germany, as merely increasing their own vulnerability to Germany. The British Government understood this well, but, with growing concern at the prospect of German rearmament, they saw little incentive to compromise an already uncertain Western security by the addition of a potential entanglement in Eastern European hostilities. Consequently the more German and Polish opposition to a multilateral Eastern guarantee scheme became apparent, the more the British welcome for it cooled. Their dilemma was that they liked even less the prospect of a direct bilateral Franco–Soviet alliance. The risk was only too clear. If France, honouring a commitment to Russia, found herself at war with Germany, Britain could be involved in hostilities in relation to an area, Eastern Europe, where, as she perceived it, she had no direct interest and in support of a Soviet Union which seemed substantially less worthy and substantially less capable than Tsarist Russia had been twenty years earlier. The views of Foreign Office officials were divided, but there was certainly much support for the view of Orme Sargent, the Assistant Under-Secretary, who saw a Franco–Soviet alliance as the first step towards the 'horrible prospect' of a return to the pre-war grouping of Powers. It might be inevitable but, in his view, every effort should be made to prevent it and to this end some alternative form of Eastern pact might be sought – a pact weak enough to be acceptable to Germany and Poland, but adequate to meet Soviet fears. It was the beginning of a desultory debate on which the political–strategic relationship of Britain and the Soviet Union was to turn and on which – in different circumstances and in a different form – the tripartite negotiations of 1939 were to founder.

Strategic assessments in 1934

It is interesting that at this time, when the Soviet Union was beginning to be seen by Britain as a factor in the international political scene, it was regarded as almost wholly irrelevant in terms of British defence assessments. Only in relation to the obsessive fear of Russian pressure through Afghanistan to India was there any specific consideration of a Soviet threat and it was noted by the Chiefs of Staff[18] that with weakening Soviet influence in Afghanistan, tribal opposition to a Russian invasion would be 'more ardent that previously'. The Chiefs of Staff did in this context note the increase in Russian military strength, although 'it would be a very sweeping assumption to think that the defects have been eliminated'. In parallel with this report, the Defence Requirements Sub-Committee conducted a major review of British needs in which, apart from a reference to the increase in the strength of the Soviet Air Force, the Soviet Union did not figure as either a positive or negative factor.

Eden in Moscow

The immediate fruit of the Vansittart–Maisky conversations in the summer of 1934 was a decision that there should be a British ministerial visit to Moscow. Vansittart argued that Russia had been 'offering indications of better behaviour' in relation specifically to Afghanistan and also, more generally, to hostile propaganda. It would, he said, be wrong to overrate the change of heart or to underrate the use to which it might be put. What mattered was to strengthen the Litvinov school of Soviet policy against the Voroshilov school of Soviet–German rapprochement. The Russians wanted a visit. 'On every ground of high and far-sighted policy' the reply should be affirmative. Endorsing Vansittart's recommendation, Eden advised his colleagues of the need to reckon with the 'intensely suspicious nature of the Russian regime' and with the fact that Russia must eventually figure in an overall negotiation, if only because Germany was constantly citing the Russian threat.[19] The possibility of a ministerial visit to Berlin was already being considered. The Prime Minister, Ramsay MacDonald, was keen that the two should be kept distinct. 'It is essential', he minuted,[20] 'that we should improve our contacts with Russia, but in nearly every respect Russia and Germany are fundamentally different propositions to us, and the fitting of Russia into a European scheme of cooperation cannot be done in the same way as Germany.' Nevertheless, the project for a Russian visit was accepted. It was decided that Simon and Eden should jointly visit Berlin and that Eden should continue to Moscow and Warsaw.

Events moved quickly. The publication of the British White Paper on Defence on 4 March, followed by the Parliamentary Debate on 11 March, brought a tantrum by Hitler, followed on 16 March by the announcement that Germany was introducing conscription. Welcoming the forthcoming talks with British ministers, Hitler remarked that any country which allied itself with the 'filthy crew' in Russia was doomed to perdition. In thoroughly unpropitious circumstances and against a background of substantial French anxiety, the British ministerial visit to Berlin nevertheless went ahead and the discussions between Hitler, Neurath and Ribbentrop on the German side and Simon and Eden on the British were in a relatively low key. The Germans were, however, wholly opposed to participation in an Eastern pact which contained provisions for mutual assistance in the event of aggression, and made much of the potential Soviet military threat. Eden noted in his diary that the total result of the meeting was very disappointing and, commenting on Hitler's obsession with Russia, he wrote that he was strongly against letting Germany expand eastwards: 'Apart from its dishonesty, it would be our turn next.'[21] From Berlin, Simon returned home to report to the Cabinet, while Eden took the train to Moscow. On the way, he composed a telegram to London concluding that there was no basis for a general settlement with Germany and that the only course for Britain was to uphold the principles of the League Covenant and consolidate against Germany all those nations which believed in the collective system.[22]

So it was that on 28 March 1935 Mr Eden, still only 37, but already a rising star of the Conservative Party and, as Lord Privy Seal with responsibility for League of Nations questions, Simon's junior in the Foreign Office, became the first British minister to visit Russia since the Revolution.[23] His first impression was of weather, streets and people all grey, sad and unending. His reception was, however, warm and he quickly got down to a detailed discussion with Litvinov, in which he gave a very full report of the Berlin talks. Litvinov, who commented that Germany was bent first upon revenge and then upon domination, asked about Eden's conclusions from the talks. For his part, Eden said, those Governments which believed in collective security should hold to it even more strongly – but he did not know the views of the British Cabinet. (Here in fact, was the weakness of his position. He might not know the latest view of the Cabinet but he knew only too well the instincts of many of its members, and so did Litvinov.) The discussion of bilateral questions was relatively brief. The British side expressed satisfaction at the working of the commercial agreement and indicated that if extra orders were forthcoming, credit might be possible. Eden made no headway when be remarked that if the two countries were to enter upon an era of friendliness and greater frankness, this could not be reconciled with the continuance of propaganda. Apart from this, he said, there were no real differences between the two Governments. The high point of the visit was a meeting between Eden, accompanied by Chilston and Strang, and Stalin, Molotov, Litvinov and Maisky. It was the first time Stalin had received a Western political leader. Eden commented upon his remarkable knowledge and understanding of international affairs, his unshakeable assurance and control and his implacable ruthlessness. The substance of the discussion was unremarkable, Stalin confirming that the Soviet Union had no desire to interfere in the internal affairs of the British Empire, speaking of the menace of Germany and Japan, urging the need for collective security and the importance, in that context, of British policy.[24] A final communiqué on the talks stated 'that there is at present no conflict of interest between the two Governments on any of the main issues of international policy ... that the integrity and prosperity of each is to the advantage of the other' and recorded the 'primary importance' of cooperation between the two countries for the 'collective organization of peace and security'. It was an endorsement of the Litvinov slogan, 'Peace is indivisible', carved in butter among the caviar at lunch. The spirit of cooperation was to prove scarcely more durable than the butter. By the summer of that year the Seventh World Congress of the Comintern was passing a resolution aligning Britain with the fascist powers: 'Great Britain is striving ... to strengthen the anti-Soviet tendencies not only of Germany, but also of Japan and Poland.'[25]

The appeasement years

The facts of British policy during the years of appeasement have been well recorded and much analysed. It is a period which, even for those of us who were in our teens at the time, is still not easy to treat dispassionately, despite the passage of more than half a century. The reader will have little trouble in sensing how I viewed British policy at the time. The years may have mellowed my criticism, but they have not changed its essence. My purpose here, however, is not to reopen the old debate, but to describe the handling of a single element of British policy, the relationship with the Soviet Union. The volume of directly relevant material is not great. Its very thinness speaks much for the quality of the relationship.

For a Soviet historian, the analysis was simple: Britain and France, motivated by fear, greed and hatred of Communism, sought to buy off the aggressors with every available concession, preferably at the expense of others, in the hope of avoiding the inevitable intra-capitalist conflict in the West and turning Germany eastwards. It is perhaps enough that the charge was made by those whose standard of international morality was set by Stalin. Yet it must be examined. The record of these years is indeed one of the search for measures which might avoid military conflict with Germany. It is, sadly, also the record of a British Prime Minister, a British Government and a large part of the British people prepared for long – but not for ever – to surrender the interests of others in this process. The principles by which they were guided were, for the most part, not ignoble. The structure of Europe after Versailles contained the seeds of its own disintegration. It may be that the year gained for British rearmament and for the consolidation of British opinion justified even that brief and shameful period during which the search for peace at almost any price left honour to weigh little in the scales of judgement. There was more of emotion than of calculation in the decisions of the British government, and emotion does not lend itself to measurement. How is one to weigh the emotions aroused by the Versailles Treaty, the sympathy with Germany's post-war plight, the instinctive anti-Soviet prejudice of a large sector of society, the passionate desire of those who had experienced the carnage of 1914–18 to spare another generation its repetition? What is relevant for this study is that these and many other emotions combined to produce policies in which the Soviet Union counted for little. But they did not produce an anti-Soviet conspiracy. In the conduct of relations with the Soviet Union the errors – and they were not insignificant – were of omission, not of commission. Ministers and officials, battered from crisis to crisis, did not consider the Soviet Union as a substantial factor in their policy until they were within a few months of the outbreak of war. Cabinet minutes, which in earlier years have entry after entry dealing with Russia, reveal almost nothing. In times of crisis there are often policies too sensitive to be recorded, but the sad fact is that policy towards the Soviet Union, open or concealed, barely existed between the spring of 1935 and the spring of 1939.

Let us now examine the facts. Sparse though they are, they make a coherent picture. The policy, or more accurately the lack of it, is not difficult to chart. Nor is the reasoning – and also the lack of it – difficult to follow. Immediately after the Eden visit to Moscow, the early summer of 1935 saw a significant realignment of the East–West relationship in Europe, with the signature on 2 May of the Franco–Soviet Treaty and on 16 May of the Czech–Soviet Treaty. With these treaties, the situation which British policy-makers had been hoping to avoid had come to pass. In the Locarno context France had already given a guarantee to Czechoslovakia and now, instead of a loosely worded Eastern pact, with which the British Government for a brief moment hoped to see Germany associated, there was a direct Franco–Czech–Soviet combination which, to those whose aim was the appeasement of Germany, brought the prospect of hostilities measurably closer. It is worth recalling the essential features of the three treaties. The French guarantee to Czechoslovakia, given in the original Locarno context, was linked with the League Covenant and provided for mutual assistance in the event of an attack resulting from failure of the respective undertakings with Germany. The Franco–Soviet Treaty, also linked to the Covenant, provided for the parties to come to each other's aid against unprovoked aggression by any European state. The Czech–Soviet Treaty was similar, but conditional upon assistance being rendered by France. The British response to the situation created by these interlocking commitments was threefold: to intensify the effort to appease Germany; to oppose any strengthening of the Franco–Soviet Treaty; and to seek to frustrate a German–Soviet rapprochement. We can see the latter element reflected as early as February 1936 in a memorandum by Sir Robert Vansittart, 'Britain, France and Germany'.[26] He saw the risk that 'if he [Hitler] were to beckon the Russian Government

... they might step forward' and argued that if a German–Soviet alliance were to be avoided, the relationship between Germany and the Western powers must be improved. He would not wish this to take place at the expense of others in Europe but if, for instance, Britain were prepared to restore the German colonies then, he argued, it would not make sense to arouse German suspicion by the grant of a loan to Russia. Delay in the ratification of the Franco–Soviet Treaty meant that it was only in September 1936 that the Cabinet considered its implications.[27] The Chiefs of Staff Sub-Committee had recommended that Britain should 'reserve complete freedom to decide for ourselves whether we should intervene in any conflict arising out of German aspirations or French commitments in Eastern Europe'. In line with this view, the Foreign Policy Committee of the Cabinet recorded general agreement 'that at some stage we should make it clear to France that we had no intention of being drawn into any troubles arising out of her Eastern commitments' and the Cabinet accepted the view that British commitments ought not to be increased by reason of the Treaty.

A year after the Eden visit to Moscow, despite a blast of organised Comintern hostility, the bilateral relationship was still in reasonable shape. In January 1936 Litvinov visited London for the funeral of King George V and took the opportunity to have talks with Eden and Baldwin, and in September Major-General Wavell attended Soviet army manoeuvres at Minsk. By then, however, the situation in Western Europe had already deteriorated sharply. On 7 March 1936 the German army's reoccupation of the Rhineland precipitated a major crisis, the effect of which was to concentrate thinking on the German threat in the West. In justifying this action, the German Government alleged that the Franco–Soviet Treaty constituted a breach of Locarno. To British ministers, not only was the allegation unfounded, but the Soviet Union seemed largely irrelevant to the whole issue. It was only in response to Labour pressure that Austen Chamberlain confirmed that British obligations under the League Covenant applied 'equally, wherever aggression takes place in the Eastern or Western parts of Europe'.[28] To Soviet policy-makers, it seemed more probable that Britain might seek to safeguard its Western security at the expense of Eastern Europe and Litvinov expressed his anxiety to Eden shortly after the German move. In reply, he received an assurance of the British desire for a peaceful settlement for the whole of Europe, not merely its Western half. It was at this time that the old problem of British and Soviet interests in access to and egress from the Black Sea once again brought a clash at the Montreux Conference. A compromise was, however, found. Relations, if not close, were stable and, in the commercial field, they were further improved by agreement on the availability of guarantees by the Export Credits Guarantee Department (ECGD) in respect of exports to the Soviet Union.

The Spanish Civil War

In the light of subsequent Soviet involvement in Ethiopia, it is interesting to recall that the Soviet Union played no significant part in the crisis over the Italian invasion of Ethiopia in the autumn of 1935 although, within the League of Nations, Litvinov was to receive an early warning of the infirmity of collective security in the face of an armed challenge. With the outbreak of the Spanish Civil War in the summer of 1936 there was, however, direct Soviet involvement. That conflict was to polarise British opinion in relation to Communism and Fascism more sharply than any other event since 1917 and to colour the sympathies of a generation. Since the ending of the Soviet–Polish war, Soviet policy had been considered by successive British Governments very much in terms of trade and propaganda. Now the struggle between Fascism and Bolshevism took the form of an armed struggle in Western Europe. As Anthony Blunt wrote:[29] 'Even for the most ivory-tower intellectual it meant that the time of not taking sides was past.' These were the years in which, on one side of the divide, idealistic British volunteers were fighting with the Government forces in Spain – the time, too, when Philby in Spain and Blunt, Burgess and Maclean in Britain were being led towards their careers as Soviet agents. On the other side a substantial – and in government circles influential – segment of British opinion, alarmed at the prospect of Communist domination of Spain, deplored Nazi and Fascist methods, but nevertheless wanted to see victory go to the Franco rebels.

It was not easy for the Soviet Union to assess British policy. At first they saw in Eden's policy of non-intervention the possibility of frustrating German and Italian ambitions and there was, at the outset of the Civil War, a brief possibility of British–Soviet collaboration, with the Soviet Union taking an active part in the work of the Non-Intervention Committee, meeting in London under British chairmanship. As the ineffectiveness of the Committee became increasingly apparent, Soviet disillusion mounted and the Soviet Union began, albeit more modestly, its own interventionist policy. In a perceptive despatch from Moscow in October 1936,[30] the Chargé d' Affaires,

MacKillop, commented that the Soviet interest in collaborating with Britain and France had at first overcome instinct and led to participation in the work of the Committee, but if there were no results, doctrine and class sympathy would come to the fore. He saw the Soviet hope of British participation in collective security as faint and if the Franco–Soviet Treaty, the cornerstone of Soviet policy, were broken, the Soviet Union would be forced into a 'defensive and anxious isolation' in which its 'specific eccentricities' would be less restrained.

The conclusion of the Anti-Comintern Pact between Germany and Japan in November heightened Soviet concern at the prospect of a threat from East and West and reinforced the logic of Litvinov's search for collective security. British opinion, on the other hand, was coming increasingly to see the Soviet Union as a complication rather than as an asset against the German threat in the West. The trial of Zinoviev and Kamenev in the summer of 1936 heralded the great Stalin purges in which the new Soviet state seemed to be tearing itself apart. They came at the very moment at which the Soviet Union had begun to be accepted on the international scene and at which a closer Soviet–British relationship might have given some substance to collective security. During the next two critical years, a healthy British repugnance at the process of mass judicial murder and a calculation of its effect upon the Soviet armed forces made the Soviet Union seem markedly less attractive as a potential friend and markedly less relevant as a factor in the European military equation.

The Soviet Government could see very clearly that the risk of an appeasement policy pursued at their expense was heightened by their identification with an ideological struggle in Spain. In November 1936 Maisky sought to persuade Eden that Soviet support for the Spanish Government was not for ideological reasons, but because of the need to prevent a German–Italian victory. He recalled the spirit of the Moscow Communiqué of the previous year, but evoked little response from Eden. By the end of the year Vansittart, with Eden's approval, was implementing the spirit of the Cabinet decision of September and warning Reynaud of the danger that any strengthening of the Franco–Soviet Treaty with a military treaty or staff talks might make an agreement with Germany more difficult to achieve. He was not to know that two and a half years later, in the summer of 1939, Soviet irritation and suspicion at the French refusal to undertake these staff talks was to underlie a Soviet refusal to accept political commitments without parallel military commitments and add a substantial complication to the negotiations for a tripartite British–French–Soviet alliance.

Despite the political hesitation, British defence planners at this time saw the Soviet Union as a potential ally rather than an enemy. The purge of the Soviet armed forces was only beginning. A major Review of Imperial Defence produced by the Chiefs of Staff Sub-Committee on 20 February 1937[31] noted that until 1931 Soviet policy had been one of open hostility to the Versailles system and in particular to the British and French Governments, but that subsequently – and especially since 1935 – the attitude towards Britain had improved *pari passu* with the deterioration in relations with Germany and Japan. It was expected that this would continue, with the proviso that, whereas it was contrary to British interests that there should be war anywhere, the Soviet Government would have no objection to a war between the capitalist powers of Europe, so long as the Soviet Union was not involved. The military development of the Soviet Union had progressed to the point at which she possessed the largest army and air force in the world and a submarine force of possibly similar dimensions. For the next few years at least, 'the British Empire and the Soviet Union are likely to have two common potential enemies in Germany and Japan as well as a common desire for peace'. The ultimate Soviet hope of world revolution had not been abandoned and, in the long run, there might be trouble over India, but there were no immediate serious causes of friction and even in relation to Spain it was unlikely that British–Soviet relations would be seriously disturbed. Finally, the report noted that in the event of a German attack on the Low Countries, Britain and France might find themselves fighting with the Soviet Union against Germany and, in the event of war with Japan, Soviet assistance might be of considerable value.

As Chancellor of the Exchequer at this time, Chamberlain was already exercising a substantial influence on foreign policy. The whole thrust of his policy was to minimise the confrontation with Germany. Like many others, he saw Eastern and South-Eastern Europe as an area in which German economic influence might well be dominant, and doubted, as did many in the Foreign Office, both the equity and the viability of the post-war settlement of the German frontier with this region. Despite the belief that frontier revision would sooner or later be inevitable, he was looking for measures by Germany which would 'reassure the Governments of Central and Eastern Europe of Germany's intention to respect their territorial integrity and sovereign independence', including 'an indirect arrangement with regard to the Soviet Union'.[32] The determination of the Foreign Office, under Eden, to avoid being drawn into an anti-Soviet bloc as the price of a better relationship with Germany may be seen in the instructions sent on 15 July 1937 to Sir Nevile Henderson, HM Ambassador in Berlin, for a meeting with Goering:

> The German Government complain that His Majesty's Government continue to cooperate with the Soviet Government in European affairs; whereas Germany would like to see the Soviet Government completely isolated. This ... raises a fundamental issue on which His Majesty's Government have made their position quite clear and on which they cannot compromise. His Majesty's Government must take the Soviet Government as they find them in the conduct of international affairs, nor refuse cooperation if its offer appears to be genuinely made, simply on account of divergence of political creed.

The Austrian and Czech crises

Immediately after Chamberlain became Prime Minister, in May 1937, the balance of political and strategic assessment began to change and, without any conscious decision, the process of excluding the Soviet Union from participation in the resolution of Europe's growing crisis began to take shape. Within the Soviet Union, Stalin's purge was exacting a toll across the population which was rising into the millions. A leadership which had brought famine and death to the countryside by the forced collectivisation was now devouring its soldiers, its administrators, its managers and its workers. In the armed forces alone, some 30 000 officers were believed to have been removed and many of them executed between 1937 and 1939. Neither in terms of moral authority nor of military power was the Soviet regime in any position to command acceptance as a partner to Britain. In April 1938 Lord Chilston forwarded to the Foreign Secretary[33] an assessment by his Military Attaché, commenting on the disastrous effect of the purge on morale and efficiency. In the Ambassador's view, 'nothing short of an immediate threat to the integrity of Soviet territory would be held by the rulers of this country to justify entry into a war': a German occupation of part of Czechoslovakia would not fall into this category and for the time being, the Soviet Union must be 'counted out of European politics'.

As the European crisis gathered force, with the German *Anschluss* with Austria in the spring of 1938 followed by the Czech crisis in the summer and autumn, the prospect of war with Germany became clearer, but British rearmament was proceeding slowly and time was needed. The resignation of Eden in February 1938 and his replacement by Halifax left the conduct of British foreign policy very much in the hands of the Prime Minister. The search for peace by the satisfaction of German demands now resulted in the exclusion of almost all other factors. Chamberlain saw no merit in an American suggestion of participation in the search for a European settlement and was well pleased at its abandonment. There was certainly no political will on the part of his government nor, it seemed, any military justification for the consolidation of relations with the Soviet Union as a partner in thwarting German expansion. There was instead a substantial reinforcement of the fear, already apparent in 1936, that too close a relationship would make even more difficult the appeasement of Germany.

Litvinov had now been struggling for five years to make a reality of the policy of collective security.[34] His belief in it was probably genuine, but he lacked the power base of Politburo membership, his instincts were not those of Stalin and he was not securing any demonstrable success. It was a tribute to his skill that the policy was not abandoned sooner. By 1938, however, the Soviet Union, increasingly irritated at the coolness of Britain and France, was beginning to hint at the alternative of a Soviet–German rapprochement[35] and similar hints were emanating from Berlin. There was no great disposition, at this point, to take such hints very seriously and the British Government, while refraining from being drawn into an anti-Soviet coalition, were equally disinclined to join the Soviet Union in one directed against Germany. In March 1938, immediately after the Austrian *Anschluss*, the Soviet Government drew attention in a statement by Litvinov to the immediate menace to Czechoslovakia and beyond it to the other states bordering on Germany as well as those further away. They formally proposed to the British and other Governments consideration within or outside the League of collective action against the further development of aggression, a proposal rejected in a formal note by the Foreign Secretary. Halifax, with a courtesy which did little to conceal his instinctive aversion, pointed out that a comprehensive conference could not be arranged, and a conference attended only by some Powers and designed less to secure the settlement of outstanding problems than to organise concerted action against aggression would not necessarily have a favourable effect.[36]

Throughout the critical year of 1938, the Soviet Government can have had few doubts about the trend of British policy. Their Foreign Office agent, Captain J. H. King, was supplying copies of secret telegrams and Maisky's reports of his talks with Halifax, Cadogan,

Vansittart, Beaverbrook, Churchill, Lloyd George and others were illustrating the range of British opinion. We may, for instance, note his meetings with Chamberlain's adviser, Horace Wilson, whom Maisky had known in a different capacity during the negotiation of the 1934 Trade Agreement. In a telegram of 11 May[37] Maisky reports Wilson's description of Chamberlain's policy: German expansion into the smaller states of Central and South-Eastern Europe would be less harmful than an early war. It would give time for British rearmament and the resulting mixture of pressures might in ten to fifteen years lead to a more moderate German foreign policy. So far as the Soviet Union was concerned, Wilson continued, Chamberlain was less hostile than Baldwin, but simply did not regard the relationship as important at that time. He was a practical man who recognised the Soviet defence capability, but saw the Soviet Union as an essentially passive factor on the European scene, of doubtful value as a potential ally against Germany. Wilson saw him, therefore, according to Maisky, as being disinclined towards any activity over the 'Russian question'.

Even against this political background, it is remarkable that, throughout the Czech crisis in September 1938, the Soviet Union was almost wholly ignored as a factor in the situation. On 27 August, Halifax had a discussion with Maisky, in which the latter said that, in the event of a German attack, the Soviet Union would 'certainly do her bit', but in the crucial Anglo–French discussions on 18 September there was no consideration of the possible role of the Soviet Union. The Soviet records show[38] that, in formal terms, the Soviet Union had indicated that it would honour its obligations and had offered joint staff talks with France and Czechoslovakia, but by 15 September, Litvinov had concluded that Czechoslovakia would be sacrificed and saw no reason to develop a practical plan for Soviet assistance. The assurance of Soviet support in the event of action by France which was given to Benes on 20 September must be seen in that light. Subsequently, on 23 September, when it seemed that a settlement with Germany was unlikely, instructions were sent to Butler in Geneva to speak to Litvinov, explain to him the supreme effort being made by the Prime Minister in his talks with Hitler at Bad Godesberg and ask for 'any precise indication of what action the Soviet Government would take in the event of Czechoslovakia being involved in war with Germany and at what point they would be prepared to take it'. Litvinov had, in fact, already stated publicly that if France were to honour its obligation towards Czechoslovakia and fight, the Soviet Government would 'come to the aid of Czechoslovakia', but he must have known that his own Government was in no position to take effective action and had no plan to do so. In any case, he could scarcely expect a productive discussion with Butler. In response to the British enquiry, he therefore refused to amplify his statement, saying merely that Russia would 'take action'. He did, however, suggest that a separate tripartite British, French, Soviet Conference might be held, together perhaps with Romania and any other 'reliable' small power, at which he would be prepared to discuss 'military and air questions'.[39] In his memoirs,[40] Lord Butler condemns the theory that Britain deliberately 'excluded Russia from Europe' and says that his interview with Litvinov 'only confirmed our conclusion that, both on political and military grounds, Russia could not be trusted to wage war in defence of interests that were not bound up with her own security'. (It would indeed have come as a surprise to Stalin that anyone might have supposed otherwise.) Litvinov's report of the meeting with Butler[41] indicates that, in response to Butler's questions, he complained that the British Government, having ignored the Soviet Union, was now wanting answers without being willing to provide any information about British policy and that the Soviet Union would not, in any case, act in advance of France. Maisky subsequently received a telegram in which the Foreign Ministry spoke of the need to give the impression of taking at face value the British 'eyewash' about 'cooperation' with the Soviet Union, although it was really all a fraud.[42]

As the crisis came to its height, the British Government was concerned that Soviet participation at any conference would be wholly unacceptable to Germany. Consequently, although the Cabinet contemplated the inclusion of the Soviet Union in a tripartite guarantee of the new Czechoslovak frontier[43] there was no question of an invitation to Munich. Munich may not have figured directly in the British–Soviet relationship, but it was critical to the Soviet assessment of British policies and to the setting of the stage for the 1939 negotiations. For Pravda it 'surpassed in shamelessness' anything since 1918. It must have been a powerful factor in that reshaping of Soviet policy which was to culminate in the German–Soviet agreement of the following summer. In London, the exclusion of the Soviet Union from the crucial policy nexus continued to be a guiding principle. By November[44] the Foreign Secretary was reporting that the French were anxious to 'disentangle themselves from the Russian connexion' and recommending avoidance of 'a position in which we might find ourselves asked to take action with France and Russia against Germany and Italy on behalf of a state which we were unable effectively to defend'. In Franco–British discussions in Paris, later in November[45] the Prime Minister remarked that it would be 'much easier for everyone' if the Czechs were to say that they did not want a Russian guarantee. There were at this time rumours of German support for Ukrainian separatist agitation and Chamberlain was able to secure from Bonnet an assurance that France's obligations would be effective only in the event of a direct attack by Germany on Russian territory.

Towards the end of the year, Lord Chilston was replaced as Ambassador in Moscow by Sir William Seeds. Seeds spoke Russian, but his only experience of Russia was as a young man in the years before the Revolution. He spoke with determination to Litvinov of the British Government's 'real desire to know – and give friendly consideration to – the Soviet Government's views of international questions', but he was heard with some scepticism and reported Litvinov as saying on one occasion that Britain would continue to capitulate and the Soviet Union would 'leave us to our own folly'. Butler also gained the impression from Maisky that the Soviet Union would now pursue a 'more isolationist policy'.[46] On 6 March, Seeds wrote a major despatch on the state of the Soviet Union in which he commented that the Government was 'as firmly established as any regime can reasonably be expected to be' and that the army, if not of great value in an offensive war, was loyal and would constitute a serious obstacle to an attacker. Of greater interest than the despatch was an important note appended to it by Fitzroy Maclean, at that time an attaché in the Embassy. 'It must be remembered', he wrote, 'that Soviet policy is purely opportunist ... were they to consider that their own interests or those of the Soviet Union required it, the rulers of this country would not hesitate to change horses in mid-stream'. His comments preceded by only a few days the speech to the Eighteenth Party Congress in which Stalin spoke of the failure of Britain and France to pursue a policy of collective security, their encouragement of Germany to turn eastwards and their plan to involve Japan and Germany in a war with the Soviet Union at the end of which the democracies would be able to dictate their own terms. Seeds warned that the 'innocents at home' should heed Stalin's advice that Soviet Russia would 'not be drawn into conflicts by warmongers who are accustomed to have others pull the chestnuts out of the fire'.

The 1939 negotiations

Throughout the winter of 1938–9, after having decided to abandon the joint guarantee of the frontiers of Czechoslovakia, the British

Government gave little more thought to Russia. The only substantial issue which they considered was the need for a visit to Moscow by the Secretary for Overseas Trade, Robert Hudson, in order to make a further effort to settle the problem of the pre-Revolution debts and, more important, to renegotiate – or, if necessary, denounce – the 1934 Trade Agreement on the ground that the Soviet Union was using its sterling earnings to purchase re-exported raw materials rather than British manufactures. Rumours of possible denunciation reached the Soviet authorities and did little to help the climate of relations.

It was only after the German occupation of the rump of Czechoslovakia on 12 March that the British Government began to consider the desirability of Soviet support in the resistance to further German aggression. A sudden panic arose as a result of an alarmist statement by the Romanian minister in London about the imminent German threat to his country and immediately an enquiry was directed to the Soviet Government as to whether they would actively help Romania in the event of German aggression. Litvinov, in reply, proposed a conference 'to discuss possibilities of common action'. It was essentially the proposal which he had made exactly a year earlier and which the British Government had declined. On this occasion, even before the Soviet reply had arrived, the Government had decided that the risk to Romania had been over-stated and that the threat to Poland was of more immediate concern. They therefore proposed instead a joint declaration by the British, French, Soviet and Polish Governments providing for immediate consultation on joint resistance to 'any action which constitutes a threat to the independence of any European state'.[47] The Soviet Government, although preferring a conference, declared themselves ready to accept, provided France and Poland did likewise. By this time, Hudson was in Moscow and was assured by Litvinov that the Soviet Government was prepared to consult with the British and other Governments 'regarding all suitable measures of resistance, whether diplomatic or military or economic'. There was, however, still no enthusiasm from the British side. Poland, as was to be expected, objected to joining with the Soviet Union in any declaration and on 22 March the Cabinet considered the matter. The Foreign Secretary commented that the essential was to secure the support of Poland, but added: 'At the same time, he would take what steps were possible to keep in with Russia'. Suddenly, on 31 March, fearing an imminent German attack on Poland, the British Government undertook to 'give all support in their power ... in the event of any action which clearly threatened Polish independence and which the Polish

Government accordingly considered it vital to resist with their national forces'.

The guarantee to Poland, in form, if not in reality, the proximate cause of the Second World War, was conceived as a deterrent and given in haste, with no prior consideration of the strategy for its implementation if it failed to deter. In giving it, the Prime Minister tried to imply the Soviet Union's indirect association by referring in Parliament to a discussion which Maisky had had with the Foreign Secretary and saying that he had no doubt that the Soviet Government 'fully understood and appreciated' the principles upon which the British Government were acting. Neither Maisky nor his Government welcomed this involvement and Chamberlain's subsequent statement that there were no 'ideological impediments' between Britain and the Soviet Union[48] can have carried no conviction.

The need for an urgent reassessment of the British–Soviet relationship was clear. There were after 31 March 1939 commitments which, in the likely event of a German attack upon Poland and the less immediate threat to Romania or Greece, would result in war between Britain and Germany. There was little practical aid which could be given to these states and, if the guarantees were to be invoked, it was desirable, both in terms of the defence of either country and in terms of the wider British defence interest, that the Soviet Union should be enlisted as an ally. So began the negotiations for a tripartite British–French–Soviet alliance. Those negotiations led to allegations of bad faith which persisted throughout the subsequent years: Soviet historians alleged that the British Government's main objective was merely to entangle the Soviet Union in hostilities with Germany as a means of diverting the threat to itself; that they never seriously desired an effective alliance with the Soviet Union; that to this end they deliberately spun out the negotiations and left them in the hands of a Foreign Office official rather than a minister; and that they refused to accompany the political negotiations with serious military contingency planning. Against this, the Soviet Government is accused of duplicity in the initiation and conclusion of an agreement with Germany behind the backs of the British and French Governments, an agreement which, by removing the risk of Soviet opposition, cleared the way for the German attack on Poland and the seizure of Polish territory by the Soviet Union itself. Space does not permit a detailed account of the negotiations, but they occupy an important place in the history and mythology of British–Soviet relations, and if we are to assess their significance in this context, it is necessary to examine briefly the main stages in their conduct.

Soviet policy in the spring of 1939 had been indicated by Stalin's speech of 10 March in which he effectively indicated the end of the search for collective security with the Western democracies and a retreat into isolation. By the time of the German occupation of Czechoslovakia, no actual change of policy had, however, been implemented and the Soviet response, as we have seen, still echoed the old policy of collective security. On the British side, there was a recognition of the possible value of Soviet support if war should break out, but certainly, as yet, no readiness for an alliance in advance of the event. On 26 March, the Prime Minister wrote to his sister: 'I must confess to the most profound distrust of Russia. I have no belief whatever in her ability to maintain an effective offensive, even if she wanted to. And I distrust her motives, which seem to me to have little connection with our ideas of liberty.'[49] On 5 April he said much the same in Cabinet: he 'had very considerable distrust of Russia and had no confidence that we should obtain active and constant support from that country'. He was supported by Hudson, who remarked that Russia would be of 'little or no assistance except for defensive purposes'. It was easy for ministers to conclude that 'the question of making any arrangement with Russia was obviously one which required a great deal of further consideration',[50] It was, nevertheless, clearly in the British interest to seek some arrangement under which, if the guarantees to Poland or Romania were invoked and Britain were involved in war with Germany, Soviet assistance would be available. The Polish Government, for their part, having received the British guarantee, had no incentive to abandon their traditional hatred of Russia. The Polish Foreign Minister, Beck, visiting London early in April, had stated bluntly that Poland would keep clear of any British–Soviet conversations and was 'not in a position to accept any agreement which would have the effect, if only indirectly, of linking Poland with the Soviet Union'. From Moscow, Seeds warned of the temptation to the Soviet Union to stand aloof and urged that the Government should prevail on Poland and Romania to accept the idea of some form of Soviet military assistance. At this stage, there was, however, no realistic possibility of this. What Britain was seeking was simply a unilateral Soviet guarantee matching the British guarantees to Poland and Romania. Such an arrangement would imply no new British commitment and, equally, no enhancement to Soviet security.

The negotiating climate had not been improved by the Prime Minister's remark, when announcing the guarantee to Poland, that he believed the Soviet Government understood and appreciated the principles on which the Government were acting. Litvinov made it wholly clear to Seeds that, on the contrary, the British action was not at all appreciated. The British Government, having first proposed a four-power declaration, had dropped the idea, despite Soviet acceptance, and had ignored the Soviet proposal for a six-power conference. The Soviet Government 'had had enough and would henceforward stand apart free of any commitments'.[51] It was an inauspicious start. Nevertheless, when a proposal for matching unilateral guarantees to Poland and Romania was put to the Soviet Government, it elicited a formal response envisaging a far closer defence relationship than the British Government was at that time prepared to consider. The Soviet Government offered a tripartite British–French–Soviet treaty for a period of five to ten years which would provide for mutual assistance, including military assistance both between the parties themselves and also to the East European states bordering the Soviet Union, from the Baltic to the Black Sea. Simultaneous political and military agreements would be concluded and there would be a commitment, in the event of war, not to conclude a separate peace.

British policy at this point was well indicated by the remark of Lord Halifax to the Romanian Foreign Minister[52] that 'it was desirable not to cold shoulder Russia too much'. There was little effort to conceal the patrician distaste at the prospect of close association with such a regime. More formally,[53] the objectives of British policy were set out in a fine quadruple negative as being:

(a) Not to forgo the chance of our receiving help from the Soviet Government.
(b) Not to jeopardise the common front by disregarding the susceptibilities of Poland and Romania.
(c) Not to forfeit the sympathy of the world at large by giving a handle to Germany's anti-Comintern propaganda.
(d) Not to jeopardise the cause of peace by provoking violent action by Germany.

On 26 April, when the Cabinet[54] considered the Soviet proposal for a tripartite pact, the Foreign Secretary suggested that the value of Russia as an ally was by no means as high as seemed to be believed by prominent members of the Labour Party. It was generally agreed that the Soviet proposal 'took too little account of the practical difficulties', prominent among which was the Polish objection, and that to go beyond matching unilateral declarations would be to run the risk of 'breaking the common front'. On 3 May[55] the matter was considered again. The Foreign Secretary noted regretfully that Mr Churchill was entirely in favour of the tripartite pact and had been quite unmoved by Lord Halifax's arguments. Halifax maintained, however, that a tripartite pact 'would make war inevitable'. If the Soviet proposal were rejected, 'Russia would sulk' and there was a bare possibility that refusal 'might even throw her into Germany's arms'. It was, however, noted that Canada, South Africa, Portugal and Spain would all cause difficulty and that Cardinal Hinsley had expressed his anxiety in a long letter to the Foreign Secretary. Accordingly, it was decided to maintain the British counter-proposals in the confidence that Russia would not break off on the spot.

At this point, in Moscow, on 4 May came the first consequence of the Stalin speech. Litvinov who, since his days in Britain during the 1914–18 war, had been intimately connected with Soviet–British affairs, was replaced as Foreign Minister by Molotov. There was at the time and subsequently much speculation about the significance of this move. Was it confirmation that the Soviet Union had abandoned the search for collective security with the Western democracies and had begun to explore, if not yet to adopt, the policy of closer association with Germany? Seeds certainly saw the risk of a policy switch. He had already warned that British policy would merely confirm the Soviet leadership in their belief that Britain was trying to evade association with them.[56] Now, with the sophisticated Jewish influence of Litvinov gone, 'the great men of the Kremlin will be more apt to plunge off into the deep if disappointed or indignant'. The policy of collective security was very much a Litvinov creation. He could scarcely have pursued it as far as he did without at least the acquiescence of Stalin, but Stalin was probably never convinced, any more than was Chamberlain, that the policy merited a full commitment. By 1939 it had suffered failure after failure, culminating in the sacrifice of Czechoslovakia. The policy and its author were discredited and the argument that the Soviet Union had no option but to act independently to safeguard its own security was powerfully reinforced. A new, harsher, spirit was needed and it must be accompanied by a more direct subordination of foreign policy to the supreme leadership of the Party. There was no good reason to trust either Germany on the one hand or Britain and France on the other. The direct threat to Soviet security came from Germany and, while the apparent infirmity of Britain and France made them less menacing, it equally made them unattractive as allies. There were moreover, enough hints of the search for a new basis of accommodation between Britain and Germany to make the possibility of a new

Munich a real one. Soviet policy was for long founded upon a calculation of the harsh realities of power and in that calculation it was Germany which was the dominant factor on the European continent. In such a situation, there was no incentive to compromise Soviet freedom of action by an alliance with Britain and France, unless the terms of that alliance were such as to bring a reinforcement of Soviet security powerful enough to offset the added risk of conflict with Germany as well as the threat from Japan. Moreover, there were signs that Germany would be glad to improve her relationship with the Soviet Union. Thus, in some respects, the considerations influencing Soviet policy were the obverse of those which had led the British Government for the past three years to eschew a closer relationship with the Soviet Union and seek its security in the appeasement of Germany. It is probable that up to the time of Litvinov's fall, no definite decision had been taken. From the German side, there was mounting pressure for a political deal with the Soviet Union which would remove the threat of a British–French–Soviet alliance. On the Soviet side, there was the beginning of a readiness to make the switch, but for the time being the Germans were stalled, while Molotov formed his own judgement as to the value of the negotiations with Britain and France.

The British reply, delivered on 6 May, to Molotov's offer of a comprehensive treaty was well calculated to intensify his suspicions. It amounted to little more than a slightly improved variant of the original proposal for a unilateral Soviet declaration and was swiftly and formally rejected, with the comment that it 'cannot serve as a basis for the organisation of a front of resistance'.[57] Nevertheless, in Seeds' view, the Soviet Government were, for the present, 'still prepared to pursue a policy of collaboration, to a degree which may be found embarrassing'.[58] Their essential requirement was for full reciprocity and this meant a formal triple alliance. So the pressure on the British Government began to mount. They had to recognise that, if they were not to forfeit the possibility of Soviet assistance, they would have to pay the price of commitment to a formal alliance, with all this meant in terms of the heightened provocation to Germany, the complication to relations with Poland and Romania, the possible alienation of support elsewhere in the world and the opposition of a large section of British opinion. To add to the pressure, rumours of a possible Soviet–German rapprochement were being revived. In Geneva, Halifax spoke to the French Premier, Daladier, of the British desire to avoid a straight triple alliance and was warned that there could be a sudden change of policy in which the Soviet Union would 'retire into isolation and let Europe destroy itself'.[59] Halifax next spoke to Maisky and received much the same warning. According to Maisky, the Soviet Union could take care of herself and enter into no obligations, in which event she might have to defend herself single-handed, but would preserve liberty of action. Alternatively she could collaborate with others and, at the price of losing freedom of action, gain the chance of preventing war. But to accept the British proposals would mean losing freedom of action without avoiding war.

While Halifax was talking to Maisky in Geneva, Foreign Office officials were putting together a memorandum summing up the dilemma[60] and concluding that, despite all the disadvantages, it might be more dangerous to have the Soviet Union completely untrammelled and playing off one side against the other than to 'collaborate with a dishonest or an incompetent partner'. It was scarcely a recipe for a whole-hearted attempt to forge an alliance.

In Parliament, meanwhile, pressure was growing. On 19 May, Lloyd George called for an end to 'this political snobbery that only wants to help a proletarian Government provided you do not rub shoulders with it'. Eden advocated a full tripartite alliance and Churchill who, cheerfully oblivious of the political realities of the smaller states of Eastern Europe, had been arguing for the construction of a solid front from the Baltic to the Black Sea, came out firmly in favour of the Soviet offer of a treaty of alliance. It was 'a fair offer, and a better offer ... than the terms which the Government seek to get for themselves; a more simple, a more direct and a more effective offer. Let it not be put aside and come to nothing'.[61] The logic of the situation could not be escaped. Within the Cabinet, even Hoare had said that he was 'more and more impressed by the serious consequences which would result from a breakdown'[62] and the Chiefs of Staff had come to the view that although the military value of Russia as an ally was 'not nearly as great as was commonly supposed', full alliance was 'a better bargain' than the kind of middle course which the Foreign Office was advocating. On 24 May, the Cabinet faced the issue squarely.[63] There was, said the Foreign Secretary, a clear choice of alternatives. The risk of a Soviet–German rapprochement 'could not be altogether disregarded'. He 'had never disguised his own views on the subject of close association with the Russian Government', but it was not possible to contemplate breakdown. Failure to oppose Hitler with a solid bloc would make war more likely and it was therefore necessary to enter into a direct mutual guarantee with the Soviet Government. Ministers decided that, if there were to be any prospect of securing Soviet support, they would have to pay the price of accepting the principle of the Molotov proposal. The Prime Minister, too, although admitting that he 'viewed anything in the nature of an alliance with Russia with considerable misgiving', agreed that it was 'impossible to stand out against it'.

So it was that the major reversal of British policy took place and on 27 May the British and French Ambassadors put to Molotov a proposal for a triple alliance, linked to the principles of the League of Nations and providing for mutual assistance either in the event of a direct attack, or in the event of a signatory being involved in war as a result of an agreement with or a request for assistance from a third country. It was a move of profound significance, intended to meet the essential Soviet requirement. The Ambassadors could, as Seeds commented, scarcely believe their ears, when Molotov gave a negative response, alleging that references to the principles of the League meant involvement in League procedures, that no concrete agreement on forms of assistance was envisaged and that the Soviet Union wanted effective action, not words. Seeds commented on Molotov as a man with the 'foolish cunning' of a peasant 'totally ignorant of foreign affairs and to whom the idea of negotiation – as distinct from imposing the will of his party leader – is utterly alien'. Nevertheless, having now committed themselves to the principle of an alliance, the British Government, with increasing desperation, sought to meet Soviet objections. A Soviet counter-draft produced on 2 June made explicit the Soviet requirement for the guarantees to the Eastern European states to include the Baltic states of Latvia, Estonia and Finland and to take effect whether or not those states so desired. Here was a major stumbling block. The British Government knew that these states, fearing the Soviet Union at least as much as they feared Germany, were opposed to a Soviet guarantee which, on the basis of an allegation of indirect German aggression, might well serve as the pretext for a pre-emptive Soviet occupation. The Prime Minister commented[64] that it was 'manifestly impossible to impose a guarantee on States which do not desire it'. In a speech of 31 May, Molotov had already indicated the resumption of commercial negotiations with Germany, but the advice from Seeds was that a German–Soviet political agreement, never more than a possibility, was now unlikely, even if the tripartite negotiations were to break down. Nevertheless, the British need for the Soviet alliance was great. In a letter to Henderson in Berlin, Halifax described the negotiations as 'now the most important factor in the situation'.[65] An offer by Eden to go to Moscow himself was rejected by Chamberlain and it was decided that the British and French Ambassadors in Moscow should continue the negotiations with the assistance, on the British side, of William Strang.[66]

Strang arrived in Moscow on 14 June and revised proposals were put to Molotov on the following day. These provided for assistance in the event of one of the three parties being involved in hostilities as a result, *inter alia* of aggression against another European State which it had *in conformity with the wishes of that state* (author's italics) undertaken to assist. Since it was apparent to all that the Soviet Union's neighbours were opposed to receiving her guarantees, this scarcely moved matters forward and was rejected immediately by Molotov. To compound the failure, it was now envisaged on the British side that the Eastern guarantees should be matched by guarantees not only to Belgium and Luxembourg, but also to Switzerland and the Netherlands, the two latter being countries which had refused to recognise the Soviet Government. Molotov therefore proposed that the question of guarantees for the minor states should be dropped altogether and that there should instead be a simple triple alliance. This, of course, would have left the British Government exposed by reason of their existing unilateral guarantee to Poland and Romania, while providing no watertight assurance of Soviet support if that guarantee were invoked.

Puzzled, Halifax wrote to Seeds asking him to find out what Molotov really wanted before any new proposals were put forward: 'You are doubtless as bewildered as I am ... We have declared ourselves ready to give him the substance of everything he requires'. Seeds had no need to consult Molotov. He spelt out bluntly the Soviet position as he saw it. The Soviet Union wanted 'assistance or connivance if they found it expedient to intervene in the Baltic States (... in conditions which we would not regard as threatening the peace of Europe) on the plea that the Governments and ruling classes as distinct from the rest of the population ... were about to compound with Germany'. The French Government had from the outset been less ready than the British to stand out for the interests of the Baltic States and the British Government now conceded once more. The guarantee would cover countries which the 'contracting country concerned felt obliged to assist'. The list of countries guaranteed might be unpublished; but if it were published it would contain the Baltic States, Poland, Romania, Turkey, Greece, Belgium, the Netherlands and Switzerland. Again the British proposal was rejected and now the Soviet Union concentrated on two points: the need for an accepted definition of 'indirect aggression' (i.e. the abandonment by one of the border countries of its neutrality or independence); and the need for simultaneous negotiation and entry into force of a military agreement parallel to the political agreement. Halifax commented in a letter to HM Ambassador in Paris[67] that the Russian business was 'quite infuriating, it blocks everything and frays everybody's nerves'. He considered reverting to the idea of a simple tripartite pact, ignoring the border states, and warning Molotov 'that he will do well not to presume any further on our readiness to yield to the Soviet Government each time they put forward a new demand'. In the end, however, the British Government again decided to concede. The principle of a guarantee covering 'indirect aggression' was accepted on a basis which excluded only 'anything capable of being interpreted as an intention of interfering in another country's internal affairs' and it was agreed that a Franco–British military mission should proceed to Moscow to conduct negotiations for the parallel military agreement. On one point, however, Britain remained firm. They would not concede a Soviet demand that 'indirect aggression' should cover situations in which one of the border countries sacrificed its neutrality or independence even without threat of force. Strang commented in a letter to Sir Orme Sargent,[68] that the negotiations had been a 'humiliating experience. Time after time we have taken up a position and a week later we have abandoned it; and we have had the feeling that Molotov was convinced from the beginning that we should be forced to abandon it.' Strang recognised that the weakness of the British position flowed inevitably from the fact that Britain, committed to Poland and Romania, needed agreement, whereas the Soviet Union had a choice of at least two other policies, isolation or accommodation with Germany. He considered the possibility of breakdown, but still recommended that, on balance, continuation of the 'indeterminate situation' of protracted negotiations would be preferable.

At this point there was a pause. The political negotiations seemed close to conclusion. Surely, the British Government thought, with all else conceded, Molotov could afford to accept a formulation of 'indirect aggression' which did not make blatantly obvious the possibility of direct interference in the border states. It would take a fortnight or so before the military teams could be assembled, briefed and transported to Moscow. Meanwhile, the initiation of the military discussions would itself serve as a warning signal to Germany. So, wrote Halifax,[69] 'Having followed a policy of concession throughout these negotiations and gained nothing by it ... there is no danger now of an imminent breakdown during the next crucial weeks ... we feel we can afford to take a somewhat stiffer line'. It is likely that, at this point, the Soviet Government, already engaged in major hostilities with Japan and conscious of the risk of war on two fronts, were approaching their crucial policy decision in favour of collaboration with Germany.[70] On 22 July, the Soviet Commissariat of Foreign Trade had announced that trade and credit negotiations had been reopened with Germany. On 25 July the Soviet Government were told of the British and French readiness to open immediate military conversations and it was proposed that an announcement should be made that 'such a measure of agreement has been reached on the provisions of the political Agreement ... that they can now proceed without delay to the consequential examination ... of practical measures'.[71] Molotov objected not merely to the relatively optimistic tone of this announcement, but to any announcement at all: the Soviet Government 'decline to associate themselves with any joint statement'. It is scarcely possible, with the advantage of hindsight, to see this refusal other than as a reflection of the preparation to move to a relationship with Germany. At this point, the Soviet Government knew that they could obtain with Britain and France an agreement which covered them against every possibility other than hostilities caused by their own intervention in one of the border states in a situation not provoked by a threat of force by Germany. If they had wished to use the prospect of the alliance as a deterrent to Germany, it was clearly to their advantage to proclaim rather than to obscure the extent of agreement. Moreover, it must have been abundantly apparent that even given maximum good will on both sides, the negotiation of a military agreement covering all the possible situations on the Eastern and Western fronts which might lead to war with Germany would require many months. Thus, the moment of initiation of staff talks was the moment at which the prospect of the alliance, if it was ever to serve as a deterrent to Germany, needed to be deployed. At this point the Soviet Government chose to remain silent.

The remaining difference in relation to 'indirect aggression' was put with perhaps excessive frankness to the House of Commons on 31 July by the Prime Minister, who indicated that the Soviet formula appeared to carry the signification of permitting encroachment upon the independence of other states. Butler then added to Soviet irritation by adding: 'The main question is whether we should encroach on the independence of the Baltic States'. The Government, Butler said, was opposed to this 'and the difficulty of reaching a formula on this point is one of the main reasons why there has been delay in these negotiations'. Accurate though his statement was, it was scarcely calculated to improve the climate for the military talks. Reporting a meeting on 2 August at which Molotov spoke of Butler's 'gross misrepresentation' of the Soviet position, Seeds commented that the negotiations had received a severe setback. It was in fact to be the last of the negotiating meetings with Molotov.

The German–Soviet Non-Aggression Treaty

In discussions between Schnurre, an official of the German Economics Ministry and Astakhov, the Soviet Chargé d'Affaires, the Germans had since May been hinting at the possibility not merely of trade negotiations, but of a more general understanding. On the latter point they received little encouragement until the beginning of August, when Astakhov said that his latest report to Molotov 'had created great interest'. But, he said, 'nothing concrete' was known of Germany's attitude'.[72] It was a fairly clear invitation to produce more detailed proposals. On 2 August Ribbentrop put to Astakhov a proposal for conclusion of a Soviet–German political protocol. There were, he said, no outstanding issues between the two countries in the whole territory from the Black Sea to the Baltic. On the following day, the German Ambassador in Moscow, Schulenburg, saw Molotov. He reported that Molotov had abandoned his habitual reserve. Schulenburg told him that, so far as Poland was concerned, the German Government 'were prepared to protect all Soviet interests and come to an understanding with the Soviet Government in the matter'. Reporting the discussion, he commented, however, that the old Soviet mistrust remained and that the Soviet Government seemed 'determined to conclude an agreement with Britain and France if they fulfil all Soviet wishes'.[73] On 12 August, the Soviet Government took the next step. Astakhov informed the German Government that the Soviet Government would be willing to open discussions in Moscow on a wide range of questions including the Polish question and the old German–Soviet political agreements.

For a further week, however, the Soviet Government played its hand with some caution, Astakhov stating that the discussions in Moscow must proceed by stages, with the political relationship as the final stage. The German pressure was, however, insistent. After negotiation in Moscow between the German Ambassador, Schulenburg, and Molotov, Tass announced on 22 August that Ribbentrop would visit Moscow for conversations on a Non-Aggression Treaty. On the following day he and Molotov signed the Treaty. Together with it, they signed a secret protocol, the existence of which was for long denied by the Soviet Union, delimiting spheres of interest 'in the event of a territorial and political transformation' of Poland and the Baltic States. 'The question whether the interest of both parties makes the maintenance of an independent Polish State appear desirable and how the frontiers of this State should be drawn' was left for determination 'in the course of further political developments'. With regard to Bessarabia, the Soviet Union secured a free hand.[74] As Stalin, Molotov and Ribbentrop celebrated the signature, Molotov toasted Stalin 'who – through his speech of March of this year, which had been well understood in Germany – had introduced the reversal in political relations'.[75]

In ignorance of the German–Soviet exchanges, the British and French military missions, having concluded that to cross Germany by train would be 'unnecessarily provocative', that no satisfactory arrangement for air travel was available and that to travel by cruiser would be 'inadvisable', were travelling slowly to Moscow via Leningrad in a small chartered passenger vessel arriving on 13 August. Their brief[76] was to go very slowly until such time as the political agreement was concluded and to try to confine the Military Agreement to the broadest possible terms – 'something on the lines of an agreed statement of policy'.[77] The Soviet negotiators, under Voroshilov, brushed aside the British draft principles on the ground that they were 'too abstract and immaterial'. What was needed, they said, was 'a complete military convention which should fix the number of divisions, artillery, tanks, aircraft and naval squadrons, which each of the three States should contribute'. In practice, however, the Soviet negotiators chose to stand on the issue that no progress could be made until the British and French Governments could secure from Poland and Romania permission for Soviet forces to transit their territory. They refused to address themselves direct to those two Governments on the ground that the Soviet Union had no military agreement with them and that the danger of aggression was most likely to affect Britain, France, Poland and Romania. It was therefore for the two former to make the approaches. It was, of course, well known to all concerned, that Polish and Romanian hostility to the Soviet Union was so deep rooted that there was no prospect of this agreement being given. Only eighteen years before the Poles had occupied Kiev and the Soviet army had thrust to the suburbs of Warsaw. Nevertheless, there ensued a week of frenzied exchanges between London, Paris, Warsaw and Bucharest. The main interest was in Poland, but the Polish Government remained obdurate. Finally, on 22 August, the day before Ribbentrop arrived in

Moscow, the Head of the French mission informed Voroshilov 'that France's answer to the Soviet question re the right of passage through Polish territory is yes as soon as Poland is at war with Germany'. Voroshilov, however, declared himself unsatisfied and declined any further meeting until the political situation was clearer. In instructing Doumenc to give this assurance, the French Government, more desperate than the British to frustrate the conclusion of a Soviet–German deal, over-stated the highly qualified assurances which were all they could obtain from Warsaw. The British Government, doubtful though they were, in an attempt to continue the discussions, authorised Seeds to support the French answer on passage through Polish territory. However, on 25 August, in response to a direct enquiry by Seeds, Molotov stated that the political situation had changed and the talks could not continue. The British and French military missions left immediately and there was no further contact between the British and Soviet Governments before the German forces moved into Poland on 1 September.

It was only after 1985 that the negotiation of the secret protocol came into the realm of open discussion in Moscow. An official commission under Aleksandr Yakovlev examined the documents, confirmed the existence of the protocol and called for 'unequivocal condemnation of the pre-war Soviet leadership's departure from the Leninist principles of foreign policy'.[78]

The record is now clear enough to justify the following conclusions:

(a) The British Government was unwilling prior to the spring of 1939 to consider any effective collaboration with the Soviet Union to resist further German expansion. The Stalin purges had heightened British abhorrence of the Soviet system and scepticism as to the capability of the Soviet forces. The Government's objective was to avoid war and it judged that a closer relationship with the Soviet Union would make war with Germany more, rather than less, likely.

(b) The British initiatives in the spring of 1939, the over-hasty guarantees to Greece, Poland and Romania and the proposal for a joint declaration with the Soviet Union, reflected an impulsive reaction to crisis rather than a considered revision of policy. The proposal for a Soviet guarantee to Poland and Romania fell into the same category.

(c) Only from the Cabinet meeting on 24 May 1939 did the British Government commit itself to the principle of a tripartite alliance with France and the Soviet Union. From this point onward, although less ready than the French to offer quick concessions, the British Government met, one by one, those Soviet conditions which lay within its own competence, reserving its position only in relation to a Soviet right of interference in Poland, Romania and the Baltic States other than in response to a threat of force by Germany. Having committed itself, it had little bargaining power and was hamstrung by the Polish refusal to accept any matching commitment in regard to the Soviet Union. Mistrustful of Soviet military capability, it sought a deterrent alliance rather than a coordinated strategy.

(d) The need to coordinate policy with France did not constrain British initiative. French policy throughout placed greater emphasis upon the need for the tripartite alliance. Consultation with Paris may have added slightly to the response time. The Soviet Government was quicker in its responses, but this is scarcely surprising in view of the fact that the Soviet response was normally a simple negative.

(e) The Soviet Government had long proclaimed the policy of 'collective security'. It had stated its intention of honouring its obligation to Czechoslovakia in September 1938, but gave no substantial evidence of this. Stalin's speech of 10 March was intended as an indication of the reorientation of policy. It probably indicated the abandonment of collective security and a determination to revert to an isolationist policy. The replacement of Litvinov by Molotov represented the implementation of that policy.

(f) The Soviet Union was deeply mistrustful of British and French policy and wholly indifferent to the rights of small states. Taking a short-term view of its strategic interests, the Soviet Union thought it had little to gain from an alliance with Britain and France. The British guarantees to Poland and Romania came as a surprise and, in the light of Munich, there must have been genuine doubt whether they would be honoured. In any case, if they failed to deter Germany, it was hard to see how they could be implemented. If they were, the consequence would be an inter-imperialist war in which the primary interest of Britain and France would be to protect their own interests. If they waged war actively in the West, a quick German victory seemed unlikely and the balance of forces would move in favour of the Soviet Union, but the Soviet interest would still be best served by non-involvement. To accept the tripartite alliance would mean that the Soviet Union might face the main burden of the combat with Germany and possibly also full-scale war with Japan. The Soviet Western frontier with Poland and the Baltic States was vulnerable. Britain and France offered no encouragement to the seizure of territory from these states, whereas Germany did. If Germany dishonoured her Treaty, the Soviet Union would still be in a better position to fight after having advanced her Western frontier.

(g) The Soviet Government used the Moscow negotiations as a test of British and French policy. From the outset, their disposition was not to commit themselves, but they decided to establish the maximum which could be obtained from this source while keeping their options in relation to Germany open. Meanwhile, they left it to Germany to make the running if it wished to supplant the British and French. The decision in principle against the Franco–British alliance was probably taken in early August, between the end of the political and the beginning of the military negotiations and the definitive commitment to the German Treaty in the final few days before Ribbentrop's arrival. It is unlikely that any different handling of the political negotiations would have enabled the British and French Governments to secure Soviet cooperation against Germany without a commitment to sacrifice the states on the Soviet Union's western border and even this might not have sufficed. The military negotiations were never serious on either side and were largely irrelevant to the outcome.

So the first British attempt to establish a politico–military alliance with the Soviet Union, bedevilled from the outset by mutual suspicion, failed and in its failing left a legacy of mutual recrimination. The pressure of events was such that, in the days which remained before the outbreak of war, the British Government had little time to reflect on this major reverse. The Foreign Secretary remarked in Cabinet on 22 August[79] that if it was true that a German–Soviet pact had been concluded, the moral effect would be very great, but the pact was 'perhaps not of very great importance in itself'. With that, the British Government, its prejudices confirmed, having included the Soviet Union in its calculations for a brief and unfruitful six months, proceeded once again with some relief to do its best to ignore it.

7
Alliance

Neutral – but in whose favour?[1]

In judging the policies of the British Government towards the Soviet Union during the period between September 1939 and June 1941, it is necessary constantly to have in mind three underlying factors:

(a) The attempt to forge a British–French–Soviet alliance in the summer of 1939 had represented a deep but brief reversal of traditional British policies and instincts. Its failure left British policy-makers with a sense of betrayal and a reinforcement of the ingrained mistrust of the Soviet Union.
(b) The trauma of Munich had left a determination to have no complicity with another apparently aggressive power in the East.
(c) The sense of standing alone after the fall of France produced a certain elation of the spirit, in which purity of motive could easily prevail over cold calculation of the odds.

Against this background, it is scarcely surprising that, after the declaration of war on Germany, the British Government had little time – and less inclination – for consideration of its relationship with the Soviet Union. The consequences of the German–Soviet secret protocol of August 1939 were soon made apparent as Soviet forces moved into eastern Poland and the formal partition of Poland was effected by a German–Soviet agreement of 29 September. The Cabinet noted with some relief that the British guarantee to Poland, now given treaty form, was applicable only in respect of the German aggression. There was at this stage no desire to engage in hostilities against the Soviet Union, but the old conviction that there was little to choose between Nazi and

Communist dictatorship was powerfully reinforced. Churchill subsequently wrote[2] that he did not give way to the general indignation in Cabinet, but instead put forward a paper indicating the possible strategic advantage of the new Soviet frontier with Germany and advocating a 'renewal of relations with Russia'. In a much-quoted broadcast of 1 October, he spoke of Russian action as 'a riddle wrapped in a mystery inside an enigma'. The key to the riddle was, for him, the historic Russian national interest which ran wholly contrary to German domination of South-Eastern Europe and the Balkans and it was with this key that, in the spring of 1941, he tried to loosen the German–Soviet link. In 1939 and 1940 there was, however, no general desire in Britain for a renewal of the British–Soviet relationship and certainly no practical possibility of bringing it about. After the collapse of Poland, with no active pursuit of the war in the West, the interest of British ministers was concentrated very largely on economic measures against Germany, including the need to minimise the leakage of strategic supplies through the Soviet Union.

The Soviet–Finnish War

Mutual Assistance Pacts between the Soviet Union and Latvia, Lithuania and Estonia provided the pretext for the subsequent introduction of Soviet forces into these three Baltic States and when, on 30 November 1939, the Soviet forces attacked Finland, the public outcry in Britain was intense. The Cabinet, however, noted that Russian expansion in the Baltic would have no direct adverse effect on British strategic interests and accepted the advice of the Chiefs of Staff against being drawn into war with Russia.[3] The lead in the expulsion of the Soviet Union from the League of Nations was taken by France, but Britain, after first seeking to avoid a vote, joined in voting for expulsion and Maisky noted an 'icy void' around his Embassy. As the war dragged on, the flow of British defence supplies to Finland, although never substantial, was gradually stepped up. It was first recognised that a certain number of specialists would need to accompany them, then the raising of a volunteer force was agreed to and finally a substantial British regular force was prepared for a landing at Narvik with the joint objective of completing the northern blockade of Germany and aiding the Finns against the Soviet Union. It was in connexion with this enterprise that Harold Macmillan, visiting Finland, acquired the white fur hat which attracted so much attention on his visit to Moscow in 1959. A formal proposal of British mediation to bring about a settlement of the Soviet–Finnish War was put forward by Maisky to Butler on 22 February 1940, but the taint of Munich was still strong. Could a British Government, still smarting at the way it had been exploited by Hitler to bring about the dismemberment of Czechoslovakia, now be seen to lend its good offices to Stalin to bring about the dismemberment of Finland? Stafford Cripps visited Moscow privately at Soviet invitation early in 1940, but his report that Molotov seemed anxious to cultivate better relations with Britain was firmly set aside. Indeed, some views expressed in the Foreign Office at this time were, if anything, more belligerently anti-Soviet than those of the Chiefs of Staff. Vansittart minuted about 'Stalin and his pseudo-Communism which it is just as necessary to destroy as Nazism'. Only Butler sounded a warning note that by never meeting the Russians we should tend to increase rather than decrease German–Russian amity.

It was at this point that French pressure was being exerted in favour of an attack upon the oilfields at Baku, on which the Chiefs of Staff advised[4] that the risk of initiating war with Russia would be acceptable only if it led to the early defeat of Germany, but that there was no action against Russia which would achieve this result. In the Foreign Office, Fitzroy Maclean commented that the risks seemed negligible in comparison with the certain advantages and his view was endorsed by Orme Sargent, with only a mild dissent from the Foreign Secretary who noted that the paper was 'rather more decided in favour of action against Russia than I am at present'.[5] With neither the Foreign Secretary nor the Chiefs of Staff showing much enthusiasm, the project did not progress very far.

A new equilibrium in Europe

Fortunately for the British Government, the Soviet–Finnish War ended in March 1940, before the major volunteer force had embarked. During the brief period between the fiasco of the British attempt to preempt the German occupation of Norway and the German invasion of the Low Countries in May, there was some consideration of the possibility of renewing trade negotiations with the Soviet Union, but it was made clear by Maisky that his Government would not buy an agreement with Britain at the price of discontinuing their economic collaboration with Germany. Nevertheless, after the attack on Holland and Belgium, there was renewed pressure in Britain for the appointment of an Ambassador to Moscow to replace Seeds, who had been withdrawn for consultation at the time of the Soviet attack on Finland. The original plan was that Stafford Cripps should act as a special emissary for the purpose of trade negotiations, but at Soviet insistence he was appointed as Ambassador and embarked upon the task of restoring relations at the most unpropitious moment, arriving in Moscow on 12 June 1940, two days before the fall of Paris.

With Churchill having replaced Chamberlain as Prime Minister, there was now the possibility of a new impulse in British–Soviet relations. Churchill's antipathy to Soviet Communism was at least as great as that of Chamberlain and his record as an active opponent of the Soviet Union went far beyond that of the former Prime Minister. Nevertheless, in the critical military situation facing the new British Government there was no place for squeamishness. Within Europe, the Soviet Union had the potential either to level the balance or to tilt it so decisively in favour of Germany as to ensure the defeat of Britain. On 25 June Cripps was sent a personal message for delivery from Churchill to Stalin[6] designed to place the re-establishment of contact between the two countries on as firm a base as possible. Churchill referred to the 1939 negotiations and stated bluntly: 'Germany became your friend almost at the same moment as she became our enemy.' Now, he continued, there was the 'prospect of Germany establishing a hegemony over the Continent'. Britain, he said, had two objectives – to save herself and to free the rest of Europe – and was ready 'to discuss fully with the Soviet Government any of the vast problems raised by Germany's present attempt to pursue in Europe the methodical process by successive stages of conquest and absorption'. On the basis of this message, Cripps had a discussion of two and three-quarter hours with Stalin. Churchill thought it 'an interview of a formal and frigid character', but it was not without substance. Stalin questioned whether Germany had the strength to dominate Europe; stated that the Soviet Union had no intention of going further into Romania or the Balkans; hinted that British assistance in the improvement of Soviet–Turkish relations might be welcome and maintained that although the trade agreement with Germany would not be broken, it would not be used against Britain. The most important part of the discussion was, however, that in which Stalin foreshadowed the post-war reconstruction of Europe. The basis of the German–Soviet agreement had, he said, been 'a common desire to get rid of the old equilibrium in Europe which, prior to the war, Great Britain and France had sought to preserve'. 'If the Prime Minister wishes to restore the old equilibrium', he continued, 'we cannot agree with him.'[7] The history of the next forty years was to be very largely the history of the steps by which the Soviet

Union first established and then maintained a new equilibrium based upon its own effective control over Eastern Europe.

The Baltic States

Stalin was at this time disposed to strengthen the security of the Soviet Union by such action as lay within his own power and certainly not to compromise it by closer association with Britain. Having already occupied Eastern Poland, his first steps towards the reshaping of European frontiers were already in train when Cripps met him. On 15–16 June, under the pretext of thwarting a military conspiracy against the Soviet Union, Soviet forces entered the Baltic States, Latvia, Lithuania and Estonia, and puppet governments were quickly established. On 27 June, faced with a Soviet ultimatum, Romania ceded Bessarabia and in the first week of August the three Baltic States were formally incorporated into the Soviet Union. This action confronted the British Government with the need to decide its policy on recognition. The Cabinet was at first inclined to accept the Soviet action as a military necessity in preparation against a possible German attack, but eventually, influenced in part by American pressure against recognition and in part by the determination of the Foreign Office not to repeat the appeasement of the previous decade, decided to recognise the incorporation *de facto*, and to withhold *de jure* recognition until after the war. Meanwhile the gold deposits of the Baltic States in Britain were held against eventual compensation for seized British property.

Throughout the summer and autumn of 1940, the British Government continued its efforts to deflect Soviet policy away from alignment with Germany. The Soviet Government, for its part, careful to preserve that relationship, informed the German Embassy in Moscow of Churchill's proposal.[8] There is, nevertheless, some evidence to suggest that fear of a British–Soviet rapprochement may have helped to precipitate the German attack on the Soviet Union. On 31 July, when Hitler announced to his generals his decision to attack Russia, he was recorded as saying: 'Russia is the factor on which Britain is relying the most ... with Russia smashed, Britain's last hope will be shattered.'[9] The elimination of Soviet power was an objective in its own right and the British factor may have been relevant only to the timing. But timing could be critical. In Germany at this time, Operation Sealion, the invasion of Britain, was still being prepared for September, but it is doubtful if Hitler was ever fully committed to it. By October when the decision was taken to postpone Sealion, the attempt to obtain air supremacy over Britain had failed and preparations for the attack on the Soviet Union were already in train.

For some months longer, the diplomatic tussle for Soviet support continued to be waged by the British and German Ambassadors in Moscow, with little enthusiasm on the part of their Governments. In October, Cripps followed up Stalin's thinking about the new equilibrium by putting to Vyshinsky a suggestion that those who helped Britain during the war might expect to 'share actively in the task of reconstruction'.[10] British successes in the Battle of Britain were having some effect on Soviet opinion, but no realistic assessment of the balance of power in Europe could have led Stalin to gamble Soviet security on a closer relationship with Britain while the reconstruction of Europe was already proceeding apace under the German armed forces. When Ribbentrop invited Molotov to Berlin, there was little hesitation about acceptance. The proposal put to him by Hitler and Ribbentrop was for a joint German–Soviet liquidation of the 'worldwide estate in bankruptcy' of the British Empire. From both the German and the Soviet accounts of this meeting, it is clear that Molotov was non-committal in his response and insisted upon German confirmation of the 1939 agreement placing Finland in the Soviet sphere. An air raid on Berlin had, on Cripps' recommendation, been timed to coincide with his talks and, as Stalin subsequently recounted to Churchill, it prompted Molotov to enquire of Ribbentrop: 'If England is finished, why are we in this shelter, and whose are these bombs which fall?' It must be doubtful whether a ready Soviet acceptance of the German offer would have served to delay the attack on the Soviet Union until after the defeat of Britain, but non-acceptance must have helped to confirm its timing for the summer of 1941. It took only a little more than a month after the meeting with Molotov before, on 18 December, the German Government took the operational decision to proceed with Operation Barbarossa, the attack on the Soviet Union. To the policy-makers in London, however, Molotov's visit seemed to demonstrate that, faced with the need to choose, the Soviet Union had, as in the summer of 1939, preferred to align herself with Germany, and on 13 November the Chiefs of Staff were instructed to consider possible military action by Britain against the Soviet Union.[11]

The preparation for Operation Barbarossa

It did not take long before the first intelligence indications of preparations for a German attack on the Soviet Union began to reach London, but British analysts found it hard to decide whether the German Government was bent upon invasion or merely intended to use the threat in order to secure concessions. It still seemed that the Soviet Union would prefer to accommodate Germany rather than fight her. The British Government had, at this time, as indeed later, little to offer by way of inducement and, as June approached, there was still no British–Soviet rapprochement. *De facto* recognition of the incorporation of the Baltic States had been conceded. The withholding of *de jure* recognition was an irritant, but the grant of it would have counted for little. The trade negotiations were given desultory attention but, as Stalin had already made clear to Cripps, what Britain could offer by way of rubber and non-ferrous metals was not enough to wean the Soviet Union away from its German trade. Indeed, the Soviet Union so misjudged its own national interest that it continued to supply strategic materials necessary for the maintenance of the German war effort right up to June 1941. British influence was used to enable the Soviet Union to improve its relationship with Turkey, but there was little negotiating leverage in this. Soviet reporting of the war showed a distinct bias in favour of Germany and the British assessment – which was probably correct – was that the Soviet Union would not prejudice its relationship with an apparently victorious Germany for the sake of a Britain still struggling to avoid defeat. Cadogan noted in his diary. 'Russia has no fear of us and we have nothing to offer. No use juggling with words and jiggling with drafts.'[12] As seen from Moscow, there were two courses open to Britain: she could seek to improve her own military fortunes by embroiling the Soviet Union in war with Germany and, additionally or alternatively, she could seek a separate peace with Germany and then join Germany in a second war of intervention in the Soviet Union. Either course would divert the thrust of German power eastwards and, given the known anti-Soviet sentiments of the British establishment, either seemed feasible.

Hitler needed to keep the Soviet Union quiet until his own attack had been fully prepared. He was, with good reason, confident of his ability to do this. In his New Year message to Mussolini, he described relations with the Soviet Union as good and commented: 'I do not envisage any Russian initiative against us so long as Stalin is alive and we ourselves are not victims of serious setbacks.' So, having secured the cooperation of Romania and Hungary, he continued his drive southeastwards with the objective of affecting the subjugation of Greece and Yugoslavia before redeploying his forces for the attack on the Soviet Union. To the British Government there seemed little reason for

Germany to attack a benevolently neutral Soviet Union. The principal theatre of land operations was North Africa and German strategy was consistent with preparations to destroy the British position in the Middle East.

In March, it had seemed that Yugoslavia would capitulate without fighting, but the revolution in Belgrade made it necessary for three Panzer divisions which were being moved into Poland in readiness for the attack on the Soviet Union to be redeployed in the Balkans. An intelligence report of this move prompted Churchill to try to persuade Stalin that the Soviet Union could best delay a German attack on itself by action to increase German difficulties in the Balkans. On 3 April, he sent Stalin a personal message informing him of both the original move and the redeployment and added, 'Your Excellency will readily appreciate the significance of these facts'.[13] Cripps' handling of the message was, in Churchill's words, 'obstinate and obstructive'. He argued that Churchill's brief and cryptic message might merely detract from the impression made by his own representations, recommended against delivery and on 11 April wrote his own warning letter to Vyshinsky. Only in response to the Prime Minister's insistence did he eventually transmit the original message on 19 April through Vyshinsky. By this time, a day before the German attack on Yugoslavia, the Soviet Government had concluded a Treaty of Friendship with the new Yugoslav Government. Stalin later professed to have no recollection of Churchill's message and it is not unlikely that this was true. It is just possible that, had the message been personally delivered with some ceremony on 3 April, it might have served to open up a direct contact with Stalin, but even then it must be very doubtful whether he would have taken any more notice of it than he did of the warnings from his own sources.[14]

Even before delivering Churchill's message, Cripps sent a further remarkable memorandum to Molotov on 18 April, proposing an immediate improvement of relations. Cripps warned of German plans to obtain Soviet supplies either by humiliating concessions or by occupation, for all of which, he said, a plan existed for that spring.[15] The memorandum, which was curtly rejected by Vyshinsky, could scarcely have had any positive effect, but might have done no harm had it not also referred to the possibility that 'if the war were protracted for a long period there might be a temptation for Great Britain (and especially for certain circles in Great Britain) to come to some arrangement to end the war'. If Soviet suspicions of a British–German understanding needed any further boost it was given by the dramatic flight of Rudolf Hess to Britain on 11 May, with proposals – promptly dismissed in

Berlin as a 'hallucination' – for a peace settlement between Britain and Germany. Soviet historians[16] later admitted that there was, by this time, no realistic possibility of British and American collusion with Germany, but Churchill recounts how, even three years later, Stalin was still fascinated by the Hess incident and disposed to see it in the context of a plot against the Soviet Union.[17]

While Soviet suspicions were concentrated on the possibility of a British–German deal, the British Government was forced to evaluate an increasing volume of evidence from intercepted German communications, pointing to the assembly of the forces for Barbarossa.[18] As spring moved into summer, it was still possible to account for these moves as a show of force designed to secure Soviet concessions. After all, German policy provided examples enough of securing the spoils of war without the need to wage it and, it could be reasoned, the temptation to pursue such a course with the Soviet Union must be strong.

The tragedy was played out even through the final weeks preceding the invasion. Cripps was so badly out of sympathy with opinion in London that on 2 June he was recalled for consultations, arriving on 11 June. Even before he arrived, the British press was beginning to carry stories of German troop concentrations and by 10 June evidence of the pending invasion had become so strong that women and children were evacuated from the Embassy in Moscow. On 12 June the Joint Intelligence Committee decided that hostilities were highly probable and that the most likely period was the second half of June. This assessment was communicated to the Soviet Ambassador in London by the Foreign Secretary, but was brushed aside as a provocation by the Soviet Government. The only response from Moscow was a Tass communiqué on 14 June, denouncing rumours of an early Soviet–German war as 'nothing but clumsy propaganda by forces interested in an extension of the war'. During the final ten days preceding 21 June, the Chiefs of Staff considered policy in preparation for the German attack. It was estimated that the occupation of Ukraine and Moscow would take the German forces something between three and six weeks and that thereafter the Soviet Government would disintegrate.[19] In terms of British interests, even a campaign as brief as this would impose a useful delay upon the German plan for the invasion of Britain and allow further time for the strengthening of British defences. As Eden put it: 'We need a breathing space.' It did not, however, provide much justification for substantial aid, even if this had been feasible, and all that was envisaged was the despatch of a Liaison Mission combined with an offer – scarcely likely to be received with enthusiasm in

Moscow – of assistance in the destruction of the Caucasian oilfields and the supply of oil in replacement.[20] Fortunately, the importance of strengthening Soviet resistance received rather more recognition in Cabinet and a formal decision to pledge aid was taken in advance of the German attack. On 15 June Churchill informed Roosevelt that 'we shall of course give all encouragement and any help we can spare to the Russians'. He refrained from speaking of an alliance, but Roosevelt's reply indicated a readiness to support any statement 'welcoming Russia as an ally'. To Moscow, nothing further was said. Mutual suspicion, founded on established antipathy and proven experience, had destroyed any possibility of advance planning.

The past flashes away

The German forces crossed the Soviet borders on the morning of Sunday 22 June 1941 and that evening Churchill made one of his most memorable wartime broadcasts. 'No one has been a more consistent opponent of Communism than I have for the last twenty-five years. I will unsay no word that I have spoken about it. But all this fades away before the spectacle which is now unfolding. The past, with its crimes, its follies, and its tragedies, flashes away.' With emotion he conjured up a picture of the Russian people upon whom a 'cataract of horrors' had been launched and declared. 'Any man or state who fights on against Nazidom will have our aid ... It follows therefore that we shall give whatever help we can to Russia and the Russian people.'

It is tempting to date a transformation in British–Soviet relations from this speech. It did indeed inaugurate a period in which the British Government was to be committed to full alliance in war and peace with the power which the British Prime Minister was subsequently to describe on his first visit to Moscow as 'this sullen, sinister Bolshevik State I had once tried so hard to strangle at its birth, and which, until Hitler appeared, I had regarded as the mortal foe of civilised freedom'.[21] The past did not, however, flash away. On the British side, it was not easy for ministers or their civil and military advisers to forget the Molotov–Ribbentrop agreement of August 1939 or to ignore the fact that the Soviet Union had sought its own salvation in a policy of benevolent neutrality towards Germany during the year when Britain was struggling alone for survival. As Churchill reminded Cripps: 'No one wants to recriminate, but it is not our fault that Hitler was able to destroy Poland before turning his forces against France, or to destroy France before turning them against Russia.'[22]

All the mistrust of the Soviet regime which had built up over the years was at its deepest in June 1941 and it undoubtedly coloured the initial British response to the German attack. With the progress of the war, suspicion did indeed gradually give way to respect and sympathy as the scale of the Soviet war effort and the depth of suffering of the Soviet people became apparent, but the day-to-day conduct of relations was rarely free from friction. There were good moments, for instance at the Teheran conference, but there was no point at which it could be said that a genuine mutual understanding had been arrived at. On the Soviet side, Churchill's innate dislike was fully reciprocated by a Soviet leadership basing its policies upon a doctrine of irreconcilable struggle with the forces of capitalism represented by the British Government. There was a measure of respect for the British achievement in continuing the war alone, but the mistrust was never wholly eradicated and, with the approach of victory, the savour of military triumph was to overwhelm all other political factors in a heady blend of Russian nationalism and Soviet doctrine. The bond between Britain and the Soviet Union, in so far as it existed, depended upon the common enemy and dissolved with its defeat.

In following the course of British–Soviet relations during this period, it will, on occasion, be convenient to depart from the chronological narrative in order to separate out the two main strands, the pursuit of the war and the preparation for the peace, intertwined though they were throughout all the intergovernmental exchanges of the period. Within the former, it is appropriate to follow separately the controversy over the opening of a second front in Europe and the problems connected with the delivery of supplies to the Soviet Union.

The initial response

The prospect of alliance with the Soviet Union had, as we have seen, been contemplated shortly in advance of the German attack and by the time the attack was launched, the basis for Churchill's speech had been established. Practical considerations meant that at this stage little more than token gestures were possible. Britain certainly had no spare supplies. The war material already on order from the United States was all urgently needed and there was little incentive to sacrifice it, with prejudice to the defence of Britain itself, if the effect were merely a slight prolongation of an apparently forlorn Soviet resistance. Memories of the collapse of France were not far below the surface and after the Stalin purges Soviet military capability was regarded as, if anything, even less reliable than that of France in the weeks before surrender. As Churchill summed up the policy: 'In the early days of our alliance there was little we could do, and I tried to fill the void by civilities.'[23] Nevertheless, a Military Mission under General Mason-Macfarlane was established in Moscow, a Soviet mission was received in London and, at the urging of Cripps, who had resumed his post in Moscow, an Anglo–Soviet Declaration was signed on 12 July,[24] in which the two Governments undertook to 'render each other assistance and support of all kinds' and neither to negotiate nor to conclude a separate peace. The Anglo–Soviet Agreement was followed by a Polish–Soviet Agreement, negotiated with British participation and accompanied by a British reaffirmation of the guarantee to Poland. By the Polish–Soviet Agreement of 30 July the Soviet Government recognised 'the Soviet–German treaties of 1939 as to territorial changes in Poland' as having lost their validity and provided for the formation of a Polish army in the Soviet Union, while leaving open the question of Poland's post-war frontiers.

Within a month of the German attack on the Soviet Union, the problem of opening a second front came to the fore. The first direct communication received by Churchill from Stalin came on 19 July,[25] immediately after the signature of the Declaration, and contained a proposal for the establishment of a front in northern France as well as a joint operation in northern Norway, where British naval and air support was sought. In terms of the pursuit of the war, there was little problem about the common objective, the defeat of Nazi Germany. The opportunity for a common strategy had, however, been largely vitiated by the conclusion of the Soviet–German Agreement of August 1939 which made possible a single-front operation by Germany against Britain and France in 1940 and, hence, a single-front operation against the Soviet Union itself in 1941. The opportunity which the Soviet Union had squandered in 1939 could not easily be reconstituted once Germany had effective control of the whole land mass of Western Europe. The logic of a two-front ground operation against Germany was, however, still inescapable and the establishment of the second front in the West was a primary purpose of Allied planning. The insistent Soviet demand for its premature implementation was to dominate bilateral and tripartite exchanges with the Soviet Union on the conduct of the war.

At the time of Stalin's first message, British land forces were still being reformed after the defeats of 1940 and were heavily engaged with the Axis forces in North Africa while, at sea, the Navy was fully stretched with the task of holding open the lines of communication upon which the country's survival depended. Even had the forces been available, there were virtually no landing craft and only over the Pas de Calais was there the possibility of establishing any effective air cover. There was no way in which, within a period of less than two years, any effective Allied landing could have been made. There was no point in concealing the reality. In his reply of July 20 Churchill was able to offer naval operations in the Arctic and the possible basing of Hurricanes in Murmansk, but in relation to ground operations, he could only say: 'The Chiefs of Staff do not see any way of doing anything on a scale likely to be of the slightest use to you.'[26] It was the beginning of a series of exchanges on this topic which was to last for two years, but before following their course we must turn briefly to the more immediate problem of Allied aid to Russia, namely the provision of supplies.

The first tripartite conference of the war was devoted almost wholly to the supply problem and came about through the joint efforts of Cripps and President Roosevelt's emissary, Harry Hopkins. It was proposed in a message sent on 12 August[27] by Churchill and Roosevelt from their conference at Placentia Bay at which the Atlantic Charter was agreed. It took place at the end of September, at a time when the German offensive was threatening to overwhelm the Soviet armies and when Stalin, in a desperate message to Churchill, had asked once again for the opening of a second front in the West, or, failing that, the despatch of 25 to 30 divisions to the Soviet Union through Iran or Archangel. It might have been possible for British troops to relieve the five Soviet divisions in Persia and thus free them for service on the Russian front, but it would have taken three months to put even two fully armed British divisions into South Russia. Stalin's request was, in Churchill's words 'utter unreality', but its very unreality reinforced the case for a British–Soviet discussion of strategy. In the event, however, although the British delegation was prepared for this, Beaverbrook so handled the conference that it was confined to a discussion of supply arrangements. As Minister of Supply, he led on the British side and Averell Harriman represented the United States. There could scarcely have been two more mutually antipathetic British representatives in one city than Cripps and Beaverbrook. For all Cripps' intelligence, his political vision and his sympathy with the Soviet Union, Beaverbrook's mixture of brute energy and political cunning was better attuned to a negotiation with Stalin and, from this point on, he was to establish himself as an advocate for the Soviet Union within the War Cabinet and in the country at large. Having effectively excluded Cripps from the conduct of the Moscow negotiations, he ended with agreement on a schedule of deliveries running up to June 1942.[28] Subsequent protocols were negotiated on an annual basis.

Concurrently with the conference, the one joint British–Soviet land campaign of the war was successfully accomplished, when, in August–September, after overcoming slight opposition from the Persian Army, British and Soviet forces linked up from north and south to open a supply route through Persia to the Caspian. The operation stemmed primarily from the British concern to safeguard the oil supplies – and indeed the whole Middle East position – against a German thrust southwards through the Caucasus, rather than from a desire to aid the Soviet Union. A formal Treaty of Alliance between the United Kingdom, the Soviet Union and Iran was signed on 29 January 1942 and the route, when opened, carried, over a period of four and a half years, five million tons of supplies to the Soviet Union.

The Anglo–Soviet Treaty

The high water mark of relations between Britain and the Soviet Union was the signature on 26 May 1942 of the 'Treaty for an Alliance in the War against Hitlerite Germany and her Associates in Europe and Providing Also for Collaboration and Mutual Assistance Thereafter'.[29] Immediately after the Beaverbrook–Harriman mission, the German offensive against Moscow was intensified and, with the partial evacuation of the city, there was concern that the Soviet Union might be forced into a separate peace, leaving the German forces, in a repeat of 1917, free to resume the offensive in the West. There was growing Soviet bitterness at the absence of any British military diversion in the West or the provision of any land forces for the Soviet front. British reluctance to declare war on Finland, Romania and Hungary served as a further irritant. Matters were brought to a head by a message from Stalin to Churchill, dated 8 November 1941, complaining of a 'lack of clarity' in relations and stating bluntly: 'As long as the present situation exists there will be difficulty in establishing mutual confidence.' Churchill had proposed a visit to Moscow by Generals Wavell and Paget, but this was rejected by Stalin unless the visit was 'with a view to concluding agreement on two fundamental questions ... , a definite understanding on war aims and on plans for the post-war organisation of peace' and an 'agreement on mutual military assistance against Hitler in Europe' as well as the immediate declaration of war on Finland, Romania and Hungary.[30] Stalin's message was received with 'pain and surprise'[31] and this was made clear to Maisky, but gradually, aided by a more moderately phrased second message, the British government accepted that, if the war effort were not to be seriously prejudiced, some positive response had to be given. So war was declared on Finland, Romania and Hungary and Eden was sent to Moscow to take, with the Soviet leadership, 'a broad survey of the war as a whole' as well as the 'post-war organisation of peace'. He made it clear, however, to Cripps, that the Government envisaged a 'gradual and tentative procedure' rather than 'to attempt prematurely to define our collaboration in treaty form'.[32] The hope was that in exchange for a relatively modest offer of additional supplies, it would be possible to secure a joint public declaration on policy for the defeat of Germany.[33]

Eden arrived in Moscow on 15 December 1941 at a moment which was perhaps the turning point of the war. In October, when the German advance guard had penetrated to the suburbs of Moscow, it had seemed that the capital might fall and the Embassies had been evacuated to Kuibyshev. Now the German advance had been stemmed and while Eden was on his way by sea, the Japanese attack on Pearl Harbor had brought the United States into the war. Much had changed since he and Litvinov had discussed the rising threat of Nazi Germany in 1935, but the Soviet position still resembled in many respects that of 1939, with the requirement for matching political and military treaties embodying commitments in respect of the conduct of the war and the future frontiers of the Soviet Union, particularly in relation to the Baltic States, Finland, Poland and Romania. Commitments relating to post-war territorial adjustments were bluntly rejected by Churchill and no text could be agreed during Eden's discussions. Matters had, however, moved a long way since the ill-fated negotiations of the summer of 1939 and now neither Britain nor the Soviet Union could afford an open breach. It was left that Eden would return to London for further discussions with the Cabinet.

Debate within the Cabinet and discussion with the United States lasted from December 1941 until May 1942. Within the Cabinet it was clear that the Polish–Soviet frontier could not be the subject of a formal commitment at this stage. It was, however, accepted that there should be a formal treaty and there was a disposition to find some way of meeting the Soviet requirement in respect of recognition of the 1941 frontiers as well as to acquiesce in a post-war commitment in respect of the integration of the Baltic States into the Soviet Union. Victory was still far off. The Soviet Union was engaged in a desperate struggle and the outcome was far from clear, but if the Allies were to be victorious the Soviet forces would certainly have to re-occupy the area within their 1941 borders. There was no way in which the Soviet Government would then accept that it should conclude peace on a basis which left it with less territory and less security than when Hitler attacked. Opposition to commitments in respect of post-war frontiers was, however, particularly strong in the United States and this carried the day. In the hope, quickly confirmed, of securing an American assurance about the opening of a second front in Europe, the Soviet Government abandoned its insistence on a frontier commitment and the Anglo–Soviet Treaty, in the form eventually negotiated between Eden and Molotov in London, left the territorial question wholly open. In retrospect, it is clear that the Soviet Union must have made the realistic calculation that victory over Hitler would leave the Red Army as a far more effective means of securing the reversal of the 'old equilibrium' and guaranteeing Soviet security than heavily qualified intergovernmental understandings. Military victory had to be the Soviet priority. The Treaty as concluded contained a preambular reference to Soviet adherence to the Atlantic Charter. The body of it was in two parts. The first, valid until the establishment of peace, provided for a formal alliance against Germany and states associated with her in acts of aggression in Europe (i.e. excluding Japan) and for no armistice or peace treaty except by mutual consent. Part II, valid for twenty years, provided for 'common action to preserve peace and resist aggression in the post-war period', measures to prevent renewed aggression by Germany and collaboration in the organisation of security and economic prosperity in Europe.

The coordination of strategy

The course of military operations must fall outside the scope of this study, but it is necessary to address the problem of the extent to which, as allies, the British and Soviet Governments – together with the United States – were able to coordinate the broad strategy for the conduct of the war. We have noted the early exchanges on the opening of a second front and the execution of the joint campaign in Persia. There was, however, in the early stages of the alliance, virtually no joint consideration of strategy. Nor, given the refusal of the Soviet Government to disclose any information about its own military planning, were any profitable exchanges possible through the Military Mission in Moscow. Shortly after the German attack, largely in response to pressure from the Prime Minister, Enigma material – i.e. intercepted German cypher traffic – was passed, with the source camouflaged, to the Soviet authorities, but because of the lack of reciprocity the supply dwindled and finally lapsed in 1944 after Soviet closure of the intercept station at Murmansk. Indeed, the British Government seem to have obtained more information about operations on the Eastern front from the interception of German communications than they did from the Soviet Union itself. A somewhat surprising agreement on collaboration in subversion and propaganda in countries outside the Soviet Union and the Commonwealth seems to have borne equally little fruit.[34] It was the resumption of Soviet pressure for the establishment of a second front in northern France which prompted the first serious consideration of strategy during the Prime Minister's visit to Moscow in August 1942.

The need for a landing in Western Europe was clear enough. The problem was one of timing. In a memorandum of 18 December 1941 Churchill defined the objective of 'liberating conquered Europe by the landing during the summer of 1943 of United States and British armies on their shore' and planning went ahead on this basis. Soviet pressure for early action was, however, intense. After the preliminary discussions on the Anglo–Soviet Treaty in London in March 1942, Molotov continued to Washington. Cordell Hull, with Roosevelt's backing, was determined to avoid the inclusion of any territorial commitment in the British Treaty and believed that the offer of a second front during 1942 'should take the heat off Russia's diplomatic demands upon England'. The President therefore authorised Molotov to inform Stalin that 'we expect the formation of a second front this year'. It was not a firm promise and it did not specify where the second front would be. The communiqué issued at the end of the Washington talks however, included a sentence drafted by Molotov to the effect that 'complete agreement was reached with regard to the urgent task of opening a second front in Europe in 1942'. Returning through London, he secured a British communiqué in the same terms, but it was accompanied by an *aide-memoire* stating: 'We are making preparations for a landing on the Continent in August or September 1942 ... It is impossible to say in advance whether the situation will be such as to make this operation feasible when the time comes. We can therefore give no promise in the matter, but provided that it appears sound and sensible we shall not hesistate to put our plans into effect.' The *aide-memoire* also confirmed that maximum effort would be put into a 'large-scale invasion' in 1943.[35] It was true that consideration was being given to Operation Sledgehammer, designed to seize the Cherbourg peninsula, but there was no plan at that time, nor could there have been, for the effective establishment of a sustainable second front in France in 1942. There was little cause for the Soviet Union to be misled, since, in addition to the formal *aide-memoire*, Churchill personally made the reservations clear to Molotov. Nevertheless, it is not improbable that a communiqué designed in part to mislead the Germans into holding an excessively large force in France may also have encouraged the Soviet leadership to cherish unrealistic hopes. Certainly, they lost no opportunity to represent it as a formal commitment.

The final recognition of the need to defer the main landing until 1943 came during British–American discussions in London in July 1942 at which the decision was taken that the principal operation for 1942 should be 'Torch', the joint British–American operation to destroy the German forces in North Africa and pave the way for the opening up of the Mediterranean. This strategic decision coincided unhappily with the decision to suspend the Arctic convoys to Russia during the summer months, a decision to which we shall return later. The Soviet Union had, ever since the Molotov visit, waged an assiduous campaign of publicity and lobbying designed to ensure the early opening of a second front and the confirmation of British reservations brought a peremptory message from Stalin on 23 July stating 'in the most emphatic manner' that the Soviet Government could not acquiesce in the postponement of a second front in Europe until 1943.[36]

Churchill in Moscow

Sir Archibald Clark Kerr, who had succeeded Cripps in the Moscow Embassy, suggested that Molotov might have failed to brief Stalin properly on Churchill's thinking and it was agreed that the Prime Minister should visit Moscow in August in order to put British strategic planning personally to Stalin. This, the first-ever meeting between British and Soviet Heads of Government, should have been a momentous occasion. On the one side was Churchill who hated all the Soviet state stood for and had, as he recollected, tried to strangle it at its birth. On the other was Stalin, the legatee of a long Russian tradition of conspiracy, terror and repression who, two years earlier, would have contentedly warmed his hands over the funeral pyre of that society of which Churchill now stood as the supreme champion. They met in Moscow at a time when the fate of the Soviet forces still hung in the balance. The immediate threat to Moscow had been contained and the front-line was stabilised to the west of the city, but in the south the threat to Stalingrad and the Caucasus was critical (see Map 2, p. 35).

Churchill's task was to secure Stalin's confidence in a revised strategy which brought little immediate and apparent relief to the Soviet Union. He did not expect the meeting to be agreeable and, on the whole, it was not, although both officially and personally he was shown every courtesy and hospitality. After a rough start, Stalin recognised the strategic merit of the North African operation, but in relation to the second front and the suspension of convoys it was not easy to receive without anger his taunts about the broken promises of a country afraid of fighting the Germans. One incidental product of the discussions was agreement on the merit of a joint operation to capture German bases in northern Norway and Finland, an operation which was close to Churchill's heart but not to that of his Service advisers. In his alternation of joviality and brutality, Stalin followed a practice which was to become familiar to all those who had dealings with the Soviet leadership. Churchill met his recriminations firmly, but refrained from reproaches about the 1939 treaty with Germany and the encounter ended with a private meeting of seven hours, culminating in dinner in Stalin's private apartment. The meeting served to establish a certain rapport between the two men, a rapport which was of some value to Stalin in the later wartime conferences.

The strategic discussion took very much the form of a British exposition of British–American planning and a Soviet interrogation. Little insight was gained into Soviet planning. Churchill was left with the impression that there was an 'even chance' that the Russians would hold, but his military advisers were less certain. The final communiqué spoke optimistically of 'an atmosphere of cordiality and complete sincerity' and 'close friendship and understanding'. What might, at best, have been claimed was the creation of a measure of mutual respect.

Further strategic differences

If proof of the impossibility of establishing a front in France in 1942 were needed, it was afforded on 17 August, immediately after Churchill left Moscow, when he received the news of the outcome of the raid on Dieppe, involving a total of some 10 000 members of all three forces. Casualties were extremely heavy. Churchill's assessment was that it had been 'a costly but not unfruitful reconnaissance in force' which, by holding German forces in the West, 'did something to take the weight off Russia'.[37] What it did was to make clear the magnitude of the task which would have to be faced when the time came to re-establish a major army in France.

One effect of the Moscow Conference was to make the commitment to open a second front in 1943 proportionately stronger. British and American planning went ahead on this basis. Two other operations designed to afford direct assistance to the Soviet Union were also considered, but neither materialised. First was Operation Jupiter, the plan for an attack on northern Norway which Churchill had discussed with Stalin but for which he was unable to secure the support of the Chiefs of Staff. Second was a proposal, which both Churchill and Roosevelt found attractive, to establish in the Caucasus an Anglo– American airforce formed early in the New Year of 1943 by the withdrawal of aircraft from the Middle East. The force was envisaged as comprising nine Fighter and five Bomber Squadrons from the Royal Air Force as well as a Heavy Bomber Group and a Transport Group from the US Air Force. It took time to move from the initial concept to a formal plan, but on 21 November 1942 Air Marshal Drummond, together with an American officer, went to Moscow to negotiate the detailed arrangements for an operation which, it was hoped, would be 'a genuine comradeship in arms'. By this time, however, the German army had been surrounded at Stalingrad and the Alamein victory had stemmed the German drive eastwards in Africa. The Soviet Union had already shown a preference for receiving aircraft rather than complete Allied formations and, with competing demands arising in other theatres, this project also faded away with a note by Churchill: 'I do not wish to force upon them what it costs us so much to give.'[38]

The strategic relationship continued to hinge on the establishment of a second front in France and as late as 9 February 1943, Churchill telegraphed to Stalin that the British and American Governments were: 'Pushing preparations to the limit of our resources for a cross-Channel operation in August ... If the operation is delayed by weather or other reasons, it will be prepared with stronger forces for September.'[39] In reply, Stalin stressed that it was 'extremely important to deliver the blow from the West in the spring or in the early summer and not to postpone it until the second half of the year'. Further exchanges took place in March, with Churchill hinting at the possibility of a strike even before August and Stalin warning 'in the strongest possible manner' against further delay. By May, however, when Churchill and Roosevelt met in Washington, it was clear to both that the major cross-Channel operation could not take place before 1944 and that, meanwhile, the conquest of Italy offered the best prospect of engaging maximum German forces and easing the task of the Soviet armies. On 2 June a message was sent through the

US Embassy with news of the postponement and this led to a further Stalin–Churchill–Roosevelt exchange in which Stalin complained that a decision which might have grave consequences for the further course of the war had been taken without Soviet participation.[40] Churchill observed to Maisky that he was 'getting rather tired of being scolded' and doubted the value of further personal correspondence, but eventually an emollient reply was sent, proposing a tripartite meeting at Scapa Flow.

Meanwhile, British and American planning for the final stage of the war was moving ahead and came to a culmination at the Quebec Conference in August 1943. At this stage, coordination with the Soviet Union became more urgent, in relation not only to military operations in Europe, North Africa and the Far East, but also to the problems of the peace which would follow. We shall turn separately to the way in which these matters were handled at the three great summit conferences, but first the final stage of the controversy over the date for the second front must be noted. In October 1943, at the tripartite meeting of Foreign Ministers in Moscow prior to the Teheran Conference, Molotov and Stalin pressed Eden to confirm that the deadline of spring 1944 held good. Warned by Churchill against the danger of letting battles be governed by 'lawyers'' agreements made in good faith months before, Eden confirmed that it would be at the 'earliest possible moment'. At Teheran, in November, a date of May 1944 was established for the main cross-Channel operation. The Soviet Union undertook to initiate a large-scale offensive at the same time and, in the event, this materialised on 23 June, a fortnight after the postponed Allied landings. So ended a controversy which had soured the relationship with the Soviet Union for much of the war.

Although on occasion it suited the Russian leadership to recall the wartime alliance, Soviet historians continued, long after the war, to write of 'blatant deception of an ally and betrayal of a promise' in the pursuit of 'a policy designed to weaken the USSR to the maximum extent'.[41]

With the advantage of hindsight, it is not difficult to envisage the disaster which would have struck an Allied invasion in the summer of 1943, not to speak of 1942. Clark Kerr commented in July 1942[42] that the weakness in the British case lay 'not in our inability to open this second front but in our having let [Stalin] believe we were going to'. If there is one lesson from these exchanges, it must, sadly, be of the rashness of using an over-optimistic forecast – no matter how carefully hedged around – in an attempt to comfort a mistrustful partner on a critical issue.

The Arctic convoys

We have followed the course of the Soviet recriminations over the date for the invasion of France. It is now necessary to turn to the other main element in the British–Soviet operational relationship during the war years, the provision of supplies, and to take up the account from the point of the Beaverbrook–Harriman mission to Moscow in September 1941. The outcome of that meeting was agreement on a schedule of deliveries running from October 1941 to June 1942. Supplies were to be made available 'at British and United States centres of production', but the only undertaking in respect of their transportation was that Britain and the United States would 'give aid to the transportation to the Soviet Union and help with the delivery'. At this most critical stage of the war in Russia, the German forces were close to the suburbs of Moscow and Leningrad, there were serious doubts as to the ability of the Soviet forces to hold out, and the United States was still neutral. There can at the time have been no serious expectation in London or Washington that the Soviet Union would in fact be able to arrange its own transportation and from the outset the primary responsibility for transportation of British and American supplies by the most direct route around northern Norway to Archangel and Murmansk fell to the British. In the second protocol, covering the period to July 1943, the British and American Governments agreed to 'supply the shipping necessary to lift that part of this programme for which USSR ships cannot be made available'.[43] In giving this undertaking the two Governments can scarcely have envisaged the accusations which would flow from it.

Despite a critical shortage of shipping, the convoys were organised and three-quarters of the merchant ships were British or American. Throughout the winter of 1941–2 the operation was surprisingly successful, only one ship being lost, but in the spring of 1942 German attacks were intensified and out of the 83 ships in the April and May convoys 11 were lost, together with an escorting cruiser. Even at a rate of three convoys in two months, a backlog of supplies was building up and there was pressure on Britain from both the United States and the Soviet Union for an increased shipping effort. The German air and naval forces in northern Norway had, however, been reinforced and, with the approach of summer, the long Arctic day gave maximum opportunity for German aerial and surface reconnaissance and attack. Disaster came with convoy PQ 17 which sailed from Iceland to Archangel on 27 June 1942. The scale of the operation was indicated by the fact that 34 merchant ships carrying 200 000 tons of cargo required a total naval commitment, direct and indirect, for escort, immediate cover and Home Fleet back-up, of 2 battleships, one aircraft carrier, 5 cruisers, 9 destroyers, 2 anti-aircraft ships, 13 submarines and 11 smaller craft. The Home Fleet could not be committed to the passage east from Bear Island and, as a result of a threatened German attack by a heavy naval force, the convoy was ordered to scatter when just to the east of Spitsbergen. The naval escort withdrew westwards, expecting to engage the German surface vessels, but, with the convoy scattered, the German forces could rely on aircraft and U-boats to hunt down the individual vessels. In all, 23 merchant ships were sunk and only 11 eventually reached Russia.

Reluctantly, Churchill accepted the naval advice that there was no realistic possibility that future convoys during the summer months would fare any better and informed Stalin that the next convoy could not be run, but that if suitable arrangements could be devised, the system would be restarted. The response was a sharp and unfriendly message[44] on 23 July in which Stalin spoke in terms of fulfilment of 'contracted obligations'. He did not, however, make much of the issue when he met Churchill in Moscow in August. A further convoy sailed in September with the loss of 12 out of 39 ships to a heavy air attack in which 24 German aircraft were destroyed. A total of 77 warships were, however, employed in this operation and the demand for naval forces to support the North African landings later in the year was such that further convoys had to be suspended until December, when an attack by a German force led by a pocket-battleship, a heavy cruiser and supporting forces was beaten off with the loss of only one merchant ship and one destroyer. In the summer of 1943, the Arctic convoys were again suspended, but before their resumption in the autumn a new controversy arose over the severe restrictions imposed by the Soviet authorities upon the small British group of service personnel stationed in Murmansk. There were problems over the use of radio equipment, over mail deliveries and over the refusal of entry visas for replacements. No one was permitted to land from a British naval or merchant vessel except by a Soviet boat in the presence of a Soviet official and, on top of other minor restrictions, permission to establish a small British medical unit to care for the casualties was refused. After other representations had proved ineffective, Churchill took up the difficulties with Stalin, asking that they might be 'smoothed out in a friendly spirit'.[45] In notifying the planned resumption, he made the point that this was 'no contract or bargain'. This caught Stalin on the raw and in his reply[46] he referred to 'a refusal of the British Government to fulfil the obligations it undertook', stated that it would be 'inadmissible to have the supplies of the Soviet armies depend on the arbitrary judgement of the British side', described the British complaints as inaccurate and made various allegations about the behaviour of the British forces. Churchill found the reply so offensive that he personally gave it back to the Soviet Ambassador. The problems were eventually resolved by Eden in discussion with Stalin and Molotov when he was in Moscow for the Foreign Ministers' Conference in October and, with Soviet expressions of appreciation, the convoys were duly resumed and ran until the end of the war.

By the time hostilities ceased, Britain had supplied over 5000 tanks and 7000 aircraft (including some of Canadian and American origin), while the United States had supplied over 7000 tanks and nearly 15 000 aircraft.[47] (By way of comparison, the operational strength of the German air force at its peak was estimated at about 6000 aircraft.) Deliveries by the Arctic route accounted in fact for the smaller part of the total supplies and it has been argued that a greater concentration upon the Persian route might have produced a better outcome at lower cost in ships and lives. Out of a total of 811 ships in the 40 Arctic convoys, 98 were lost from various causes. In terms of the goods carried, the loss rate of 15 per cent for the period to April 1944 and $7^1/_2$ per cent for the whole war compared with only 0.7 per cent on the Atlantic convoys.[48]

The bald figures, striking though they are, cannot convey the full significance of this remarkable operation, demonstrating at one and the same time the best and worst aspects of the wartime relationship. The intergovernmental exchanges illustrated only too clearly the classic problems of British–Soviet cooperation and the deep difference of approach. As with the controversy over the opening of the second front, the Soviet Union made it a matter of national pride to regard British help as a contractual obligation and having done so, left the British Government to regret having embodied a goodwill gesture in a formal document. Even at a time when the two countries were allied in a common struggle for survival and the British individuals concerned were suffering in the common cause, the rigidity of Soviet bureaucracy could not be eased, nor could normal considerations of humanity be made to prevail without the personal intervention of the Prime Minister. A seaman might survive for no more than two minutes in the Arctic waters, but such was the suffering of the Soviet armies that the conditions counted for little. In an operation which at the personal level required courage of a singular order and a remarkable devotion to a common cause, trust and confidence were sadly lacking at the governmental level. Perhaps it could not have been otherwise.

Planning for victory and peace

We have seen how the problems of the Western frontiers of the Soviet Union were raised during the early months of the Alliance and how any commitment in this respect was excluded from the Anglo–Soviet Treaty. A crucial issue was the future of Poland. Neither the politicians nor the public in Britain forgot that it was for Poland that war had been declared and Poland's future remained the subject of British–Soviet discussion throughout most of the war, the tone and tempo of the discussion reflecting both the progress of military operations and the emotional impact of such climactic events as the Katyn massacre and the Warsaw uprising, as well as the death of General Sikorski. On the wider issues of post-war planning, a first abortive attempt to initiate informal talks was made by Clark Kerr in February 1942, but he was rebuffed personally by Stalin, who made it clear that the Soviet Union was not interested in such talks unless they were designed to lead to a binding agreement. Planning went ahead within the Foreign Office, but it was not until the summer of 1943, when Mussolini had fallen, the Soviet forces were advancing and the prospect of victory was beginning to be more real, that a substantial and wide-ranging discussion with the Soviet Government was initiated. Churchill had already made the suggestion of a tripartite meeting at Scapa Flow and the suggestion of such a meeting was raised again in a note sent on 7 August, immediately before the Quebec conference,[49] explaining that the President and Prime Minister were to meet with the Chiefs of Staff to review future operations in Europe and the Far East, that the Soviet Government would be kept informed, but that the Prime Minister hoped for a meeting of the three Heads of Government. Eventually agreement was reached on the holding of a Conference of Foreign Ministers in Moscow from 19 to 30 October, to be followed by the Conference of Heads of Government in Teheran from 28 November to 1 December.

The meeting of Foreign Ministers was businesslike and productive, covering not only the pursuit of the war, but the political preparations for victory. Eden had prepared well and succeeded in covering many distinct and substantial problems. The primary Soviet interest was, as we have noted, in the arrangements for the opening of the second front in 1944. There was discussion of the possibility of bringing Turkey and Sweden into the war, of Yugoslavia and of the disposal of the Italian fleet. A formal Declaration (to which China adhered) was agreed on the prosecution of the war and the need to establish a 'general international organisation ... for the maintenance of international peace and security'. There was agreement on the establishment of the European Advisory Commission, the body of British, American and Soviet officials which was to draw up the zones of occupation and the plans for the administration of a defeated Germany, and also on measures for the re-establishment of democracy in Italy, the independence of Austria and the punishment of war criminals. The Soviet Government was not ready for substantive discussion of the treatment of Germany and blocked two of Eden's desiderata, a declaration on the disclaiming of 'separate areas of responsibility' and on the formation of 'associations' of the smaller countries of Europe. (The Foreign Office obsession with the idea of establishing federations in Eastern Europe formed one of the more engaging oddities in British foreign policy from the 1930s onwards. The theory of a stable buffer between Germany and Russia had obvious attraction, but it is difficult to see how a federation of small states would have been capable even of surviving its internal tensions, let alone resisting determined pressure from East or West.) The Conference was, however, generally regarded as something of a personal triumph for Eden. He was well received by Stalin, even Molotov was in a good mood and it seemed that the Soviet representatives at last wanted to establish relations on a footing of permanent friendship. Vyshinsky spoke of it as opening 'a new and happy chapter'.[50]

The road to military victory, to the post-war political structure of Europe and to the international framework within which it should be set was plotted, albeit with varying degrees of clarity and effectiveness, at the three great tripartite conferences, Teheran in November 1943, Yalta in February 1945 and Potsdam in July 1945. For an analysis of the objectives of the participants, the conduct of the conferences and the consequence of the decisions reached, the reader must turn to more specialised studies. We examine them here as a pivotal point in the development of the British–Soviet relationship and do so from two broad aspects: as establishing the international structure within which the British–Soviet relationship in the post-war world would have to be developed; and as determining certain enduring elements in that relationship, in particular the twin problems of the independence of Poland and the mutual relationship with Germany.

Teheran – 'Friends in fact, in spirit and in purpose'

The Teheran Conference, following closely on the preparatory meeting of Foreign Ministers in Moscow, ran from 28 November to 1 December 1943 and was the first meeting of the three Heads of Government, Stalin, Roosevelt and Churchill. By this time the German armies had been ejected from Africa and were in retreat along the whole of the front from west of Moscow to the Black Sea. The Soviet Union could plan with some confidence to move within a matter of months into Poland and the Baltic States, while Britain and the United States could at last plan a similar timing for their re-entry in force into France. The primary purpose of the conference was the coordination of these military arrangements and there began to be some sense of common strategic purpose, if not of detailed coordination. It was confirmed that the landings in northern France should take place in May 1944, that they should be accompanied by a landing in southern France and that a Soviet offensive should be timed so as to prevent the transfer of German forces from East to West. On the main strategic issues, there was little division of opinion, but on the possible use of a part of the forces already in the Mediterranean theatre to open up the Aegean, bring Turkey into the war and link up with the southern flank of the Soviet forces, Churchill had to concede in the face of American opposition. It was, however, agreed that action should be taken to try to bring Turkey into the war on the side of the Allies. Despite the marked change in the military prospects of the Allies, the strategic discussion still turned almost wholly on the future deployment of British and American forces. To a certain extent this reflected the greater range of options open to them by comparison with the more concentrated Soviet objective which limited the Soviet commitments to the timing of the Eastern offensive to coincide with the landings in France and a possible declaration of war on Bulgaria.

While the military discussions at Teheran led to formal conclusions, the political did not. There was only very preliminary discussion of the treatment of Germany, but Poland was a more immediate issue. It had been the subject of many bilateral exchanges between Britain and the Soviet Union. Now it was dealt with in formal tripartite conference and, largely at Churchill's instigation, the question of Poland's frontiers was discussed in some detail. Churchill's objective was, he said, a 'strong and independent Poland friendly to Russia'. Britain had given no commitment to the restoration of Poland's 1939 frontier and the outcome at Teheran was a broad measure of agreement on the proposition that the eastern frontier should be based generally upon the Curzon Line, while the western should be that of the Oder. Much was left open, including the southern extension of the Oder Line and the treatment of Lvov, but Churchill certainly committed himself to the general proposition and remarked that he 'was not going to make a great squawk about Lvov'. He made it clear that he had no mandate to take formal decisions, but indicated that he would recommend the outcome to the Poles. So, in effect, was decided the future shape of Poland (see Map 3, p. 76). So far as the re-establishment of relations between Poland and the Soviet Union was concerned, the future controversy was clearly indicated in the Soviet objection to dealings with the London-based Polish Government in exile.[51]

The conference was used as the occasion for the presentation by Churchill to Stalin of the Sword of Honour given by King George VI in token of 'the homage of the British people to the steel-hearted citizens of Stalingrad'. The gesture was well received and helped to cement the personal relationship with Stalin which Churchill was beginning to enjoy and which was, without doubt, a key element in the intergovernmental relationship. In his memoirs, he noted: 'It would not have been right at Teheran for the Western democracies to found their plans upon suspicions of the Russian attitude in the hour of triumph.'[52] For each of the leaders, the conference seemed a success. There was, indeed, every reason why it should be. It took place at the point when thoughts could be turned to victory, when the strengthening of Soviet confidence lessened the impulse to recrimination, when the natural coincidence of strategic interest made joint planning a real possibility and when the political problems of the post-war world were still below the horizon. In the failure of Churchill's attempt to secure the use of British and American forces in a northward thrust into the Balkans came the first erosion by the United States of the British dominance in the wartime relationship with the Soviet Union, but it was an inevitable reflection of the changing power relationship. There was even a momentary ring of truth about the joint Declaration of 1 December: 'We came here with hope and determination. We leave here friends in fact, in spirit and in purpose.'

It was in the course of 1944, between Teheran and Yalta, that the victories of the Allied armies in West and East combined with the work of the Foreign Ministries of the three great powers to form the first elements of the pattern within which the East–West confrontation of the post-war world was to be played out. The coordinated military strategy agreed at Teheran was largely effective. The Allied landings in France were deferred only from May until early June and the Soviet offensive in the east followed little more than two weeks later. By the beginning of February 1945, as the three leaders met again in Yalta, the Soviet armies had occupied most of Poland and were poised to enter Germany from the east, while the British and American forces, having liberated France, were already inside Germany and preparing for the crossing of the Rhine. The halting of the Soviet offensive outside Warsaw had stirred a major controversy, to which we shall return, and attempts to coordinate Allied bomb-lines on the southern sector of the Eastern front had proved unrewarding. At one critical point, when the German counter-offensive in the Ardennes had posed a major threat to the Western advance, the Soviet winter offensive had been brought forward in order to ease the pressure, but for the most part the operations in East and West had each progressed according to their individual momentum. It was this momentum, coupled with the effect of German defence strategy, rather than detailed inter-Allied coordination, which had brought them more or less simultaneously to the German frontier.

Planning for the peace went ahead swiftly during 1944 and was concentrated on two major topics, on the one hand the arrangements for the occupation and future political structure of Germany, including the problem of reparations; and on the other the establishment of some wider international structure to maintain the peace. The structure of the occupation regime was worked out in the European Advisory Commission which had been agreed at the Conference of Foreign Ministers in Moscow, prior to Teheran. The meetings took place in London and the outcome was largely the work of Strang. Progress was slow, particularly on the part of the Russians, but it was the United States which posed the major problems of substance. The allocation of zones between Britain and the United States and the eventual provision for a French zone caused difficulty and at one point the planners were wondering whether they would be able to reach agreement on the terms of a German surrender before the surrender took place. Eventually both the boundaries and the terms of the occupation were agreed, and the Commission's work, ratified by subsequent quadripartite agreement and consolidated by the accumulation of precedents, established the basis for Allied rights in Berlin, for the eventual frontier between the German Democratic Republic and the Federal Republic of Germany and hence for the East–West frontier through Central Europe.

In parallel with the work of the European Advisory Commission, the second main task of political planning was the creation of a comprehensive international organisation. This, like the work of the European Advisory Commission, stemmed from a British initiative at the meeting of Foreign Ministers in Moscow in October 1943, but subsequent work was more American-oriented. Tripartite conversations were carried out in Washington during the first half of 1944 and led, through the Dumbarton Oaks Conference in August–September of that year to the tripartite decisions at Yalta and the eventual establishment of the United Nations at the San Francisco Conference from April to June 1945. The negotiations were directly relevant to the British–Soviet relationship as it was to develop in the post-war years, in that they established the permanent British membership of the Security Council and thus, in a certain measure, the continuation, albeit less directly, of the great power relationship between the two countries which had existed prior to 1939 and had been at its peak in the wartime conferences. Throughout the negotiations leading up to San Francisco, British–Soviet diplomacy played a full part and the Soviet Union made much of the Commonwealth analogy in its bid for independent representation of its constituent republics.

A third, less obvious aspect of the preparatory work of 1944 must be noted. With the approach of victory over Germany, the British Chiefs of Staff began to consider the military problems of the post-war era. Work was put in hand in the Post-Hostilities Planning Committee. It was accepted that the primary object of British policy must be the preservation of a unity of purpose among the three powers. What concerned the Chiefs of Staff was the risk that this might not be achievable. In that event, they saw the only possible future enemy as the Soviet Union and the only route to British security in the formation of some Western European organisation, with which Germany – or part of it – would need to be associated and for which American support would be important.[53] This line of argument was also advanced by Duff Cooper, at that time British representative with de Gaulle, who recommended to Eden in May 1944 that, rather than relying solely on the new World Organisation, Britain would need to seek a system of Western European alliances as a protection against Russian domination of Europe. Western European unity was in line with Foreign Office thinking, but a military alliance against the Soviet Union was not. Pursuit of the Chiefs of Staff line might, in their view, create the very danger it was intended to avoid. Eden regarded the Chiefs of Staff's paper as 'terrible' and Duff Cooper was told that any West European system would need to be based squarely on the Anglo–Soviet alliance: 'A Western group organised as a defensive measure against the possibility of Russia embarking at some future date on a policy of aggression and domination would be a most dangerous experiment which might well precipitate the evils against which it was intended to guard.'[54]

Churchill's own concern at this time was beginning to be directed not so much at the possible organisation of post-war alliances, but rather more at what he described as 'the upsurge of Communist influence which slid on before, as well as followed' the westward movement of the Soviet forces.[55] He was deeply moved by the ordeal of the Polish population in the struggle to liberate Warsaw. In view of the position of Poland in the British–Soviet relationship the facts merit a brief restatement. In the last week of July, the German forces in Poland were hard pressed. The Soviet forces were ten miles from Warsaw and on 29 July Moscow Radio broadcast an appeal from the Polish Communists urging the people of Warsaw to begin 'direct, active struggle in the streets'. Then, faced with a difficult crossing of the Vistula, the Red Army halted at the outskirts of the city for some six weeks, while, with appalling violence, the German forces destroyed much of the city and people of Warsaw. After first offering to supply arms themselves to the Polish Home Army in Warsaw, the Soviet Government refused permission for British or American aircraft to land on Soviet airfields after supply drops (thereby reducing the effectiveness of the operation and adding to the Allied losses) and Stalin informed Churchill that 'the Soviet command must dissociate itself from the Warsaw adventure'.[56] Ministers considered hard whether a further effort could be made to drop supplies, but an accurate drop required a low-level approach across German positions and losses in the first attempts had been high. On 11 September, the War Cabinet endorsed the opinion of the Air Staff that 'a large-scale operation to assist the Poles in Warsaw would be militarily unjustifiable'. Shortly afterwards the Soviet forces gave some assistance to the Poles and permitted American landings at Soviet airfields, but by then it was too late.[57] On 25 September Stalin told Clark Kerr that 'all idea of a frontal attack had been given up'.[58] On 2 October the Polish forces surrendered.

It is not easy to assess Soviet policy. The difficulty of the Vistula crossing and the immovability of the Soviet bureaucracy in its dealings with the Western powers were real factors, but it is hard to resist the conclusion that underlying it all was the calculation that, with the destruction of the Polish Home Army in Warsaw, the subsequent control of the country by the Moscow Lublin Committee would be substantially facilitated. In 1944, Polish–Soviet relations had not recovered from the shock of the murder of some 6000 Polish officers and men at Katyn. The fate of the Poles who were deported, many of them to Siberia, when the Soviet Union seized eastern Poland in 1939 is a story deserving fuller treatment than it can be given here. It must suffice to note that among the total, believed to be close to 2 million, were some 60 000 who, with 30 000 women and children, were allowed to leave the Soviet Union in 1942 and fight with the Allied forces. (Did Stalin perhaps have recollections of the Czechs in Siberia in 1918?) Some 13 000 officers remained unaccounted for, and when the discovery of mass graves at Katyn was announced by Germany in 1943, it was generally accepted in London that the Soviet Union was responsible.[59] At that time, the British Government, concerned primarily with the pursuit of the war and the avoidance of a rift between Poland and the Soviet Union, had not forced the issue and in its short-term impact on British–Soviet relations it was soon overtaken by Churchill's successful visit to Moscow. Against the long history of Polish–Russian conflict, however, and on top of the shock of the Katyn massacre, the emotional effect of the Warsaw tragedy was to bring a new depth of bitterness into Polish–Soviet relations and, in the longer run, to heighten British awareness of the policies and methods of the Soviet leadership in the Stalin era.

With the advance of the Soviet forces into Poland, the problem of the country's political future was urgent. Was control to lie with the Polish Government in exile in London or with the Soviet-sponsored Lublin Committee? The need to resolve this issue was to the fore when Churchill proposed his second bilateral meeting with Stalin in Moscow in October 1944.[60] He was also concerned more generally with the position in Eastern Europe and with the problem of voting in the World Organisation which had not been resolved at Dumbarton Oaks. At his first meeting with Stalin on 9 October Churchill scribbled out the celebrated list of percentages:

Romania
  Russia 90 Others 10
Greece
  Great Britain (in accord with USA) 90
  Russia 10
Yugoslavia 50–50
Hungary 50–50
Bulgaria
  Russia 75 Others 25

As Churchill explained the percentages afterwards to his colleagues, they were not intended to define rigid spheres of interest, but were an indication of the relative 'interest and sentiment' of the British and Soviet Governments. So the paper, with Stalin's tick on it, was left with Churchill. There was a full discussion of military planning, in which, for the first time, the Russians gave valuable indications of their further operations against Germany. Political discussions ranged from the future of Germany and Austria, to revision of the Montreux Convention and the entry of the Soviet Union into the war against Japan. On the central issue of the future of Poland, for which delegations from the London and Lublin Poles were present, little progress was made, but at least the principle of a merged administration seemed to be accepted. Churchill was, by the end, left with the feeling that he had got closer to his Soviet ally than ever before. He could scarcely have thought, as he left Moscow, looking forward to the tripartite summit at Yalta, that almost fifteen years were to elapse before a British Prime Minister again visited Moscow.

Yalta – 'Their word is their bond'

The hopes entertained by Churchill in Moscow as regards the future Government of Poland were quickly proved vain. Correspondence, primarily between Roosevelt and Stalin, was acrimonious. Stalin accused the London-based Poles of undertaking 'terroristic actions creating a threat of civil war in the rear of the Red Army' and on 31 December 1944[61] the Lublin Committee was recognised by the Soviet Union as the Government of Poland. It was against this background that Churchill went to Yalta to 'talk all these matters over, not only as isolated problems, but in relation to the whole world situation both of the war and the transition to peace'.

The tripartite meeting was preceded by a meeting between Churchill and Roosevelt at Malta. It is perhaps not irrelevant to the subsequent course of relations that the very natural process of close and continuous British–American consultation throughout the war, vital though it was, must to some extent have increased the Soviet Union's feeling of isolation and heightened their already extreme sensitivity. We may also, however, well note the remark by Sir Llewellyn Woodward[62] that, at Malta, 'The President and his entourage continued to assume that, unlike Great Britain, Russia was not an "imperialist" Power.' The temptation to seek an American–Soviet understanding at British expense was not wholly absent during the tripartite discussions.

The Yalta Conference itself ran from 4 to 11 February 1945. Much has been written about its significance in determining the structure of post-war Europe. In reality, however, that structure was already largely determined by the progress of military operations, which, as we have noted earlier, had brought the British, American and Soviet forces, by

Map 4   European battlefronts, January–May 1945

the time of the Conference to the borders of Germany both in the East and the West (see Map 4). In so far as the Soviet military grip on Eastern Europe was in large measure established, it could not realistically be challenged. The fate of Poland was sealed. Militarily, central Europe remained open, but the work of the European Advisory Commission had effectively pre-determined the area of Soviet control in Germany. Considering these facts, the Declaration on Liberated Europe agreed at Yalta,[63] with its commitment to representative interim governments and free elections and its operational clause providing only for consultation, could represent little more than a pious aspiration. The future of Poland played a major part in the proceedings of the Conference and agreement was eventually reached that the existing Provisional Government should be 'reorganised on a broader democratic basis, with the inclusion of democratic leaders from Poland itself and from Poles abroad'. The reorganisation was to be the subject of consultation between Molotov and the British and American Ambassadors in Moscow and, after a new Government had been formed, elections were to be held. The three Governments would then recognise the new Polish Government of National Unity. The eastern frontier of Poland was agreed broadly on the basis of the Curzon Line, but the western boundary was left for decision at the Peace Conference because of the difference of view as to whether it should, in the south, be based on the eastern or western branch of the Neisse River. In verbal terms, the compromise settlement was not unreasonable. In real terms, it did not and could not significantly change the Soviet plan for the establishment in Poland of a subservient satellite regime.

On the wider front, there was satisfaction that it had been possible to reach agreement on the future World Organisation. Churchill felt that Stalin had been helpful over Greece and Stalin accepted his pleas for French participation in the occupation of Germany. There was also agreement in principle on the need for the eventual dismemberment of Germany, but on this and other matters such as reparations it was recognised that further discussion would be necessary.

One of the matters dealt with at Yalta was the repatriation of those citizens of the three powers who had been liberated during the advance from West and East. The British Government was greatly concerned to secure the swift repatriation of British prisoners-of-war from camps in Poland and eastern Germany and had not been disposed, in preliminary negotiation in Moscow, to complicate matters by seeking to distinguish between Soviet prisoners-of-war and deported civilians or to deal separately with those Soviet citizens wearing German uniform. Controversy has subsequently raged over this issue, but at the time it seemed clear to the British Government that, as the Allied armies moved into the debris of Europe, a general return home was the only feasible solution. The administrative difficulties were substantial, but despite some division of opinion in the United States, tripartite agreement on the principles governing the repatriation arrangement was reached with no difficulty at Yalta. It was this repatriation which provided me with my first contact with the Soviet forces. On a British troop-ship, the *Staffordshire*, we picked up the Russians from Liverpool, Marseilles and Naples and took them back to Odessa. They came on board dirty and squalid, mostly in American uniforms, indistinguishable in rank or status. Some had tried to commit suicide. The others were wild with joy at the prospect of returning home. With the help of one young officer from the Soviet Military Mission we changed them from a rabble to a tidy and disciplined body of troops who disembarked in Odessa to the welcome of a military band. We never discovered what they had done. Nor could we be certain of their fate. We could only suspect that it was cruel. But at my humble level, the balance of moral and practical considerations did not seem very different from the way it did to Eden. It was a brief lesson, but it left impressions of the frightening and erratic power of the system represented by that young officer as well as the strange mixture of warmth and brutality in the Russian character. It was already apparent that accommodation to the reality of Soviet power would be the dominant problem for post-war Europe. I remember feeling uneasy at the prospect. But it made me want to see more of the country and its people.[64]

By the time of Yalta, the US Government was beginning to be increasingly concerned about the need for Soviet entry into the war against Japan and a bilateral US–Soviet agreement was reached on this point. In relation to the future of Europe, the full impact of Roosevelt's announcement that American troops would not stay in Europe for more than two years after the end of the war was slow to develop, but it cannot have been lost on the Russians. In Britain there was anxiety about the future, and, in presenting the results of Yalta to Parliament[65] Churchill warned of the danger of 'some awful schism' with the Soviet Union. However, he declined 'absolutely to embark on a discussion about Russian good faith'. 'Their word is their bond', he said. He knew of 'no Government which stands to its obligations, even in its own despite, more solidly than the Russian Soviet Government'. So far as the future of Poland was concerned, Churchill's public expression of confidence was not shared by the twenty-five Members of Parliament who, led by a group of Conservatives, voted for an amendment to the motion of confidence on the outcome of the Conference.

'An Iron Curtain is drawn down'

There is a sorry symmetry to the role of Poland in British–Soviet relations at the outbreak of the war and at its end. In the summer of 1939 the Soviet Union had chosen partition of Poland by agreement with Germany in preference to defence of Poland in alliance with Britain and France. As the war was approaching its victorious conclusion in the spring of 1945, it was the fate of Poland which, following the Soviet disregard of the Declaration on Liberated Europe and the installation of pro-Soviet regimes in Hungary and Romania, symbolised the disintegration of the alliance. Within weeks of the end of the Yalta Conference, it became clear to the British Government that the Soviet interpretation of the agreement on Poland was very different from that which might have been expected. Having already precipitated a substantial crisis within his own party by placing his faith in Soviet implementation of the agreement, Churchill was the more determined to ensure it. He saw the fate of Poland as the crucial test of Soviet willingness to cooperate in the wider problems of the post-war settlement. In that test, the central element was the setting up of a representative Polish Government which Britain and the United States could recognise. As he put it to Roosevelt on 13 March: 'Poland has lost her frontier. Is she now to lose her freedom?' Failure, in his view, would represent an utter breakdown of what had been agreed at Yalta.[66]

The arrest and trial of members of the Polish Home Army by the Soviet authorities augured ill and the negotiations between Molotov and the British and American Ambassadors in Moscow on reconstruction of the Lublin Government proved fruitless. The Allied relationship with the Soviet Union was souring quickly. There had been intense Soviet suspicion that the Western powers might conclude a separate peace and sharp exchanges took place over Soviet charges of British and American bad faith in relation to Soviet participation in possible surrender negotiations by the German forces in Italy. There was tension with Yugoslavia over Trieste and the communisation of Eastern Europe was proceeding swiftly. Some thought was given to the possibility that bargaining leverage might be secured if Berlin, Prague and Vienna were to be reached first by British or American forces, but even if this had proved militarily possible – as, in the case of Prague, it almost certainly was – there was no American enthusiasm for it. It was plain that, in practical terms, Britain had little more chance of securing the independence of Poland in 1945 than in 1939. By 29 April Churchill was warning Stalin of a future in which the English-speaking nations and their associates might be drawn up against the Communist states in a quarrel which would 'tear the world to pieces'.[67] Stalin was unmoved. Some progress was made as a result of a visit to Moscow by the American emissary, Harry Hopkins, and a new Polish government, including Polish representatives from London, was eventually recognised by Britain and the United States on 5 June. Mikolajčik placed some reliance on the ability of the Polish people to determine their future through free elections in accordance with the Declaration on Liberated Europe, but the Western powers had effectively recognised a Soviet *fait accompli*.

The danger of Soviet domination of Europe was heightened in Churchill's mind by the probability that, with the end of the war in Europe at midnight on 8 May, there would be a swift withdrawal of American forces. On 12 May, he telegraphed to Truman[68] that an 'iron curtain' had been drawn across the Soviet front and that it would be open to the Russians to advance to the North Sea and the Atlantic. It was vital, he urged, to come to an understanding with the Soviet Union before the British and American armies were weakened and before the withdrawal of those forces which, when hostilities ended, were in occupation of substantial areas – up to 100 miles in depth – to the east of the agreed border of the Western occupation zones.

In an attempt to secure such an understanding, the last of the great tripartite conferences was arranged at Potsdam. Before it could take place, there was, however, an incident which revealed graphically the change in the relationship with the United States after the death of Roosevelt. Churchill was, to his astonishment, told of an American proposal that Truman, who, since becoming President had not met either Stalin or Churchill, might meet Stalin bilaterally somewhere in Europe prior to a tripartite meeting. This proposal probably stemmed from Truman's natural and sensible desire to make his own private assessment of Stalin, before embarking on the main conference. It may also have reflected an American feeling that the sharp deterioration in relations with the Soviet Union was an essentially European phenomenon in which Churchill, reverting to his long-standing hostility to the Soviet regime, was aggravating the tensions and perhaps prejudicing the attainment of American objectives in relation to the pursuit of the war against Japan and the subsequent organisation of the post-war world. At this point in history, the potential problems of the projection of a new Soviet power onto the international scene were less vivid in the perception of many Americans than the colonial issues represented by British imperial power. The trend of American opinion was well illustrated by a telegram from Lord Halifax, Ambassador in Washington, to Churchill, shortly before the opening of the Conference. Halifax spoke of American unresponsiveness to pleas about the risk of the spread of Communism and of nervousness at his portrayal of the clash of Soviet and Western influence on Europe. He saw the United States as 'half expecting to play, or at any rate to represent themselves as playing, a moderating role between ourselves and the Russians'.[69] An American–Soviet meeting would have represented a staggering reversal of the tradition of prior bilateral British–American consultation. Churchill had already made it plain that, on this basis, there would be no tripartite meeting. He would not agree to British participation in any meeting except 'as equal partners from its opening'.[70] The proposal was dropped, but it had been a clear reflection of those realities of power which were to complicate the handling of the British–Soviet relationship in the early post-war years.

Potsdam

The date of 15 July for the opening of the Berlin, or, as it is more commonly known, the Potsdam Conference, was established by correspondence between Truman and Stalin. It fell oddly in relation to the British General Election which was to take place on 5 July, in that the delay in receiving postal votes from the forces overseas meant that the result would not be declared until 26 July. Churchill sought to bring the date forward, hoping that this might make it possible to hold the conference before the withdrawal of British and American forces to the agreed occupation zone border. In this he failed. The US Government insisted on prior withdrawal to the lines established by the European Advisory Commission and a potential bargaining counter – albeit of very doubtful utility or applicability – was given up.

The British view of the political scene at the time of Potsdam was well illustrated by a Foreign Office memorandum by Sargent, 'Stock-taking after VE Day',[71] an attempt to assess Britain's international position in the post-war years. There had been some evolution of policy since the controversy over the report of the Post-Hostilities Planning Committee. The objective of three-power cooperation was still central to British foreign policy, but it had to be pursued in the context of a divided Europe, in which Britain would need by its diplomacy to compensate for its lack of material power. On the question of Soviet long-term objectives, Sargent was cautious, but realistic. Stalin's obsession with security and his fear of Germany were recognised. It was assumed that he did not want and could not afford another war in Europe and that his objective was the consolidation of Soviet power in Eastern Europe rather than further territorial expansion. In a contest for influence in Europe between Britain and the Soviet Union, Britain would need the support of the United States, but there was a risk that the United States would prefer the 'less arduous role' of mediator and that the two supreme world powers might be content to arrange matters between themselves, a 'misconception' which Britain would need to combat. Britain, he argued, should not be afraid of an independent, anti-totalitarian policy and should be ready to take the lead in challenging Communist penetration in Eastern Europe. It might have to be accepted in Romania and Hungary, but in Finland, Poland, Czechoslovakia, Austria, Yugoslavia and Bulgaria the challenge could be realistic.

The agenda for the Conference reflected the major issues on which the contest would turn: the future of Germany; policy towards Italy; the application of the Declaration on Liberated Europe with particular reference to Poland; and the peace settlement with Germany's former East European satellites. Japan had not yet been defeated and it was only after the conference opened that the news was received of the successful test of the atomic bomb. With Germany defeated, this was, in Churchill's terms, the final opportunity to come to an understanding with the Soviet Union on the future of Europe. On 10 July Eden sent the Prime Minister a note[72] on 'what cards we hold for a general negotiation with the Russians, in the shape of things which the Russians want from us and which it is in our power to give or withhold'. The list covered credits (which would have to be American), German industrial equipment, the Italian fleet, modification of the regime in the Straits, participation in the regime for Tangier and recognition of the Soviet acquisition of the Baltic States. There was little in this list to encourage expectations that the Soviet Union could be persuaded to relax its grip on Central and Eastern Europe. Eden remarked that he found 'the world outlook gloomy and signs of Russian penetration everywhere'.[73]

In its outcome,[74] the Conference did not substantially affect the British perception of the relationship with the Soviet Union. Churchill's own performance was disappointing. Much of his time was taken up with discussion of the Polish question, in particular the Polish–German border. Eden found him under the spell of Stalin, having failed to read his briefs, 'confused and woolly and verbose', while Cadogan said he 'talks the most irrelevant rubbish and risks giving away our case at every point'.[75] He left for Britain on 25 July and, after the Labour victory in the General Election, Clement Attlee returned as Prime Minister, with Bevin as his Foreign Secretary for the final days from 28 July to 1 August.

This was the first occasion since Ramsay MacDonald had appointed the first British Ambassador to Moscow at the end of 1929 that Labour had had the opportunity to conduct relations with the Soviet Union. During the election campaign, they had made a certain amount of play with the argument that Left could talk to Left. In practice, however, the change made little difference to the outcome of Potsdam. As Deputy Prime Minister, Attlee had been fully associated with the handling of relations during the war and had accompanied Churchill for the first part of the Conference itself. Bevin could draw not only on his Cabinet experience, but on his knowledge of Soviet policy towards British Labour during the 1920s and 1930s. Neither had any illusions about the nature of the problems they faced. They had no wish to offer a new challenge to the Soviet Union, but there was little room for constructive initiative on any of the major issues and they were in no mood to concede. Like Churchill, they had to devote most of their time to Poland. The reality had to be accepted that the German territory lying east of the line of the Oder and the Western Neisse had been handed over by the Soviet Union to a Polish Government which the Western powers had already been forced to recognise. Bevin was, however, determined to extract what price he could for the territorial concession by making it part of a larger package and securing concessions from the Poles in respect of the holding of elections. In this he had some success. He succeeded from the outset in making his personality felt, but he could have little confidence in the value of the assurances he received.

With the principles of the occupation regime for Germany already settled, discussion at Potsdam turned largely on economic questions, in part those flowing from the Soviet demand for reparations and in part the problem of feeding the industrial areas of the Western zones, in particular that occupied by the British. Here were visible some of the problems which were eventually to precipitate the economic reform of the Western zones and the Berlin blockade, but that still lay far in the future. In terms of the conduct of British–Soviet relations during the immediate post-war years, the Conference took a key decision by establishing the Council of Foreign Ministers, with its Secretariat in London. By doing so, it had provided a machinery through which, if the will existed, the powers of the wartime alliance might shape the peace and through which the British Government might try to work out its relationship with the Soviet Union. On his return from Potsdam, Attlee reported to his colleagues, paying a warm tribute to Bevin and commenting that 'on the whole we could be very well satisfied' with the outcome.[76]

The experience of alliance

With the Potsdam Conference, the wartime partnership between Britain and the Soviet Union had, in just over four years, run its course. Immediately beset by the internal and external problems of adjustment to the post-war world, Attlee had little time for reflection on the quite remarkable experience which it represented. From time to time during the Soviet era the alliance was recalled with nostalgia as an illustration of the possibility of cooperation in a common cause. Today's circumstances are happily very different, but it may still be appropriate briefly to examine the nature of the wartime relationship.

Governments, no matter by what ideology they are guided or to what external and internal pressures they are subject, are composed of individuals. The alliance was what it was made by the politicians, the diplomats, the bureaucrats, the members of the armed forces – all those individuals in whose hands rested the actual conduct of relations. Singly and collectively, in Britain and in the Soviet Union, it was they who, guided by their instinct, their training, their emotion and their experience would determine whether the alliance would amount to more than a greeting between two vessels whose courses briefly coincided. For all of them, personal experience and historical perception, whether true or false, were a potent factor in shaping their response to the new fact of the alliance. Their comments give a little of the flavour of thinking, for which a recital of facts and dates is no substitute.

The fact that in the summer of 1941 German forces crossed the Soviet border could not, of itself, destroy the Soviet recollection of British participation in the intervention or of their ostracism by the pre-war British Conservative Governments. It could not erase two decades of indoctrination about the irreconcilable struggle between the forces of socialism and capitalism. It could not make the British public forget the Stalin purges. The diplomats, the sailors and the soldiers who had conducted the abortive 1939 negotiations still remembered how they had been left to pack their bags while Stalin, Molotov and Ribbentrop raised their champagne glasses in celebration of a new-found friendship.

It is hard to judge from first-hand evidence the evolution of opinion towards Britain in the Soviet Union between 1941 and 1945. Nor, from a British perspective, is it easy to form a valid assessment of such evidence as is available. From the summer of 1941 to the summer of 1944 the German forces were on Soviet soil and the whole people of the Soviet Union were engaged in a struggle to the death to eject them. In such a situation, the only thing which mattered – as it mattered to Lloyd George in the different circumstances of 1917 – was the pursuit of the war, and the only relevance of Britain was in the extent to which she could contribute to that end. The quality of the alliance, in Soviet eyes, was measured in these terms. The practices of Russian bureaucracy, with roots deeper than 1917, could not, as we have seen in the problems at Murmansk, easily be changed. At the official level, the records are filled with accounts of the frustration of the Military Mission in Moscow and the difficulty of securing any useful information about the conduct of Soviet operations. Even when, in preparation for the cross-Channel landings, the Mission sought permission to inspect German beach defences constructed at Odessa, this was refused. When the Foreign Secretary was at Yalta, Sir Alexander Cadogan sent him a briefing telegram[77] in which he stated, 'Russian attitude to our mission in Moscow has been throughout deliberately uncooperative and both before and after D-Day there has been no attempt to work on basis of reciprocity … As a matter of policy, very little information about the Red Army is given and practically no worthwhile information on the course of fighting in progress.'

In February 1943, Clark Kerr devoted the whole of a longish talk with Stalin to a plea that he might be allowed some contact with the country in which he was serving as Ambassador. Reporting his remarks to the Foreign Office,[78] he said that he had pointed out the wide contacts which Maisky enjoyed in London, whereas 'after some ten months in this country, I found myself isolated and friendless. Day in and day out, I saw no-one but my staff … I was allowed to see nothing'. In April he was able to report 'a consciousness that feeling towards us has been taking a kinder shape', perhaps as a result of some Kremlin edict, but the effect did not seem to have percolated very far. In the Foreign Office archives is a bitter letter[79] dated 20

January 1944 from the Moscow correspondent of the *News Chronicle* complaining. 'We are making no progress here getting nearer to the Russians ... The position is becoming stickier, contacts are fewer, obstruction is greater ... They are an impossible crowd to work with, close, secretive, jesuitical and, unless they can use you, indifferent.' There is a sad little story, familiar enough through the decades, of the lady who was rash enough to give Russian lessons to one of the British in Moscow and was last heard of in the Lubyanka. Yet against this can be set examples of warmth and kindness by individual Russians and instances such as the performance in Baku of a remarkable little play celebrating the heroism of the British and Soviet sailors engaged in the Arctic convoys.

In London, Maisky was constantly pleading for British understanding of the Soviet inferiority complex in dealing with Britain. His countrymen, he said, were inexperienced in the conduct of diplomacy and felt themselves 'country cousins'. Clark Kerr had some sympathy. He wrote on 10 August 1943:[80] 'I feel indeed that we are still holding these people at an arm's length. We have not yet let them into the club. They are still scrutinised by the hall porter, stared at by the members and made to feel that they do not really belong, whereas we fall over ourselves to make the Americans feel at home. In a word, we consult Washington and we inform Moscow.'

There must have been much substance to the concern of the two Ambassadors. Yet there were instances of solid practical cooperation, not merely in the pursuit of the war but also in the more contentious task of preparing for the peace. In Britain, many of the responsible officials were those who had experience in dealing with the Soviet Union before the war. Among them, one may single out William Strang who, after his 1939 experience, can have had few illusions. He took the lead in the work of the European Advisory Commission and, although he had cause to complain of Soviet delay, he was cited in the spring of 1944, in a Foreign Office Minute[81] as saying that his Soviet counterparts 'genuinely want to cooperate and in so far as they fail to do so there is little to choose between them and the Americans'. Subsequently, in his memoirs, he wrote of this work: 'Though for eighteen months we relied again and again on unrecorded oral understandings and undertakings never once, so far as I can recollect, was there ever any serious misunderstanding amongst us or any breach of given word.'[82] When one considers how little experience the diplomats of the two countries had had of joint work, either bilaterally or in the work of the League of Nations, the achievements of the Commission and of those concerned with the preparatory work for the United Nations were the more noteworthy.

The most remarkable feature of alliance diplomacy was undoubtedly the series of summit meetings. By 1941, Stalin had been in power for seventeen years. His only contact with a British Minister had been his meeting with Eden in 1935. Between 1941 and 1945 he was to meet Churchill twice in Moscow and three times at the tripartite summits. It has been convenient to chronicle much of the British–Soviet wartime relationship by reference to the voluminous and often acrimonious correspondence between them. There is a risk, in doing so, of underrating the contribution of others, but the wartime relationship was exceptional. The summit correspondence was no mere set of formal exchanges. Churchill was personally responsible for the drafting of many of his messages. In the other direction, it is hard to judge how far Molotov's pen was responsible, but the result is probably a fair reflection both of the personalities of the two men and of the relationship between their two countries.[83] There can be little doubt that Churchill greatly relished the contact; that he tried by every means to use it for the direct exercise of personal diplomacy on major issues; and that he had some success. Eden, however, clearly had doubts about this method of diplomacy. He observed in his memoirs that the summits 'had their merits, though the orderly despatch of business was not one of them' and remarked of Churchill's handling of them: 'The spoils in the diplomatic game do not necessarily go to the man most eager to debate.' Cadogan noted after Teheran that Eden was 'rather in despair about this hazy conference'.[84] By contrast, Eden greatly admired Stalin's tactics at Yalta: 'He never wasted a word. He never stormed, he was seldom even irritated. Hooded, calm, never raising his voice, he avoided the repeated negatives of Molotov ... By more subtle methods he got what he wanted without having seemed so obdurate.'[85]

On other occasions, Stalin deployed the classical alternation of anger and joviality to unsettle his negotiating partners. At the first tense meeting in Moscow in the summer of 1942, when Churchill broke the news of the deferment of the second front, he had to endure a full session of Stalin's bitter reproaches, yet, by the end, he was able to report to his colleagues: 'I feel I have established a personal relationship which will be helpful.'[86] At Teheran, in the autumn of 1943, he noted Stalin's brutality, but also his 'captivating manner when he chooses to use it'. By the spring of 1944, he was thoroughly gloomy about the personal relationship. The mood of Teheran was fading. Cordell Hull had spoken of a possible need for a show-down and

Churchill was inclined to agree. He minuted to Eden:[87] 'Although I have tried in every way to put myself in sympathy with these Communist leaders, I cannot feel the slightest trust or confidence in them. Force and facts are their only realities.' He did not want to go back on the effort to establish a friendly relationship, but felt that 'courteous and even effusive personal approaches' had done no good and that a few months of 'moody silence' would be useful. Foreign Office officials were disposed to attribute Soviet behaviour to 'ignorance and clumsiness' rather than 'ill-will or careful calculation'. Eden was less hopeful. He admitted to 'growing apprehension that Russia has vast aims and that these may include the domination of Eastern Europe and even the Mediterranean and the "communisation" of much that remains', but advised: 'On the whole I would be inclined to let matters drift a little longer before considering a show-down with Stalin.' Yet, six months later, at Churchill's second bilateral meeting in Moscow, there was for the first time a significant supply of military information about Soviet operations against Germany and plans for entry into the war against Japan. Churchill's report spoke of an 'extraordinary atmosphere of goodwill' and 'an atmosphere of friendliness and frankness which is an enormous advance on anything we have known before'.[88] At Yalta, with Roosevelt close to death and Stalin confident of victory, lavish Soviet hospitality contributed to a certain euphoria, which did nothing to further the achievement of British objectives. On balance, whatever the defects of this summitry, it is probable that, without it, the wartime relationship would have been worse, the losses which were sustained through the Soviet control of Eastern Europe would have been no less, and the agreements reached in other areas such as the foundation of the United Nations would have been harder to secure.

Four years of war had shown Britain that where a direct Soviet strategic interest, whether real or perceived, was at stake and where the Soviet Union could, without risk, secure it by force, concession to the spirit of the alliance was not to be expected and verbal understandings were ineffective. The Soviet leaders expected Britain to be equally ruthless in protecting its security interest in Western Europe. Where the issues were in the longer range area of national interest, the normal processes of official diplomacy and the extraordinary processes of summit diplomacy could be effective, but the validity of the result had yet to be tested. The mistrust had been eased only slightly, if at all. The relationship was excessively concentrated at the summit, thin among the diplomats, even thinner among the military. As we shall see, it was, by 1945, possible for Whitehall to appraise Soviet policy with some accuracy. Whether Soviet appreciations were as accurate we cannot say. What is certain is that among the policy-makers on both sides mutual mistrust was still deep and that, on the British side, it was for the first time aggravated by apprehension about Soviet military power. Nevertheless, as the war ended, the popular mood in Britain, largely untempered by the reality of direct contact, was still one of respect for a gallant, if unlovable, ally and readiness to embark on a joint effort to create a safer structure of international society. A policy of open confrontation would have found little support among the electorate in the summer of 1945.[89]

8
Post-war Confrontation

The breach with Russia and the division of Germany

Chapters 5–6 have traced the sequence of events which culminated in the failure of the pre-war Conservative Government to establish an alliance with the Soviet Union against Nazi Germany. Now, after the brief interlude of the wartime alliance, we have to trace the evolving British perception of Soviet policy in the post-war world and the gradual hardening of the response until, ten years after the end of the war, the British–Soviet Treaty of Alliance was formally annulled and Britain and West Germany were allied in defence against the possibility of war with the Soviet Union.

In the summer of 1945 and well into 1946 the British Government still based its policy on the hope of developing a cooperative relationship with the Soviet Union. Later in 1946 and throughout 1947 and 1948 a progressive and almost uninterrupted deterioration in relations marked the descent into that state of political and military confrontation which became known as the Cold War, a term which the Foreign Office reluctantly accepted and proceeded to define as 'a struggle against Stalinist Communism on a world-wide scale not involving a world war'.[1] The early hopes were replaced by a realisation that for many years to come the best that could be expected was that the confrontation with Soviet power and Soviet ideology could be contained without the danger of war or the erosion of essential British interests. The history of the next forty years was the history of that containment.

The policy of 'containment' has acquired a certain doctrinal significance as a result of its advocacy by George Kennan in 1947. He defined it as meaning that the West should 'confront the Russians with

1 The British landing in Vladivostok, 1918. *The Hulton Picture Company.*

2 Propaganda leaflet, 1918–19, with the original florid translation. *The Hulton Picture Company.*

3 Chicherin and Litvinov at Genoa, 1922. *The Hulton Picture Company.*

4 1924 election poster warning John Bull not to let his pockets be emptied by Labour's Bolshevik friends. *The Illustrated London News.*

5 Police raid Soviet Commercial Offices in Moorgate, 22 May 1927. *The Illustrated London News.*

6 Departure of the Soviet Chargé, 1927. *The Hulton Picture Company.*

7 Eden leaves for Moscow, 1935. *The Hulton Picture Company.*

8 Stalin, Molotov and Ribbentrop celebrate signature of Non-Aggression Treaty, August 1939. *Popperfoto*.

9 Stalin, Truman and Churchill at Potsdam, 1945. *Bettmann/The Hulton Picture Library*.

10 A Russian girl sniper in London, 1942. *The Hulton Picture Company.*

11 Hurricanes at Murmansk, January 1942. *Imperial War Museum.*

12 A Ministry of Information wartime poster. *Crown Copyright HMSO/The Public Record Office.*

13 Eden, Bidault and Dulles prepare for the 1954 Berlin Conference. Author second from left at top.

14 Sir Anthony Eden and the Russian leaders Marshal Bulganin and Mr Khrushchev, signing the official communiqué at the Foreign Office, 26 April 1956. *Popperfoto.*

15 Soviet forces in Hungary, November 1956. *The Hulton Picture Company.*

16 Macmillan and Selwyn Lloyd with Khrushchev and Gromyko in Moscow, 21 February 1959. *Popperfoto.*

17 The author and wife in the Moscow Embassy. *Photograph Anne Pringle.*

Foxtrotsky

The farewell for our ambassador leaving Moscow, Sir Curtis Keeble, had Muscovites gaping as the British 'community' danced in evening dress to a jazz band on board the ss Maxim Gorky. It would have disgruntled Stalin, for whose use the ship was built in 1934. The only pity was the captain did not feel able to chug downstream to salute the Union Flag flying on the British Embassy opposite the Kremlin. The palatial establishment was a constant annoyance to Stalin, who tried for years to evict the British from their embankment site.

"All right! Who told the ambassador that it was fancy dress?"

18 Farewell to Moscow.
© *Cartoons International.*

19 While Sir Geoffrey Howe and Mr Eduard Shevardnadze sign a Memorandum of Understanding in Moscow, March 1987, the Prime Minister and the General Secretary continue their discussion. *Novosti/Camera Press.*

20 Mrs Thatcher and Mikhail Gorbachev in St George's Hall in the Kremlin. *Camera Press/TASS.*

21 New British Embassy in Moscow. *Photograph by Peter Cook.*

22 President Yeltsin and Queen Elizabeth II. *GAMMA Presse Images, Bassignac-Benainous.*

23 President Putin of Russia meets Tony Blair. *GAMMA Presse Images, Ian Jones/FSP.*

unalterable counter-force at every point where they show signs of encroaching upon the interests of a peaceful and stable world'. There are those who, ignoring the popular mood of 1945, argue that Kennan's policy was over-cautious and that the West, with its monopoly of the nuclear weapon, could have enforced the liberation of Eastern Europe. Others have argued that, by basing their policies upon an exaggerated fear of Soviet expansion, the British and American Governments created the very danger they had then to overcome. It is only too easy to quibble with Kennan. He himself was not completely happy that his article became a doctrinal text, but he summed it up rather well later as: 'Stand up to them, but not aggressively and give the hand of time a chance to work.'[2] That, by and large is what the post-war British Governments did and I believe they were right. The real world was never a simple Marxist world of socialists and imperialists, nor, irrespective of the tensions created by the 'irreconcilable struggle' of Marxism–Leninism, was it naturally peaceful or stable. We may regret that the United States did not more quickly realise the threat posed by the Soviet Union, but even fewer Europeans would have supported a 'roll-back' policy in 1945 than in 1951. Equally, with the East–West border already on the Elbe, no responsible British statesman could have afforded to gamble British security on Soviet goodwill. My purpose in this chapter is not, however, to argue the doctrine of 'containment'.[3] I use the term merely as a factual description of the policies of successive British Governments as they tried to create a structure of international relations which would withstand the pressure of Communist doctrine and Soviet subversion and would provide a credible defence against the Soviet armed forces, while seeking at the same time to reduce the inherent tension by dialogue with the Soviet Union.

The years 1945–50 saw the framework established within which the East–West confrontation was to be played out over the next thirty years. The diplomatic exchanges with the Soviet Union, for all their sterility, were arguably more significant than the great wartime summits.[4] Throughout the first three critical years, while the nations of Western Europe picked themselves up from the rubble, and opinion in the United States first hesitated and then hardened, the British Government, although handicapped by severe economic constraints, was able very largely to set the tone and the substance of policy towards the Soviet Union. When the Labour Government took office, the wartime alliance had all but run its course. Its fruit had been military victory. The Soviet state which Churchill had hoped to break, which Austen Chamberlain had kept 'as distant as possible' and to which Neville Chamberlain had allowed no voice in the fate of Czechoslovakia, had won its right to play a dominant part in the shaping of the post-war world. It had become, in the opinion of Admiral Leahy, President Truman's Chief of Staff, the 'unquestioned all-powerful influence in Europe'. It had done this by harnessing the total human and economic resources of the state to the attainment of military power. It had done it at the price of 20 million lives and the devastation of large areas of the country. Britain, too, emerged victorious, uninvaded, its national self-confidence enhanced by the recollection of the year during which the British Empire had stood alone against German hegemony. Its loss of life had been only a fraction that of the Soviet Union, but the repair of an economy dependent upon external trade, shipping and finance was in some respects a more complex task than that faced by the Soviet Union. The will to play the full part of a great power was still there, but there was a consciousness of limited means, of resources far inferior to those of the United States, of a need to base foreign policy on cooperation rather than dominion. In parallel with the change in the power ratio was the creation of new machinery, within which the British–Soviet relationship had in large measure to be conducted. The Council of Foreign Ministers was established as the body in which the victorious great powers, together with France and China, would prepare the peace treaties and seek to resolve the immediate problems of the transition from war to peace, while the Security Council of the United Nations would provide for their cooperation in handling the tensions of the post-war world. The peacetime provisions of the Treaty of Alliance were clearly going to be tested in very different conditions from those which governed the pre-war relationship.

Many of the features which were to determine the course of British–Soviet relations throughout the next forty years had already been established by the outcome of the conflict in Europe. In Bulgaria, Hungary, Romania and Poland, the Soviet Union had established a form of government subservient to its own control. British policy had to be based upon recognition that, for better or for worse, Eastern Europe was now an area in which Soviet power would be dominant. In relation to Poland, for whose independence Britain had gone to war, this was a bitter outcome. Of itself, however, it did not constitute a threat to British interests and there was still some room for hope about the way in which that power would be exercised. Elsewhere in Europe, the extent to which the Soviet Union could secure control over

Finland, Czechoslovakia, Austria and Yugoslavia remained to be tested, as did Soviet ability to influence the political scene in Greece, Turkey, Italy and France. Possible Soviet ambitions in terms of the extension of power and influence westwards and southwards in Europe, the Middle East and Central Asia, and the wider policies which the Soviet Union would pursue in the newly established United Nations Organisation (UN) were all a matter of speculation. It was, however, Germany which had once again to be the key to European security and the central issue in British–Soviet relations. Where, in the new Europe, would the power to control its centre reside and how would that power be exercised? For the four powers, Britain, France, the United States and the Soviet Union, this was the issue which underlay the assumption of quadripartite control in Germany.

For its part, the Soviet Union must also have felt the need to test British and American policy. Would Britain adapt to the reality of the new structure of international power in the post-war world? Would she seek, with American help, to restore the old structure of imperial power, to constrain the Soviet Union within its own boundaries, perhaps to challenge its domination of Eastern Europe? Or would the imperialists, under pressure, move aside in order to accommodate the Soviet Union, not merely as dominant in Eastern Europe, but as exercising that role in relation to global policy which the structure of the Security Council envisaged? So far as Britain was concerned, the conclusion must have been that, given the chance, a British Labour Government would still seek to re-establish Churchill's 'old equilibrium'; but that its resources were limited, it could not be sure of American support and, lacking the firm hand of Churchill, it could well be forced to concede positions of power and influence to the Soviet Union. Now, however, it was the United States which, alone among the great powers to end the war with its economy greatly strengthened, constituted the stronghold of imperialist power. Would she assume the responsibilities of leadership, or would her people, as in 1918, prefer to stand aside from Europe's troubles? To Stalin, it must have seemed that, with so much still open, to hold back would be to risk forfeiting the fruit of military victory; to consolidate the gains already made was essential; and to press beyond them was worth trying.

The Soviet mood at that time was a strange mixture of confidence and uncertainty. Victory had given them every reason for confidence in their ability to defeat any conceivable threat based on conventional military force and to play, in the widest international arena, the role of a great power. With the explosion of the atomic bomb, that confidence in military invulnerability was now tinged with doubt and the doubt was aggravated by each indication of a hardening Western policy. It soon became apparent that Britain and the United States were maintaining their claim to world-wide power and influence, extending even to areas of critical importance to Soviet security such as the entry to the Black Sea, while denying to the Soviet Union any comparable influence, for instance in the Mediterranean and in Japan. The Soviet mood was well sensed by Frank Roberts, who was in charge of the Moscow Embassy for much of this period. He sent a telegram to the Foreign Office on 28 September 1945,[5] in which he reported how Stalin had said to visiting US Congressmen that Britain and the Soviet Union had little to give one another, whereas Soviet–American relations were all important. This was more than mere flattery. There can be little doubt that Stalin was on the one hand genuinely reflecting the Soviet assessment of the reality of post-war power and on the other playing to American suspicion that hard-line British policies might precipitate an unnecessary split. Roberts went on to describe the Soviet mood as 'a dangerous mixture of suspicion with a temporarily uncertain sense of power', a combination which made the leadership the more determined to safeguard its own strategic interests and to 'pocket whatever may be going before the general world situation crystallises'. He saw many 'frankly imperialist aspects of Soviet policy', but thought recent Soviet intransigence more a matter of genuine suspicion and advocated a recognition of the respective British and Soviet spheres of influence. Roberts found a surprising ally in Bertrand Russell who wrote in the *Manchester Guardian* on 2 October, arguing that the history of British policy towards Russia 'is not creditable either to our intelligence or to our virtue'; that present difficulties arose out of Soviet imperialism; that appeasement was wrong; but that the right course was to concede the Soviet Union a free hand in Eastern Europe other than Greece and Turkey in exchange for acknowledgement of the British interest in the Mediterranean. For the present, 'we must trust to expedients, hoping that in time the Russian regime may become more liberal and more cooperative' and build up a Western bloc 'not hostile to Russia, not subservient, not susceptible to political penetration by Communist totalitarianism'. The *Manchester Guardian*'s leader writer was somewhat more emollient when he wrote on 20 December of the Soviet Union, 'anxious for the friendship of the two Great Powers, but more than half anticipating their enmity' and arguing the need to 'extend to the Russian ideas and needs the sympathy and respect which we expect for ourselves'.

Having ample advice but little direct evidence of Soviet thinking, the British Government could be guided only by the external manifestations of Soviet policy. It was scarcely to be expected that Soviet diplomacy, in this new and strange set of international relationships moulded by force of arms, would be marked by much subtlety, and indeed it was not. Little enlightenment and no comfort were to be derived from the obduracy with which Molotov handled both procedural and substantive questions in the Council of Foreign Ministers. On the ground, where the Soviet Union held power, that power was exercised ruthlessly in the Soviet interest and it could only be assumed that, given the opportunity elsewhere, Soviet policy would be similar. In consequence, British opinion – and in particular Bevin's opinion – steadily hardened throughout the sequence of frustrating meetings in London from 11 September to 2 October 1945, in Moscow from 16 to 26 December 1945, in Paris from 25 April to 16 May and 15 June to 12 July 1946, in New York from 4 November to 12 December 1946, in Moscow again from 10 March to 24 April 1947, and finally in London from 25 November to 15 December 1947.

The first meeting of the Council was the occasion for an immediate trial of strength with Molotov. Eastern Europe might be a lost cause, but President Truman was not disposed to write it off and, although the US Secretary of State, James Byrnes, vacillated, Bevin sought an independent inquiry into the maintenance of democratic liberties in Bulgaria and Romania. Molotov, in return, challenged the status of France as a party to the peace treaties with the Eastern European countries and staked the Soviet Union's own claim to trusteeship over Tripolitania. The meeting ended in procedural disagreement on the question of entitlement to participation in the preparation and conclusion of the peace treaties. In substance it changed little, but as a first test of the peacetime relationship it was depressing. Soviet tactics had squandered much of the wartime stock of public goodwill in Britain and to the British Government it seemed that the Soviet Union was seeking to develop from its established bridgehead in Eastern Europe a wider thrust of power and influence. Bevin did not, however, wish to aggravate the dispute in public. In his report to Parliament on 9 October, he spoke of 'temporary breakdown', but looked forward to the 'present divergencies' being overcome.[6] As Roberts saw it in Moscow, the Soviet Union had been surprised by the force with which the United States had challenged their position in Eastern Europe, sought to exclude them from the Far East and tried to dilute the three-power monopoly of major policy. He spoke of their need to 'consolidate their position in Eastern Europe before the Anglo-Saxon democratic counter-offensive gathers strength'.[7] It must indeed have appeared to the Soviet Government that Britain and the United States were determined to maintain a global supremacy and deny the Soviet Union its rightful place as a world power.

The next meeting of Foreign Ministers in Moscow in December 1945 was not formally a meeting of the Council. It was held without France and China – the latter did not again participate – and was somewhat more productive in that agreement was reached on various aspects of the peace-making process. In terms of British–Soviet relations, it was noteworthy for a long talk between Bevin and Stalin, in the course of which Bevin suggested a possible extension of the Anglo–Soviet Treaty to fifty years, but also pointed out that there was 'a limit beyond which we could not tolerate continued Soviet infiltration and undermining of our position'.[8] It seemed to Bevin, however, that Byrnes, who had taken the initiative in arranging the meeting, was disposed to curry favour with the Soviet Union at Britain's expense and the mutual irritation was aggravated by the sharp British reaction to the American attempt to use the terms of the UK–US Loan Agreement to break open the Commonwealth trading system.

As Soviet policy developed throughout 1946 and 1947, it appeared to have four major elements which caused concern to the British Government: the consolidation of the Soviet hold on Eastern and Central Europe; the strengthening of the position in Germany; southwards pressure against Turkey and Iran; and a virulent publicity campaign against the Western democracies. In Germany, the early frustration of the attempt to coordinate policy on a quadripartite basis in the Allied Control Council owed more to French than to Soviet intransigence. Soviet policy was directed towards the establishment of Communist control over the political process in eastern Germany, with the ambition that, from this base, a 'Popular Front' type of Government could eventually be established throughout Germany. With this political objective and with the economic objective of securing reparations from the Western Zones, it was to Soviet advantage, while exercising total control in its own Zone, to maintain the principle of a united Germany under quadripartite control. The first substantial political move was made early in 1946 with the forced amalgamation of Communists and Social Democrats in the Soviet Zone to form the Socialist Unity Party on a basis which provided for effective Communist control by Walter Ulbricht.

At the same time, Roberts was reporting from Moscow a series of Soviet pronouncements on the theme of the power of the Soviet

Union, without whom, from Greece to Iceland, no decision could be taken; the mixture of British weakness and hostility; and on the way in which the Labour Government had 'completely taken over the reactionary policy of the Conservatives'. In March 1946, he summed up the scene in a series of three important despatches on the basis of Soviet policy and its implications for Britain. They provide a good summary of the British assessment of the Soviet Union in the early post-war years. Painting a 'sombre picture' of pressure in Europe, the Middle East and the Far East, Roberts saw the Soviet Union seeking to profit from the fluid state of Europe and making a desperate effort to seize advanced positions before the reaction set in. He was impressed by the 'tremendous revival of orthodox Marxist ideology, which left the impression that the Soviet peoples were a chosen people, and that they were surrounded by a hostile world, composed largely of reactionary capitalists and their willing tools in the social democratic movement' and wondered 'whether the world is not now faced with a modern equivalent of the religious wars of the sixteenth century'. Ideologically and economically, the Soviet Union was a closed community, governed by a small handful of men cut off from the outside world, men with a Jesuit-like belief in their own ideology, absolute confidence in their system, suspicious and mistrustful, with no regard for human relationships. They might not now proclaim the doctrine of world revolution, but their aim was to make the Soviet Union the most powerful state in the world, to weaken the capitalist and socialist democratic countries and encourage 'liberation' movements among the 'so-called oppressed colonial peoples'. Yet the friendly Russian people, with their 'streak of laziness, indiscipline and inefficiency', were not the German people, the new Soviet threat was not the pre-war German threat, Soviet objectives did not call for a war of aggression 'except possibly for a limited aim' and issues were not likely to be pressed to the point of serious conflict 'except as a result of the miscalculation of forces'. On British policy, he admitted to finding it 'easier to draw the conclusion that none of the methods adopted over the past thirty years should be repeated than to put forward any very positive or inspiring substitute for them'. His prescription was a mixture of the old and new diplomacy, firmness and politeness, closer contacts and normal trade. 'Be strong, look strong, but strength should not be paraded unnecessarily' and there should be no sabre-rattling. He summed it up as the 'distant realism' which had for three centuries been a not unsuccessful basis of relations with the old Russia.[9]

Roberts' despatches were well received. They coincided in most respects with the thinking of Bevin and his officials. Indeed, they had to some extent been anticipated by the development of opinion in London, and the Foreign Secretary had them circulated to the Cabinet. The situation was, in some respects, not dissimilar to that of the early years after the First World War, when British opinion had been much exercised by the threat of Soviet propaganda in the Empire and the danger of a Communist Germany. Now, however, the doctrinal challenge was backed by Soviet military power.

Within the Foreign Office there was a general recognition of the need to counter the twin elements of Soviet policy, the direct actions of the Government and the indirect use of Communist propaganda. Bevin had no illusions, but he was still inclined towards patience. It was Churchill who, in his speech at Fulton on 5 March 1946, while Roberts was composing his despatches, put into words the new assessment of Soviet policy which ministers and officials were beginning to accept but not yet publicly to enunciate. The Soviet Union, he said, did not desire war: 'What they desire is the fruits of war and the indefinite expansion of their power and doctrine.' He spoke of the Iron Curtain drawn across Europe and called for a special relationship between Britain and the United States, with close defence cooperation. Russia should be welcomed to 'her rightful place among the leading nations of the world' and was entitled to security against Germany, but Russia admired nothing so much as strength. Unity of the western democracies must be the basis for 'a good understanding on all points with Russia'.[10] In substance, the speech was not remarkable, but Churchill spoke with the authority of his unheeded warnings of the Nazi threat and the tone and timing of the speech were well chosen to catch and develop the trend towards a harder policy on both sides of the Atlantic. In Moscow, it was seen by Stalin as an ultimatum to the non-English speaking nations to accept the rule of Britain and the United States.[11] In April, the new mood was marked within the Foreign Office by the re-formation of the Russia Committee, originally constituted in 1918, in order to examine Soviet policy and propaganda throughout the world. In an interesting sidelight on the way British officials still saw the United States playing a secondary role, the Committee was also to examine the 'degree of support to be looked for from the USA' in dealing with the Soviet threat.

It was, however, in relation to Germany rather than to the Soviet Union that there was an acute need to formulate British policy. Britain was in desperate financial straits and its Zone of Germany was proving an impossible economic burden. Thus economic and political considerations began to coincide in forcing the British Government to abandon the reality, while maintaining the form, of quadripartite control and to reply to the communisation of the Soviet Zone with an economic and political reorganisation of the Western Zones. Bevin warned his colleagues[12] that the danger of Russia in Europe was 'certainly as great as and possibly even greater than, that of a revived Germany' but he was still anxious that if there were to be a break the Russians should be seen to be responsible for it. So, while the moves were set in train which resulted in the amalgamation of the British and American Zones and the effective abandonment of Potsdam, a further effort was made to improve relations with the Soviet Union.

In December 1945 Bevin had mentioned to Stalin the possible extension of the Anglo–Soviet Treaty and when, in May 1946, Sir Maurice Peterson succeeded Sir Archibald Clark Kerr as Ambassador in Moscow he brought with him, as six years earlier Cripps had brought Churchill's letter, a goodwill letter from Attlee to Stalin proposing replacement of the wartime treaty by a fifty-year treaty of alliance.[13] In presenting the proposal, Peterson raised various British grievances: the Soviet press showed 'deep underlying hostility' to Britain and there appeared to be a 'certain mistrust' of Bevin personally; British trade with countries in the Danube basin was being frustrated; the Soviet delegation at the Paris Peace Conference was blocking progress; could not the Russians, who knew 'nothing at all' about the Arabs, accept that the Middle East was 'our area'? The British approach was scarcely calculated to produce acceptance of a fifty-year treaty and it did not. Stalin replied point by point and remarked that he saw no good in prolonging the treaty if account were taken of the present British attitude towards the Soviet Union. In public, Bevin was still reluctant to accept that the relationship was now set firmly on a downward course. In the Foreign Affairs debate on 4 June 1946 his tone was described by Churchill as 'sombre and patient'. Reviewing the problems of negotiation with the Soviet Union in Europe and world-wide, his theme was the need to create mutual respect and confidence.[14] The Prime Minister, speaking of the 'iron curtain between minds' took a similar, if scarcely flattering line: 'We have to look upon the Russian people to some extent as people who have been born and lived in a dark forest. They do not seem to understand the sunlight, wind and air of the free democracies. It would be a fatal thing to accentuate in any way this line of division between Eastern and Western Europe because we have to try to get across the barriers and get a mutual understanding. At the same time we have equally to try and understand the Russian mind and Russian history and why they take the line they do.'[15]

The second half of 1946 brought some easing of the outstanding problems with the Soviet Union and progress was made on the conclusion of peace treaties with Italy, Finland, Hungary, Romania and Bulgaria. Much to the surprise of the British Government, the Soviet Union also suddenly agreed to the British request that the Dodecanese should be incorporated into Greece without insisting upon satisfaction of its own claim to Tripolitania. The conclusion can only be that, for the Soviet Union, the one absolute essential was control over the territories lying directly between Germany and its own western frontier. Outside this area, and even on its northern flank, in Finland, objectives could be more flexible. By this time, however, the downward trend in relations with Britain was not easily reversible. The Foreign Office had already begun the preparation of a campaign to counter Soviet propaganda and in January 1947 they revised the 1945 'Stock-taking' memorandum. It was noted that the phase of American non-involvement in what had been thought of as an Anglo–Soviet conflict was apparently over and the United States was 'tending to claim leadership of any forces in the world which were willing to stand up to excessive Soviet pretensions'. It was thought unlikely that the Soviet Union would seek war within the next five years, but it was clearly bent on using Soviet power and the 'fifth column' of a world Communist movement completely subservient to Moscow 'to undermine British and American influence in all parts of the world and where possible to supplant it'. After eighteen months experience, three-power cooperation was now dismissed as unreal.[16] While the Foreign Officer paper was being written, Field Marshal Montgomery was engaged on a visit to the Soviet Union, after which he observed that Russia was immensely acquisitive, but wanted a long period of peace: 'She will watch very carefully that she does not overstep the mark anywhere by careless diplomacy and thus start another war.' During the visit Stalin spoke of the need for a British–Soviet alliance and spoke of the 1942 Treaty being 'suspended in the air' as a result of the formation of the United Nations, to which Bevin responded with confirmation that in the British view Part II, which dealt with post-war relations, remained in force.[17]

By the beginning of 1947, with Kennan's despatches from Moscow commanding increased attention in Washington and George Marshall replacing the vacillating Byrnes as Secretary of State, American policy was turning increasingly towards a more positive effort to contain Soviet expansion. Nevertheless, it was in large measure the British

Government which, through Bevin, determined the next steps in the relationship with the Soviet Union. It did so more from weakness than from strength. The point of decision was policy in relation to Germany and the occasion was the meeting of the Council of Foreign Ministers held in Moscow in March. Bevin's handling of this meeting was conditioned by the realisation that Britain could not afford to sustain its role in relation to Germany unless either the whole country – or, failing that, the Western Zones – could be set on the road to economic recovery. If the Soviet Union were to take reparations from current German production, Britain and the United States would be left to 'feed the German cow in the West while it was milked in the East'. The process of recovery had been started by the fusion of the British and American Zones of Occupation. It now needed to be taken further. If progress were to be quadripartite, there would have to be a revision of the Potsdam arrangements and the Soviet Union would have to accept that the taking of further reparations was subordinated to the need for economic recovery. Otherwise the Western Zones would have to go ahead on their own.[18] He therefore set out requirements for the future handling of reparations and the restoration of effective four-power control over Germany in terms which were likely to prove unacceptable, content that, in the event of failure, responsibility for the breakdown of quadripartite control would rest with the Soviet Union.[19]

The commitment of the United States to a general policy of resistance to Communism was proclaimed by President Truman on 12 March, just after the opening of the Council. Its immediate cause was the need for the United States to take over from Britain the economic burden of support for Greece. The linking of Turkey with this programme was a direct signal to the Soviet Union in relation to access to the Eastern Mediterranean. When, on 5 June, George Marshall made the offer of American aid which set in train the process of Western European recovery, it was Bevin who took the lead in coordinating the European response. Although the offer was formally open to the Soviet Union and the countries of Eastern Europe, it was scarcely conceivable that, in the climate of 1947, a coordinated programme could have been formulated with Soviet participation, and there was little surprise when, on 2 July, Molotov withdrew from the preliminary meeting with Bevin and Bidault. Thus the first formal organisational breach between the two halves of Europe was signalled and a further step was taken towards the division of Germany. Czechoslovakia, having originally indicated acceptance, withdrew. Vyshinsky commented: 'The world is now divided into two camps.'[20]

During these early post-war years, the menace of Soviet military power was a source of unease, rather than a direct and immediate threat to Western Europe. The tightening of the Soviet grip on Eastern Europe had certainly proceeded remorselessly and it was intensified after mid-1947. There was evidence enough that Soviet policy was based firmly on the classic Leninist doctrine of irreconcilable struggle with the capitalist world and incitement to the subversion of the 'old equilibrium'. The creation of the Cominform on 23 September 1947 marked the sharpening of this type of attack and the strength of the French and Italian Communist Parties left no room for complacency. Faced with a firm Western position, the Soviet Union had, however, withdrawn its forces from Iran, and in Greece, where British forces were committed, Soviet involvement was marked by a certain caution. On the whole, outside Eastern Europe, the deterioration in relations stemmed rather more from a well-founded fear of what the Soviet Union might do than from what it actually was doing. The need for Britain to take the lead in the formation of some kind of Western European security grouping had been apparent even before the end of the war, but so long as there was any slender hope of cooperation with the Soviet Union the Foreign Office was reluctant to prejudice this. There was consequently still a lingering uncertainty as to whether the objective of a Western European grouping should be to contain a resurgent Germany, or whether Germany should be associated with it in order that it might contain an expansionist Soviet Union. As the hope of cooperation faded, such qualms as there were about the need for Western European unity soon disappeared. The course was set which was to lead to the establishment of the North Atlantic Treaty and the incorporation of Western Germany within it.

Defence against the Soviet Union could not, however, be secured from a Western European base alone. In 1946 British military planning was much occupied with the control of the Middle East, not only as a source of oil and a key element in imperial communications, but also as a base from which in the event of war a bombing effort could be mounted against the main industrial centres of the Soviet Union. Attlee was unhappy with policies which seemed based upon this contingency. When the Chiefs of Staff pressed for the maintenance of the British position in the Eastern Mediterranean and aid for Greece and Turkey, he argued the case for agreement with the Soviet Union that this area should somehow become a neutral zone and wrote on 1 December to Bevin: 'Of course, it is very difficult to tell how far Russian policy is dictated by expansion and how far by fear of attack by the US and ourselves. Fantastic as this is, it may very well be the real grounds of Russian policy. What we consider merely defence may seem to them preparations for an attack.'[21] Again in January, in a minute to Bevin, he questioned the Chiefs of Staff's proposals for defence of imperial communications against a possible Soviet threat. Their broad conclusion that 'The only possible enemy is Russia' and 'the only bases from which Russia could be attacked are situated in the Near East' was, he said, a strategy of despair. In its place, he urged the need to reach agreement with the Soviet Union on points of friction 'unless we are persuaded that the USSR is irrevocably committed to a policy of world domination and that there is no possibility of her alteration'. He put three questions: 'How far is the ideology committed to the conception of the necessity of world revolution? Is it possible to convince the USSR that we have no offensive intentions? What prospects are there of changes in the Russian mentality?' In the margin an unidentified hand has scribbled the answers 'Completely', 'No' and 'Very few'.[22] Attlee was, at that point, far from being persuaded that cooperation was unattainable, but Bevin persuaded him that there was no merit in leading from weakness. The Treaty of Dunkirk between Britain and France, signed on 4 March 1947, was designed to afford reassurance against a revival of the German threat and it was not until the final unsuccessful meeting of the Council of Foreign Ministers in London in December of that year that military planning began overtly to reflect the breach which had already been signalled in the economic field.

The final episode of 1947 in the field of British–Soviet relations was the signature on 31 December of a new Trade Agreement providing not only for an exchange of goods, but for the settlement terms in respects of credits under the 1941 agreement on civil supplies and the waiver of claims in respect of supplies directly concerned with prosecution of the war. It was a personal success for the young Secretary for Overseas Trade, Harold Wilson, and was to influence his later handling of relations with the Soviet Union as President of the Board of Trade and later as Prime Minister. Any political influence it might have had, was, however, wholly overshadowed by the failure of the December meeting of the Council of Foreign Ministers. To the surprise of none of the participants and probably, although it could not be admitted, to the satisfaction of each, the meeting established that there was no prospect of quadripartite control of Germany working on a basis which would satisfy all their requirements. For the British Government, this marked the point at which the dream of a post-war world built on cooperation among the great powers had finally faded.

In a party political broadcast on 3 January 1948, Attlee summed up the threat in terms which were to become a standard description of Soviet policy: 'Soviet Communism pursues a policy of imperialism in a new form – ideological, economic and strategic – which threatens the welfare and the way of life of the other nations of Europe.' Interestingly, however, he was careful not to align Britain wholly with the United States, but rather to speak of it as lying geographically and from the point of view of economic and political theory between the Soviet Union and the United States.[23]

The Soviet leadership could scarcely be surprised by the progressive hardening of British policy, but it must be highly doubtful whether they understood the way in which it had evolved any better than they had understood it in the summer of 1939. For its part, the Soviet Union still felt itself in a minority position, striving to assert its claim to great power status against the opposition of Britain and the United States. Its conduct in the areas which it controlled, deplorable though it was in Western eyes, reflected its minimum security requirement against Germany. There is no reason to suppose that the Soviet intelligence service did not know, through their British agents, of the contingency planning of the British Chiefs of Staff and, prudent though such planning might be, it was scarcely calculated to alleviate their mistrust. The Soviet Union might well consider that it had not pressed its own strategic claims outside Eastern and Central Europe with any great force; that it had eventually agreed to withdraw from Iran; that it had shown restraint in relation to Greece and Turkey and moderation in its dealings with Finland; that since 1945 the diplomatic initiative had lain more with Britain and the United States; and that a temporary consolidation of imperialist forces followed by conflict between them was what a prudent Marxist–Leninist theoretician might have predicted. It was scarcely surprising that the Soviet leadership failed to see the world scene in 1948 as it appeared to the British Government.

Attlee had, as we have seen, clung longer than Bevin to the hope of a post-war world built on cooperation with the Soviet Union. Now he was proclaiming to the British public the threat which Bevin had already seen rather earlier and against which Bevin's policies had been directed ever since 1945. Both Bevin and Attlee had been conditioned by the experience of the 1920s and the 1930s, when the Soviet ideology was a menace, and Bevin, in particular, through his trade union experience, was well aware of Soviet techniques for the manipulation of political power. In many respects, however, the Soviet Union itself had been distant and unknown, its armed forces largely ignored in the

European balance. The countries of Eastern and Central Europe, on the other hand, troublesome and turbulent though they were, had formed part of a European family of nations. Now, after 1945, the whole political structure of Europe had been upset. Soviet troops stood some 600 miles westwards of the Soviet Union's 1939 frontier and, at their closest, were a mere 100 miles from the North Sea coast. The main mass of Continental Europe east of the Elbe was under Soviet control and, throughout it, democracy had come to mean 'People's Democracy'. The strength of Communism in France and Italy was uncertain, but alarming. Germany had been destroyed as a political entity. Most of Western Europe was in a pitiable state of economic privation and Britain itself no longer capable of sustaining the financial burdens of a major power. If Soviet hostility had to be accepted as a fact, the 'correlation of forces' against Britain was substantially worse than it had been when Europe was threatened with German domination in 1939. Having seen the Soviet Union demonstrate only too clearly the ruthlessness with which it would control the countries of Eastern Europe and the Soviet Zone of Germany, Attlee and Bevin could not afford to gamble on Soviet restraint. Nor did the intransigence of Soviet diplomacy and the tone of Soviet propaganda give them any encouragement to do so. They could see no margin of safety, nor any prospect of security save in close association with the United States. The British Government had no desire for, and could ill afford, a still deeper breach with the Soviet Union, yet the only policies which would offer any prospect of guaranteeing the security and prosperity of Western Europe were certain to produce it. They had to assume that, faced with the opportunity of a Western European power vacuum, the Soviet Union would fill it.

It was in this sense that Attlee, extrapolating from Eastern European experience, could justifiably speak of the threat of Soviet imperialism. Only the small body of Communists and one or two on the left wing of the Labour Party were inclined to contradict him. Equally, however, there was no reason to suppose that, if the vacuum were filled by Britain and the United States, the Soviet Union, having already adequately ensured its own security, would be prepared to run the risk of war in order to extend its power further westwards. It was therefore possible to carry forward the process of consolidating Western Europe in reasonable confidence that, although the result would be to deepen and institutionalise the East–West split, the relationship with the Soviet Union which would emerge would, despite increased tension, be inherently more stable and more secure. The basis for British policy in this new situation was set out by Bevin in a series of Cabinet papers[24] which included, *inter alia*, a plan to counter Communist propaganda.

Despite initial French hesitation, the response to the Soviet consolidation of Eastern Europe was developed with remarkable speed in the first half of 1948. With the integration of the French Zone of Germany into the combined British–American Zone, the political and economic structure began to be created which would make possible a revival of the West Germany economy. In February the Soviet-inspired coup in Czechoslovakia, ten years after Munich, brought a swift justification, if one were needed, of Attlee's assessment. On 17 March the process of forming a Western European security structure was taken a stage further with the negotiation of the Brussels Treaty, in which the Anglo–French alliance was extended to include the Benelux countries, and in British–American discussions later that month the first steps were taken which were to culminate in the North Atlantic Treaty. The Benelux countries were also consulted about the plans for the economic and political restructuring of Western Germany, worked out at a British–French–American Conference in London. To this, the Soviet Union responded with a call, backed by the Eastern European countries, for the formation of a 'provisional, democratic, all-German Government'.

The Berlin blockade

Berlin now became the focal point of the European confrontation, not so much in its own right, but rather as a test of will between the Soviet Union and the Western powers over the future of Germany. The risk that the Soviet Union would act against the Western position in Berlin had been foreseen, but Bevin argued[25] that delay in the Western programme would lead to intensified Soviet pressure, demoralisation of Britain's friends and even the risk of a Russo–German combination. The build-up to the blockade was gradual. The first limited restrictions on Western access to Berlin were enforced in April 1948, but the Western plans went ahead. A new currency was introduced on 18 June into the Western zones and shortly thereafter into West Berlin. After introducing its own currency reform, the Soviet Union precipitated the full crisis on 24 June by severing all rail, road and canal access to Berlin from the West. The challenge to the Western position in Berlin was clear.

The Soviet action raised the immediate issue of response by force. At one extreme of British opinion was Churchill who, in April, had suggested that the time had come 'to tell the Soviets that if they do not retire from Berlin and abandon Eastern Germany, withdrawing to the Polish frontier, we will raze their cities'.[26] In practical terms, however, once the blockage had been established, the only options were to negotiate a settlement under pressure, to break through by land or to organise supply by air. The British and American Commanders in Germany were in agreement that they could not guarantee, with the forces available, to break through by land. Plans existed for the supply of the British garrison by air and, on 25 June the Cabinet over-rode the doubts of the Deputy British Military Governor and took the decision to try to supply the civilian population also by air.[27] An attempt to break the blockade by the use of ground forces would have meant the initiation of hostilities by the Western side. Aircraft flying through the designated corridors could be blocked only by direct hostile action from the Soviet side, either by aircraft, surface weapons or barrage balloons. The risk of opposition by air was accepted and the decision was taken that if barrage balloons were used they should be shot down. It was calculated correctly that the Soviet Union would not wish to run the risk of war for the sake of gaining control of West Berlin. The British Government's policy on the other hand, required that, in the event of miscalculation, this risk would have to be accepted. The joint British–American airlift began on the following day.[28] The British response was, in the early stages, both more determined and swifter than that of the United States and, for this, much of the credit must go to Bevin. His achievement was the more remarkable in that, with British resources stretched to the limit, he was grappling simultaneously with the termination of the Palestine mandate. On 30 June, he put his policy to Parliament, warning that it might be necessary to face a 'grave situation', but that there was no alternative than surrender 'and none of us can accept surrender'.[29] The response was wholehearted parliamentary support. At the same time, diplomatic action was instituted with the despatch on 6 July of identical British and American notes to the Soviet Government and, in order to add force to the proclaimed determination to stand firm, the British Government agreed to the stationing in Britain, without prior conditions, of a force of American B29 bombers. These aircraft were known to constitute the American nuclear bombing force and, although those initially stationed in Britain had not been adapted for this role, the gesture must have had its effect.

The diplomatic notes were followed by tripartite discussions in Moscow at which the British representative was Frank Roberts who, after his service in Moscow, had become Private Secretary to Ernest Bevin. A weakness of the Allied position was that the arrangements for access to Berlin stemmed in part from the recommendations of the European Advisory Commission and in part from ad hoc arrangements between the commanders of the occupation forces. The Soviet position was firm: any rights which the Western allies enjoyed in Berlin flowed from the quadripartite arrangements for Germany as a whole and until these were restored there could be no restoration of normal communications with the city. No progress could be made. The British Military Governor in Germany, General Robertson, did not believe that Berlin could be supplied by air through the winter and was 'convinced that in the course of time the Soviets will steal the city from under our noses'. A land convoy was dismissed as impracticable, but the British Government was determined not to concede. Measures were taken to put the armed forces 'into a better position to fight'[30] and Bevin, rejecting the argument that the allocation of extra resources for defence would delay economic recovery, argued that 'unless a firm stand were made now, our position in Europe would be hopeless'.[31]

The failure of the Moscow discussions was reported to Parliament by Bevin on 22 September. He indicated that there had been some British readiness to compromise, in that once the blockade was lifted and four-power control over trade between Berlin and the West restored, the Soviet currency could circulate in Berlin under four-power control. The restoration of normal communications must, however, precede discussion of quadripartite control and, as Bevin put it, he would not accept that once a line had been drawn 'you wake up to demands, revolutions, stirrings up of your people and upsetting of your institutions and everything else to promote an expansion at a very cheap price without war'.[32] On 29 September the British Government referred the Berlin question to the Security Council. The Soviet Union announced its intention not to participate in the proceedings. The airlift was sustained throughout the winter and, by the spring, the Soviet Union accepted the failure of the blockade. In private discussions between the Soviet and American representatives (the latter acting for the three Western Governments) agreement was reached on a face-saving formula which provided that all restrictions on movement would first be removed and that on 23 May a meeting of the Council of Foreign Ministers would be convened 'to consider questions relating to Germany and problems arising out of the situation in Berlin, including also the question of currency in Berlin'. On 4 April the North Atlantic Treaty had been signed and on the day the Council met, the Federal

Republic of Germany was constituted. On 30 May, the Soviet Union responded with the creation of the German Democratic Republic (GDR), followed by a series of purges in Eastern Europe and the intensification of Soviet pressure against Yugoslavia. The division of Europe, already created in practice by the outcome of the war and symbolised by the outcome of the Marshall Aid negotiations, had now begun to take its definitive political shape.

The Berlin crisis was the only occasion on which the Soviet Union directly challenged, with the backing of its own armed forces, a position held by the forces of the Western powers. Up to this point, the Soviet threat had been inferred by British ministers from Soviet action in Eastern Europe, Soviet diplomacy and Soviet propaganda. With no precedent to guide them, the British Government had to construct policy *ab initio*. Against a background of initial American hesitancy, there can be little doubt that, had Bevin not been prepared to commit Britain to the airlift, the Western position could not have been sustained. Beyond the immediate consequences, a precedent for further Soviet encroachment on Western positions would have been established, with a greater risk of subsequent miscalculation. As it was, the Soviet Government made the initial miscalculation over Berlin, but from the point that the airlift was initiated, both parties understood one another and there was no escalation. Bevin had assessed the situation correctly in Cabinet on 26 July 1948: 'As regards Berlin, to yield to Soviet pressure there would lead to further withdrawals by the Western allies and in the end to war. On the other hand, if we maintained a firm attitude we might reckon on ten years of peace during which the defences of Western Europe might be consolidated.'[33]

The bounds are set

The ending of the Berlin blockade reduced the tension, but did nothing to resolve the struggle for power between the Soviet Union and the Western allies. Over the course of the next twenty-five years, the Soviet Union gradually developed the full military potential of a nuclear superpower. Blocked in Western Europe, where the East–West frontier was now secure, it sought to extend its power and influence in the Third World. The character of the British–Soviet relationship evolved significantly. The development of the Communist threat outside Europe introduced a new dimension, in which it was not easy to determine the extent of Soviet involvement or the appropriate nature of the response. The breakdown of the old European-based imperial structures, the creation of new independent states in Asia and Africa and the rise of Communist China brought a substantially more complex pattern of international relationships. At the same time, the escalation of nuclear weaponry by the Soviet Union and the United States led to a new bilateral superpower relationship. Nevertheless, the attempt at quadripartite regulation of major issues continued intermittently until the failure of the Paris summit in 1960. Even then, the absence of a definitive settlement of the German problem left a remnant of the key element in the post-war quadripartite relationship. The role of Germany in British–Soviet relations and the continued quadripartite occupation of Berlin made that remnant of more than formal significance.

Successive British Governments, grappling with the problems of restoring the British economy and adjusting to the radically new post-imperial world, had no thirst for confrontation with the Soviet Union. Yet Soviet power could not now be ignored as it had been in the 1930s. Throughout a succession of crises, stretching through more than thirty years, the extent of Soviet involvement was not always easy to determine. When the Soviet armed forces entered Hungary, Czechoslovakia and Afghanistan, or Soviet missiles were introduced into Cuba, there could be debate about the appropriate response, but little doubt as to the underlying facts. The pattern of involvement – military, political or economic – in other areas was more complex. The emergence of new states from the old imperial structures offered opportunities for the extension of Soviet power and influence. In Korea, Indo-China, Indonesia, Malaysia, Egypt, Angola, Mozambique, South Yemen and Ethiopia the crises were to erupt as competing factions fought for control. The extent of Soviet involvement in the stimulation or prosecution of revolutionary wars was open to argument, but Soviet theorists maintained the classic doctrine of the struggle against all those who did not accept Soviet socialism and, inconclusive though the evidence might sometimes be, it was difficult for any responsible British statesman to see the combination of Marxist–Leninist doctrine, Russian imperial instincts and Soviet armed force as other than a threat to the whole structure of international society. Throughout these decades the problem of dealing with the Soviet Union rarely occupied the first place among the issues claiming the attention of the British Government, but it was continuously present and in so far as ministers saw one predominant opponent and one predominant threat to British security, it was the Soviet Union.

The primary response to this perceived threat lay in the consolidation of Britain's other relationships, military, political and economic, in the Atlantic Alliance, in the Commonwealth and the Third World and in Western Europe. The direct relationship with the Soviet Union remained almost wholly intractable. It was necessary to sustain a strategic defence capability within the Alliance, sufficient to deter the Soviet Union from the direct use of armed force against any essential British interest. Yet it was consistently recognised that armed force could not be used for the ultimate resolution of disputes between nuclear powers. The confrontation with the Soviet Union had therefore to be contained at a level below that which might involve recourse to force and, to this end, the search for a productive dialogue had to constitute a central element in British political strategy. The pattern of the 1950s, 1960s and 1970s was one in which the search for some basis of understanding was repeatedly instituted, broken off and resumed. In this fluctuating relationship there was a basic change of motivation from the pre-war years, when policy had alternated with the alternation of political power between Left and Right in Britain. From 1945 onwards, the ideological alignment of the Labour and Conservative Parties was less significant and a certain consensus developed in which the trend of British policy was largely responsive to the changing manifestations of Soviet policy.

Germany and Korea

In the final years of Stalin's regime, British policy was concentrated almost exclusively on realising the full potential of the alliance which had been created in 1949 and bolstering it with the strength of Western Germany. There was no basis here for agreement with the Soviet Union. The Council of Foreign Ministers met as planned in Paris on 23 May 1949. Of the original post-war members, only Bevin remained. Acheson and Schuman represented the United States and France, while Vyshinsky, whose role as prosecutor in the first Stalin show trials did little to inspire confidence on the part of his Western interlocutors, now spoke for the Soviet Union. Agreement was recorded on the normalisation of relations between the Eastern and Western sectors of Berlin and the respective zones of Germany and on the basis for further work on the Austrian Peace Treaty. In substance, however, the agreement was meaningless, except in so far as it ratified the lifting of the blockade. There was deadlock in the negotiation of the Austrian Peace Treaty and no basis for agreement on a unified Germany. The existing relationship between the two alliances was unchanged and the existing differences were unresolved.

A year later the stakes had been raised. The first Soviet nuclear explosion was detected by Britain and the United States in September 1949 and nuclear deterrence, previously a monopoly of the United States, would from that time on constrain the policies not only of the Soviet Union, but also of the Western powers. The control of nuclear energy, one of the first subjects to engage the attention of the UN, became more urgent and the chance of Soviet acceptance of its internationalisation on the basis of anything like the original Baruch plan even more remote. The victory of the Communists in the struggle for the control of China brought a new menace, while the declaration of non-alignment by India seemed to the Soviet Union to deal a major blow to British imperial power. In Britain itself, growing economic difficulties weakened the base on which Bevin had to construct his diplomacy and made reliance upon the United States the more necessary.

At the election in February 1950, policy towards the Soviet Union was no longer a major issue. Churchill called for a new summit meeting, 'a supreme effort to bridge the gulf between the two worlds, so that each can live their life, if not in friendship, at least without the hatreds and manoeuvres of the cold war'. His appeal was, however, dismissed by both the British and Soviet Governments as an election stunt. The outcome of the election, a Labour majority of only six, made it inevitable that there would be a second appeal to the electorate within a fairly short time. In the interim, the Government was increasingly preoccupied with domestic issues. The international scene was tense. Bevin's health was failing. He was still determined to press on with the development of the Atlantic alliance and even less disposed to make concessions to the Soviet Union. The Foreign Office did in fact examine the Churchill proposal,[34] but concluded that there was no likelihood of agreement on the major practical issues and that a summit would enable the Soviet Union either to lull Western opinion into a false sense of security or to brand Western Governments as warmongers. A *Times* leader of 10 April was quoted with approval: 'In a war of ideologies the definition of strict spheres of interest is an anachronism.' In May the Foreign Secretary circulated a paper to the Cabinet in preparation for a meeting of the Atlantic Council in which he considered whether the 'time was ripe for any attempt to reach a settlement by negotiation with the Soviets'. His conclusion was that 'general negotiations are unlikely to succeed until such time as we have built up a situation of strength in the West'. The French and American Governments both felt slightly more need to show at least some readiness for negotiation, though there was pressure within the United

States to 'heat up the cold war'. It was not too hard to agree that in any case the time was not ripe. The work of the Russia Committee of the Foreign Office at this time was becoming very much oriented towards the threat in Asia and Africa and to the means by which the West might mount a counter-offensive in the ideological struggle.[35] This trend was reflected in the meeting of British, French and American Foreign Ministers in London on 13 May 1950. Although they were concerned primarily with policy regarding Germany, the communiqué envisaged 'a new joint and Western drive to combat Communist imperialism in both Asia and Africa'.

In their concern about the Soviet threat in Asia, the British Labour Government of 1950 were echoing a theme which had been apparent in Conservative policies in the years following the Revolution, when Curzon had been preoccupied with the need to safeguard British India against the threat of Soviet penetration from the north and in 1927 when concern about Soviet instigation of disorders in China played its part in the events leading up to the breach of relations. With the outbreak of the Korean War on 24 June 1950, the new threat in Asia materialised more quickly and more dramatically than had been expected. The conflict had ominous implications, not only for the position of the Western powers, particularly the United States, in the Far East, but also as a portent for what might be expected elsewhere on the fault lines where the stresses of the Communist and non-Communist worlds were concentrated. It had its origin in the post-war division of Korea between the Soviet occupation zone in the North and that of the United States in the South. The extent to which the North Korean attack had been directly instigated by the Soviet Union was uncertain. It is likely that the Soviet Union believed the United States to be unwilling to fight for the independence of South Korea and saw advantage in a quick campaign by the North Korean forces. Initial Soviet moral and material support was clear. The first stage of the Chinese intervention may also have seemed attractive to the Soviet leadership in so far as it tied down a substantial American force in an inherently profitless campaign. Only when the extension and intensification of the conflict began to pose a significant threat did a recognition of the need for restraint begin to gain the upper hand in Soviet policy.

Although British troops were included in the UN forces in South Korea, the military operations and the associated diplomacy were primarily conducted by the United States. The war was, however, of significance to British–Soviet relations in various respects. In particular, hostile action by a Soviet client state in a divided country in Asia was an uncomfortable precedent for similar action in Germany and undoubtedly contributed to the case for a defence contribution from Western Germany. Churchill repeated his call for an attempt to arrive at an understanding with the Soviet Union while the United States still held nuclear superiority, arguing in a major parliamentary speech, applauded from both sides of the House, that it was in Europe and not in the 'Far East diversion' that the world cause would be decided.[36] Equally significant was the change which the war marked in the respective roles of Britain and the United States in relation to the Soviet Union. The pressure for action now came primarily from the American side, where anti-Communist emotion rose to a new pitch, and the British Government found itself torn between the need to retain American confidence and the fear of escalation. A moment of some tension in the British–American relationship came in December when Attlee, concerned at the risk of all-out war between the United States and China, flew to Washington to dissuade President Truman from using the atomic bomb, a course which the President had in fact already rejected.

The difference of approach between Britain and the United States was heightened by the fact that one aim of Soviet policy was to enable the Communist Government to take the Chinese seat at the United Nations. Britain had already recognised the Communists as the Government of China, although diplomatic relations had not at the time been established. The United States had not recognised it and the Soviet Union had boycotted Security Council meetings in protest against the non-admission of Communist China. Soviet absence had made it possible for Britain and the United States to secure the establishment of the United Nations force in Korea. At the outset of the war, the British Government tried to persuade the Soviet Union to use its influence with China to end hostilities. The Soviet response in July 1950 was to propose discussion in the Security Council in which Communist China should be included. This would have meant that, without any prior guarantee of the withdrawal of North Korean forces, the Soviet Union would secure Chinese participation and restore its own power of veto over subsequent developments. The Cabinet had no hesitation in rejecting the Soviet proposal, but, with the recollection of the outcome of bilateral contacts during the Berlin blockade, it was decided to continue discussions.[37] The Soviet Union was asked to use its influence with North Korea to cease hostilities and withdraw to the 38th parallel, but it was not until a year later, on 23 June 1951, when the United Nations had effectively regained control of the South, that the Soviet Ambassador to the United Nations, Y. Malik, proposed discussions for a ceasefire based on a mutual withdrawal from the 38th parallel. The British Government welcomed the suggestion and did what it could to follow it up, but to such an extent was the diplomatic initiative left in American hands that when Sir Alvary Gascoigne replaced Sir David Kelly in Moscow in November 1951 he was dissuaded from even raising the issue of the armistice negotiations in his initial talks. The only discernible result of bilateral British–Soviet talks in Moscow was to secure the eventual release of the British envoy in Seoul, who had been captured by the North Korean forces. It is not easy to judge the subsequent Soviet role in the final settlement, but on the Western side it was undoubtedly American diplomacy backed by American military power which was crucial. The Soviet Union had, since 1945, been clear that its principal opponent was now the United States. The Korean War powerfully reinforced the trend towards a bilateral superpower relationship, but it was to take another decade before, with the Cuban crisis, the full implications of this trend became apparent.

Policy on trade with the Soviet Union

The Korean War also caused the British Government to reconsider its policy for trade with the Communist countries. In the pre-war years, British exports to the Soviet Union had fluctuated between a low point of £4 million in 1923 and 1933 and high points of £19 million in 1925 and £20 million in 1937, while imports had fluctuated around an average of a little more than £20 million a year. Despite moments of British enthusiasm, the development of a policy of economic autarky by Stalin in the 1930s had meant that the potential of the Soviet market had never been fulfilled. After 1945, British purchases of grain and timber had brought a substantial rise in imports, but by 1948 British exports were a mere £7 million and subsequent growth had been handicapped by the introduction in April 1949 of a ban on the export to Eastern Europe of certain machinery which was of direct military value. By 1950, when the Korean War broke out, Britain was, as it had been in 1935, the Soviet Union's principal Western trading partner, but this position now reflected very largely the devastation of the economies of Western Europe during the war. The Soviet market, at £14 million, accounted for only 0.6 per cent of total British exports. Now, however, the Government was faced with

American pressure for a much more comprehensive strategic embargo which would have blocked certain British industrial exports as well as hindering the procurement of coarse grains and timber. Some reduction in British sales of critical items such as machine tools was agreed and the Commercial Section of the British Embassy in Moscow was closed. The gestures were largely symbolic, but the problem was to remain for many years as an irritant both to British–Soviet and to British–American relations. Indeed, it became, as it had been in 1921, a focal point in the doctrinal controversy over the nature of East–West relations.[38] Was the purpose of Western policy, as the United States tended to see it, to do everything possible, short of open warfare, to weaken an irredeemably hostile Soviet Union? Or was it rather, as the British Government saw it, not gratuitously to increase the military capability of the Soviet Union, but at the same time to help both the British economy and the international climate by seeking to develop all that network of commercial and other links which might in time build up a genuine community of interest? By the time of the invasion of Afghanistan in 1979 and the Polish crisis in 1982, the issue was still being debated in very much the same terms, and the respective stance of the British and American Governments had not evolved very far from that of 1950.

The rearmament of Germany

The general policy of the British Government towards the Soviet Union after the outbreak of the Korean War was set out in a paper prepared by the Foreign Office for the tripartite meeting of Western Foreign Ministers in New York in September 1950.[39] In it lay the essence of the Cold War strategy:

> The Soviet Union probably does not wish to become involved in general war in the immediate future. It may, however, engage in further aggression by proxy, either in the guise of Civil War or of attack across frontiers by satellites without involvement of Soviet forces, *even at the risk of provoking general war* [author's italics]. It will in any case continue its sustained effort to subvert free peoples and undermine their will to resist aggression.

The Western policy which the Foreign Office recommended was intensification of the military, political and economic defence of the Western European 'keystone', the avoidance of unnecessarily provocative action, attempts to relieve tension on specific questions, exploitation of difficulties between the Soviet Union and its satellites and an 'expanded, intensified and coordinated' Western effort in the 'struggle for men's minds', seeking to 'convince them of the falsity of the Kremlin's championship of peace, nationalism and social reform'. The paper was noteworthy both for its assessment – which many would now consider to have been over-pessimistic – that the Soviet Union might have been ready to run the risk of provoking a general war; and also for the call for a counter-offensive in the ideological struggle which was to lead to the reinforcement of the publicity campaign, both direct and indirect, against Soviet Communism which the Foreign Office had initiated in 1947.

At the outbreak of the Korean War the NATO forces in Europe consisted of some 14 divisions, while the strength of the Soviet army was estimated at 175 divisions. At the September meeting in New York, following a meeting of the Atlantic Council, the need for some German contribution to European defence was accepted and, in recognition of French objections, the concept of a European Army was evolved. There was concern in the Foreign Office and the Ministry of Defence about the possible Soviet reaction to any such move, but, given the overriding importance of maintaining the American contribution to the defence of Europe, the Prime Minister decided against raising this aspect with President Truman. While work on European defence went forward, so did the exchanges with the Soviet Union on a possible ministerial meeting. In December 1950, Bevin put one of his last papers to the Cabinet.[40] The Soviet Union, seeking to prevent West German rearmament, had proposed a new meeting of the Council of Foreign Ministers to consider carrying out the Potsdam Agreement in relation to the demilitarisation of Germany. Bevin accepted that there was 'considerable feeling in Parliament and the country as a whole' against a completely negative reply. As he saw it, however, the Soviet purpose was merely to play upon French susceptibilities and delay the strengthening of Western defences. The British proposal, put forward at Paris in 1949 and pursued subsequently at official level, was for free all-German elections under international supervision. This had elicited no direct response. The Soviet counter-proposal for the formation of a Council with equal representatives from East and West Germany to prepare for an all-German provisional Government seemed only too clearly designed to maximise the opportunities for Soviet interference by proxy in Western Germany. The only armed forces in Germany at this time, other than the occupation forces of the Four Powers, were the militarised East German police units, and Bevin saw the risk that a demilitarised Germany, with occupation forces withdrawn, could easily become a power vacuum, vulnerable to the Soviet Union. In his lengthy paper Bevin considered all the options for either a limited or a global solution to the relationship with the Soviet Union, seeking some means of reducing tension without sacrificing essential interests. Uncharacteristically, perhaps because of his illness, he left his recommendations open and it was eventually decided that officials of the Four Powers should meet to see whether it was possible to work out an agenda for a meeting of Foreign Ministers.

Exchanges with the Soviet Union dragged on through the first half of 1951, until in July they were suspended. By the time of Bevin's death in April 1951, British policy was firmly on course. One of the Labour Government's last papers before the General Election in September was a brief for meetings between Bevin's successor, Herbert Morrison, and his American and French colleagues. On their agenda was a 'Survey of progress in the policy of containment of the Soviet Union and its Satellites'.[41] The brief recorded a measure of success in the policy of building up positions of strength and a series of Soviet setbacks. Two potential dangers were seen. There was a risk that the Soviet Union might be driven to a full war economy, or even to preventive war, if the West overlooked or misjudged the Soviet reaction in relation to 'sore spots in their security' such as air bases near the Soviet border. In this respect American impulsiveness was seen as a risk. The second potential danger lay in a failure to be constructive and positive, but it was still thought that the time was not yet ripe for full-scale negotiations. In relation to Germany, Morrison considered it right to press on with the arrangements for German participation in Western defence, in default of which there could be a risk that a disillusioned Western Germany might eventually move into the Soviet camp. The risk of a Soviet preventive war in 1951 was not discounted by Sir David Kelly, Ambassador in Moscow. The Politburo, even Stalin, he argued, might be more human and impressionable than Ministers assumed. They might not feel confident that time was on their side, and 'from the purely military point of view ... there is quite a case for a preventive war by the Russians (and Chinese) this year'. In reply, the new Foreign Secretary assured him on 4 July that the risk had been 'long and carefully weighed', but the conclusion was that the Soviet leaders were 'realistic enough to appreciate the appalling risk' and would refrain 'unless they were to feel themselves under imminent threat of attack'.[42]

Maclean and Burgess

We have noted the hardening of British official opinion in relation to the threat of Communist subversion of free institutions. One consequence of the coup in Czechoslovakia had been the announcement by the Government on 15 March 1948 of measures to exclude known Communists from work affecting the security of the state. In the United States the mood of virulent anti-Communism had mounted almost to a state of hysteria as Senator McCarthy began his drive against Communist or quasi-Communist activities in public life. At the height of the Korean War, in May 1951, British opinion suffered a severe shock with the news of the flight of the two Soviet agents, Donald Maclean and Guy Burgess, to the Soviet Union.[43] The two men, part of the group whose Communist sympathies had first been kindled during the Spanish Civil War, had been operating on behalf of the Soviet Union for many years. Burgess, a squalid and disreputable junior official, had been an Assistant Private Secretary to Hector McNeil, Bevin's Minister of State, then a member of the Far Eastern Department of the Foreign Office and later, to general surprise, posted to the Washington Embassy. Maclean, the senior of the two, an unstable, tortured character, a potential high-flyer of the Service, had spent most of the post-war years in Washington before becoming Head of the American Department. Between them they had access to – and passed to their Soviet controllers – many of the key papers on the development of British foreign policy and, in the case of Maclean, on Anglo–American nuclear cooperation. There can be little doubt that, as a result of their activities, the Soviet Union was well briefed on the development of British and American policy throughout the critical stages in the development of the Cold War. Soviet nuclear espionage had been well exposed as early as 1945 by the confession of the British scientist, Nunn May, and no doubt his work, together with that of Fuchs, helped to accelerate the Soviet development of nuclear weapons. Combined with Maclean's briefing on strategic thinking, it must have been as gravely prejudicial to British and American defence interests as was the work of Philby to British counter-intelligence operations.

In the political field, on the other hand, fascinating though the intelligence must have been to the Soviet leadership, it is doubtful whether it materially affected the course of policy. The key decisions on questions such as the rearmament of Germany had, by their very nature, to be publicly aired, and on other matters which have occasionally troubled Western consciences, such as the organisation of active counter-measures against Communist subversion, the knowledge can have come as no surprise. It may well be that the most significant influence of Burgess and Maclean – and subsequently of Blunt, Cairncross and Philby – lay in the shock to British and American opinion caused by the revelation of the route which led from the Communist sympathies prevalent in certain small but well-placed sectors of British pre-war society, through the wartime alliance and homosexual blackmail to active espionage on behalf of the Soviet intelligence service. American opinion was excitable and the scandal did much damage not merely to the British–American nuclear relationship, but more widely to the confidence which, largely as a result of Ernest Bevin, had been developed between the two Governments.

The scandal of the Foreign Office spies led to a substantial tightening of security procedures within British Government Service as well as to an intensification of the drive against the intelligence activities of Soviet officials in London. The strand of intelligence and counter-intelligence work which had been woven into the British–Soviet relationship from its earliest days, emerging above the surface with events such as the British interception of Soviet communications in 1920 and the Arcos raid in 1927, was reinforced and remained a significant element to the present day. Even now, after the dissolution of the Soviet Union and the initiation of cooperation in intelligence work against drug traffickers and other common enemies, the old-style agent has not gone out of business. Nor has the whole elaborate apparatus of technical surveillance been dismantled. The brief has changed, but it would be a rash observer who would conclude that the hostile use of intelligence agencies to penetrate national security will not, in the future as in the past, feature in the relationship between the two countries.

9
The Khrushchev Years

The Conservative Government under Winston Churchill which took office after the General Election in October 1951 found the British–Soviet relationship at its nadir. It had inherited from Labour a hard-line policy based on a broad British–American unity of purpose in containing the Stalinist threat. There had been some fraying of the unity during the Korean War but, on the whole, it had held. There could scarcely have been a more marked contrast with pre-war experience than the progress by which the Churchill and Eden Governments sought, while carrying forward Labour's policy of the Western alliance, to establish a sounder basis for relations with the Soviet Union and to restrain the United States from belligerent anti-Communism, only to find themselves, five years later, almost simultaneously threatened with rocket attack from the Soviet Union and bankruptcy by the United States. Within a further year, under Macmillan, Britain and the United States were to be realigned in opposition to a newly perceived Soviet threat of global domination. The scope for developing the British–Soviet relationship in the final years of Stalin and throughout the tumultuous Khrushchev decade was determined in part by the uncertain evolution of the Soviet Union and in part by the realities of a divided Europe set in a post-imperial world. This was the era in which, with the first thermonuclear explosions by the United States, the Soviet Union and the United Kingdom, the threat of nuclear destruction came to play an increasing part both in public perception and in the reality of East–West rivalry. Thus there began a concentration of the relationship with the Soviet Union on the problem of controlling nuclear weapons and the development of a bilateral superpower relationship. First, however, came another stage in the struggle of Britain and the Soviet Union over Germany's place in Europe.

In a Foreign Affairs debate on 19 November 1951, Eden, commenting on the state of relations created by the Korean War, observed: 'There is now virtually no diplomatic contact between East and West either side of the iron curtain. That is something new and entirely to be deplored.' East–West relations were, however, already close to the point at which both sides would recognise the need for change. With Truman's dismissal of MacArthur, the decision had been effectively taken to limit the scope of the Korean War and, although fighting was to continue for a further two years, the military stalemate meant that the focus could begin to move to Germany and Indo-China. For the time being, there was no change in British policy. At the first meeting of Churchill's Cabinet, the main point of concern to Eden, back at the Foreign Office, was the defence of Egypt. On Germany, policy was moving steadily ahead and the need to come to grips with the Soviet Union on the whole complex of issues arising from the integration of Western Germany into Western Europe could not long be evaded. Behind all the manoeuvring, the issue was a simple one. What place was Germany to hold in post-war Europe? The British objective was to press ahead with the integration of Western Germany into Western Europe, without prejudice to the eventual reunification of Germany on the basis of free elections. The Soviet objective was to retain control of East Germany, frustrate the Western plans for West Germany and permit reunification only in the unlikely event of it being on terms which would permit the extension of Soviet control, direct or indirect, over the reunited German state.

On 10 March 1952 a Soviet note was received, proposing a meeting of Foreign Ministers to discuss a German Peace Treaty, with the participation of an all-German Government. Eden saw this as no more than an astute manoeuvre, a specious appeal to the German desire for reunification, without any commitment to the holding of free all-German elections under independent supervision. Throughout the summer of 1952 the exchange of notes continued, with the British Government holding firmly to the view that the correct sequence of events was the holding of elections, the formation of an all-German Government, the negotiation of a peace settlement and the withdrawal of occupation forces. Under the Soviet proposals the order would, in key essentials, have been reversed, and the holding of elections would have followed the negotiation of a peace settlement with a provisional government based on representation from the two halves of Germany.

Between the summer of 1952 and the spring of 1953 the British–Soviet relationship itself remained stagnant, but major changes occurred in the international environment within which it would in future be conducted. On 24 May 1952 the signature of the 'contractual arrangement' with the Federal Republic of Germany represented a major step towards the ending of the occupation regime in the West, save for the Western sectors of Berlin; on 27 May the treaty establishing the European Defence Community (EDC) was signed and the British and American Governments formally linked it to their NATO commitment by undertaking that any threat to the integrity or unity of the Community would be regarded as a threat to their own security; the birth of the European Coal and Steel Community (ECSC) marked a new stage in the long process of the economic integration of Western Europe; on 4 November the victory of President Eisenhower brought a Republican Administration to the United States, with John Foster Dulles, the advocate of rolling back Communism, as Secretary of State in place of Dean Acheson; and on 5 March 1953 Stalin died.

As the post-Stalin era opened, the French Government was still engaged in its long and eventually fruitless battle to secure ratification of the treaty establishing the EDC. The Korean Armistice Agreement was not concluded until 27 July 1953 and in Indo-China and Malaysia fighting was continuing. Nevertheless, Britain and her allies could embark with some confidence on the task of establishing relations with Stalin's successors. It was to be pursued at a series of Conferences of Foreign Ministers and Heads of Government in Berlin and Geneva during 1954 and 1955 which carried forward the process of determining, in a trial of political and military strength, the frontier of the Communist-dominated area in Europe and Asia.

In the summer of 1953, neither the British nor the American Government had any clear view of the policies which might be expected from the new and largely unknown Soviet leadership. Would expansion or stability be the priority task? The return of Molotov to the Foreign Ministry offered no encouraging prospect, but the impact of Malenkov as Chairman of the Council of Ministers and Khrushchev as Secretary (later First Secretary) of the party remained to be seen. It was, however, clear that a new era was opening and both Eisenhower and Churchill appealed to the new Soviet leadership to make a fresh start. Mr Churchill made a major Parliamentary statement on 11 May in which he proposed 'a conference on the highest level between the leading powers without long delay'. Justifying it, he said:

> We have been encouraged by a series of amicable gestures on the part of the new Soviet Government ... These have so far taken the

form of leaving off doing things which we have not been doing to them and it is very difficult to find a specific case in which to match their action ... I think it would be a mistake to try and map things out too much in detail and expect that grave and fundamental issues which divide the Communist and non-Communist parts of the world can be settled by a single comprehensive agreement.

He recalled a telegram of 29 April 1945 in which he had warned Stalin not to under-rate the divergences which were even then opening up and had seen 'not much comfort in looking into a future where you and the countries you dominate plus the Communist parties of many other states are all drawn up on one side, and those who rally to the English speaking nations and their associates are on the other'. Now he looked forward to the Russian people taking 'the high place in world affairs which is their due, without feeling unsettled about their own security' and sought to assure the Soviet Union that 'so far as human arrangements can run, the terrible events of the Hitler invasion will never be repeated and that Poland will remain a friendly power and a buffer, though not a puppet state'.[1]

A month later, the first crisis of the post-Stalin era erupted with anti-Soviet demonstrations in East Berlin and in several places in the German Democratic Republic, as the Soviet Zone of Germany had now become. I was at this time serving as Deputy Political Adviser to the British Commandant in West Berlin and recollect driving through East Berlin on the morning of 17 June. The normal life of the city had come to a halt and crowds of demonstrators were roaming the streets. At one point my car was immobilised by an obstruction in the roadway and was freed by the advancing crowd. It seemed discourteous to accelerate away in a cloud of dust and for a few embarrassing moments the rioters had at their head a British Military Government car flying the Union Jack. The crowds had, however, no political organisation. As the Soviet tanks rolled through the city, the demonstrators, save only for a small number of casualties, went home to supper. The Soviet action was relatively restrained, as was the reaction of the British Government. Churchill's primary interest was in the renewal of high-level contact with the Soviet Union. He was in no mood to inflate the issue and it had remarkably little effect on the course of British–Soviet relations. What it did, however, was to reawaken sympathy in West Germany for their countrymen in the East, to exacerbate feelings against the Soviet Union and to make the new Soviet leadership, by now uncomfortably aware of the precarious nature of their hold on

Germany, the more determined not to prejudice it by rashness in negotiation with the West.

The Four-Power meetings of 1954 and 1955

Churchill's enthusiasm for an unprepared, informal summit was shared neither by Eden nor by his officials. It was, however, in line with the mood of the time. The question came to Cabinet at a bad moment in the summer of 1953, when Eden was out of the country, incapacitated by a severe operation followed by prolonged convalescence, and just after the Prime Minister himself had suffered a stroke. It was consequently in the absence of both Prime Minister and Foreign Secretary that, on 6 July, the Cabinet considered the complex of German–Soviet issues. Much had happened since the last fruitless meeting of the Foreign Ministers of Britain, France, the United States and the Soviet Union in 1949. The divergence of British and American opinion was beginning to reach significant proportions. Lord Salisbury, in charge of the Foreign Office during Eden's illness, put forward a lengthy paper[2] on policy towards the Soviet Union in the light of changes since Stalin's death. The nub of it was that, although longterm Soviet policies had not changed, there were signs of change in the Soviet Union itself which might even go so far as to modify the nature of the regime. Such moves as there had been to reduce international tension might stem partly from a desire to weaken and divide the West and there might be no readiness for serious discussions, but the possibilities ought to be tested. Salisbury was concerned at the 'new and dangerous American tendency ... to interpret the situation behind the iron curtain as already shaky and to advocate new, although unspecified, measures to encourage and even promote the early liberation of the satellite countries'. This was the period in which the Dulles philosophy of 'rollback' was in the centre of American thinking. Salisbury's recommendations were to discourage 'dangerous new initiatives' by the United States; to continue existing policies in relation to Germany, with West German membership of NATO as a reserve solution if the EDC were to fail; to reject neutralisation; and to persuade the Americans to keep the door open for informal high-level four-power talks. The Cabinet also took a paper by the Prime Minister[3] stressing the importance of the EDC and the goal of German reunification. He was confident that Germany would not within the next twenty years join Russia against the West, saw the only solution in a 'real UNO' and recommended that in the meantime the objective should be early ratification of the EDC, followed by a four-power conference. In a decision reflecting the incapacity of the Prime Minister and the Foreign Secretary, the Cabinet accepted both Salisbury's paper and the Prime Minister's recommendations.

The Berlin Conference of 1954

There was no chance of early French ratification of the EDC and the American Government were determined that a four-power conference should not delay the process even further by introducing a beguiling but unrealistic search for a means of avoiding the need for European defence. By the autumn, Eden was back at his desk and still firmly opposed to an ill-prepared summit. He wrote later in his diary about Churchill's speech that: 'It must be long in history since any one speech did so much damage to its own side,'[4] and argued with Churchill for a preparatory meeting of Foreign Ministers such as he had had in Moscow in 1943 to prepare for Teheran. It was eventually agreed that the best course was to satisfy public desire for a meeting as quickly as possible and to propose that it should be held between the four Foreign Ministers in Berlin, the location preferred by the Soviet Union, in January 1954. The Western aim was, as it had been in 1950, to discuss the organisation of free elections and the establishment of an all-German Government as the first steps towards a solution of the German problem. The whole of British and American policy was now based on the integration of Western Germany into the European–Atlantic structure and it was reasonable to hope that a Germany reunited on the basis of free elections would voluntarily choose the path of association with Western Europe on which the Federal Republic had already embarked. The course of Soviet policy in Eastern and Central Europe since 1945 and the experience of the Korean War had removed any temptation British ministers might have had to gamble on the alternative of a neutralised Germany. In notes of 4 August and 15 August 1954, the Soviet Union held to its policy that the formation of a provisional government and the holding of a peace conference should precede the elections; they also proposed that the conference should include China and should consider a wider range of world problems. From their point of view, the gamble of German reunification made sense – if indeed it made sense at all – only on a basis which effectively preserved the existing East German regime as forming half of the first all-German Government, and formally excluded any defence linkage between a reunified Germany and the

Western powers. The Soviet objective was perceived by Eden[5] as being to secure an American withdrawal from Europe and to prevent the resurgence of a strong, united Germany integrated with the West. He was entirely correct. As the official Soviet history put it: 'Every new Soviet proposal was a further obstruction to the remilitarisation of West Germany and its inclusion in aggressive military blocs.'[6] After a year's experience of post-Stalinist Russia, the British Government concluded that there was still no evidence of a fundamental change in Soviet foreign policy.

None of the participants embarked on the Berlin conference with any expectation of success. It was in large measure a public contest in which each side hoped to influence the more malleable sections among the Western Europeans – and in particular the Germans – by a public demonstration of the other's intransigence. Shortly before the conference opened, Churchill invited the Soviet Ambassador to lunch at Chequers, and spoke in terms which, he hoped, would help to disabuse the Soviet Government of hopes of exploiting British–American differences. His assurance that the British Government had no desire to change the situation in the Soviet Union's 'satellites' by war was no more calculated to arouse enthusiasm than was his hope that if it proved necessary to break off at Berlin, this might be merely for a year. It was, perhaps, not surprising that when Eden conveyed the Prime Minister's greetings to Molotov at Berlin, the response was 'in no way cordial',[7] or that later Malik should have launched at Roberts a 'rather venomous attack' on Churchill, who was 'no friend of the Soviet Union and had never been one'.[8]

Mistrust played a major part in British–Soviet relations at this time. Misunderstanding did not. British expectations were proved correct, even in the handling of the administrative arrangements for the Berlin Conference. The four Commandants were given the task of making the arrangements for the Conference. Was Berlin one city or four sectors? Were there two sides or four parties? Should there be one meeting place, two, or four? The finer points of occupation theology were at issue as we laboured through a succession of all-night meetings before eventually agreeing that the ministers should meet for one week in West Berlin, followed by one week in the East and a final week in the West. In a final bizarre moment the Soviet Commandant, having been instructed to propose this eminently sensible compromise, was so startled by our immediate acceptance that he refused to agree to his own proposal without first returning to his headquarters for confirmation from higher authority. Such were the minutiae of the four-power relationship.

The Conference, which began on 25 January 1954, proceeded on predictable lines. The agreed Western proposal was put forward by Eden and was countered by the Molotov proposals for a peace treaty providing for the withdrawal of foreign forces and the constitution of a German national army. The Soviet Union continued to insist upon the establishment of a provisional government of representatives from East and West prior to the holding of elections. Molotov spent much time on public denunciation of the EDC and NATO hoping, in Eden's view, to promote enough dissension in the Western ranks to bring about an American withdrawal from Europe. Deadlock over Germany continued throughout the conference and was extended to Austria, despite Western acceptance of an earlier Soviet draft peace treaty. The only agreement reached was that a subsequent conference should be held in Geneva, with Chinese participation, to consider the problems of Korea and Indo-China. Reporting back to Cabinet, the Foreign Secretary noted the extreme rigidity of the Soviet position over European problems, a rigidity which he thought stemmed from a sense of weakness.

The relaxation of strategic controls

The Prime Minister, neither surprised nor deterred by the outcome of the Berlin Conference, turned his thoughts, as Lloyd George had done in 1919, to the possible expansion of East–West trade as 'evidence that we were continuing to try to find peaceful means of living side by side with the Soviet Union'. A mission of British businessmen had returned from Moscow in January with the offer of substantial contracts, only to learn that more than half the goods the Russians wanted to buy were subject to strategic export control applied in accordance with arrangements agreed at the Allied Coordinating Committee (COCOM). Ministers were soon locked in dispute with the United States over the need for relaxation of the controls. Political instinct and commercial interest coincided and on 24 March the Prime Minister wrote to President Eisenhower: 'I am anxious to promote an easement of relations with Soviet Russia and to encourage and aid any development of Russian life which leads to a wider enjoyment by the Russian masses of the consumer goods of which you speak.' He spoke of relaxing both the 'grim discipline' of the Russian people and the international tension and remarked that the real peril, the development of the hydrogen bomb was 'nearer and more deadly to us than to you'.[9] In the event, some relaxation of controls was agreed.

The Geneva Conference and Indo-China

The focus of British–Soviet relations now moved away from Germany. The Geneva Conference of Foreign Ministers which opened on 26 April 1954 was primarily concerned with the problem of Indo-China. Here again, as in Korea, was part of the legacy of 1945 and here again the role of the Soviet Union in the doctrines and policies of a worldwide expansion of Communist power and influence had to be tested in the environment of post-imperial Asian nationalism. Britain was heavily and in the end successfully engaged in defeating Communist insurgency in Malaya. It had no standing in the Indo-China dispute other than that which flowed from membership of the Security Council in relation to international disputes and of the Council of Foreign Ministers in relation to the post-war settlements. The French resistance against the Viet Minh forces in Indo-China was already heavily dependent upon American aid and before the conference opened the French Government had appealed for direct American military intervention. The course of the conference need not concern us in terms of British–Soviet relations. The co-chairmanship of Eden and Molotov served, however, to enhance the British role in the eventual agreement on the effective partition of Vietnam and encouraged the hope that a more fruitful bilateral relationship could lead to a measure of agreement on the broader East–West relationship. It is difficult to judge the accuracy of Eden's diary assessment that Molotov 'clearly thinks that he and I have a special task in this conference to try and facilitate agreement'.[10] Agreement was in fact reached and both Britain and the Soviet Union made a contribution to it. It was reached in terms which gave the Communists half of Vietnam, with undertakings regarding reunion which, in the circumstances of that unhappy country, doubtless left them feeling confident about its eventual forcible reunion under their control. Ten years later, the North Vietnamese attack and US intervention found Britain once again seeking to use the relationship with the Soviet Union to secure a settlement, but by then the attempt was doomed to failure. Of the Geneva Conference, Eden's biographer comments[11] that, churlish and unimpressed though the Americans and part of the British press were, 'others recognised one of the most remarkable diplomatic achievements of the post-war world'. Eden had indeed conducted a skilful piece of diplomacy, but the Geneva agreement was little more than a post marking the first stage on the road to Communist control of Vietnam.

'A measure of tolerable agreement'

One other outcome of the Geneva Conference of Foreign Ministers was agreement on the holding of a further conference at the level of Heads of Government, also in Geneva, a year later. Before it occurred, however, Churchill took a remarkable personal initiative in an attempt to arrange a summit conference. There was in mid-1954 a concentrated Soviet campaign on the theme of 'peaceful coexistence' in which British policy was contrasted with the 'so-called policy of strength' of the United States. Churchill himself had, on 30 April, made a speech to the Primrose League in which he spoke of the need to 'establish with Russia such relations as, despite all the irritations, misgivings and disagreements, will convince the Russian people and the Soviet Government that we wish them peace, happiness and ever-growing prosperity ... and that we wish to see them playing a worthy and glorious role in the leadership of mankind'. In Washington, in June, he had expressed the view that 'we ought to have a try for peaceful coexistence'[12] and Eden, in Parliament, had expressed the more modest ambition of 'a measure of tolerable agreement'.[13] Sir William Hayter in Moscow and the officials in the Foreign Office wrote lengthy minutes to one another – and also to the Prime Minister – on the doctrine of 'peaceful coexistence' – or, as it was more cynically but more accurately described in one minute, 'hostile co-existence'.[14] Hayter quoted Dryden:

> 'Tis all a cheat; yet filled with hope
> Men favour the deceit.

Nevertheless, any easing of the tension of armed confrontation was welcome in Britain. The stabilisation might, as Hayter believed, be only superficial and subversion might continue, but if the Soviet Union no longer saw advantage in adventure, this was all to the good. William Strang, now in the House of Lords, thought that a peaceful coexistence which meant merely absence of war was attainable but 'a positive spirit of harmony and concord' was not to be hoped for.[15]

While the debate was continuing, Churchill, sensing the mood, was itching for action. On 4 July, on his way home from Washington, he despatched a personal telegram to Molotov suggesting a meeting with Malenkov as a prelude to a possible wider meeting. Within two days he received a welcoming response. Churchill's action had, however, not been cleared with his Cabinet and it provoked a substantial storm. The

Prime Minister had in mind a bilateral meeting which would enable him to explore whether a basis could be created, for instance by a Soviet gesture over the Austrian Peace Treaty, for a three- or four-power meeting with Malenkov.[16] He claimed to be doing no more than following up his speech of 11 May 1953 and also a parliamentary motion of 5 April 1954 calling for an 'immediate initiative' towards a meeting of Heads of Government. His colleagues doubted both the wisdom and the propriety of his action. In Cabinet, Eden noted the anti-American tone of Soviet statements at the end of the Geneva Conference and, although loyally supporting his master, was clearly unhappy. Lord Salisbury was particularly critical of Churchill's move and his remarks confirmed the way in which British opinion was turning against the Dulles policy and the general anti-Soviet mood in Washington. He held firmly to the relationship with the United States as the cornerstone of British policy and was concerned that bilateral talks with the Soviet Union might encourage the development of independent American policies. The Cabinet minutes, however, report him, *inter alia*, in the following terms: 'Some believed that the greatest threat to world peace came from the Russians. He himself believed that the greater risk was that the United States might decide to bring the East–West issue to a head while they still had overwhelming superiority in atomic weapons and were comparatively immune from atomic attack by Russia.'

Churchill had, in fact, cleared his policy with a somewhat reluctant Eisenhower, but his colleagues were unimpressed and the Cabinet's dilemma was only resolved by the Soviet Union choosing this moment to launch a new initiative to prevent the incorporation of West German forces into the alliance by proposing a conference of all European Governments on the establishment of a system of collective security in Europe.[17] Thankfully, the Cabinet agreed that the proposal for a bilateral summit should be left in abeyance. This was the last major intervention of Churchill in the conduct of a relationship in which he had played a prominent part ever since 1917. Having advocated the crushing of the Bolsheviks, urged the breaking of relations, forged the wartime alliance and set the philosophical basis for the Cold War, now, as Harold Macmillan was to put it: 'His last service was to have the vision to realise that the Soviet monolith would itself begin to undergo changes inseparable from growth and the lapse of time.'[18]

A month later, with the refusal of the French National Assembly to ratify the EDC Treaty, the British Government had to turn its mind back from the relationship with the Soviet Union to the reconstruction of the Western alliance. There was little doubt where the priority lay. Without the presence of American forces in Europe and substantial American support for the European defence effort, there would be no effective counter to Soviet force in Europe and the whole carefully constructed Western system might disintegrate. A European, and above all a German, contribution to European defence was seen as a political necessity in the United States and the only route by which it could now be achieved was German membership of NATO. At the end of 1954, after one defeat and by a narrow majority on the second vote, the French National Assembly ratified the Paris agreements which established the basis for German entry into NATO. Britain independently undertook to maintain forces on the European mainland. As Eden put it in his memoirs: 'Germany was now a sovereign partner in the defence of Europe.'[19] The union of the greater part of Germany under a right-wing Government in a military alliance with the United States and Canada as well as Britain, France and most of the rest of Western Europe, was the combination which the Soviet leadership had foreseen when they tested Allied policy in Berlin in 1948. Now it had come about and in terms of the 'correlation of forces', it marked the failure of ten years of post-war Soviet diplomacy.

Detente and the status quo

The response by the new Soviet leadership to this culminating act of Western policy was summed up by Hayter in the summer and autumn of 1955[20] as being the adoption of a policy of detente and the status quo. In other words they wished to reduce the tension in their relationship with the West, but to do so at no cost to their established gains. In Hayter's view, the ultimate Soviet objective of the triumph of Communism was unchanged and there would be determination not to prejudice the position in Eastern Germany, but 'practical, limited, short-term bargaining' might be possible. Before Hayter formed this view, there had, however, already been signs of the erratic course which British–Soviet relations were to follow through much of the Khrushchev period. It was soon to become apparent that although preservation of the status quo might be the Soviet objective in Europe, it certainly had no part in Soviet policy outside Europe. In September 1955 the Soviet decision to supply arms to Egypt brought a fruitless exchange of correspondence between Eden and Bulganin and heralded a sequence of events which was to bring both the end of Eden's premiership and the virtual extinction of the Soviet presence in Egypt. That, however, was for the future.

In the field of bilateral relations, one immediate effect of German membership of NATO was Soviet annulment of the bilateral treaties with Britain and France, an action notified on 20 December 1954 and implemented on 7 May 1955. The treaty was not seen in Britain, as it had been by Stalin, as 'a mere scrap of paper'.[21] The British Government expressed their regret, but were firm that they could not 'allow themselves to be deflected by any threat from their chosen course' and the treaty died quietly.

The Austrian State Treaty

In the summer of 1954, Churchill had hoped that a Soviet gesture on the Austrian Peace Treaty might open the way for a summit meeting at which wider issues might be resolved. What happened instead was that the entry of West Germany into NATO opened the way to the Austrian State Treaty. The Soviet Government saw the Western objective as being to include Austria in NATO and turn it into an 'Alpine fortress'.[22] In order to ensure that Austria did not go the way of Germany, they hastily decided to gamble on neutralisation and, in three days of negotiation with the Austrians in Moscow, agreed to immediate signature of the Austrian State Treaty and the withdrawal of occupation forces in exchange for a guarantee of permanent Austrian neutrality. In consequence, the Austrian State Treaty was signed by the four powers on 15 May. With its signature, a major potential source of friction was removed and Austria, politically neutral, was free to develop its natural economic and cultural links with Western Europe. Ten years had passed since the time when Britain and her partners had been concerned that Austria, Finland, Czechoslovakia and Yugoslavia might all fall into the group of Eastern European Communist states wholly subservient to the Soviet Union. The 1948 coup had brought Czechoslovakia under Soviet control, but the independence of Finland had been secured and when the new Soviet leadership came to terms with Yugoslav independence of Moscow and signed the Austrian State Treaty, the balance sheet was not bad. The Austrian outcome was rightly seen as a remarkable achievement. It brought direct benefit to Austria and it also demonstrated that the East–West relationship in Europe need not be a zero-sum game. With time, there would come a more general recognition of the mutual benefit in settlements which removed the points of direct confrontation and recognised the heterogeneity of Europe. Some observers might wonder whether that time would have come more quickly if the West had been prepared to gamble on a more flexible response to the Soviet scheme for Germany in 1954. The answer must be that the circumstances were wholly different and the stakes were too high. A year and a half after the Austrian Treaty Soviet tanks were on the streets of Budapest. Khrushchev had to build the Berlin Wall before Gorbachev could recognize that it had to be demolished.

The Geneva Summit

On 6 April 1955, Churchill's post-war administration came to an end. Eden succeeded him and Harold Macmillan took over the Foreign Office. With the security of Western Europe now on a more solid base than at any time since 1945, Britain could turn back to the search for a resolution of the underlying problems in East–West relations. As Churchill wryly remarked, Eden's dislike of summits waned swiftly after his move into Downing Street and on 10 May 1955 a tripartite proposal was put to Moscow for a meeting of Heads of Government which would hopefully provide the basis for a subsequent meeting of Foreign Ministers and initiate a long diplomatic process, designed to lead, through specialised meetings at various levels, to the gradual resolution of the complex of East–West problems. The outcome was the Geneva summit from 26 October to 17 November 1955 at which President Eisenhower, M. Faure and Eden met the two Soviet leaders, Marshal Bulganin and Khrushchev, the latter having already ousted Malenkov and established his own supremacy. This was the first meeting at Head of Government level between the Soviet Union and the Western powers, either jointly or individually, since Potsdam and, with the failure of the Paris summit in 1960, it was to prove the only quadripartite meeting at that level. As a meeting, despite its unique character, it is now virtually forgotten. The preparatory Cabinet paper noted that there were as yet 'no signs of any new flexibility in the Russian attitude'[23] and, in the event, the substantive discussion of the German problem opened up no new perspectives. Eden was, however, impressed by the fact that the Soviet Union seemed 'more apprehensive of the resurgence of Germany than of encirclement by the United States' and that its leaders were 'genuinely anxious to secure ... a friendlier relationship with the Western powers'. Various schemes of 'disengagement' designed to lessen the armed confrontation in Europe were beginning to be developed at this time and the conference also enabled Eden to put forward a package of proposals for European security including a plan for joint inspection of forces in Eastern and Western Europe. In Moscow, Bulganin spoke of the Eden plan as 'likely to have a positive influence' and, although the subsequent meeting of Foreign Ministers from 27 October to 16 November proved wholly fruitless, this phase of summit diplomacy did reduce the degree of misunderstanding and lessened the tensions, including those between the United States and China. The Soviet Union made much of the 'spirit of Geneva' and Eden was able to take the opportunity to issue an invitation to Bulganin and Khrushchev to visit Britain in the following year.

Bulganin and Khrushchev in Britain

The consolidation of Khrushchev's power was marked by the Twentieth Party Congress in February 1956, at which he made his celebrated denunciation of Stalin and affirmed the policy of peaceful coexistence for the conduct of relations with the Western powers. It did not, however, greatly change the British assessment of Soviet policy. The Labour Party was beginning to be restive for an end to the 'cold-war posture', but the Government was waiting for deeds rather than words.[24]

In Moscow, Hayter pondered upon the question whether the Soviet Union was becoming conservative rather than expansionist and concluded that it was too early to say whether the hope 'that this state should cease to be expanding, cease to be genuinely Marxist and in fact cease to be a nuisance to the world as a whole' might be realised. The Soviet Union might seek to lull the free world rather than intimidate it, but a 'genuine agreement to live and let live with an expanding Marxist state' was a contradiction in terms. He saw the Soviet Union continuing by a sort of force of inertia to carry out revolutionary activities which had little relevance to its real interests or desires.[25] Lullabies were, in any case, scarcely Khrushchev's style. The first quarter of 1956 was marked by what Hayter described as a 'high pitch of synthetic cordiality', but the tone changed when, baulked in Europe, Khrushchev and Bulganin made a foray to India and Burma, in the course of which and subsequently both men attacked Britain in such violent terms as almost to cause the Cabinet to withdraw Eden's invitation to visit Britain. Eventually, however, Ministers concluded that a policy of coexistence might better be pursued 'until we were in a position to bring all the neutral powers within the Western orbit',[26] and the visit took place from 18 to 27 April 1956.

This visit by Marshal Bulganin as Chairman of the Soviet Council of Ministers and Khrushchev as leader of the Communist Party of the Soviet Union was the first occasion since the October Revolution on which the country's top leadership had visited a Western country.[27] Lenin had indeed spent much of his exile in the West, and part of it in London, but he did not visit it after 1917. Stalin also never visited Western Europe after the Revolution (unless one counts the Potsdam Conference) and it was to be almost another thirty years before Mikhail Gorbachev set foot in Britain.

There was no expectation on the British side that this visit would lead to any early and substantive results. There were many major international issues which might usefully be discussed between the two countries, but few which were susceptible of bilateral negotiation. It was seen essentially as an opportunity to begin the creation of mutual confidence by establishing a personal link with the new Soviet leadership, and in this it had a measure of success. The discussions ranged widely over the problems of Europe, the Middle East, the Far East and disarmament. They were not easy, but they were substantial. The final communiqué dealt with the relaxation of international tension; the problems of the Middle East where British concern was growing quickly and on which Eden felt he had obtained concrete results; disarmament and trade. There was talk of the purchase of up to £1000 million of British goods over five years and agreement was reached on increased technical, scientific, sporting and artistic exchanges. A visit to the Palace for tea with the Queen passed off uneventfully, but a dinner with the Labour Party was marked by a sharp quarrel. George Brown, at that time on the Opposition front bench, had a temper as volatile as Khrushchev's and when, as one of the British hosts, he questioned the Soviet leaders about the treatment of Social Democratic politicians in Eastern Europe, the dinner ended in disarray. It was only after the Soviet leaders had returned to Moscow that the news of the death of a British naval frogman, Commander Crabb, revealed the sorry outcome of an unauthorised operation, delicately but transparently veiled as 'trials of certain under-water apparatus', in the vicinity of the naval vessels which had brought them. The incident caused some embarrassment to the British Government, which made a formal expression of regret, but although Pravda spoke of a 'shameful operation' the Soviet Government appeared neither greatly surprised nor seriously concerned.

The public reaction to the visit was mixed. The Government received numerous letters of protest, but on balance any move towards an easier relationship was welcomed. In his memoirs, Eden summed up the visit by saying: 'As a result of ten days spent together in almost constant contact, I felt that I knew these Russians as no volumes of despatches could have revealed them to me.'[28] To his colleagues, he spoke of the candour and realism with which both sides had conducted the discussions[29] and in his diary he noted, 'I do not believe that the Russians have any plans at present for military aggression in the West. On the other hand are we prepared with other weapons to meet the new challenge? This seems to me the major issue of foreign policy.'[30] In a broadcast, he remarked that in the long history of diplomacy, suspicion had done more harm than confidence and spoke of the discussions as 'the beginning of a beginning ... It may be – I think it is – true that the immediate danger of war has receded and that is good.'[31]

Hungary and Suez

The danger had not receded very far. Immediately after the visit, it was noted that the Soviet Union's exchanges with Britain were at a higher level than with any other country, but the new mood was soon to be sharply disrupted. It was Stalin who had fastened the Soviet grip on Eastern Europe and his denunciation by Khrushchev must have aroused latent aspirations to freedom which threatened to disrupt the Soviet imperial structure. The focal points were Poland and Hungary. With Gomulka as the new leader of the Polish party, the crisis in that country was contained. For a time, it seemed that Hungary, under the moderate Imre Nagy, might establish its own, less repressive brand of socialism, with its subordination to the Soviet Union loosened and its links with the West increased. But the threat that Hungary might breach the Soviet defence *glacis* by withdrawing from the Warsaw Pact was too much. After an early indecisive appearance in Budapest, the Soviet forces launched a mass attack on Sunday 4 November 1956 and in the succeeding days heavy civilian casualties were sustained. The Hungarian resistance was estimated to have cost 20 000 lives. Public opinion in Britain was outraged and the Archbishop of Canterbury castigated Her Majesty's recent guests as 'instruments and slaves of the devil', but the Western Governments were wholly preoccupied with the Suez crisis. The British airborne attack on Port Said took place on 5 November and on the same day Marshal Bulganin wrote to the Prime Minister warning of Britain's vulnerability to rocket attack and expressing 'determination to use force to crush the aggressors'. In Moscow, a carefully organised mob invaded the British Embassy.

Although the United Nations General Assembly duly called for the withdrawal of Soviet forces from Hungary, Britain was effectively paralysed and virtually the only direct British response, other than verbal reproaches by the Prime Minister, was the cancellation of a planned visit by the Sadlers Wells Ballet and the boycotting of the Soviet celebration of the anniversary of the October Revolution. There was a certain feeling that Dulles' strong language had created in Eastern Europe an expectation of more effective Western support, but Eisenhower was quite clear that nothing could be done by force to help the Hungarians. So, as Britain withdrew from Suez and Eden from Downing Street, Khrushchev proceeded methodically to re-establish control over Hungary.

Macmillan and nuclear arms

The remarkable feature of relations during the Khrushchev years was the speed with which they alternated between the promise of coexistence and the threat of war. In 1955, Macmillan, as Foreign Secretary, had been complaining that the accommodating attitude of the Soviet Union at the General Assembly was placing the solidarity of the anti-Soviet front in jeopardy.[32] Now, as Prime Minister after Suez, he was to construct a new relationship with the United States and secure British–American collaboration in nuclear weaponry on the basis of resistance to the Communist threat.[33] At Bermuda, in March 1957, he anticipated Reagan when he told Eisenhower: 'You cannot be neutral in a war between two principles, one of which – Communism – is evil.'[34] Hungary had demonstrated the readiness of the Soviet Union to apply force ruthlessly in order to retain control in a key area of Central Europe. The potential consequences of the use of force between nuclear powers were, however, increasingly alarming British public opinion. This was the time of the Aldermaston peace marches and, apart from the intrinsic need for detente, Macmillan needed to make some gesture to the growing demand for an effort to reach an understanding with the Soviet Union. The Rapacki plan for an atom-free zone in Europe was attracting attention and the whole question of arms control and disarmament was moving towards the central position in East–West relations, which it was to hold intermittently throughout the succeeding years. It is a theme which cannot be comprehensively treated within the confines of this study, but it was of particular significance in the development of the British–Soviet relationship during Macmillan's premiership.

In April 1957, Macmillan received a 10 000-word letter from Bulganin, the theme of which was that it was 'exceptionally important' that 'the present tension in relations between the Soviet Union and Great Britain should be replaced by good friendly relations'. In substance, the letter concentrated on disarmament and, in particular, the prohibition of nuclear testing, an awkward point for Britain, since the first thermonuclear tests were due in the following month. In reply, Macmillan pointed to the need for progress in both conventional and nuclear disarmament as well as in matters such as the removal of jamming from BBC broadcasts and of restrictions on the sale of British books and newspapers.[35] It was to be the beginning of a brief but useful exploitation of the bilateral relationship, in which a British Prime Minister once again took the lead in the conduct of relations by the Western powers.

The repair of the British–American relationship, begun at Bermuda, was dramatically accelerated by the launch of the first Soviet inter-continental ballistic missile in August 1957 and the first Sputnik earth satellite on 4 October 1957. The new mood of extrovert Soviet self-confidence, symbolised by Khrushchev, was having a remarkable effect on the United States. The suppression of Hungary had demonstrated the imperial ruthlessness of the Soviet regime. The recollection of the Soviet Union's wartime achievements had not faded, and it was beginning to seem that the concentration of power in a single-party state of such size might place at the service of a hostile ideology and an ambitious leadership a formidable combination of economic and military power. The spectre of the Soviet Colossus rose from time to time before Western policy-makers and in Khrushchev's final years it assumed a menacing aspect. At a Cabinet meeting on 21 October[36] the Prime Minister told his colleagues of his acceptance of an invitation by President Eisenhower to visit Washington and consider how the collective strength of the free world might be mobilised against the Soviet threat. In Macmillan's view, the US Government 'appeared to be convinced that, in order to counter the Soviet threat, of which the earth satellite was the most recent and most spectacular warning, the whole structure of Western collaboration needed to be re-examined'. The result of Macmillan's visit was to repair the breach with the United States and to align the two countries in a recognition that 'no single country, however powerful, could alone withstand the Soviet threat' and that there had to be 'a common policy for countering Soviet encroachment, not only by military preparations, but also by political, economic and propaganda measures'.[37] The formal British–American

Declaration of Common Purpose of 25 October spoke significantly of the Soviet Union's 'formidable material accomplishments' and provided for joint measures of security against 'the threat of International Communism' and the 'danger of Communist despotism'. What was significant was not merely that Khrushchev had provoked this response, but that in doing so he had provided the means for healing the Anglo–American breach and that this had happened at a crucial point in the British relationship with the newly forming European Economic Community (EEC). The British concentration upon the trans-Atlantic relationship as the central element in the organisation of resistance to the Soviet Union re-emphasised the priorities of British policy, complicating the already difficult problems of participation in the movement towards closer integration of Western Europe and hardening de Gaulle's mind in favour of a veto on the subsequent British application for full membership of the Community.

The Berlin crisis and Macmillan's visit to Moscow

In reinforcing the defence potential of Britain within NATO and securing the future of the British nuclear deterrent, Macmillan did not lose sight of the parallel need to eliminate the causes of tension. Selwyn Lloyd put to the Cabinet a typically cautious Foreign Office paper on relations with the Soviet Union.[38] The Soviet leadership, he said, was less unattractive to Western public opinion than it had been in the Stalin years, but Soviet imperialism remained a major threat. It behoved the British Government to show willingness to negotiate, but unfortunately on the Soviet side there seemed to be no willingness to negotiate about anything, merely a process of discussion by public statement designed to manoeuvre the West into unilateral concessions. Nevertheless, it was Macmillan's belief that, if war could be avoided, the offensive features of Soviet communism might eventually become 'blurred, blunted and perhaps softened'.[39] A lengthy process of NATO consultation and correspondence with Khrushchev about a possible summit ensued, but throughout 1958 relations deteriorated, first over the Middle East and then over Quemoy and Matsu, leading Macmillan at one point to cite to Dulles the much-quoted minute of Palmerston in 1853 to the effect that 'the policy and practice of the Russian Government has always been to push forward its encroachments as fast and as far as the apathy and want of firmness of other Governments would allow them to go, but always stop and retire when it was met with decided resistance'. In Moscow, Sir Patrick Reilly had succeeded Sir William Hayter as Ambassador and Macmillan raised with him the possibility of taking up the invitation, originally issued to Eden, to visit Moscow. Shepilov had now briefly replaced Molotov in the Soviet Foreign Ministry. Molotov's removal seemed good news, but with each change, Khrushchev's power was enhanced. Reilly was concerned at his apparent megalomania and commented that, although now waged with different weapons, the Soviet Union's world-wide campaign was still the Cold War which it had been called over ten years earlier.

There was indeed a frightening unpredictability to Soviet policy and the crisis erupted when on 10 November Khrushchev demanded the withdrawal of Allied troops from Berlin, following this up with a note stating that the Soviet Union regarded the existing arrangements about Berlin as null and void, but did not intend to change the procedures for military traffic for six months and was prepared to negotiate for a 'demilitarised free city'. He then proposed a peace conference with the two German states, after which the Soviet Union would relinquish its functions in respect of communications between Berlin and West Germany. For the West, the situation was more complex than in 1948. Two German states now existed, despite the fact that only one was recognised. West Berlin itself was no longer a city of wartime ruins surviving at subsistence level. Its economy could not be sustained by an airlift. In any case, there was no direct threat to civil supplies. It was arguable that in the circumstances of 1958 there was no reason why the Soviet Union should maintain the fiction of wartime occupation in order to enable the Western powers to maintain their position in Berlin. The very existence of a prosperous West Berlin constituted a challenge to the drab East German state and the flow of refugees was both an economic handicap and a political embarrassment. If the Soviet Government chose to place responsibility for access to West Berlin in the hands of the GDR, the Allies could scarcely blockade themselves by refusing to accept German controls. Nor could they go to war because a German official had replaced a Russian. Yet to recognise the GDR was to take a further step back from the reunification of Germany. To abandon West Berlin, the symbol of resistance to Soviet pressure, was unthinkable.

At this point Macmillan took the lead, as Bevin had done ten years earlier, in shaping the Western response. The Soviet Government accepted his proposal for a ten-day visit beginning on 21 February 1959 and so, the first British Prime Minister to visit Moscow since the end of the war, wearing his Finnish fur hat, he returned to the city which he had first visited as a tourist nearly thirty years before. He presented the visit as a reconnaissance rather than a negotiation, but he achieved something more. He found Khrushchev an 'excitable, petulant, occasionally impossible, but not unlovable extrovert', a 'mixture between Peter the Great and Lord Beaverbrook'. Macmillan's reception typified all the volatility of Khrushchev's temperament. His decision to give a visit to the dentist precedence over an out-of-town visit with Macmillan was a thinly disguised snub and throughout the visit Macmillan was subjected to a typical Russian alternation of flattery and brutality, lavish hospitality and calculated discourtesy, charm and anger. Yet, in the end, the visit did good. The final communiqué recorded disagreement on Berlin and Germany, but it was agreed that an urgent settlement was necessary and, in the course of discussion, the six-month ultimatum was effectively dropped. Agreement was also recorded on the need to halt nuclear testing under an effective system of international inspection and control. In the field of bilateral relations Khrushchev offered a non-aggression treaty but this, in Macmillan's view, should be a multilateral agreement representing the end of the road, not a bilateral agreement at the outset. His counter-offer of a joint declaration was not taken up. On his return, Macmillan reported to the Queen that he had found in Khrushchev 'certain elements of sincerity'. At his initiative the Great Britain–USSR Association was set up in order to foster personal contacts between citizens of the two countries and a new British–Soviet Trade Agreement offered a stimulus to the development of trade. Beneath the surface, the intelligence communities were, as ever, active. Within a few years, the Soviet agents in Britain, the Krögers and Gordon Lonsdale, and the British agent in Moscow, Oleg Penkovsky, with his collaborator, Greville Wynne, were all to be arrested. For the time being, however, Macmillan had a favourable bilateral relationship on the basis of which he could pursue his broader aim of developing the route through a Foreign Ministers' Conference to a meeting of the four Heads of Government.

'Why should the UK try to stay in the big game?'

Two sets of negotiations were opened in Geneva in the first half of 1959, a meeting of the four Foreign Ministers, with the association of German representatives, on the problems of Germany as a whole and Berlin in particular and a lower-level negotiation on the halting of nuclear testing. Macmillan's hope was that, without too much delay a basis could be established which would justify the holding of a four-power summit. Adenauer and de Gaulle were both, for their own political reasons, taking a hard tactical line and ready to exploit any sign of British appeasement, while Eisenhower, guided no doubt by Dulles and sensitive to his own political standing, was determined to secure some assurance of positive results before agreeing to a summit. Macmillan, equally determined to maintain the substance of the Western position in Berlin, wanted to encourage any readiness for compromise on Khrushchev's part and put it to Eisenhower that 'we and our allies should do and should be seen to do what ordinary people would think reasonable'.[40] This meant that, in relation to Berlin, there should be no military measures until, at least, a summit conference had been tried. Suddenly, without prior consultation, Eisenhower invited Khrushchev to visit the United States, possibly in connexion with a four-power summit in Canada. Khrushchev accepted the bilateral visit, leaving the summit open. Macmillan saw his careful diplomacy thrown into confusion and wrote angrily in his diary, 'Everyone will assume that the two Great Powers – Russia and the US – are going to fix up a deal over our heads and behind our backs ... People will ask, "Why should the UK try to stay in the big game? Why should she be a nuclear power?"'[41]

Macmillan's perception was accurate, but premature. The next stage was to be not the fixing up of a deal, but the precipitation of a rupture. Eisenhower's invitation was exactly the kind of initiative for which British opinion was hoping and Macmillan was given credit for having pursued the policy which brought it about. His policy received a further boost when Khrushchev's visit gave Eisenhower the basis for agreement to the holding of the four-power summit in Paris on 15 May 1960. Meanwhile the 1959 General Election had returned Macmillan to power with an increased majority. The election had turned largely on domestic issues. Public opinion was still considerably exercised about the hazards of a nuclear confrontation with the Soviet Union, but Gaitskell's success in holding the majority of the Labour Party against abandonment of the British nuclear deterrent meant that there was no direct party confrontation on the issue of relations with the Soviet Union. The depth of concern within the Labour Party and in the country at large was, however, such that Macmillan had a clear mandate to pursue, as an 'honest broker' his search for measures to reduce the sources of East–West confrontation. As the Conservative election manifesto put it, both sides had to learn to live together and the 'steady improvement in relations with the Soviet Union' had to be maintained.

The Paris Summit of 1960

The meeting of the Heads of Government of the Soviet Union, the United States, the United Kingdom and France, scheduled to take place in Paris on 15 May, brought the post-war process of four-power summit diplomacy to an end in a quite remarkable diplomatic fiasco. A fortnight before it was due to open, a high-altitude American photographic reconnaissance aircraft, the celebrated U2, was brought down over the Soviet Union and the pilot captured. The US Government, at first uncertain whether the real purpose of the mission was known, issued a series of evasive and contradictory statements which did nothing to ease the tension. Khrushchev's anger was rising with each apparent affront to the majesty of the Soviet Union. He took his delegation to Paris, but on the way there – possibly as a result of a meeting with his colleagues immediately before his departure – decided to harden his stand and, on arrival, demanded an apology in terms which no American President could have accepted. Dismissing Eisenhower's assurances as inadequate, he returned to Moscow, the three Western Heads of Government went their separate ways and the new era of confrontation between the two nuclear superpowers began to take shape.

Macmillan had worked hard to set up the summit. He did all he could to save it and the failure caused him deep distress. The outcome, however, was in the hands of the Soviet Union and the United States. Might it have been different? The President had foreseen the risk and had ruled, when authorising the U2 flight, that it should be the last of the series. After the incident, a quick expression of regret might have permitted the summit to proceed. Alternatively, if Khrushchev had wanted, he could have accepted Eisenhower's assurances in Paris and emerged from the whole affair with his own standing and that of the Soviet Union much enhanced. The ways of Western policy are such that he might indeed have secured a gain in terms of the arms control negotiations. To ask whether the Cuba crisis could have been avoided is to push speculation too far. What is certain is that, had the summit taken place, it would not have changed the reality of the new superpower relationship. Summit or no summit, from 1960 onwards, the British–Soviet relationship was to be conducted in a different context.

The Berlin Wall and Cuba

President Eisenhower's term was now nearly at an end and Khrushchev left the Berlin crisis to simmer through the second half of 1960 before his trial of strength with John Kennedy. The emerging pattern of East–West relations was symbolised by Kennedy's proposal to Khrushchev for a personal exchange of views between the two, without any attempt at negotiations. The meeting, held at Vienna on 3–4 June 1961, seems to have left Khrushchev, now at the height of his power, with the impression that the new young President might usefully be subjected to pressure. The situation in Berlin at this time was never far from flashpoint. Over the years since the end of the blockade, half the city had become a showplace for some of the more glossy manifestations of Western culture and the other half for some of the more repressive aspects of the socialist state. Between the two halves, the military personnel of the occupying powers and the civilian population of East and West moved freely and the various intelligence organisations conducted their multifarious operations. The escape route from East Germany into East Berlin, from East Berlin into West Berlin and from there to West Germany was simple. Between 1949 and 1961 more than two and a half million of East Germany's reluctant citizens had left, most of them by this route. Khrushchev's ultimata had increased tension to such a point that in July 1961 the flow reached 30 000. The Soviet Union had three possible courses: to let its East German satellite waste slowly away; to enforce the ultimatum and force the West out of the city; or to block the escape route at the simplest point. The building of the wall, begun on 13 August was, in one sense, a challenge to Western insistence on the unity of the city. More accurately, it could be seen as a defensive act, taken in near desperation, a humiliating confession, at a time when the Soviet Union was brandishing its new power, of total failure to meet the need of the German people for their basic material and moral sustenance. Macmillan's diary shows his deep concern about the possible consequences of Khrushchev's action: 'We may drift to disaster over Berlin – a terrible diplomatic defeat or (out of sheer incompetence) a nuclear war.'[42] But the lessons of the blockade had been learned. American and Soviet tanks confronted each other at the centre of Berlin, but no action was taken by the West to prevent the construction of the wall or by the East to obstruct the movement of British, French or American forces.

The building of the Wall eased Khrushchev's immediate problem, but it did not remove Berlin from the international agenda. In December 1961 a further long personal message to Macmillan renewed the demand for the withdrawal of Western forces and suggested that West, but not East Berlin should be made a free city. To this Macmillan responded with a suggestion which, in essence, went a long way to meet the main Soviet preoccupation in Europe:

> Just as we do not seek to upset the existing order in Eastern Europe, though we cannot approve of it, so you for your part should respect the existing positions of the Western Powers. This means that, until such time as we can reach agreement on a permanent solution for Germany, neither side should seek to frustrate the arrangements and the policies which are vital to the other.

Six months had passed since the death of Dulles, the advocate of 'roll-back'. Kennedy believed in solving the Berlin problem by negotiation and if Khrushchev really wanted, as Hayter had suggested, detente and the status quo, it was effectively on offer so far as Britain was concerned.

Macmillan's letter to Khrushchev was more than a mere stage in a verbal duel. The Soviet Union had resumed the atmospheric testing of major thermonuclear weapons and the United States was ready to follow suit. Macmillan was reflecting continuing and widespread British concern when, early in 1962, he put to Kennedy a proposal to seek a more general basis for detente, through negotiations with the Soviet Union, initially between the Foreign Ministers, on nuclear testing, non-proliferation, disarmament and European security. Kennedy and Khrushchev accepted the proposal for the initial meeting and, with France holding aloof, the American Secretary of State, Dean Rusk, and his British counterpart, Lord Home, had a meeting with Andrei Gromyko in Geneva, only to find him more rigid than ever in refusing to permit on-site inspection in the Soviet Union. Macmillan wrote in his memoirs: 'The controversy ran tediously on, losing itself like some great river in the sands and never reaching the sea.'[43]

Concurrently with the problems of nuclear weapons and the tussle over Berlin, British–Soviet relations were directly engaged as a result of a Soviet proposal to the British Government, based on the co-chairmanship of the 1954 Geneva Conference, to convene a multilateral conference on the situation in Laos. The Conference, in which fourteen nations participated, formed a stage in the continuing British involvement with the Soviet Union in the attempt to resolve the hostilities in Indo-China, an involvement which was to continue, and indeed to be intensified, during the period of the Labour Government. The 1961 Conference led to a measure of agreement on the independence, neutrality and territorial integrity of Laos, but the realities of the Vietnam War and the conflicting interests of the superpowers made it largely ineffective. The Soviet Union in these years was riding high on what the Twenty-Second Congress of the Party saw as the 'common interests of world socialism and the world national liberation movement'. Its growing power was placed behind the 'peoples fighting for liberation from imperialist oppression' in a move to 'deflate imperialism's omnipotence'.[44] Here was a line of development, easy enough to perceive in the Soviet Union's objectives from the earliest years, proclaimed during Khrushchev and Bulganin's Indian tour in 1956 and brought to a dominant position in East–West relations through the increase in Soviet power and global ambition at a time when the post-war disintegration of the old imperial structures had reached an advanced stage. It was a trend of Soviet policy which was to persist through the remainder of Khrushchev's years and for the greater part of Brezhnev's tenure of office.

While the disarmament negotiations were meandering on, the Cuban missile crisis of October 1962 made the possibility of nuclear war seem something more than a theoretical hazard. The failure of the Paris summit had marked the last stage in the post-war quadripartite relationship. Now, with a direct armed challenge and counter-challenge between the superpowers, the new structure of East–West relations was being tested. The details of the crisis do not belong here. What does belong is an assessment of the British role and of the consequences for future British policy towards the Soviet Union. The United States Government in the post-war years, like the British Government in the 1920s and 1930s, had been exercised by the threat of Communist subversion, but the threat to its own territory had been remote. The military aspect of the fight against Communism could be conducted in Europe and Asia. The development of Soviet rocket technology had created an awareness of potential vulnerability, but it was the emplacement of Soviet missiles in Cuba which made the potential threat seem a real one. As Macmillan observed, it was a far less significant threat than that under which the Europeans had long been living, but that did not lessen its psychological impact. Nor did it count for much, in the American reaction, that the Soviet Union was already open to attack by American land-based missiles in Turkey as well as by air-launched missiles from European bases. What mattered, for the purpose of this analysis, was the simple American perception of a direct Soviet nuclear challenge to the territory of the United States. It was a challenge which was bound to happen at some time. The Cuban revolution, the fiasco of the Bay of Pigs, the mood of confidence in the

Soviet Union and the erratic judgment of Nikita Khrushchev meant that it happened in Cuba in the autumn of 1962. Throughout the Cuba crisis there was close, full and personal consultation between Kennedy and Macmillan. The outcome proved the judgment of Kennedy and Macmillan correct and that of Khrushchev wrong. The Soviet missiles were removed from Cuba and, by tacit agreement, the American missiles were subsequently withdrawn from Turkey. Macmillan felt himself to be at the centre of events: 'We were in on and took full part in and almost responsibility for every American move ... The whole episode was like a battle; and we in Admiralty House felt as if we were in the battle HQ.'[45] In reality, for all that he felt himself to be at the HQ, Macmillan was not part of the command structure. The decisions which precipitated the crisis and those which ended it were American and Soviet decisions. Because of its very nature, the crisis had to be resolved directly between the two superpowers and, once they had been so engaged, the structure of East–West relations was changed.

10
Between the Europeans and the Superpowers

Britain's changing role

Henry Kissinger has spoken of the relationship with the Soviet Union as 'a persistent preoccupation for post-war American foreign policy'.[1] It has also been a preoccupation for British foreign policy, but there is a danger, when teasing out the thread of British–Soviet relations from the whole international fabric in which it is set, of giving the British–Soviet relationship a greater prominence in the calculations of British Governments than it has actually possessed. There is a danger, too, of tracing a misleadingly direct course for the bilateral relationship through the complex texture of a Government's many preoccupations. These qualifications apply with particular force to the period after 1962.

After the relative simplicity of an armed struggle, the post-war international scene presented the British Government with an increasingly complex set of circumstances into which the relationship with the Soviet Union had to be fitted and in terms of which its value had to be judged. From 1962 onwards there was an accentuation of this gradual, qualitative change. The relationship with the Soviet Union was still an issue in its own right for the British Government, but the formulation and implementation of a coherent policy required the integration of the day-to-day bilateral relationship with the approach to the Soviet Union as a European state and a nuclear superpower. The present chapter will trace this process through the 1960s and 1970s. For the greater part of that time the leadership of the Soviet Union was held by Leonid Brezhnev, and although Soviet diplomatic historians continued to force events into a Marxist–Leninist format and described the era as 'characterised by further advances in the world revolutionary process',[2] it has subsequently been seen as a period of progressive stagnation in the development of the Soviet Union itself. It was, for Britain, a period which frequently saw the country's diplomacy tossing uneasily in the intersecting wave patterns of the celebrated three circles – Europe, Atlantic and Commonwealth.

While struggling with the problems of an economy in travail and an imperial structure in the throes of reconstruction, successive British Governments had, as we have seen, from 1945 to 1955 to counter the threat of Soviet expansion in post-war Europe and to enlist the power of the United States in a European cause. At this stage, the task, difficult and unrewarding though it was in terms of relations with the Soviet Union, was relatively clear-cut, since the process of welding together Western Europe was an essential element in British policy in its own right and in relation to both the Soviet Union and the United States. The British concept was, however, one of a Europe organised on a basis compatible with Britain's existing internal policies and external obligations. In pursuing a policy of cooperation rather than integration, the British Governments of the post-war years, still conscious of the victory of 1945, were influenced by a mixture of emotions: belief that Britain could, mixing their metaphors, indefinitely ride the troika of Europe, the Commonwealth and the United States; reluctance to merge sovereignty into a federal Europe; doubt as to whether the Europeans themselves would welcome full British participation; and alarm at the incompatibility of the European concept with existing British obligations. The preferred pattern was that of the Organisation for European Economic Cooperation (OEEC) and the Council of Europe rather than new supra-national organisations. In this spirit Britain had cooperated with rather than joined the European Coal and Steel Community and the Atomic Community and had agreed to support, but not to join, the European Defence Community. Prior to 1956 this policy appeared – and indeed was – sustainable. The decision not to join in the first Schuman Plan discussions was unfortunate, but the conflict between the European and Atlantic aspects of British policy was still reconcilable.

The significant divergence began with the decision to stand aside from the critical stages in the inception of the European Economic Community (EEC) in 1955–6. From this point on, the growth in the economic power of Western Europe – and above all of an independent West Germany – began to coincide with the recognition by the Soviet Union and the United States of the nature of the new superpower relationship. The whole pattern of Britain's external relations had to adapt to the new scene and it had to do so at a time when the country was, once again, beset by economic problems. The ability to sustain the global responsibilities of a first-order power had been sapped and Suez had laid bare British vulnerability. As a factor in Soviet policy, Britain's significance was declining and, although the Soviet Union remained a major factor in British defence policy, there was progressively less room for Britain to do much about it.

To the extent that Britain was able to pursue the relationship with the Soviet Union during the period in which the integration of Western Europe was being determined, it was doing so in much closer cooperation with the United States than with France and Germany. This was a trend of greater significance for the future of British–Soviet relations than was, perhaps, realised at the time. It reflected in part the realities of nuclear weaponry and in part the political scene in the countries concerned.

The symbolic realignment of British policy was marked politically by the first formal application in 1961 for membership of the EEC and militarily by the withdrawal from east of Suez. The process was, however, a slow one. Despite all the policy papers of the Foreign Office and the speeches of ministers, it was in reality more a matter of gradual adaptation to evolving circumstances – an adaptation frustrated by the de Gaulle vetoes of 1963 and 1967 – than of a single conscious re-evaluation of the British role. The instinctive reluctance to tie Britain's fate irrevocably to continental Europe, the 'great power' syndrome, the attachment to the Commonwealth link and the technical problems of Commonwealth preference remained for many years powerful factors. Full membership of the Community seemed to many to be a betrayal of the Commonwealth and even if Britain had been ready at an earlier stage to join in the European process, success might well not have resulted.

In relation to the Soviet Union, membership of the EEC would constrain Britain's ability to operate an independent commercial policy, one of the traditional elements in the bilateral relationship. This was not, however, seen as a major issue by Britain and indeed the question of British relations with the Community was treated in isolation from the British–Soviet relationship. Technically, this was correct, but more deeply, in relation to the British Government's concept of its role in world affairs, there was a linkage. The 1963 veto on British membership of the European Communities cannot be attributed wholly to de Gaulle's reaction to the British–American nuclear defence relationship. The evolutionary process in Britain, in Europe, in China, in the Third World and in the two superpowers was moving swiftly but asynchronously. Paradoxically, both prior to and immediately after the Cuba crisis and the negotiations with the EEC, there was a period in which the British role in East–West relations was enhanced by the rigidity of Adenauer in respect of the East–West relationship in Europe and the determination of de Gaulle to stand aloof from the negotiations over the Berlin crisis and the Test Ban Treaty. The post-war quadripartite relationship even gave way briefly to a British–American–Soviet relationship. The power ratio in the early 1960s was, however very different from that of the war years. For the Soviet Union, British policy was significant not so much in its own right, but rather to the extent that it might influence American policy. This was in no sense a recreation of the wartime tripartite relationship.

Nuclear weaponry was now emerging as the central issue in relations with the Soviet Union. Britain, as a nuclear weapons power, was critically dependent upon the United States, Germany was excluded from the nuclear equation and de Gaulle was bent upon the restoration of the power and self-esteem of France. Before long, however, the natural evolution of the political process brought about a situation in which Germany, and to a lesser extent France, began to set the pace in dealing with the Soviet Union as a European power, while on the world-wide scale the American–Soviet bilateral relationship, dominant in its own right, was enhanced in its effect by the open breach between the Soviet Union and China. The Sino–Soviet clash had its origins in 1956 and by 1963 was both profound and public. For the Soviet Union it represented the greatest adverse change in the correlation of forces since the October Revolution and was a major factor in the redefinition of the whole pattern of East–West relations. Its effects were, however, slow to be felt in terms of British policy towards the Soviet Union.

In the new situation of the 1960s and 1970s that policy still turned on a familiar axis. The quadripartite responsibility for Berlin and Germany as a whole gave Britain a special position in respect of the stabilisation of the German–Soviet relationship, which was the prerequisite for the movement towards European detente leading to the Helsinki Conference. The co-chairmanship of the Geneva Conference also gave Britain some continuing role in the search for a solution to the war in Indo-China. The strategic nuclear arms negotiations had to be conducted at the superpower level, but Britain was actively involved in other aspects of the arms control process and from the mid-1960s to the mid-1970s British diplomacy remained active in both the European and the global relationship with the Soviet Union. Bilaterally, too, the process leading from Macmillan's first visit to Moscow in 1959 to Wilson's last in 1975 resulted in the most comprehensive network of agreements and exchanges since the time of Lloyd George and Ramsay MacDonald. Nevertheless, this must still count as a period during which the British role in the conduct of relations with the Soviet Union, although extremely active, was less significant in relation to wider issues than at any time since the war. That it coincided in part with a period of Labour Government in Britain was largely irrelevant. The factors which brought it about had already been determined.

The Nuclear Test Ban Treaty

Macmillan's final success in dealing with the Soviet Union was the signature on 5 August 1963 of the Nuclear Test Ban Treaty with the Soviet Union and the United States. The negotiations had been taking a weary and inconclusive course for some years, before Khrushchev, provoked perhaps by the deepening rift with China and the knowledge that the first Chinese nuclear explosion could not be far off, wrote to Macmillan and Kennedy offering a concession on inspection procedures which Macmillan was able to seize upon as a spur to reopen negotiations. Macmillan was very aware of the pressure of public opinion on this question and his letters to Kennedy doubtless helped to overcome some of the doubts in Washington, although the President was not prepared to accept, on the basis of the limited Soviet inspection offer, an agreement covering underground as well as atmospheric tests. The final tripartite negotiation was conducted on the British side by Lord Hailsham and Sir Humphrey Trevelyan, who had by then taken over the Moscow Embassy. Edward Heath, as Lord Privy Seal, visited Moscow for the signature. The limiting factors were set by the American and Soviet Governments, but the substantive issues were of considerable importance in terms of British defence policy and the successful outcome was an example of the way in which the British–Soviet relationship could be used to good effect.

After Macmillan's resignation in October 1963, the Douglas-Home Government decided to continue negotiations in an attempt to improve East–West relations.[3] At the Foreign Office, Butler commented to officials that the Soviet Union seemed to be lying low. They replied that this might flow from a preoccupation with internal problems and with the quarrel with China. They saw the main aim of Soviet policy as being to avoid any direct military confrontation with the West which might involve the risk of nuclear war. Short of this, at worst, the Soviet

Union would continue to work for the collapse of the capitalist system, but, at best, 'with increasing wealth and increasing political moderation, the Soviet Union will gradually abandon its mission to recast human society in its own image and settle down to enjoy its own prosperity, leaving the rest of the world to enjoy theirs'. While the West should guard and prepare itself against the first possibility, it should do all it could to encourage the second.[4] So, encouraged, Butler, who had visited Moscow for the signature of the Test Ban Treaty in August 1963, returned the following summer. This was the first official visit by a Foreign Secretary since Selwyn Lloyd had accompanied Macmillan in 1959. He found no movement on any of the main international issues. On Germany, Khrushchev continued to reject all-German elections and to argue for a Peace Treaty which 'recognised the existing facts', i.e. one which consolidated the hold of the East German regime. Nor was he prepared for any serious discussion of Laos. Nevertheless, it was felt that the dialogue had been useful and ought to be continued. On the bilateral front, it was agreed that the Anglo–Soviet Trade Agreement should be prolonged for five years and a Consular Convention negotiated.[5] There was, however, no time for Butler to take matters further before Labour came to power in the 1964 General Election.

The Labour Governments of 1964–70

With Harold Wilson's election victory in 1964, there began a strange period in which the Prime Minister, personally committed to a successful British–Soviet relationship to a greater extent than most of his predecessors, found himself operating in circumstances which made it peculiarly difficult to secure substantive results. Wilson took office a day after the fall of Khrushchev, when Brezhnev took up the post of First Secretary of the Party and Kosygin that of Prime Minister – and coincidentally a day after the explosion of the first Chinese nuclear weapon. Throughout the life of his first two Governments, from October 1964 to October 1970, the East–West relationship was conditioned by two major factors, the Vietnam War and the rift between the Soviet Union and China, while the British political scene was dominated by a succession of industrial troubles and financial crises. A study of the Foreign Office documents for the period shows Foreign Office officials – and for the most part their Ministers also – repeating the theme that the Soviet Union might evolve, but that it would remain committed to an ideological confrontation and at best only a slow and modest improvement could be expected in British–Soviet relations. The Prime Minister, while not contesting this, was constantly seeking to enhance the British role as a senior partner in a British–American–Soviet relationship and believing he had found a Soviet response. He may on occasion have made his officials wince. But he was following some distinguished and only occasionally more successful predecessors.

The thickening of bilateral relations

Wilson had to deal with a new, but not wholly unfamiliar Soviet leadership. *The Times*, looking back over the tumultuous Khrushchev years, was perhaps generous when, instead of echoing *Pravda*'s denunciation of 'hare-brained' policies, it commented that Khrushchev's 'pursuit of relaxation between the two great camps was his greatest and most substantial work'. It was generally expected that a less personal collective leadership of younger men – Brezhnev was still in his fifties – would wish to continue with the search for a better relationship, but that there would need to be a period of marking time.

Sir H. Trevelyan's advice from Moscow was that there were no great prospects of more flexibility in Soviet policy until the Soviet leaders had either succeeded or failed to get their dispute with China onto a new plane. The Foreign Office briefed the incoming Foreign Secretary, Patrick Gordon-Walker, in much the same terms as they had briefed his Conservative predecessor: The hard centre of Soviet policy was likely to remain unchanged. Cuba had been a major political defeat and they would not pursue a high-risk strategy. Soviet and Western policies were bound to remain in conflict so long as the Russians behaved as if it were their mission to win the world to Communism, but it was 'not unreasonable to deduce that this element in their policy was likely to diminish with the passage of the years ... and we must seek to encourage that process'.[6] Trevelyan also took the opportunity of the change of leadership in the Soviet Union and of the Government in Britain to send the new Foreign Secretary a series of thoughtful despatches analysing the British–Soviet relationship:

> We have at times been actively hostile to the Soviet Government, but neither often, nor for long, nor profitably. We have no liking for either the Tsarist or Soviet systems of government ... In two world wars we found ourselves, though not altogether wholeheartedly, on the same side ... Each of us has, on occasion, harmed the other, yet

after these occasions, each of us has found it expedient to ignore the harm done for the sake of getting back to tolerable and profitable if never entirely satisfactory relations.

Those relations, he argued, had 'been less bad than they might have been' and it seemed 'a reasonable aim of policy in the short term to ensure that our relations with the Soviet Union are never unnecessarily bad, and in the long term to try to change the basis of our relationship to something rather better'. Nevertheless, 'so long as the Communist Party of the Soviet Union regards itself as obliged to conduct a non-military but otherwise comprehensive struggle against us, our relations with the Soviet Government cannot be those of friendship and trust. Nor can they be stable'. Analysing the doctrinal basis of Soviet foreign policy, he pointed out that the new leaders were still thinking in orthodox terms of a strategy designed to yield successive victories until mankind was living under communism. What had changed was the basis of the argument for avoiding measures which might lead to military conflict with major powers: 'Stalin's policy of peaceful coexistence could be described as a policy of provisional but somewhat reluctant non-belligerence, dictated by the relative weakness of the Soviet Union at the time. The policy of his successors could be described as one of non-belligerence for an indefinite period, dictated by fear of modern weapons'. These despatches triggered an interesting argument between the Foreign Office and the Embassy on the classic theme of the relative importance of ideology and interest in Soviet foreign policy. Thomas Brimelow, at that time Minister in the Embassy, had drafted the despatches and pointed to the continuity of Soviet policy. But continuity did not mean immobility: 'The essence of the bureaucrat is that when he turns over a new leaf, he intends to make it a continuation of the same file'.[7] Under his influence the Embassy held out for the dominance of ideology. The ideology of class conflict was, he argued, pulling the cartload of Soviet national interest in the wrong direction; one day the cart would wear out the horse, but the horse was not dead yet and the new leaders were neither willing nor able to cut the harness and let the cart run backwards under its own weight.[8] This, albeit reluctantly, the Foreign Office accepted.

At the time he took office as First Secretary, Brezhnev was a relatively unknown figure and it was natural that Wilson's principal direct relationship should be with Kosygin, who was initially taking a rather larger role in foreign relations than was customary for the Chairman of the Soviet Council of Ministers, a post which was concerned primarily with internal affairs. As President of the Board of Trade, Wilson had known Kosygin in the early post-war years and did his best to capitalise on the existing relationship. He led a Labour Party delegation to Moscow shortly before the 1964 election and on that occasion spoke on Soviet television about Britain dealing with the Soviet Union on behalf of the Western alliance. His advocacy of annual quadripartite summits at the United Nations was a short-lived initiative, but on a bilateral basis he came close to achieving it, with three further official visits, in February and July of 1966 and January 1968 for meetings with Kosygin and Brezhnev, and a visit to Britain by Kosygin in February 1967 at which Wilson spoke of the relationship as being 'at an all-time high'. Brezhnev did not take up the invitation extended to him, but between the beginning of 1965 and the summer of 1968 there came from the Soviet Union the Foreign Minister, the Minister of Culture, the President of the Academy of Sciences, the Minister of Foreign Trade, the Minister for the Coal Industry, the Chairman of the State Committee for Science and Technology and delegations from the trade unions, the Supreme Soviet and the Communist Party. An equivalent flow of British ministers and delegations travelled to Moscow. A Consular Convention was signed, as were agreements on the establishment of a 'hot line' between the Kremlin and Downing Street; on the settlement of certain claims in respect of British property in the Baltic States; on technological cooperation; and on navigation. A joint working group on cooperation in electric power was set up and negotiations were started for a new trade agreement.

This progressive thickening of the texture of bilateral relations, particularly in the commercial and cultural areas, reflected a process which had been initiated during the Khrushchev years, in particular as a result of the Khrushchev and Bulganin visit to Britain in 1956 and the Macmillan visit to Moscow in 1959. On the British side there was something of the hope which had inspired Lloyd George, that the normal process of international intercourse would wean the Soviet Union away from the contest of power and ideology. The hope was not realised. Nevertheless Wilson remained perpetually optimistic. After his visit to Moscow in February 1966, he telegraphed to President Johnson that it had been 'hard pounding', with absolutely no progress on Vietnam. Nevertheless he had found Brezhnev a 'very impressive and more extrovert figure' than Kosygin and was 'more than content with the general atmosphere and with the fact that blunt talking did not mean an atmosphere of hostility'.[9] His July visit yielded just as little: 'No give whatever in the Soviet position over Vietnam. Kosygin quiet (and at all times courteous and friendly) but bitter and tough ... His purpose is clearly to work for your [Johnson's] increasing isolation and friendlessness with world opinion.' Michael Stewart and George Brown both found meetings with Gromyko equally unprofitable in 1965 and 1966.

While Soviet propaganda continued its unremitting ideological offensive and Wilson's repeated pleas for the release of an imprisoned British lecturer met with no response, the proposal for the conclusion of a bilateral Treaty of Friendship and Cooperation, originally made to Macmillan and resumed by Kosygin in a speech to both Houses of Parliament on 9 February 1967, was received with some caution on the British side by all except the Prime Minister. Foreign Office doubts were echoed by a large group of British academics who wrote to the Prime Minister on 11 May, arguing that 'a treaty from which no practical consequences would follow could only serve to confuse real issues and might, by erecting an empty verbal symbol, suggest the acceptance of practices which remain deeply alien to the British people'. Nevertheless, the British Government went ahead and handed over in Moscow a draft dealing purely with bilateral relations. This was rejected as 'wishy-washy' by the Soviet Government, who then made plain their own concept by producing a draft treaty on Cooperation in European Security directed clearly against the British position in NATO. This in turn was rejected as 'not offering a reasonable basis for discussion' and the idea was dropped for another thirty years.[10]

British–Soviet trade after 1959

By the time the Wilson Government took office, there was already the expectation of increased British–Soviet trade, and Britain was in dire need of its realisation. The commercial department of the British Embassy, closed in 1950, had been reopened when the new trade agreement was signed in 1959. The planned long-term expansion of trade was a major feature of Kosygin's visit and he was enthusiastically received by British industry. There were indeed perceptible results. During the 1960s Britain was one of the Soviet Union's leading capitalist trading partners and in 1967 moved briefly into first place as a supplier. A British consortium set the pace in major contracts with the construction of a polyester fibre plant. In total, however, results were unexciting. Exports to the Soviet Union, valued at £53 million in 1962, had doubled in cash terms, but not in real terms, to reach £102 million in 1970. As a proportion of total British exports they failed, however, to regain even the modest 1.7 per cent recorded in 1961. Despite major promotional efforts, including the holding in Moscow of a British Industrial Fair and an exhibition of British scientific equipment, the British share of the Soviet market gradually declined in the late 1960s in the face of growing competition from other European suppliers as well as from Japan. At this stage, American competition was a minor factor. As a purchaser of Soviet products, Britain remained significant, but the total British share of the Soviet Union's turnover with the industrial West, which had been 29 per cent in 1950 remained more or less static around 14 per cent during the 1960s, before declining to the range of 4–7.5 per cent in the 1970s and 1980s.

Vietnam

In all the exchanges between Wilson and Kosygin, the dominant political issue was the Vietnam War. Wilson sought to use the British relationship with the Soviet Union as a means of bringing about a cease-fire between the United States and North Vietnam. The involvement of the British Government, and of the Prime Minister personally, forms a remarkable contrast with British diplomacy in the rather different circumstances of the Korean War, almost twenty years earlier, when Attlee's principal intervention was his hurried, and fortunately unnecessary, visit to Washington to dissuade Truman from the use of nuclear weapons. The Geneva Conference of 1955 provided a *locus standi* for Britain in relation to Vietnam, but Wilson's proposal for the reconvening of the conference was not accepted and Soviet representatives showed growing irritation at its reiteration. Their objective was clear. The conduct of the war by North Vietnam may have been largely independent of Soviet control, but there was a direct Soviet interest, backed by Soviet supplies, in a North Vietnamese victory. It was, however, in the Soviet interest that victory should come about with no more than a controlled escalation of the fighting, in circumstances which permitted the Soviet Union to consolidate its own position in Vietnam and ideally which weakened the United States without providing any opening for China. To the extent that the British Government could help to bring about a reduction in the scale of military operations and leave the resolution of the conflict to be concluded by the mixed political–military offensive in which North Vietnam excelled, the Soviet Union would encourage British mediation. It had, however, no incentive to promote a settlement on terms acceptable to the United States. The route to control of all Vietnam by Hanoi was only too obvious. It would have taken a great deal of good fortune for the British Government to have succeeded in bringing about a pause for negotiations and stabilising the situation in response to the suspension of American bombing of the North.[11] Cabinet minutes in 1966 and 1967 show the Prime Minister constantly seeing signs that the Soviet 'attitude might become flexible', their 'tone less harsh', 'no longer wholly negative', 'anxious to know our views', 'friendly and constructive', 'wishing to use Britain as an intermediary' and seeking 'to create the impression of restoration of the wartime comradeship'.

Sadly, the most appropriate commentary on the Soviet reception of Wilson's efforts was perhaps that given by the Soviet spokesman who was asked why Kosygin did not stop off in London after a summit meeting with President Johnson in June 1967, despite having called on de Gaulle twice in a fortnight: 'We have a special relationship with President de Gaulle but not with Mr. Wilson. Why should we want to talk to the servant after spending hours with his master?'[12] *Krokodil* chose to illustrate the point with a cartoon showing a piratical American President on the bridge of a warship bristling with missiles, stretching out a long arm to steer the half-submerged raft which an anxious Wilson is paddling alongside him. The harsh reality was that no British mediation would have led the Soviet Union to cease its support for North Vietnam, or the United States to accept in the early stages of direct military intervention the route to a settlement which, in defeat, it had to accept in 1973.

After the rejection of the second British attempt to join the EEC, the devaluation of sterling and the decision to withdraw from South East Asia and the Gulf, the Soviet leaders must have correctly assessed the weakness of Britain's position, but found little opportunity to benefit from it. Michael Stewart found Gromyko in a typically negative mood when he visited Moscow in May 1968. The course of events in the succeeding years demonstrated both the immobility of the superpowers in a situation where one or the other was militarily committed and the limitation upon the exercise of effective influence by powers such as Britain and France.

Against this background the Foreign Secretary commissioned in 1968 a major study of relations with the Soviet Union and Eastern Europe. It painted a gloomy picture. There were those in the Soviet Union – a small, but vocal and growing minority – who were seeking greater individual freedom. They were pointing the way to the future, but measures that would make economic sense ran counter to ideological prejudice, vested interests and Party authority and it was impossible to predict whether or when a more liberal and cooperative regime would emerge. Meanwhile, the basic approach to the West was still one of hostility and bilateral political relations were 'somewhat worse than usual'. So, the Foreign Office concluded, far from yielding to Soviet pressure 'we intend to be just as tough as they are ... pursue with vigour those activities which bring practical benefit to us ... engage in discussion when the moment seems right ... not appear to be running after them'.[13]

Czechoslovakia

In one form or another, the Soviet proposal for a conference on security and cooperation in Europe had been around for more than a decade. It was eventually to become the symbol of detente in the 1970s, but it looked decidedly unpromising on 20 August 1968, when Soviet and East European armed forces entered Czechoslovakia, as Tass put it, 'to help the working people of that country safeguard their revolutionary achievements against encroachments by internal and external enemies of socialism'. Dubcek had come to power twenty years too soon. In 1968 the Soviet Union under Brezhnev was in no mood to relinquish the grasp which Stalin had fastened on Czechoslovakia in 1945 and consolidated in 1948. In 1956, when the Soviet forces entered Hungary, the Western world had been politically incapacitated by the Suez crisis. In the summer of 1968 the British Government were taken by surprise. They had watched with a mixture of hope and anxiety as Czechoslovakia moved towards the creation of a free society and, on the whole, they believed almost to the end that the Soviet Union would acquiesce. As the Soviet forces moved in, Europe was on holiday, the war in Vietnam was unresolved, President Johnson was close to the end of his term of office and the Wilson Government could already see the omens of its defeat at the polls. The Cabinet noted that 'there was at present a general understanding that the West would not intervene against the Soviet Union in Soviet bloc countries'.[14] Parliament was recalled. It was, in Wilson's words, 'quiet, shocked, determined – and impotent'.[15] Beyond the cancellation of some cultural events and ministerial visits, there was little that the Western powers, either individually or collectively, could do. Wilson spoke of the need to prevent a relapse into the 'frozen immobilism of the cold war',[16] but thought it right that the strength and unanimity of feeling throughout the country should be registered. Since 1938, Czechoslovakia had possessed a particular symbolic significance in

British foreign policy. The public reaction was strong. The TUC severed contact with Soviet trade unions and even the Communist Party of Great Britain issued a critical statement. The force of this response did not go unnoticed. In a formal note, Gromyko complained of the British Government 'complicating and aggravating the relations between our two countries' and *Pravda* spoke of policies 'inspired by the spirit of the cold war'. The Soviet Union subsequently described Britain as 'among the most active proponents of a policy of gradually separating individual socialist countries from the socialist community'[17] and Brezhnev proclaimed the doctrine that the Soviet Union had the 'right to intervene, by force if necessary, to protect socialism' in a fraternal country.

For its part, the British Government felt it appropriate to rethink the longer-term implications of Soviet policy in the light of the Czechoslovak crisis. Looking five–ten years ahead, it assumed no fundamental change in the pattern or the attitudes of the Soviet leadership, but well beyond that time scale it expected far-reaching changes in Soviet society. So, it concluded, the right policy was to settle for a very long haul, not actively and publicly seeking the break-up of the Soviet empire, but unobtrusively encouraging the process of gradual change in Eastern Europe and the Soviet Union; maintaining the American link with Europe; and increasing the strength and unity of the West. Meanwhile, it expected the Soviet Union to pursue relatively cautious and pragmatic policies, but not to abate its fundamental hostility to the Western system.[18] For the Wilson Government this broadly correct prognosis was effectively the end of the road so far as policy towards the Soviet Union was concerned.

Walking warily

On 18 June 1970 Edward Heath moved into Downing Street and his priority task was to resume the attempt to secure British membership of the European Community (EC), a task which was successfully concluded on 1 January 1973. The relationship with the Soviet Union never seemed to fascinate him in the way it had some of his predecessors from Lloyd George to Winston Churchill and Harold Macmillan. A meeting with Gromyko in London brought a useful assurance about the status of West Berlin, some progress on trade relations and a declared resolve 'to work in all possible ways to develop relations' but, for the most part, as Europe began to explore the meaning of detente, the Foreign and Commonwealth Office (FCO) under Sir Alec Douglas-

Home proceeded to implement a policy as cautious and pragmatic as that which they had attributed to Moscow in 1969. They did not, however, do so without some serious examination of the room for a more active policy, which was being urged upon them by Sir Duncan Wilson in Moscow. His first despatch, arguing that a more flexible policy might 'bring important dividends not only in trade, but in the longer term also in encouraging political and social change in Eastern Europe and the Soviet Union itself' brought a sharpish rejoinder: 'We should walk warily ... The plain fact is that in the near future our national interest is to develop our relations with Western rather than Eastern Europe.'[19] Wilson was undeterred: 'The Soviet Union is undergoing changes which may in the long or even medium term produce a different mixture – and different in some potentially very important respects ... There is much need for some change of style in our relationship.' On 8 February 1971 he came back again, arguing that it was misleading to concentrate on Marxist doctrine in assessing Soviet policy. In ten years or so the younger party leaders might see the need further to modify in practice a whole range of doctrines if party and state were not to petrify. In such a situation, he argued, British policy needed a new style, more in line with the policies of her main future European partners. Again he was met with caution: 'Apart from all the other considerations, the coming period may not be a suitable one for establishing or maintaining any new kind of relationship with the Soviet Union ... We must be very careful to ensure that our change of style is never used, whether or not it produces benefits, as an argument for less firmness where firmness is necessary.'

In some respects the arguments were those that had been used since the 1920s and were still being used right up to the final collapse of the Soviet Union. But in 1971 as in 1927, it was Soviet intelligence activities in London which for a while were to dictate the course of events. The occasional exposure and arrest or expulsion of individual intelligence officers was a normal feature of relations with the Soviet Union and, indeed, it has continued subsequently. Episodes ranging from the early escapades of Reilly and other British agents in the immediate aftermath of 1917 to the Arcos Raid, the Soviet nuclear espionage, the high drama of Maclean, Burgess and Philby, the Wynne–Penkovsky penetration of Soviet intelligence and the Lonsdale–Kroger operation caught the public eye and added an extra aggravation to an uneasy relationship. More recently, sophisticated electronic analysis and satellite surveillance provided more intelligence with less public excitement. But old habits die hard. London was a pleasant and useful posting for the Soviet intelligence services and by 1971 their combined strength, operating under various forms of diplomatic and official cover had grown to such a point that on 24 September the Soviet Government were notified that 90 of their agents in the United Kingdom would be expelled and another 15 forbidden entry. Dismissed later by the Foreign Secretary as a necessary spraying of the greenfly, it was in fact unprecedented in scale. It had been the subject of most careful consideration by Ministers over a long period and there was no doubt that it was founded on solid evidence. Revealing as it did the extent to which Soviet overseas representation had been exploited for intelligence purposes, it was a significant blow both to the esteem of the Soviet Union and to the effectiveness of its intelligence apparatus. The Soviet reaction was sharp, but direct reprisals were at the lower end of the expected range. Seventeen British personnel in Moscow were either expelled or blacklisted. This was enough to cause some disruption of normal work, but staff numbers are no guide to the effective functioning of an Embassy at the political level. It was a deliberate policy on the part of the Soviet authorities to freeze the political relationship. For two years they maintained a demonstrative sulk. Not until 1973 did Sir Alec Douglas-Home first visit Moscow as Foreign Secretary.

There is no doubt that in technical terms the expulsions were justified and that the whole operation represented a useful little victory for the United Kingdom in the continuing conflict of intelligence and counter-intelligence. But the operation has to be assessed against a wider background. The period from 1968 to 1973, when British–Soviet relations were largely inactive, was one in which the East–West relationship was moving into a distinct new phase of development, as Germany under Brandt and the United States under Nixon set out to reshape the relations with the Soviet Union as a European power and a superpower. The issues involved were, by their very nature, ones to which the British–Soviet relationship was not of central relevance, but they were of direct importance to vital British interests and the British role was perforce less active than it might have been. The expulsions were a factor in this, but there is no reason to suppose that they substantially affected the wider political balance. After all, only three years had passed since the Soviet tanks had moved into Prague. British diplomacy towards the Soviet Union has consistently been marked by a readiness to face unpleasant facts rather than to gloss them over and by a belief that it is more useful to gain respect for plain dealing than to trade implausible insincerities. So it was on this occasion. But it was not to be long before the case for a more active British diplomacy became cogent.

The German agreements

For a quarter of a century after 1945 the Western part of Germany had been moving swiftly from being a non-country, an occupied area where the struggle with the Soviet Union for control of the European heartland was at its sharpest, to becoming a substantial power with the ability to shape, by its own policies, the East–West relationship in Europe. By September 1969, when the Brandt Government took office in the Federal Republic, the 'frozen immobilism' of which Wilson had spoken was already becoming unrealistic in relation to Germany. In some respects the situation had to remain immobile. The trial of strength had brought the consolidation of Western Europe and the securing of its outermost position in Berlin, while the Soviet Union had demonstrated its will and ability to retain its control over those parts of Central and Eastern Europe which it had held since the end of the war. The unreality of a Western challenge to Soviet armed force in Hungary and Czechoslovakia or a Soviet challenge to the Western position in Berlin had both been demonstrated with equal force. The confrontation of the conventional and nuclear forces of NATO and the Warsaw Pact made disturbance of the status quo too dangerous for either party to contemplate. What was needed was a policy which recognised the unreality of any forcible challenge to it, but provided a new basis for intra-European cooperation across the East–West border.

For its realisation, such a policy required the participation of the Soviet Union, the United States, Britain and France, not only by reason of their residual wartime responsibilities, but as a matter of political reality; of the two German states themselves; and of the other nations of Eastern and Western Europe. The key was, however, in German hands. The first moves towards a rethinking of German–Soviet relations were already being made by the CDU–SPD Grand Coalition in the 1960s. In 1967 NATO itself, with the Harmel Report, had looked towards measures to promote European detente and the balanced reduction of armed forces on the continent. In July 1968 the signature of the Nuclear Non-Proliferation Treaty marked a further stage in the process of East–West negotiation on nuclear arms control which had been initiated five years earlier by the Test Ban Treaty. In retrospect, it is remarkable that the trauma of the Soviet action against Czechoslovakia in 1968 was so quickly overtaken. It is doubtful whether any government in the Federal Republic could have maintained the old policies throughout the 1970s, but the victory of Brandt's SPD in 1969 provided the necessary spur for the realisation of the new German

Ostpolitik and, with it, for more extensive change in the East–West relationship in Europe.

The formal elements of the new German policy were the treaties which the Federal Republic signed with the Soviet Union on 12 August 1970, with Poland on 7 December 1970, with the German Democratic Republic on 21 December 1972 and with Czechoslovakia on 11 December 1973. Without foreclosing the possibility of peaceful territorial change, their essence lay in the mutual renunciation of territorial claims by the Federal Republic and the Soviet Union and respect for the territorial integrity of all European nations within their present frontiers. Of themselves, these treaties represented a substantial achievement for Soviet foreign policy in so far as they legitimised the German Democratic Republic (GDR). The Federal Republic, however, retained the goal of peaceful reunification, enshrined in its Constitution. The Quadripartite Agreement on Berlin, signed on 3 September 1971, effectively confirmed the Allied position in Berlin on the basis that West Berlin remained formally not a part of the Federal Republic. With the conclusion of the Berlin Agreement, the way was cleared for conclusion of the Treaty between the two German states, for the ratification in May 1972 of the German–Soviet Treaty and for the establishment of relations between Britain and the GDR.

The establishment of relations enabled me, after a lapse of twenty years, to return to Berlin. The new British Embassy was housed in modest premises on Unter den Linden, across the road from the viceregal palace of the Soviet Ambassador. In practice, East Berlin was the capital of an independent state, but the juridical status of the occupying powers was retained. I was in the anomalous position of an Ambassador accredited to a state which had its seat of government in a city which we did not recognise as part of its territory. It was a situation which typified the new East–West relationship in Europe – a practical compromise reflecting a balance of political and military power which made possible the pursuit of normal relations, while enabling all concerned to protect the slightly tarnished purity of their political principles.

This reshaping of the central nexus of European relationships was a matter of major and direct concern to Britain. As a nuclear power, Britain was one of the initiators of the Non-Proliferation Treaty; within NATO the British Government was supporting – though not without reservations – the movement towards detente; and in the negotiation of the Berlin Agreement it had a direct role, in which it was represented by the Ambassador in Bonn, Sir Roger Jackling. The impetus for the detente process in Europe came, however, primarily from the governments of the Federal Republic and the Soviet Union and was given added force by the desire of the US Government to integrate this aspect of East–West relations into the wider relationship between the superpowers. Three decades later, looking back on the early 1970s, it is easier to agree with the more open policy which Sir Duncan Wilson had been advocating when he took over the Moscow Embassy than with the caution with which he was met in London. He was perhaps a little ahead of his time, but these were years when events were beginning to move in the direction which was to lead to the disintegration of the Soviet imperial structure and they were years during which, on the whole, the British–Soviet relationship counted for rather little. Not until the final stages of the Helsinki negotiations was there a distinct change towards a more positive British policy and a corresponding increase in British influence. Should that more positive policy have been adopted at an earlier date? The answer is probably 'yes'. The Soviet Union had to reconcile two objectives. It needed to maintain a public posture of seeking detente in order to secure influence in the West, but imperial control over the East was best served by the maintenance of a sharp dividing line between East and West in Europe. The best way of avoiding conflict between these objectives was by policies which would place upon Western Governments the apparent responsibility for tension in East–West relations. As was so often the case, British policy was to judge the Soviet Union by its deeds rather than its words. This is hard to fault. But it made Britain appear negative and, paradoxically, may for a brief time have eased rather than hindered Moscow's diplomacy.

Strategic relations between the superpowers

In parallel with the German negotiations, the Nixon–Kissinger diplomacy of the early 1970s set the parameters of a new superpower relationship in a form which was to continue into the Gorbachev era. The Soviet Union had largely remedied the disparity in strategic nuclear arms of which it had been acutely aware at the time of the Cuban missile crisis, and in November 1969 the US–Soviet negotiations for the first Strategic Arms Limitation Treaty (SALT) were opened in Helsinki. These negotiations and those for the Anti-Ballistic Missile (ABM) Treaty between the Soviet Union and the United States ran concurrently with the British negotiations for entry into the EC and were followed in

September 1973 by the opening of the Helsinki Conference on Security and Cooperation in Europe. Over a period of five years since the Soviet action against Czechoslovakia – a period during which the British–Soviet relationship had been at a low ebb – the tone and content of Western Europe's relations with the Soviet Union had, it seemed, been transformed. The transformation was part of a wider adjustment of the international balance, reflecting the American decision to withdraw from Vietnam and the need of both the Soviet Union and the United States to adjust to the new role of China.

While British–Soviet relations remained in the post-1971 chill, President Nixon's visit to Moscow in May 1972 marked a major evolution in the superpower relationship. It was not, as Sir J. Killick reported,[20] a Soviet–American love feast, but rather a mutual acceptance by the United States and the Soviet Union that neither could dominate or destroy the other by the application of material power. The FCO noted sadly: 'It is striking how much of concern to us all is treated as essentially a bilateral matter between the two superpowers'.[21] Within this new context, both in terms of strategic relationships and in terms of European policy, the British–Soviet relationship had to be reshaped.

In a report on 'The Soviet Threat'[22] the Joint Intelligence Committee (JIC) acknowledged that the extent of US–Soviet communication and even agreement was likely to grow and might give the Soviet Union opportunities for wedge-driving between the United States and its allies, but the bilateral dealing was regarded as essentially tactical on the Soviet side and in a 'relationship of underlying antagonism' it was not expected that the United States would neglect NATO interests. The Committee seemed to have some difficulty in their assessment of the Soviet leadership, describing them, correctly, as 'grey, cautious, suspicious, persistent and opportunist', but with a view of the world which was 'dogmatic, dynamic and confident'. They warned that by using military, political and economic means of influence and relying on their own consistency of purpose and on any infirmities on the part of the West, the Soviet Union might acquire a position of dominance in key areas, including, most seriously, Western Europe. This report served in effect to reinforce the policy of caution, vigilance and robustness with which the FCO had greeted the siren voices of Soviet-style detente. London was disinclined to abandon a strategy of trench warfare, but the Soviet leadership were already looking towards a more active relationship with an eventual Labour Government in Britain.[23]

Helsinki and detente in Europe

As the EEC negotiations had dominated the foreign policy of the Heath Government, so the renegotiation of the entry arrangements was a major commitment for the Labour Government under Harold Wilson which took office in March 1974 and was confirmed by the second General Election in the autumn of that year. The Helsinki Conference was by this time approaching its final stage. British Government policy in relation to it had evolved significantly from early resistance to the whole idea of a Conference, which they had seen as liable to serve the Soviet Government's objective of reaffirming the post-1945 status quo, consolidating the Soviet Union's hold on Eastern Europe, weakening the integration of Western Europe and adding to the pressure for withdrawal of American forces from Europe. The Cabinet minutes of 1967 record Wilson as having 'sought to persuade Kosygin not to pursue the proposal … which could not be expected to have any useful outcome in present circumstances'.[24] An FCO Planning Committee paper of 1970 had grudgingly concluded 'that a conference was unlikely to do the West much good; that the harm it might do could probably be contained; and that there was no reason for Britain either to encourage or to oppose the movement towards a Conference which seemed to be increasingly inevitable'. As the preparatory work moved ahead, the FCO remained sceptical: 'When in doubt we must continue to err on the side of being branded cold warriors'.[25] Gradually, however, 'working on the principle of the coral reef rather than the prefabricated house'[26] British representatives strove to ensure that by asserting Western beliefs in the freedom of movement, information and cultural contacts, the resulting agreements would 'spread the contagion of liberty'. This work was, for the most part, done in the various multilateral groups in which British diplomacy was both constructive and effective.

On the bilateral front a major advance was effected by a visit to Moscow by the Prime Minister and Foreign Secretary in February 1975. A package of agreements[27] included a long-term programme for the development of economic and industrial cooperation, a ten-year programme for scientific and technological cooperation and an agreement on cooperation in medicine and public health. A separate protocol provided that the Foreign Ministers or their representatives should meet annually for consultations on virtually the whole range of international and bilateral problems and included a specific provision for contacts on any situation which 'in the opinion of the two sides endangers peace, involves a breach of the peace or causes international tension'. The two Governments confirmed their adherence to the principles of peaceful coexistence, which they defined as 'long term, fruitful and mutually beneficial cooperation between states, irrespective of their political, economic and social systems, on the basis of full equality and mutual respect'. In the hope of expanding British exports, agreement was reached on the availability of substantial British credit. There was also provision for the establishment of an Anglo–Soviet Round Table with representatives of public life, science, culture, commerce, the press and other fields; for parliamentary exchanges; and for an exchange of visits between representatives of the armed forces. (It may in passing be noted that for some years the chairmanship of the Soviet side of the Round Table was held by Yevgeniy Primakov, who was in consequence well known in Britain when in 1998 he became Prime Minister of the Russian Federation.) The package could with some justice be described as marking 'a new phase in Anglo–Soviet relations'. It was a phase which in its character and motivation recalled the relationship which Lloyd George had set out to establish in 1919 and Macmillan to revive in 1959. It was in line, too, with the sentiment of most sectors of British political opinion. The question remained: what would it amount to in practice?

The bilateral agreements of February were followed on 1 August by the conclusion of the Conference on Security and Cooperation in Europe, with the Final Act signed at Helsinki by representatives of the European Governments as well as of the United States and Canada. The provisions of the Final Act, described by Wilson as the 'start of a new chapter in the history of Europe', dealt with questions of security, of economic cooperation and of respect for personal as well as national rights and freedoms. Establishing principles such as the inviolability of frontiers and the territorial integrity of states, the Helsinki Final Act, while still leaving open the possibility of peaceful change, appeared to place its seal, thirty years after the end of the war, upon the political structure of post-war Europe. The Soviet Union felt that it had gained an assurance of stability justifying the concession it made to other signatories in respect of the safeguarding of human rights. The British Government, conveniently forgetting its earlier doubts, felt that it had moved towards a detente in which, in Wilson's words, Europeans could 'marry whom they want, hear and read what they want, travel abroad when and where they want, meet whom they want'. Meeting Wilson at Helsinki, Brezhnev expressed the 'hope that the two countries could move forward in a bold way and talk in a still more frank and friendly manner'. The Prime Minister, referring to his earlier meeting in Moscow as a turning point, described Brezhnev and himself as 'custodians of detente, as defined in the documents which they had signed'.[28]

The Helsinki process was a fascinating exercise in diplomacy. Stabilisation rather than expansion was by this time the primary objective of Soviet policy in Europe and it must have seemed to the Soviet Government that, while demonstrating their devotion to high-sounding ideals of human rights and freedom, they would be able to maintain control over their Eastern European satellites and their strategic interest in the Eastern half of Germany. For the Western powers, at a time when rivalry in nuclear armaments still represented a major threat, there was merit in anything which might appear to ease the intra-European tensions and provide some basis for a freer flow of people, goods and ideas across the East–West barrier. What in fact happened – and to some extent it happened because of the British insistence upon practical measures to give effect to lofty declarations of principle – was that holes were driven in the Iron Curtain, holes which permitted first a trickle and then the flood which fourteen years later would overwhelm the Soviet imperial structure.

For a brief period, British–Soviet relations developed in the spirit of Helsinki. At the superpower level the negotiations for the second SALT Treaty took the central role. Among the European powers, for all Wilson's words, Britain was seen by the Soviet Union as a less significant bilateral partner than the Federal Republic and less enticing than France, both of which were pursuing an active combination of political and commercial diplomacy. In April 1976 James Callaghan succeeded Wilson as Prime Minister and in the following year David Owen as Foreign Secretary visited Moscow to sign with Gromyko an agreement, similar to ones negotiated with France and the United States, on measures to prevent an accidental outbreak of nuclear war. The first glow of Helsinki began to fade as the authorities suppressed the human rights movement in the Soviet Union. The threat of a Communist take-over in Portugal was also a matter of some concern. Wilson and Callaghan had warned Brezhnev personally in Moscow and again in Helsinki that if this happened it would ruin the prospect of a successful outcome to the negotiations. In the event, the Portuguese crisis was resolved, but in the winter of 1975 the Soviet-supported intervention began in Angola and in 1977–8 the use of Cuban forces, backed by a Soviet airlift of military advisers and supplies, in support of the Marxist leaders in Ethiopia raised new fears that detente in Europe might be accompanied by the expansion of Soviet power and influence in the Third World. It was therefore appropriate that when Owen saw Gromyko he should not only raise the issue of respect for human rights, but also call for the extension of detente to Africa, where Britain was hoping that the Soviet Union might support – or at least not actively frustrate – the search for a settlement to the Rhodesian problem.

The Moscow Embassy

To permit the freedom of contact envisaged at Helsinki was, of course, to admit the possibility of change in the very nature of society; change brought about by the assertion of individual will rather than through party doctrine or government decree. It was scarcely surprising that this challenge was one which the Soviet state viewed with some distaste and the whole Helsinki process was already running into difficulties when, in the traditional diplomatic uniform, with plumed hat, gold braid and sword, I presented my credentials as HM Ambassador in Moscow to the Vice-President of the Presidium in the spring of 1978. I found the relationship between Britain and the Soviet Union in an uneasy state. Despite the political, commercial, cultural and technological contacts established in 1975, the substance of British–Soviet relations was still thin and the flavour was becoming increasingly sour. We could not expect an easy relationship, but we could expect that, with time, there would come change and it seemed to me, as it had done to so many of my predecessors, that, if that change were to be in the direction of a slightly safer rather than a significantly more dangerous world, we could best contribute to it by seeking to build a more active, broadly-based and productive British–Soviet relationship. This was, indeed the policy which had been established by Mr Callaghan. In fact, after a brief period of relative freedom from major tension, the whole climate of East–West relations was to change abruptly with the entry of Soviet forces into Afghanistan at Christmas 1979. My remaining three years in Moscow were a period in which the bilateral relationship was brought back to a level not markedly better than that which had prevailed during the earlier periods of East–West confrontation, while the Soviet Union itself declined slowly into the economic, political and social stagnation of Brezhnev's final years.

With the collapse of the Soviet Union, the work of the Moscow Embassy and the environment within which it operated underwent a profound change. The processes of diplomacy do not, however, change in their essentials and some description of the way in which the Embassy functioned in the final years of the Brezhnev regime may still be of value. In 1978, if the ambitions expressed in the 1975 agreements were to be realised, the work of the Embassy needed to develop in parallel in its three main traditional sectors. We had to ensure that the British Government was as well informed as possible on the domestic and foreign policies of the Soviet Union; to promote British exports, institute direct bilateral exchanges in culture, science and technology and support the businessmen, students and others involved in them; and to seek to influence Soviet foreign policy in respect of wider international issues.

The Moscow Embassy still occupied the fine mansion which the British Government had acquired on lease when diplomatic relations were resumed in 1930 and which the Soviet authorities had, since the end of the war, been seeking to repossess. Rebuilt in the 1890s by a wealthy merchant Kharitonenko to the designs of the leading Russian architect Shekhtel and decorated in a strange mixture of French Imperial gilt and German–Flemish baronial woodcarvings, it had been taken over by the state in 1917 and had served variously as a state guest house, a headquarters for the Danish Red Cross and a residence for Litvinov as Commissar for Foreign Affairs. Its grandeur, with a ballroom which would comfortably have housed the whole of my London house, was matched by the view, unsurpassed by any British Embassy in the world, of the gilded cathedral domes rising above the red brick of the Kremlin wall across the narrow Moscow River. It had seen much of the history of British–Soviet relations. Lockhart had been entertained there in the last years of Imperial Russia, H. G. Wells had stayed there in the 1920s, Clare Sheridan had come to make a bust of Lenin, Churchill had entertained Stalin during the war, Khrushchev and his colleagues had celebrated with erratic joviality the revival of relations after the death of Stalin, and through it all, with the classic techniques of eavesdropping, observation, blackmail, subversion and electronic interception, the KGB had wound their tedious way. Superbly suited for the formal, representational function of an Embassy, it was inconvenient as a dwelling for the Ambassador and his family; its three bedrooms provided much grandeur but little scope for the accommodation of visiting ministers; its kitchens were separated by seventy stone stairs from the dining room; and its office accommodation on the ground floor was marked by a sad, overcrowded grubbiness of filing cabinets, tape machines and dirty cups, with Kharitonenko's cornices hidden under plaster board and his carved woodwork giving way to steel doors. For all its inconvenience, all its absurdity, all its tensions, my wife and I recall it with affection. Now, in the very different circumstances of the Embassy to the Russian Federation, negotiations initiated with the Soviet authorities have at last come to fruition. The old house will serve as a residence for the Ambassador, some members of the staff and official guests, while the Embassy offices will be transferred to a fine new building on the Smolensk Embankment.

In any country, the formal inter-governmental business has necessarily to be conducted with those who hold official position in one sphere of activity or another and nowhere was this more the rule than in the Soviet Union, where the interlinked machinery of party and state permeated the whole life of the country. The avoidance of foreign contamination combined with the acquisition of foreign technology was a long-standing Russian tradition, only partly modified by Peter the Great and resumed with enthusiasm by successive Soviet Governments. During the Gorbachev regime contacts became much easier. Now, in the new Russian Federation, society is almost at the opposite pole and the work of the Embassy has been transformed A tattered state machine is hard put to establish its authority, while effective power is dispersed through sectional and regional interests, to all of which foreign representatives have access. In 1978, however, the traditional inhibitions prevailed.

Despite these inhibitions on wider contacts, the Embassy's working relationship with the Foreign Ministry, the Ministry of Foreign Trade and bodies such as the State Committee for Science and Technology functioned, on the whole, efficiently. We had our frigid moments, as, for instance when I had to complain of the attention paid by the KGB to members of my staff. We clashed over questions of human rights, when any reference to Helsinki was rejected as interference in the internal affairs of the Soviet Union. We found difficulty in distinguishing between deliberate obstruction and the natural cumbersomeness of Soviet bureaucracy, and the harassment of visitors to our cultural section was a distasteful reminder of the reality of Soviet life, but it was possible to feel that some progress was being made. I dealt normally with the Deputy Foreign Minister responsible for our affairs, but when I needed to see Gromyko personally, I was usually able to do so. Our exchanges were courteous and businesslike, but on the whole unrewarding. All his long experience and substantial ability were devoted to the well-rehearsed deployment of sterile policies and it was hard to break through into any genuine interplay of ideas. Brezhnev himself was virtually never encountered by Western Ambassadors except on the occasion of a visit by a foreign Head of State. The deterioration in his condition since I had first encountered him in Berlin some years earlier was marked and such brief exchanges as we had in Moscow were not facilitated by the trouble he seemed to have with his hearing aid. The messages which, on occasion, I had to deliver to him were transmitted either through the Foreign Ministry or through a singularly uncommunicative member of his personal staff. Yet for all his incapacity Brezhnev still seemed able, when necessary, to dominate his colleagues on the Politburo, the body which held the destiny of the Soviet Union in its hands and which we saw as a grey group of ageing men, mounting the Lenin mausoleum on ceremonial occasions, but as individuals – with the exception of Gromyko – scarcely more accessible to foreign diplomats than was the General Secretary himself.

All of us in the Embassy saw it as perhaps our most important task to break through the wall of formality and establish a more open relationship with the individuals who were shaping the Soviet Union, whether in the party, the administration, the economy, the arts, on the land or in the factories and mines. The moments of success – and they did occur – were cherished. In our dealings with the administration, there were issues such as arms control or the law of the sea on which serious and productive British–Soviet discussion was possible. There were on occasion useful exchanges on Middle Eastern problems which, if they did not bring a solution much nearer, at least brought a measure of mutual understanding. On technical matters, there was a good relationship with several of the Soviet industrial ministries.

The thinness of contact at senior level did not prevent us from understanding the processes by which Soviet policy was formulated and we were able to assess with reasonable accuracy its broad trend. It took no great perceptiveness to recognise the stagnation of those years, the morass of inefficiency in the economy and the widespread yearning for a more decisive leadership. We relied heavily upon careful study of the Soviet press, which, deciphered with the care devoted to an Egyptian hieroglyph, could prove surprisingly informative. The leader writer who said, 'Provided I start with Lenin and end with Brezhnev, I can put what I like in the middle', may have been exaggerating, but the pseudonyms indicating the origin of the more authoritative pieces were identifiable and the grains of truth could be extracted from the mounds of official chaff. What one lacked was a feel for the balance of power and the policy debate within the leadership. Speculation over the hawks and the doves in the Kremlin was a popular pastime, but the categorisation may be misleading. There must have been genuine differences of opinion. We might infer them, but we had no direct evidence. The occupation of Afghanistan caught us by surprise. In retrospect, the portents were there for us to see, but policy decisions of this type are closely guarded in any country and we did not draw the threads together. During the Polish crisis of 1980–1 we could recognise clearly enough the preparations for military intervention and could infer the policy debates which must have led to the long hesitation before the decision to stake all on Jaruzelski. Of Gorbachev's stand in relation to the events of those years we had no inkling.

The lack of contact with the centres of Soviet political power constituted a particular handicap in that part of an Ambassador's duties which is concerned more with the presentation of British policy and the exercise of influence over the process of Soviet policy formation than with the reporting and evaluation of Soviet policy. If this is to be done effectively, one needs to be able to go beyond the formal presentation of policy documents and to inspire in one's interlocutors a degree of confidence in the authority and reliability of one's own judgement, a process which is rendered substantially more difficult when personal contact is restricted. This area of an Ambassador's work is ultimately a test of personal qualities, but it can also be crucially affected by the extent to which his own Government demonstrates its confidence in him. His arguments cannot expect to carry weight with a foreign Government unless it is apparent to them that he carries equal weight with his own. In the British Diplomatic Service, the relationship between career diplomats and ministers has, with a few sad exceptions, worked well and I was fortunate in that, appointed by a Labour Government, I enjoyed the full support of their Conservative successors.

As a matter of reciprocity, the access to senior ministers accorded to the Soviet Ambassador in London was held at a level broadly comparable to that which I enjoyed in Moscow, but in other respects his opportunity for access to all sectors of opinion in an open multi-polar society was on a scale which no Western Embassy in Moscow could enjoy. Whether his reporting was correspondingly illuminating, we cannot tell. The telegrams and despatches of Ambassador Maisky in the period leading up to the outbreak of war in 1939 provide a good illustration of the range of reporting possible to an energetic Soviet representative in London, and any inadequacy in Soviet reporting is more likely to have resulted from the attempt to interpret British policy in Soviet ideological terms than from any lack of access.

In the closed society of Moscow in the Brezhnev years the normal gossip of diplomacy tended to acquire an extra interest. The practice of regular consultation among EC, NATO and Commonwealth Ambassadors was time-consuming, but it could be useful in the assessment of Soviet policy. There was a long-standing and valuable tradition of close cooperation in Moscow among the Ambassadors of Britain, France, the United States and the Federal Republic. Each was, at one point or another, in a leading position in the day-to-day relationship with the Soviet authorities. Each had a distinctive base for that relationship, yet the extent to which our assessments coincided was remarkable. We also profited from discussion with the small group of Western correspondents in Moscow, most of whom had a good understanding of the country and could more easily maintain contacts of a kind which, given the inhibitions of diplomatic propriety, were sometimes difficult for the Embassy.

If we were to help Britain to understand the Soviet Union, we had to go to those roots of national sentiment which made the party and state what they were and would determine their future. We had to understand the people of Russia and all the other hundred or more nationalities which make up the Soviet Union, to develop some feeling for their way of life, for the challenges of a land mass almost the size of China, India and the United States put together. This was a field of diplomatic activity as rich and varied as the contacts with the machine were arid and stereotyped. Fortunately the restrictions on travel by diplomats in Moscow did not operate in such a way as to prevent Ambassadors from moving throughout most of the country. Our movements were of course known to the authorities, our hotels were booked by them, our appointments arranged by them. There is no doubt that we saw what they wanted us to see and met those whom they wanted us to meet. So, from the Finnish border to Odessa, from Northern Siberia to Kirghizia, my wife and I duly admired the Potemkin villages, the schools, the housing developments, the crèches, the sports arenas, the restored churches, the museums, the factories, the farms, the mines and the power stations. We met the local leaders, we exchanged toasts to peace, to friendship, to the children and to the fallen. Behind the façade, however, one gradually came to learn the reality. The 'peace industry' as it was described by a Moscow playwright was more efficient than most sectors of Soviet industry, but it was built on the basis of a personal experience or parental experience of war which commanded respect. Russian patriotism was exploited as a basis for Soviet patriotism, but it was real enough in its own right. So, too, was the recognition that, for all its failings, the socialist state had brought tangible gains. The prefabricated flats were shoddily built and cramped, but for those of middle age or over they represented a dramatic improvement on the squalor which they replaced. The younger generation, more cynical, was harder to satisfy, intolerant of the rigidity of the system, impatient for the consumer society.

The administrative and industrial stagnation of the Brezhnev years, now officially acknowledged, was apparent enough at the time. We now know, as we could then only suspect, the extent to which statistics were falsified. But the practical deficiencies of the planned economy were as apparent to us as to every citizen. It could lead the world in rocket technology, but it could not, as a senior official lamented, make women's tights. There were industrial and mining enterprises in Siberia run on a scale which reminded me of the major ventures of multinational corporations and controlled by men in their forties who had the intelligence and ability to command the same success. Even *Pravda* had, however, to bemoan the fact that, sixty years after the Revolution, the production quota for light domestic metalware was set in tonnage terms, with the result that it paid a factory manager to make nothing but large metal buckets, leaving an unsatisfied demand for everything from saucepans to corkscrews. The press had its reports of corruption and even in the theatre and in works such as Aitmatov's book, *A Day is Longer Than a Century*, the current of criticism could be sensed. There is no need to prolong the description. The more graphic examples which we experienced have been surpassed by the reality now paraded by the apostles of the new era. It was all summed up by the story of Stalin, Khrushchev and Brezhnev, travelling together by train. The train stops. Nothing happens. Stalin: 'Shoot the driver.' Khrushchev: 'Sack the station-master.' Brezhnev: 'Pull down the blinds and pretend we are moving.'

Although it was easy enough to identify the circumstances which made the Gorbachev restructuring essential, it was by no means easy to be sure about the nature of likely change. There were many who were actively promoting a return to Stalinist policies. I still have a lapel badge of Stalin given to me by one self-acknowledged Stalinist official. It was no surprise to be shown, in Georgia, his birthplace preserved as a shrine, but more remarkable to be accosted on a train in Uzbekistan by an elderly woman selling Stalin mementoes and to notice a Stalin sticker on the back window of a Moscow car. It was symptomatic of a mood in which, for many, the recollection of the evil of the Stalin years was outweighed by the desperate desire for a leader who would take the country out of a slough of maladministration. Most foreign observers at that time over-estimated the ability of the Party to cling to power. Yet, for all that the Soviet system was in many respects a monstrous criminal fraud perpetrated on a long-suffering Russian people, it responded to something in their character. Twenty years on, with the power of party and state demolished and the country's resources plundered by a new oligarchy, they still sought that leader.

The limping Soviet economy offered opportunities to British industry and ample credit was available for British exports, but in some respects we were less well placed than our European competitors. American export figures were swollen by the Soviet contracts for the purchase of grain, but at this time, during the Carter administration, the US–Soviet relationship was in a thoroughly unsatisfactory state and the Soviet leadership, irritated by a President whom they never understood, seemed only too happy to seek any opportunity to damage American interests. France and Germany, on the other hand, both conducting an active diplomacy in Moscow, were being wooed and it seemed that their success in securing major contracts reflected, at least in part, a political assessment. With recollections of 1941, it was surprising to hear my German colleague comment: 'We have good friends here. We always have had.' Recollecting the thinking of Austen Chamberlain, it was easier to agree with the Soviet official who put it differently: 'They take us more seriously.'

The breakdown of detente

After the fall of Nixon and the American withdrawal from Vietnam, the Soviet leadership found themselves in an odd position. They had felt that they understood the Nixon–Kissinger diplomacy. Now, suddenly, the correlation of forces had swung in their favour, but they were uncertain how to handle their opportunity. It was as difficult for them to grapple with President Carter's effort to establish a morally-based American policy as it has been for the West to deal with doctrinally-based Soviet policies. The Carter morality represented a clear and enduring strain in American policy, but it did not make for stability or predictability in relationships with the Soviet Union, and America's allies could not avoid being caught up in the confused waters of the American–Soviet relationship.

After an initial setback, the Salt II Treaty was signed at the Carter–Brezhnev summit of June 1979, immediately after the Conservative victory in the British General Election. Although, after Lloyd George's first efforts, it had been British Labour Governments which had taken the main steps in the establishment of relations with the Soviet Union, the British–Soviet relationship had not, in later years, swung with changes in the balance of political power in Britain. It was thought in Moscow that there might be a sharper tone to British policy, but there was no expectation of radical change. I was on an official visit to Georgia when Mrs Thatcher moved into Downing Street and, with a nice touch, my Georgian hosts presented me with a plaque of Queen Tamara of the Georgians leading her knights into battle. Neither for Britain nor for the Soviet Union was the other partner in the forefront of attention at this time and the impetus of the 1975 agreements was dwindling. The wider international scene was such that I saw little prospect of genuinely constructive British–Soviet cooperation, but it was still possible to expect a period of reasonable stability in the bilateral relationship.

The Duke of Edinburgh visited Moscow in 1979, as President of the International Equestrian Federation, in connection with the preparations for the 1980 Olympics and, although a new source of friction arose over the possible supply of Harrier aircraft by Britain to China, the Prime Minister was able to have her first, and reasonably substantial, discussion with a member of the Soviet leadership when, on her way to China in the summer of 1979, she stopped briefly at Moscow airport, where she was met by Kosygin, the Chairman of the Council of Ministers. The developing relationship was abruptly changed when, a few months later, the Soviet forces entered Afghanistan. Their action and the Western response to it inaugurated the next swing in the oscillating British–Soviet relationship.

The Soviet action in Afghanistan was different in kind from the earlier use of Soviet forces. Deplorable though the Soviet action in Hungary and Czechoslovakia had been, these countries had been accepted by the Western powers as falling within the imperial ringfence of the Soviet Union. In Africa, the attempt to extend Soviet influence through military intervention had involved the use of Cuban rather than Soviet forces. Now Soviet forces were directly committed to an operation designed apparently to push forward the imperial frontier in Central Asia. Despite some preliminary indications of Soviet activity, the operation came as a surprise. Yet, in retrospect, it was not wholly surprising. The Afghan revolution of 1978 had, in Brezhnev's words, created a 'qualitatively new relationship' with the Soviet Union. When the ability of the Afghan Government to hold power came into question, it must have seemed that there was a risk that the gains of 1978 would be lost and that an example might be set for counter-revolution elsewhere. The temptation to implement a combined politico–military operation to ensure the maintenance of a pro-Soviet regime was strong. Carter's foreign policy adviser, Zbigniew Brzezinski, had, a year earlier, drawn attention to the 'arc of crisis' along the shores of the Indian Ocean which was of 'vital importance' to the United States. Nevertheless, the Soviet leadership were doing their best to aggravate the humiliation of President Carter over the American hostages in Teheran – whereby they must incidentally have improved the prospect of a Reagan victory a year later – and doubtless calculated that an operation in Afghanistan could be completed without any risk of a direct military clash with the West. Extrapolating from earlier experience, they could expect that the emotional reaction would soon subside.

The scope for a British response was limited. The world had moved a long way since Lloyd George had secured the 1921 assurances about non-interference in Afghanistan. Aid to the Mujaheddin would, in due course, be possible, and, in its consequences, more effective than seemed likely, but there was no direct action which could be taken to halt the Soviet operation. In the assessment of Soviet policy and in discussion of the handling of the Afghanistan crisis, there was an encouraging measure of collaboration among the major Western European Embassies and with the United States. We all had our separate interests and differing approaches, but we all recognised the need to make the Soviet Union understand that a concept of limited detente which left open the use of military force in support of the extension of Soviet imperial control in the Third World was no basis for the establishment of a sound relationship with either the Western powers or the Third World. So, in parallel with the demonstration of international outrage in the United Nations, the British Government adopted a policy which amounted in effect to the ostracism of the Soviet Union. It was a controversial policy, but I believe it was right. It involved the deliberate severance of contacts which we had been trying, against heavy odds, to develop and which would have to develop again if there were ever to be any genuine understanding between the two countries. It involved gestures such as non-attendance at the great ceremonial occasions of the Soviet calendar. We boycotted the May Day and October Revolution parades. It had its element of farce as when our wives, after much serious deliberation, concluded that they could properly accept the invitation to the International Women's Day reception given by Mrs Brezhnev, but should not stay for the dancing. Most controversial of all was the decision to boycott the Olympic Games, a decision which required my temporary withdrawal from Moscow. Politics should have no place in the Olympics, but for Moscow the games were a major political event and the British competitors could not evade the political implications of their presence or absence. It was scarcely surprising that the pressure for a boycott should have caused considerable dissension among the competitors, for whom the price of absence was a heavy one, and many of the British team decided to participate. In the commercial field, the effects were slight, the principal measure being the American embargo on grain exports. In the field of arms control, the Soviet action dealt a blow to any chance of ratification of the Salt II Treaty and, more widely, it contributed to the mood which led to the installation in Western Europe of the intermediate range nuclear weapons constituting the response to the Soviet SS20 missiles.

The political dialogue was not wholly severed. The 1975 Protocol provided for bilateral consultations in a case such as this. I had a number of exchanges with the Foreign Ministry. During the UK presidency in the EC, Lord Carrington, as Foreign Secretary, came to present the proposals of the Community members concerning a basis for the withdrawal of Soviet forces from Afghanistan and spent a totally unproductive day of discussions with Gromyko. The Western response to the Soviet action in Afghanistan was a strange rag-bag, part planned, part haphazard, but it was soundly conceived. I believe it had its effect and the vast majorities against the Soviet Union in the United Nations were an important part of that effect. The detente of the 1970s was not illusory. It was a necessary stage in the gradual maturing of the relationship with the Soviet Union, but another cycle in the evolutionary process was necessary.

While the situation in Afghanistan remained in deadlock, the Soviet Union was confronted with the rise of the Solidarity movement in Poland. In Moscow, we watched as, throughout 1980 and 1981, the situation in Poland deteriorated and the tension with the Soviet Union rose. The tone of Soviet official comment grew more strident and it seemed clear that the political and military preparations for Soviet armed intervention were at an advanced stage. Still, the leadership hesitated and eventually, control was regained, at Soviet insistence, as a result of the installation of Jaruzelski and the imposition of martial law. Had Jaruzelski failed, I think it probable that the Soviet forces would have been used as they had been in Hungary and Czechoslovakia. We still do not know what was said in the Politburo discussions, but it is not unreasonable to assume that the international response to the Soviet action in Afghanistan was one factor in strengthening the Soviet desire to avoid the use of its own forces in Poland. It was sad to see the suppression – only temporarily – of Solidarity, but Europe had avoided a military operation which might have proved the most dangerous since 1945.

Again the question of a Western response arose, and on this occasion the dissent between the United States and her European allies was significant. With President Reagan in the White House, both the tone and the content of American policy had been sharpened. The rhetoric was that of the 'evil empire', but the room for new practical measures was limited. The strengthening of American weaponry was embarked upon but, in relation to the Soviet Union, the only intensification of the earlier response which seemed feasible was the extension of the existing strategic controls on exports to the Soviet Union. This, in essence, raised the old issue of the validity of economic sanctions. There was little dispute about the principle of preventing the export of advanced equipment directly connected with the development of Soviet military potential, but the central issue became the supply of foreign equipment for use in connection with the project to bring Siberian natural gas to Western Europe. This project was of interest to British equipment suppliers and of rather greater interest to other European countries, in particular France and Germany, both as equipment suppliers and as gas consumers. The disagreement within the Alliance was vocal and public and such measures as were taken proved insignificant, even as a gesture.[29]

The final episode of my period in Moscow was the need for discussion with the Soviet authorities on the Falklands War. It provided an interesting contrast between the formal and public Soviet denunciation of British colonialism and the practical recognition not only by the Soviet public but also, I believe, by some Soviet officials, of the justice of the British case. The risk of a potentially serious incident as a result of the presence of Soviet submarines in the South Atlantic was not negligible and the fact that it did not occur must have owed something to the prudence of Soviet policy.

Nevertheless, by the time I left Moscow in the autumn of 1982, relations with the Soviet Union had been reduced to the barest formality of diplomatic contact, a trickle of trade and a handful of academic exchanges. I commented at the time that the Soviet Union had been forced to recognise that it could not sustain a concept of detente under which it remained free to develop its military superiority in Europe, pursue destabilising policies world-wide and repression within its own sphere, and at the same time maintain a stable strategic relationship with the United States. The essential hostility of the Soviet and Western systems was displayed with full clarity: each had the military capacity to annihilate the other and the political relationship was a sullen stalemate.

Within the Soviet Union, the economy was in a bad way and the system was showing the stress of its imperial burden. The preoccupation of the Soviet leadership would have to be with internal policy, but they would not, I thought, refrain from challenging Western interests if they believed that they could secure profit to themselves without incurring any risk. The inertia of the whole state was symptomatic not only of the leadership, but of the system itself. It was clear that a full cure could need something closer to revolution than to reform and the political and ideological opposition was too strong to permit anything more than an ineffective tinkering. We could see that Brezhnev could not last long. My advice was that when he died his senior colleagues would share the spoils of office between one another, but that within five years we could expect this group to be replaced by men in their fifties. They would inherit a tired ideology, a strained economy, a restless empire, a hostile relationship with the major powers and a massive military power. We were approaching a period of major change of a kind which happens rarely in history and the men who would have to manage it were almost wholly unknown to us. In this situation, the task for the Western powers, as I saw it, was to get to know this new generation of potential leaders and to plan a progression from the necessarily negative policies of the post-Afghanistan period. We had first to achieve a safe management of the confrontation and then to establish a dialogue in which we could offer the prospect of a more constructive relationship, with the emphasis on the community of interest rather than the clash of ideology. In this whole process I saw Britain as well placed to take the lead. The Prime Minister's standing was high and her words would, I thought, carry weight.

I left Moscow in the early autumn of 1982, shortly before the death of Brezhnev provided the spur for the reassessment of British–Soviet relations. Mikhail Gorbachev was already visible as a contender for power, but, as we had expected, his seniors had to have their turn. Andropov's previous responsibility as head of the KGB was a less than encouraging augury, but he was thought to have the intellectual qualities necessary to analyse the sorry state of both the internal and the external policies of the Soviet Union. His illness and early death, followed by the appointment and equally early death of Chernenko, gave little opportunity to test the possibilities, but it is to the credit of the

British Government that, during this virtual interregnum, they were among the first to realise that the strident rhetoric and negative policies of the crisis years, necessary though they had been, would have to make way for yet another attempt to bring the Soviet Union into a less confrontational relationship with the remainder of the international community. Britain could indicate its readiness for such a development and this Margaret Thatcher did in speeches to the Conservative Party Conference on 14 October 1983 and a month later, at the Lord Mayor's Banquet, the forum chosen by Lloyd George for the initiation of his Russian policy in 1919, at which she set out the aim of reaching a 'broad understanding' on the 'common interest in peace and security at a lower level of weapons'. The British Government's policy was supported in the following year by other NATO Governments and the alliance committed itself formally to the pursuit of a more stable relationship through dialogue and cooperation and to the search for a genuine long-term detente.[30] A change of policy could, however, be made effective only if there were also in the Soviet Union a leadership which recognised the need for fundamental change and had the ability to initiate the necessary policies.

11
The End of Confrontation

The essentially confrontational relationship between Britain and the Soviet Union throughout most of the period since 1917 reflected the response of a society based on parliamentary democracy and individual rights to the challenge of a collectivist, revolutionary ideology claiming universality and backing that claim with ever-increasing military power. In March 1985, the accession of Mikhail Sergeevich Gorbachev to the General Secretaryship of the Communist Party of the Soviet Union set in train a process which was first to end the underlying confrontation and then to cause the dissolution of the Soviet Union. The decade of the 1990s found Britain and her partners facing the task of establishing a new relationship with a new Russia.

The April Revolution of Mikhail Gorbachev

A schoolboy during the war, Mikhail Gorbachev had studied law at Moscow University in the early post-war years, joined the Communist Party in 1952, a year before the death of Stalin, and made his career as a party official in the agricultural region of Stavropol in south Russia. He remained in Stavropol, progressing through the local hierarchy, until on appointment as a Party Secretary in 1978, he moved to Moscow. In 1980, with the Soviet Union locked in sterile confrontation with the Western powers, he became a full member of Brezhnev's Politburo. At this point, holding the twin appointments of Party Secretaryship and Politburo membership, he was in the clear line of succession to the leadership. The Leningrad-based Romanov, the only competitor in his own generation, was vulnerable and Gorbachev needed only to avoid disaster while death removed his elders, first Suslov, and then in quick succession the three General Secretaries,

Brezhnev, Andropov and Chernenko. A professional, a lawyer by training, his whole career was within the party, his direct responsibility was heavily concentrated on the markedly unsuccessful agricultural sector and he had no background in defence or foreign affairs. To the diplomatic community in Moscow he was known as a man of power in the party, but there had been little opportunity for any Western observers to form a personal impression of his qualities. In a major speech on 22 April 1983, in connection with the anniversary of Lenin's birth, he had spoken of the need for change and had taken up his favourite theme that Marxism–Leninism was not a collection of stale recipes. He had been uncompromising in his analysis both of the ills of Soviet society and of the ideological clash between socialism and imperialism. In many respects he was echoing familiar language, and it was reasonable to expect that he would inject a new vigour into the machinery of party and Government. At an ideological conference in 1984 he spoke of the need for openness, *glasnost*, but it was still hard for a Western observer, or indeed a Soviet citizen, to judge with any confidence the extent of the changes which he would introduce. Few, if any, could foresee their unintended consequences.

Almost immediately upon Gorbachev's assumption of the General Secretaryship the programme of *'perestroika'*, restructuring, was initiated. It was to be, as Gorbachev expressed it, a period of 'revolutionary change'. First at a Central Committee Plenum in April 1985 and then at the Twenty-Seventh Party Congress in February 1986, the two primary themes were the introduction of the discipline of a market economy into the socialist framework and the enhancement of the moral authority of the party by processes of internal democratisation. The implications of the latter process were then debated, in conditions of remarkable openness, at the Party Conference which began on 28 June 1988. With these major party gatherings successfully carried through, the doctrinal and organisational base for Gorbachev's reforms had been laid down. Their future course was uncertain, but the clear intention was that they would be conducted through the party and within a socialist framework. Here was the reason why earlier, less ambitious attempts at reform had failed and here lay the seeds of Gorbachev's own eventual failure.

The British–Soviet relationship was a matter of interest to Gorbachev even before his assumption of the General Secretaryship. In December 1984, a Delegation of the Supreme Soviet was invited to visit Britain for an exchange of views among parliamentarians. It was significant that, with his eye clearly set on the leadership, Gorbachev took advantage of this opportunity for a first substantial discussion with a Western leader. His personal impact was immediate. This was a man of determination, ability and charm, firm in his defence of socialist principles and Soviet interests, but able and apparently willing to cut through the standard ideological clichés and construct a practical working relationship with the West. On the personal level, it was the start of a relationship with Margaret Thatcher which, in its blend of mutual interest, personal respect and ideological antipathy typified the relationship between the two countries. In other ways it was, however, unique. Never before had there been a Soviet leader who enjoyed engaging in genuine debate at a personal and intellectually stimulating level with a British Prime Minister. After their first encounter, the Prime Minister observed: 'I like him. We can do business together'. But sadly – and strangely for one who had risen to the leadership of the Party – his executive ability did not match his intellectual curiosity.

Two years later, in March 1987, the Prime Minister visited Moscow and bilateral agreements were signed on the familiar topics of scientific and cultural cooperation as well as on the construction of new Embassies in London and Moscow.[1] 'It was', said Mrs Thatcher, 'a significant visit at what could be a turning point in history'. The substance of the formal agreements was of less significance than the thirteen hours of frank and private exchanges between the two leaders on the whole contemporary scene, both within and outside the Soviet Union. Divergent though their views were, it was possible to discuss them 'frankly and in a spirit of friendship.' With this visit, not only was the political dialogue resumed, but official and unofficial exchanges of all kinds were revived. Gorbachev stopped briefly in Britain in December for a meeting with the Prime Minister before his visit to the United States and in an interview to Soviet television described British–Soviet relations as 'better than at any time since the war'.

The developing British–Soviet dialogue had, as in earlier years, to find its place within the context of the differing evolution of US–Soviet and European–Soviet relations. The dominance of the superpower relationship and, within that relationship, of the balance of nuclear weaponry was inescapable, but it was significant that the first substantial product of the four Gorbachev–Reagan meetings between 1985 and 1988, the agreement on the abolition of intermediate range nuclear missiles, had a European focus. The whole issue of the intermediate range nuclear missiles was the subject of intense debate and controversy in both Britain and the other countries of Western Europe. It was necessary to take account of the heightened public emotion about the danger of nuclear weapons and at the same time to meet the differing security interests of the United States, the United Kingdom and the other Western European powers, in particular Germany, before seeking a balanced settlement with the Soviet Union. In the extraordinary calculations of a possible nuclear exchange, the intermediate range weapons which might, in theory, have engaged the superpowers in conflict at the nuclear level within Europe, were needed by NATO in order to counterbalance the long reach of the Soviet SS20 as well as the Soviet superiority in conventional forces. The ideal for Europe was therefore that the removal of intermediate range nuclear weapons should be accompanied by a disproportionate reduction in Soviet conventional forces. This was achieved, and for that achievement Europe had reason to be grateful to Gorbachev. Followed by the final withdrawal of Soviet forces from Afghanistan, by a unilateral reduction of Soviet ground forces and by the initiation of negotiations for the further multilateral reduction of non-nuclear forces in Europe, it reinforced the case for re-examination of some of the basic assumptions about East–West relations. With the Soviet Union pressing for abandonment of the NATO plan to modernise short-range nuclear weapons and for the eventual removal of all nuclear weapons from Europe, the long-term basis of Western defence policy began to come into question and divergent views opened up within the alliance.

The visit to Britain by General Secretary Gorbachev in April 1989 came at a significant point in the reform process. In an important speech on 27 October 1988, Sir Geoffrey Howe had set out logically and convincingly the case for a recognition of legitimate Soviet interests, a pragmatic testing of the new foreign policy concepts and a search for opportunities to work in partnership with the Soviet Union. He ended by asking: 'Are we entering, really, a new, more constructive era in East–West relations? It is too early to be sure, but I earnestly hope we are. Certainly we are witnessing some of the most important developments of our lifetime ... And Britain is ready – and more than ready – to play her part in turning hope into reality.' In both domestic and foreign policy the rigidity of the Soviet system was beginning to give way. The West could sense advances achieved and more to come. Gorbachev could justly claim in a speech at the Guildhall: 'The range of trust has expanded.' It was in the Western interest that it should continue to expand and that the Gorbachev reform process should succeed. But the road ahead was not easy to plot and the part which Britain could play was by no means clear. Within months the leaders in East and West were to be overtaken – some swept on, some swept away – by the torrent of events.

The collapse of the Soviet Empire

Decade by decade the political, economic and military structures which supported the Soviet state and maintained control of its empire had been eroded. Whenever a beam here, a truss there had come close to collapse, it had been shored up. In Berlin in 1953, Budapest in 1956, Prague in 1968 the Soviet army had held control. In Poland in 1981 the imposition of martial law had been successful. But in Afghanistan the massive Soviet military intervention had failed. By the beginning of 1989, although the main structures were superficially still in place, the decay was apparent.

To trace the process of collapse, as a mixture of economic reform, nationalist sentiment and political restlessness came to a turbulent, frothing head would take us beyond the scope of a book on British–Russian relations. By the end of 1989 the demolition of Soviet rule in Central and Eastern Europe was virtually complete. There was a certain irony in the fact that, of all the Communist leaders in the area, Ceausescu, who had at one time been hailed in Britain for his independent line towards the Soviet Union, was the only one to make a brief and disastrous attempt to use force to sustain his regime. Elsewhere the transfer of power had taken place with remarkably little disturbance. The opening of the frontier between Hungary and Austria opened a route for an exodus of citizens of the German Democratic Republic (GDR). Gorbachev's visit to East Berlin in October 1989 must have left Honecker in no doubt that he was about to be abandoned. It was a short route from there to the breaching of the Berlin Wall in November and the fall of the East German regime. East Germany had a symbolic importance for the Soviet Union which far outweighed that of any of the East European satellites. For a generation of Russians, the fall of Berlin in 1945, the establishment of a satellite regime and the maintenance of massive Soviet forces in East Germany had constituted a guarantee that their country would never again suffer the fate of 1941. Within a year not merely had the regime collapsed, but the East German state itself had disappeared from the map, merged with the Federal Republic and incorporated into NATO. The Red Army which had entered in triumph in 1945, withdrew in ignominy. It never forgave Gorbachev.

The collapse of Soviet control over Eastern Europe was in itself a major component in the British–Russian relationship and it is necessary to ask what part Britain played in it. Meeting Gorbachev six times in a five-year period, Margaret Thatcher had been consistent in her support for him, but as the reform process in the Soviet Union appeared to slow down and events ran out of control in Eastern Europe, she began to have doubts. They were not allowed to appear during the meeting in Moscow on 23 September 1989 when she spoke of his 'bold, courageous and visionary reforms', but immediately on her return to Britain she held a seminar at Chequers to consider his prospects of success in the 'near impossible task' which he had set himself, and the consequences for the West if he were to fail.

As the pace of the Communist collapse accelerated, the British Government's public response had been relatively restrained. A measure of practical help was given by the Government when in the summer of 1989 it established the Know How Fund 'to help with advice and expertise to assist Poland to move towards democracy and a free market economy'. £25 million was then added for Hungary. On 22 January 1990 the Fund was extended to the remainder of Eastern Europe and in November 1990 to the Soviet Union itself. Britain also took a leading part – although some saw it as a diversionary tactic from the pressure for monetary union – in arguing the case for European Community (EC) support to Eastern Europe and the Soviet Union.

In Parliament on 14 November 1989, immediately after the opening of the Berlin Wall, the Prime Minister allowed herself a characteristic burst of triumphalism when she claimed: 'There was at one time a doctrine in the West that we had merely to contain Communism. After that we put freedom on a peaceful offensive and it is partly that and partly defence that has led to the remarkable results that we now see in Eastern Europe.' To this came the opposition response: 'The absurd and incredible attempt to claim credit for the collapse of Communism by the disciples of Thatcherism is as unhelpful as it is shamelessly dishonest.'[2] *The Times* summed up much of public opinion in the headline to an article by Tom King, the Defence Secretary, on 18 November: 'Time of Hope – and Danger'. There was indeed some apprehension mixed with the hope and, as Mr Waldegrave put it in December, the Government's position was 'welcoming but careful'. Describing her own policy later in her memoirs, Margaret Thatcher wrote in similar terms:

> I was not going to allow euphoria to extinguish either reason or prudence ... War could not be ruled out ... essential to go carefully and avoid actions which would be deemed provocative by either the

Soviet political leadership or the military ... nothing was more likely to stir up old fears in the Soviet Union than the prospect of a reunited, powerful Germany, possibly with renewed ambitions on its eastern flank.[3]

Against the earlier experience of East Berlin, Hungary, Czechoslovakia and Poland it seemed almost inconceivable that the whole structure of Soviet power in Central and Eastern Europe could vanish in a matter of months, as easily as a bursting soap bubble, with no intervention by the imperial power.

The fact was, however, that successive Western Governments, maintaining the conduct of a working relationship with the Soviet Union while containing the expansionist pressure of Communist imperialism, had allowed Kennan's 'hand of time' to do its work. The basis for the 1989 revolution in Eastern Europe had been developing for half a century as national sentiment and growing frustration at Soviet control were stimulated by the example of Western society, based on democratic political systems and market economies. In Moscow itself the academic foreign policy specialists had for some time been growing sceptical about the basis of Soviet policy.[4] With the New Political Thinking of the early Gorbachev years, it became possible to talk in terms of cooperation in a Common European Home rather than in terms of the old Brezhnev doctrine. By 1989 the weakening of the Soviet imperialist drive had brought matters to such a point that military intervention to halt the process of democratic reform in Eastern Europe was no longer a practical possibility.

The reunification of Germany

It was in relation to Germany that the British Government had a direct and formal role in determining the shape of post-1989 Europe. Although the detail of the negotiations does not belong here, their long-term significance for the British–Russian relationship must not be underestimated. The structure of two German states, the Federal Republic of Germany (FRG) and the German Democratic Republic (GDR), with British, French and American garrisons still in West Berlin and Soviet forces in the GDR confronting the NATO armies in the Federal Republic all flowed from the four-power post-war arrangements as modified by the agreements of 1971. For many years British governments had been careful to uphold those arrangements and, while publicly accepting the goal of German reunification, had seen neither any likelihood of its early achievement nor any need to press for it. The collapse of the Soviet-backed regime in Eastern Germany suddenly brought the issue into sharp focus. The initial British reaction was unenthusiastic. Stopping over in Moscow on her return from a visit to Japan in 1989, Margaret Thatcher recorded her 'resolve to slow up the already heady pace of developments' and carried back to a Paris meeting in November the message that 'any attempt to talk about either border changes or German reunification would undermine Mr. Gorbachev and also open up a Pandora's box of border claims right through central Europe'.[5] Even Chancellor Kohl initially envisaged a five–ten year transition.

At this point, British policy was overtaken by the sheer pressure of events, by the force of long-suppressed public opinion in East Germany, by the political ambition of the Chancellor and by the power of the Deutschemark. The negotiations for the 'final settlement' for Germany took place in the Two-plus-Four Group (the two Germanies plus Britain, France, the Soviet Union and the United States), but the essential elements of the settlement were reached in bilateral negotiations between Kohl and Gorbachev. By January 1990 Gorbachev had accepted the principle of German reunification and, in order to secure the formal agreements, Kohl paid the Soviet Union 15 billion DM, primarily in relation to the cost of withdrawing Soviet forces. These were negotiations which subsequently led to recrimination in Russia, particularly in relation to an alleged assurance about the future expansion of NATO to the East. But in 1990 events were moving at a gallop and on 12 September the Treaty on the Final Settlement for Germany was signed in Moscow. At this crucial point in the shaping of the new Europe, Britain played its part, but cannot be said to have exercised a decisive influence. The British–Russian relationship was not a significant factor. Now, as on occasion in the past, it was the German–Russian relationship which counted. At Rapallo in 1922 and Moscow in 1939 the world had seen German initiatives towards the Soviet Union. From 1945 to 1989, while holding half of Germany hostage, the Soviet Union had given primacy to the nuclear superpower relationship with the United States. It was, however, the German agreements of 1970–2 which had opened the way to the years of detente and the CSCE agreements. After 1989 first the Soviet Union and then the successor Russian Federation were to emphasise Russia's role as a European power and in that relationship a reunited Germany was likely, for better or for worse, to establish, some would say re-establish, a 'special relationship' with Russia.

The *coup* of August 1991

Internal and external factors combined to destroy the political power of Mikhail Gorbachev. Externally, he had brought to an end the policy of confrontation with the Western powers, had accepted the humiliation of the withdrawal of Soviet forces from Germany and had presided over the dissolution of the Soviet empire. His people could sense the ending of external tension, but at the price of a national humiliation which brought no compensating material gain. Internally, the liberalisation of the regime had brought freedom of political debate, but it had not brought effective economic reform. The planned economy disintegrated, production slowed and hardship degenerated into misery. From the Politburo members at the apex of the pyramid of power down to the ordinary party members at its base a great army saw its privilege, its power and its prosperity under threat. Year by year, advisers were changed, new plans were formulated, but nothing effective was done. Gorbachev retained power by virtue of his leadership of the Communist Party, but it was a party which was as reluctant as it was incompetent to carry through fundamental economic reform. Ever more unpopular in his own country, Gorbachev retained a substantial measure of verbal support from those foreign leaders who recognised the debt which the world owed him for having brought to an end the Cold War. There was, however, little incentive for them to offer material support for the maintenance of the old command economy and by 1990 there were growing doubts about the prospect for radical economic reform under his leadership. Unwilling to contemplate the outright abolition of the apparatus of state control in favour of a full-blooded market economy, he could not do other than watch its progressive disintegration while, on the political front, the independence movements within the Soviet Union gained strength. So he came to the final crisis of power.

Margaret Thatcher had been the first to support him, but she was beginning to waver:

> In my last year in office doubts were increasingly raised about the wisdom of supporting Mr Gorbachev in his reforms. But I continued to do so and have no regrets ... The two obvious threats to peace were a takeover – covert or overt – by hardliners in the Soviet military or the violent break-up of the Soviet Union ... I now believe that all of us in the West overestimated the degree to which a Soviet Empire whose core was provided by Marxist ideology and a

communist nomenklatura – an empire constructed and bound together by force – could survive the onset of political liberty.[6]

As the inconclusive debate over economic reform dragged on in Moscow, Britain joined with other Western powers in making clear the limitations on any economic aid: 'Any help from the summit seven as a group should be tied to the introduction of genuine market policies and to encouraging the Soviet Union to mobilise its own extensive resources ... It is not our purpose to provide an oxygen tent for survival of much of the old system.'[7]

At this point Boris Yeltsin began to be taken more seriously in the West. A former Party head from the defence industry town of Sverdlovsk (Ekaterinburg), he was a contemporary of Gorbachev, approaching sixty, a self-proclaimed man of the people with no intellectual pretensions. Having been brought to Moscow by Gorbachev and appointed to the key post of Party boss of the city, he was then forced out of that appointment by Gorbachev. Combining a keen sense for the popular mood with a powerful, erratic, headstrong personality, Yeltsin was everything which Gorbachev was not. The clash between them was dramatic. When it began, Gorbachev must have felt that he held all the cards. It ended within a little more than a year in the destruction of Gorbachev, of the Party and of the Soviet Union. But when Margaret Thatcher met Yeltsin for the first time in London on 27 April 1990, she could not have sensed what lay ahead. She found him 'self-confident without being self-assertive, courteous, with a smile full of good humour and a touch of self-mockery'.[8] As he argued the case for decentralisation of power in the Soviet Union, it seemed to her that he had thought through some of the fundamental problems much more clearly than had Gorbachev who, elected only by the Supreme Soviet and increasingly unpopular both with the people and with the Communist establishment, had no effective mandate for his policies. Increasingly concerned by his failure to carry through effective economic reform, Western governments still respected Gorbachev for his massive achievement in bringing the Cold War to an end and, in any event, so long as he was President and for all practical purposes head of Government of the Soviet Union, the British Government continued to give him at least verbal support. The Prime Minister made clear this support to Yeltsin, but the very fact that she needed to do so was significant.

On 29 May Yeltsin was elected Chairman of the Supreme Soviet of the Russian Federation. The following month he issued a formal challenge to the central Soviet power by means of a declaration of Russian sovereignty and in July he resigned from the Communist Party of the Soviet Union. The way was clear for him to challenge Gorbachev. Declarations of sovereignty had already been made by the three Baltic States, Latvia, Lithuania and Estonia, where the movement for full independence had been swiftly gathering strength. Together with its NATO partners, the British Government had never accepted the legitimacy of the forced incorporation of the three states into the Soviet Union, but hesitated to give formal recognition of their regained independence until it was established in practice as well as in theory. For the time being they called only for the issue to be settled by negotiation.

The growth of nationalist feeling in the other Republics was also beginning to be felt. Margaret Thatcher visited Moscow in June 1990 for discussions with Gorbachev about Germany and NATO and went on to Kiev to open a major exhibition of the British way of life. She recorded that after the visit she was 'doubtful whether the Soviet Union could – or should – ultimately be kept together'.[9] Of the three Baltic States it was Lithuania which presented the most direct challenge to Gorbachev. His vacillation between attempts at negotiation and half-hearted recourse to force was met with total intransigence by the Lithuanian President, Landsbergis, and resulted in Gorbachev's one serious breach with the West. The anti-reform forces were already mustering against Gorbachev. Shevardnadze, resigning as Foreign Minister in December 1990, warned of a possible *coup* by the hardliners. On 13 January 1991 Soviet forces attacked the Lithuanian television station. The British Government's response was immediate. On 16 January, the Foreign Secretary, Douglas Hurd, formally condemned the use of force by the Soviet army in Lithuania and informed Parliament of an EC decision that cooperation with the Soviet Union would be suspended if the situation in Lithuania were prolonged or extended to the other Baltic States. At the same time the Government set in train a unilateral review of its bilateral cooperation with the Soviet Union and raised the Lithuanian problem in the CSCE.[10] The strength of the British reaction reflected the long-standing British sympathy with the Baltic States since their forced incorporation into the Soviet Union. Nevertheless, not wishing to precipitate all the uncertainties which might have flowed from dissolution of the Soviet Union, the British Government held back from formal recognition of Lithuania as an independent sovereign state.

In November 1990 the ousting of Margaret Thatcher and the succession of John Major as Prime Minister almost symbolically ended the close relationship with Gorbachev. Neither before nor after taking office did Major evince that personal interest in the Soviet Union which had been shown by Margaret Thatcher. Violently hostile or solidly supportive, depending upon her assessment of Soviet policy, she had always been involved. Had she remained in office, however, it is hard to see that she could have followed, or would have wished to follow, any more active policy during the events of 1991. Throughout the spring and early summer of that year, the British Government watched with concern and frustration the growing chaos in Russia, as one by one the fifteen constituent Republics stepped up their assertion of independence. While Gorbachev struggled to bring them together on a looser basis in a new Union Treaty, Yeltsin secured a popular mandate through election as President of the Russian Federation, thereby giving himself a legitimacy which Gorbachev never attained.

When the *coup* against Gorbachev took place on the morning of 19 August 1991, it seemed to many in the West that the attempt to reform the Soviet Union had failed. No immediate contact was possible with President Gorbachev who, held prisoner in his holiday residence in Crimea, was dependent on the BBC World Service for news of events in Moscow. Britain joined with the other NATO and EU powers in suspending aid and demanding the re-establishment of constitutional government, but it seemed almost too much to hope that the *coup* organisers, nominally in control of all the main organs of power in a state where central control of power had been absolute, should prove to be one of history's most incompetent groups of plotters. On 20 August and again on 21 August, with the *coup* faltering in the face of Yeltsin's rallying of popular support, John Major was able to speak to Yeltsin, the first Western leader to do so. He expressed British concern at the *coup*, asked what support the West could give to democratic institutions, congratulated Yeltsin personally on his bravery and expressed the hope that they would be able to meet in the near future. With Gorbachev nominally restored to power, Major spoke to him on 22 August, when Gorbachev gave an account of his views on the events surrounding the *coup* attempt and welcomed the prospect of a visit by the Prime Minister.[11]

From the moment the *coup* attempt failed, Yeltsin's supremacy over Gorbachev and the supremacy of the constituent Republics over the Soviet centre were effectively established. On 1 September, Major met both Yeltsin and Gorbachev in Moscow and declared his conviction that they were 'ready to work in harness to prevent Russia from sliding into chaos'. He also met the Prime Ministers of Latvia, Lithuania and

Estonia, promised to work for their admission to the United Nations and agreed that the United Kingdom would set up diplomatic missions in their capitals as soon as practicable. It was necessary to pretend that Yeltsin and Gorbachev would work together, but there was never the slightest prospect of this. Gorbachev's resignation from the CPSU on 24 August came too late to carry any conviction. On 6 November Yeltsin banned the Party from all activity on Russian territory; at a meeting at Belovezhskaya Pushcha on 7–8 December, with the leaders of Belorussia and Ukraine, he announced agreement on the annulment of the 1922 Treaty establishing the Soviet Union and on the formation of the Commonwealth of Independent States (CIS); at Alma Ata on 21 December the leaders of the other Republics with the exception of Georgia and the Baltic States formally established the Commonwealth; on 25 December Gorbachev, a President with no country, resigned. Belovezhskaya Pushcha: it is a name virtually unknown to the public and, indeed, to most politicians in the West. Yet the agreements concluded there, almost haphazard and certainly without thought for the practical implications, by three rather drunken men, were as significant for the lives of 250 million people and for the structure of international relations as, in a different sense, was the Treaty of Rome for Western Europe. The state established by the political power of Lenin and the military power of the Red Army, heirs to Imperial Russia, had grown sick. Its preservation, as a 'renewed federation of equal sovereign states' had been endorsed by a referendum in March 1991 but, with the discrediting of the central political structure of the Party, the will and the ability to sustain the Union in the face of popular demands for independence from the Baltic States and, critically, from Ukraine, had gone. Like a concerned son at the deathbed of a terminally ill parent, Gorbachev could do no more than bid it a dignified farewell.

In a matter of six years – the same length of time as the Second World War – the political map of Europe, the balance of international power and the postulates of Western defence had once again been transformed. During those years, and in particular during the last two, which must rank among the most significant periods in the twentieth-century history of Europe, Germany had at one point played a decisive part, while Britain, along with her other NATO allies, could do little more than stand watching on the sidelines, supporting peaceful change to the extent that they were able, but hesitant even in their applause. On 31 December 1991, with barely a whisper, the Soviet Union, moribund since August, formally ceased to exist. It was all over. Or was it?

Before we turn to the prospect for the relationship between Britain and the new Russia, it may be helpful to look back briefly over the sequence of events traced in earlier chapters as successive British Governments sought to adapt their policies to the evolving relationship with the Soviet Union. In some respects the Soviet Union which Gorbachev inherited in 1985 bore a depressing resemblance to the Soviet Union created by Lenin in 1922. The nightmare years of civil war, terror and invasion belonged to the past, but it was by no means a distant past. The Party still held – albeit in palsied hands – all the levers of power from the Politburo down to the factory floor, from the Kremlin to the most remote collective farm. The tentacles of the KGB, like some invasive growth, still penetrated every cell in the body politic. The army might be on the point of admitting defeat in Afghanistan, but from Berlin to Vladivostok it was the guarantor of the security of the state. The contest in defence technology had strained the economy to breaking point, but it could still sustain the systems of a nuclear superpower. The population was cynical, disillusioned, greedy for Western consumerism, but politically passive. The restless intellectuals were on the fringe. The media were tightly controlled. So, in large measure, was the Church.

Against this background it was not surprising that by the beginning of the 1980s British policy towards the Soviet Union was still oscillating, as it had done for the past 60 years, between hopeful dialogue and reluctant confrontation. The sacred Marxist–Leninist texts governing relations with the world outside the Soviet Union had undergone continual exegesis, but as late as 1980 the official History of Soviet Foreign Policy maintained the cardinal point of doctrine that, with the October Revolution, 'there appeared an entirely new foreign policy', a change in 'the nature of foreign policy, its aims and tasks, the source of its strength and its methods'.[12] In his book on the restructuring of international relations, published in 1978, Academician N. I. Lebedev followed the well trodden argument that the influence of the October Revolution was felt in every aspect of the life of mankind and that the struggle between socialism and capitalism conditioned 'not only the foreign policy of states with different social systems, but the development of the whole system of international relations'.[13] Thus, as late as 1975, Brezhnev could find it appropriate to put his name to a work entitled *Following Lenin's Course*, and to proclaim that the whole course of international relations was governed by the fact that 'the world outlook and class aims of socialism and capitalism are opposite and irreconcilable'.[14]

A proclamation of irreconcilable conflict had never, of course, constituted a sufficient basis for the practical conduct of relations. It was clear to the leaders of the Soviet Union, from the earliest days, that if the irreconcilable class struggle in its pure form were also to determine the governmental relationship with Western Europe and the United States, the result might well be mutual disaster. Marxist–Leninist theory required the inevitable revolutionary triumph of socialism, but it was necessary to construct a theory which, by differentiating between the methods employed in pursuit of the long-term class conflict and those employed in the conduct of inter-state relations, would minimise the risk of armed conflict during the intervening period. Through the application of the doctrine of peaceful coexistence the Soviet Union secured the flexibility which it needed in pursuing the practical conduct of day-to-day relations with the capitalist states, but it was a doctrine explicitly limited to the conduct of inter-state relations and never regarded as implying an abandonment of the 'revolutionary class struggle' or the 'liberation struggle of the oppressed peoples'. It was compatible with Soviet support for Communist activity wherever this seemed profitable and with the use of force in order to prevent the 'export of counter-revolution'. With the progress to socialism held to be scientifically inevitable, regression from that path could easily be attributed to exported counter-revolutionary forces and the basis established for the use of the Soviet army in the German Democratic Republic, Hungary, Czechoslovakia and Afghanistan.

The progressive refinement of the doctrine of peaceful coexistence formed a large part of the theory of Soviet foreign policy. In the early years it was seen as an essentially transient stage and, in relation to the capitalist states, the formal distinction between inter-state relations and revolutionary activity was preserved by the mechanism of the Comintern. In the post-war years, and notably from the time of Khrushchev onwards, with less opportunity for revolutionary activity in Western Europe and the United States and the new hazard of nuclear war, the time scale lengthened and peaceful coexistence came to be regarded as a policy of indefinite duration. But at no time did it imply abandonment of the objective of a constant movement of the 'correlation of forces' in favour of socialism.

The Soviet concept of the 'correlation of forces' embraced the whole range of factors on which national power might be based, from the motive power of ideology, through the structure of society, the political system and the economy, to the ultimate power of the armed forces. Throughout the years of Soviet power, that correlation changed dramatically in certain respects as between the Soviet Union and Britain. In 1917 the infant Soviet state, heir though it might be to the territory and power of imperial Russia, was only just capable of survival. Britain, by contrast, with its Empire intact, might lack the economic muscle of the United States, but still briefly commanded an unrivalled combination of world-wide political, economic and military power. To the Soviet Union, New York and London were the twin citadels of capitalism and a defeated Germany the proving ground for the next move to the triumph of socialism. In 1922 Lloyd George could regard Rapallo as the alliance between the two pariahs of international society and the Soviet Union and Germany knew that they were so regarded. Throughout the 1930s, despite the swift decline in British fortunes, the British attitude towards the Soviet Union was still marked by a conscious sense of military, political, economic and moral superiority and the Soviet leadership was in no position to contest this. It was natural that Britain should hold the initiative in determining the relationship and inevitable, given the political orientation of the parties, that it should be unproductive. Until the early summer of 1939, so far as the Soviet Union was of any interest at all to the British Government, it was not as a military power, but as a potential market for British goods, a source of subversion of the British worker and a focus of revolution internationally. It was in these terms that relations were conducted.

Except in conditions of active warfare – and sometimes even then – the perception of power may matter more than its reality. The differing perception of the two sides was well illustrated by the casualness with which Chamberlain pursued the tripartite negotiations of 1939, the decision of the Soviet Union to conclude the Molotov–Ribbentrop agreement and the brusqueness with which Stalin rejected Churchill's approach in 1940. It was the direct use of military power which enabled the Soviet Union to secure and sustain its post-war grip on Central and Eastern Europe, and throughout the years of the Cold War, it was the awareness of Soviet military power which conditioned the British relationship with the Soviet Union. The politics of the years from 1945 to 1953 were essentially an extrapolation from the facts of 1945, with military power and territorial control setting the parameters. What happened through the following 38 years was that military power continued to dominate the relationship, despite the fact that it was becoming increasingly irrelevant as an instrument of relations between major powers. Again what mattered was the perception. For perception is the essence of deterrence. The perception mattered equally to both Britain and the Soviet Union. Khrushchev's own personality was itself a symbol of the confidence of the Soviet Union in its power and it was a challenge of power to which, in their various ways, Churchill, Eden, Macmillan, Eisenhower and Kennedy had to respond. It was the military balance between the two superpowers and the projection of Soviet military and political power into the Third World which determined the major items on the agenda of East–West negotiation. In this situation, the limited political effectiveness of the very high level of bilateral activity between Britain and the Soviet Union during the late 1960s was not surprising. From time to time the Soviet Government, in pursuit of a policy of peaceful coexistence, would undertake some new initiative apparently designed to further the cause of peace and possibly to emphasise the positive elements in its relationship with Britain. The normal British response was to scrutinise the Soviet proposal with extreme scepticism, seeking to judge whether it could in fact serve a useful purpose or whether its aim was simply to confuse international opinion and provide the basis for some shift in the correlation of forces in favour of the Soviet Union. At the same time, most British Governments took the view that the closer the dialogue with the Soviet leadership – and, more important, with the Russian people – the greater would be the chance that the more aggressive aspects of Soviet policy would be softened and a notional 'peaceful coexistence' might become a genuine recognition of a common interest in maintaining peace and security and developing mutually profitable trade. Unfortunately, from Litvinov's collective security, through the wartime alliance to the 1975 agreements with their redefinition of peaceful coexistence, each period of hope turned quickly to disillusion as Soviet policy seemed to return to its basic principles.

By the beginning of the 1980s, despite the depressing continuity of so many features of the Soviet state, the correlation of forces had changed dramatically. Soviet analysts were speaking less of the balance changing in favour of socialism and more of the complexity and danger of the international system. The drive to project Soviet power had passed its peak. The attempt to subjugate Afghanistan was like a wave which obscures for a time the ebbing of the tide, but which, as it in turn ebbs, reveals yet more starkly the reefs and shoals. Soviet ideology had lost its force both in Europe and in the Third World. The economy was drifting slowly into the stagnation of the late Brezhnev years. Only in the earlier technology of space and in the production and deployment of the less sophisticated forms of conventional and nuclear military hardware could the Soviet Union still outstrip the West. The deterrent power of nuclear arms was the greatest single factor in the history of international relations since 1945, but by 1985 the one threat which the Soviet Union did not face was the threat of armed attack. For a state whose power was constrained by an outdated ideology, a senile leadership, a disillusioned citizenry, a sclerotic economy and a restless empire, the strategic rocket force, the pride of the Soviet armed forces, was as irrelevant as Khrushchev's shoe – and rather more expensive.

It was understandable that, in so far as the Soviet Union maintained a doctrine of confrontation, the West should perceive that threat in military terms and should try to neutralise it by means of arms control agreements, primarily at the superpower strategic level, but also in terms of the balance of nuclear and conventional forces within Europe. In ideological terms the Western democracies had since the 1950s done what they could to counter the Soviet offensive in the Third World and, especially by broadcasting, to open up the closed Soviet system. By the late 1970s, as they took advantage of the CSCE Final Act to increase the exposure of the Russian people to ideas of democratic politics and freedom of expression and belief, Moscow was struggling to maintain its ideological defences. Thus, while, Britain and her partners were still superficially alternating between hopeful dialogue and reluctant confrontation of a Soviet challenge, the terms of that confrontation had changed. They had changed because Marxist–Leninist ideology, for all that it had built the Soviet state, had failed the Russian people. What Gorbachev then did was twofold. Calling for 'liberation from dogmatic ideas and from conclusions which ... had ceased to correspond with the realities of our days', he attempted to reshape the ideology and institutions of the state in such a way as to make them serve the interests of the people; and, seeking a new *modus vivendi* with the West, he formally ended the doctrine of confrontation: 'We are fully justified in refusing to see in it [peaceful coexistence] a special form of the class struggle ... The struggle between two opposing systems is no longer a determining tendency of the present era.' [15] It is important to note that this formal abandonment of the doctrine of confrontation and practical implementation of new policies took place while the Soviet Union still existed. The destruction of the Soviet state was not a precondition for it.

The challenge for the 1990s was for Russia to demonstrate that, liberated after 74 years from the rule of the Communist Party and the constraint of Marxist–Leninist doctrine, it could build a society which would meet the aspirations of its people; and, for Britain and her Western partners to demonstrate that, freed from the need to meet a Soviet doctrine of confrontation, they could find a new basis for a productive relationship with the new Russia.

12
A New Russia

The early years

Even before the final disintegration of the Soviet Union, it had become clear to British policy-makers that its relevance to Western security was changing in character. Hostile though the old Soviet Union had been, its stability had, even during the Brezhnev years, made possible the containment and gradual reduction of the nuclear threat. Under Gorbachev that process had been accelerated. The confrontational basis of Soviet policy had been abandoned and in its place had come a 'New Political Thinking' leading to a policy which made cooperation with the West a primary objective. To many observers it seemed that a new and hopeful era was opening in international relations. If this were the case, there would be significant implications for British foreign policy.

It was also increasingly apparent that, even if the central Soviet government survived, power would move increasingly to the governments of the individual Republics. The process would carry a substantial risk of instability and a possibility of armed conflict between the centre and the periphery or around the periphery. Prior to the break-up of the Soviet Union, 30 per cent of its long-range nuclear weapons were deployed in Ukraine, Kazakhstan and Belarus. Tactical weapons were in all fifteen Republics. Negotiations to reduce the level of mutual threat were proceeding quickly, but it was clear that any disintegration of the control structures for the Soviet nuclear forces would carry exceedingly grave risks. In this situation, although the reshaping of the Soviet Union was clearly a matter for the Governments of Russia and of the other Republics, it was in the interest of the United Kingdom, together with its European partners and the United States, to do whatever was possible to assist in an orderly transformation. This would require assistance in promoting economic stabilisation and the establishment of such political relations as would promote mutual confidence and make possible the exercise of influence in the early stages of reconstruction.

With the formal dissolution of the Soviet Union, this task became urgent. Among the Republics, the Russian Federation was by far the most significant and was in many ways the natural successor, particularly in relation to control of central strategic forces. The stability of its reform-minded Government was an important objective. Its status as successor in all relevant respects was quickly given formal recognition, while the other fourteen republics were recognised as independent sovereign states. Ukraine and Belarus already had UN membership; the Baltic States, as members of the former League of Nations, had a clear claim to it; and the remaining Republics in their turn were accepted. Russia took the seat of the Soviet Union as a permanent member of the Security Council. Diplomatic relations were established with each of the new Republics and, while Embassies were being set up, HM Ambassador in Moscow was given multiple accreditation.

Precipitate though the dissolution of the Soviet Union had been, Western governments, Britain among them, could be content that it had for the most part been accomplished with a remarkable lack of violence. On his way to a meeting in the United States in search of economic aid, President Yeltsin stopped briefly in London on 30 January 1992 and was warmly received. *The Times* hailed him as: 'A Russian Hercules ... a courageous, principled democrat ... as decisive in office as he was trenchant in opposition ... presiding in hazardous solitude over a country engulfed in political, economic and social turmoil and under pressure from a combination of former communists, bureaucrats, military hardliners and disillusioned nationalists'. A formal state visit followed on 9–10 November, and on that occasion a Treaty on the Principles of Relations between the Russian Federation and the United Kingdom[1] was signed. In it, the two governments committed themselves to a range of high-sounding principles – peace, friendship, democracy, respect for human rights and the peaceful settlement of disputes, as well as to the promotion of commerce and to practical cooperation over a wide area of governmental activity. In parallel they signed a document on Partnership – a new word in their bilateral relationship – for the Nineties. It was some thirty years since the idea of a treaty of friendship had been aired between Harold Macmillan and Nikita Khrushchev and seventeen years since Harold Wilson had concluded a set of bilateral agreements in the glow of post-Helsinki optimism. By 1992 the circumstances had been transformed, but it remained to be seen what fruit the treaty would bear. As a symbol of the new relationship, the Queen and Prince Philip agreed in principle to take up an invitation issued three years earlier by President Gorbachev for a state visit to Russia.

The dream fades

Within Russia, the strength of Communist and nationalist representation in the Russian Supreme Soviet, the lingering resentment of all those who had supported the 1991 *coup* and the discontent with the economic state of the country, meant that President Yeltsin's position was still far from secure. In June 1992 Foreign Minister Kozyrev wrote that 'the party of war, the party of neo-Bolshevism' was raising its head[2] and Yeltsin himself, speaking to both Houses of Parliament during his London visit[3] warned that there were still forces in Russia interested in a revanchist *coup*. The showdown with the Supreme Soviet was not long in coming. Yeltsin might disavow the Leninist tradition, but remained true to it in the exercise of power. With none of Gorbachev's scruples, he carried through an unconstitutional dissolution of the Supreme Soviet, provoking its Chairman, Ruslan Khasbulatov, and his own Vice President, Alexander Rutskoi, into an armed challenge which was resolved on 4 October 1993 by the shelling of the White House, the scene of Yeltsin's own defiance of the *coup* two years earlier. The Russian Supreme Soviet, elected while Russia was still within the Soviet Union, lacked meaningful democratic credentials and Khasbulatov and Rutskoi had never endeared themselves to foreign opinion. Nevertheless the dissolution of a parliamentary body by the President's shellfire, an action more brutal even than Lenin's dissolution of the Constituent Assembly in 1918, was one for which it would be hard to find a parallel in any democratic state. For the British television viewer it made a horrifying spectacle. But Yeltsin, rushing ahead with the transfer of the old state corporations into the private property of former managers and new carpetbaggers, had been enjoying increased Western support. The IMF had pledged an initial $1 billion in July 1992 and a further pledge of support had been given by the Group of Seven major industrialised countries in April 1993. A successful referendum on his policies had given him added authority. Douglas Hurd, in Moscow at the time of the shelling, doubtless earned Yeltsin's approval – and did not much surprise the average Russian – by his outspoken support for action against 'a discredited and undemocratic body' which was 'using violence to exploit Russia's fragile democracy for thoroughly dangerous and non-democratic ends'.[4] It was a line of argument which must have rung oddly in Gorbachev's ears when he recalled the Western denunciation of his own hesitant use of force in Lithuania. But then, in the crude demonology of late-Soviet and post-Soviet Russia, the Lithuanians, like Yeltsin, were listed as staunch fighters for democracy, independence and human rights.

The following year saw the inauguration of a newly elected Russian bicameral Parliament, a visit to Moscow by John Major, and in October, just a year after the shelling of the White House, a highly successful visit by the Queen and the Duke of Edinburgh. The British–Russian relationship had indeed turned full circle. But the mood of euphoria was short-lived. Elections in 1995 gave the Communists and nationalists a small majority in the Duma. A strongly Presidential Constitution limited their power, but could not prevent continued friction with the President. Yeltsin had already been calling for a more assertive policy both towards the West and towards Russia's partners in the Republics of the former Soviet Union, now – with the exception of the three Baltic States – constituted as the Commonwealth of Independent States (CIS). With its forces engaged in hostilities with secessionist groups in Moldova and Georgia and caught up in the conflict between Armenia and Azerbaidjan over Nagorny Karabakh, Yeltsin's Russia seemed far from stable, but it was Chechnya which caused the most serious concern in Britain. The Chechens had over the centuries responded to brutal Russian repression by developing their own unique blend of nationalism and thuggery. Formally a constituent part of the new Russian Federation, they declared independence. Yeltsin's reaction was the same as that of Brezhnev when, fourteen years earlier, Afghanistan had threatened to slip from the Soviet Union's imperial grasp. The Soviet armed forces embarked on a bloody and futile conflict which sorely tested the West's support for his regime. It was not, the Foreign Secretary said, in the British interest that the Russian Federation should degenerate into chaos; but the force used was 'brutal and disproportionate'. The British Government, he explained, supported the reform process in Russia, not the personalities, and the Prime Minister left President Yeltsin in no doubt about the cloud that Chechnya cast over that process.[5] By implication, British support for Yeltsin was weakened. But in other respects he still seemed the main guarantor of Russian reform. Given that Chechnya was a part of the Russian Federation, the parallel with Afghanistan was not exact and, although there was a pause in the developing cooperation, no formal sanctions were applied against Russia.[6] Nor, if they had been, is it likely that they could have substantially influenced for the better the fate either of the Chechens or of Russia.

There is no doubt that different standards were applied in relation to the possible break-up of the Russian Federation from those which had applied in relation to the break-up of the Soviet Union. So, indeed, they well might be. The status of the constituent elements was different. So, too, were the potential consequences. In any event, the alternative, as NATO Governments have learned in Kosovo, would not have been easy to apply against Russia. After the humiliating failure of Russia's first attack it seemed that a certain vagueness about Chechnya's independence within – or, as Chechnya would claim, outside – the Russian Federation might be allowed to endure. Despite the taking of British hostages, the war did not loom large in British–Russian relations. On the bilateral front mutual espionage expulsions from London and Moscow followed a traditional pattern but with less than the old rancour. The respite in Chechnya was, however, brief. A more violent onslaught in 1999 reflected the readiness of Yeltsin and Putin to pander to the growing strength of Russian nationalism and assert Russia's right to deal in her own brutal way with an internal affair. The portents were not good.

New Labour in Britain

In May 1997 the new Labour Government under Tony Blair found a complex state of affairs in Russia. For earlier Labour Governments, from Ramsay MacDonald through Clement Attlee to Wilson and Callaghan, the conduct of relations with the Soviet Union had taken a prominent, albeit in the later years diminishing, and for the most part frustrating, place in their foreign policy. In 1997 matters were different. The new Russia was still poised uncertainly. President Yeltsin had secured re-election in 1996, but his behaviour was erratic and the durability of his recovery from a major heart operation remained to be seen. His Government, committed to a market economy, was unpopular; the nationalist/Communist majority in the Duma was vocal; Moscow was prosperous but large sectors of the population were in deep distress; and the economy was only just beginning a long overdue stabilisation. There was much to play for. The next few years might determine whether an increasingly prosperous, democratic Russia would move forward in political and economic cooperation with the Western powers or whether, with a limping economy and a restless, impoverished population, it might retreat into economic autarky, nationalism and xenophobia. The outcome would be of considerable significance for the future conduct of British foreign policy, but to the extent that the British Government could influence matters it would be very much less through bilateral actions than through wider groupings. Nevertheless, despite the pressure of many more immediate concerns the new Foreign Secretary and the Prime Minister both paid early visits to Moscow and among the first fruits was the signature of an agreement on joint action to combat crime. Modest in scope but useful in its practical effect, this typified the nature of the continuing bilateral relationship. The British presidency of the EU and the Group of Seven in the first half of 1998 also offered the opportunity for the new Government to demonstrate its desire to work with the Yeltsin Government in the framework of wider international cooperation. Russia was not high on the British Government's priorities for these meetings, but the expansion of G7 to accommodate Russia served as a symbolic gesture of support for the Yeltsin reforms. The effectiveness of that symbolic support was soon put to the test.

The marked pro-Western orientation of Soviet foreign policy during the early Gorbachev years had, even before the end of 1991, begun to give way to a more assertive line. The underlying mood of the Russian people was demonstrated by the success of the Communists and nationalists in the Duma elections and it was not easy for Yeltsin's Russia to resist the temptation to support the Bosnian Serbs. As the UN confrontation with Iraq deepened, Russia played an independent hand in seeking diplomatic mediation. In the Security Council she was aligned with France and China against Britain and the United States, but her weakness was such that no Russian Government could afford the luxury of more than gesture politics in the international arena.

The decision of the NATO Governments to extend membership to Poland, Hungary and the Czech Republic, initiated during the Major Government and implemented under Blair, was grist to the nationalists' mill. When Gorbachev acquiesced in NATO membership for an enlarged Germany – not that he had much in the way of options – it was claimed that he had been given an oral assurance that further expansion was not intended. There is no public record of any such assurance and it seems certain that there was no formal undertaking. Nevertheless, something may well have been said in the course of informal discussion and there is no doubt that the Russian Government believed they had been misled, when, under pressure from Germany and the United States on one side and the East

Europeans on the other, NATO went ahead. The proposal was fiercely resisted by the Russian Government, producing a situation which was described by Yeltsin as 'the most serious dispute since the Cuban missile crisis'.[7] But Russia had no trump cards to play and had to be content with the acceptance of a 'Founding Act on Mutual Relations, Cooperation and Security' under which a NATO–Russia Joint Council was established. The arrangement was described as giving Russia 'a voice but not a veto' and so, indeed, it was. The Parties declared that they did not consider each other adversaries, but although the Joint Council was to be competent to reach agreements on matters where the Parties were able to do so, it was specifically prohibited from restricting the freedom of action of either side. As a further concession to Russia, it was agreed at the same time that the 1990 Treaty on Conventional Forces in Europe should be adapted to reflect the new situation resulting from the dissolution of the Soviet Union and the independence of its constituent Republics. For better or for worse, with the British Government's concurrence, a new frontier had been drawn across the Continent and the seeds of future tensions had been sown. A hand was extended across the frontier, but it still left Russia on the Asiatic rather than the Atlantic side.

In March 1998 the international community was once again plunged into a brief period of uncertainty when the President dismissed his Prime Minister, Viktor Chernomyrdin and the whole of his Government in order to appoint the 35-year-old, largely untried Sergei Kiriyenko. Kiriyenko sought to continue the reforms on lines approved by the IMF, but tax reform was necessarily a slow process and the power of the new oligarchs hindered the radical measures which were needed. The burden of external debt was heavy. The prospect of servicing it, already slender, was virtually eliminated by the slump in oil and gas prices which, combined with internal mismanagement and the side-effect of the Asian economic crisis, brought turmoil in the financial market, a devaluation of the rouble and a new political crisis.

Yeltsin, by this time was visibly failing in health. A sad, shambling, incoherent figure, reminiscent of Brezhnev in his final years, he retained the will for power, but had lost the ability to make effective use of it. Kiriyenko survived barely half a year, before he in turn was dismissed and, after much wrangling, replaced by the 68-year-old Yevgeny Primakov. Primakov was well known in Britain as head of one of the Soviet foreign policy institutes, in which capacity he had led the Soviet side in Round Table discussions on foreign policy (see chapter 10). A firm exponent of Soviet policy, he had, nevertheless, earned the respect of his British interlocutors. Subsequently, under Yeltsin, he had taken charge for a time of the Russian foreign intelligence service. As Prime Minister he took a carefully judged middle-of-the-road position which enabled him to command widespread support within the Duma and among the population. Some retreat from the purity of IMF free market doctrine seemed inevitable, but he claimed to do no more than Roosevelt had done with the New Deal and the air of crisis was calmed. It was an uneasy calm. The economy remained stagnant and the banking system largely inoperative. As 1998 ended, Russia was forced to appeal not only for yet further external financial aid, but also for EU and US food aid to see it through the winter. Food aid, at least, was possible, but for the most part, Britain and her partners could do little more than watch as Yeltsin's Russia – and Yeltsin himself – tottered on the edge of collapse. In June 1999 Yeltsin removed Primakov and appointed Sergei Stepashin who survived only until September when he was replaced by the former KGB officer Vladimir Putin. The changes were essentially a part of the political manoeuvering in preparation for the Duma and Presidential elections and did not, in themselves, present the British Government with new issues of foreign policy. The need was for a stable and effective government in Russia with which they could develop a possible relationship. It had not yet been achieved, but at least the political system, sorely tested, was still functioning and the people, even more sorely tested, seemed in no mood for violence.

Economic relations

After 1991, the abolition of the whole Soviet structure for control of the economy removed the principal obstacle to the integration of Russia into the global market so far as trade and finance were concerned. An interim agreement between Russia and the EU was signed on 17 July 1995 and was replaced by a Partnership and Cooperation Agreement which came into force on 1 December 1997. This covered a wide range of trade, commercial and economic issues and instituted a political dialogue between Russia and the EU. The Group of Seven major industrialised countries, which had extended only a grudging and partial participation to Gorbachev's Soviet Union, was extended to Seven plus One and in May 1998 formally became the Group of Eight. Membership of the World Trade Organisation (WTO) remained an objective of Russian policy, but the 1998 economic crisis made this seem a very distant aim. According to official figures GDP fell by about

40 per cent between 1990 and 1996, but so much economic activity took place in the 'grey economy' that the actual decline was probably rather less. By 1997, with the help of external finance and after a revaluation of the rouble by a factor of 1000 had effectively written off the old currency, the economy began to stabilise. The ordinary Russian consumer had at last, after years of sharply falling living standards, the prospect of some benefit from the move to a market economy. Inflation was being held at a tolerable level, but there were still very significant wage arrears. Tax collection was improving, but was still not adequate. The external trade balance was positive, but even before the 1998 crisis the budget was still not under control. The economy had undergone a financial restructuring through its transfer into private hands and a great deal of wealth had been generated for a small segment of the population, but it had been generated by asset-stripping and short-term trading rather than by productive investment. Corruption was rife and criminal gangs had creamed off much of the country's wealth into overseas accounts. The resources necessary for the substantive rebuilding of Russian industry were available, but the process had barely started. By 1999 the recovery in oil prices brought a welcome boost, but with growing concern at the scale of corruption, after seven years of reform, Russia approached the new century as a less reliable – albeit in some respects more congenial – partner in economic affairs than the old Soviet Union.

In those seven years the new Russia received substantial financial support for economic reform through the IMF and the World Bank as well as by individual governments and foreign banks. Total assistance provided by the OECD countries during the period 1990–3 amounted to US$120 billion and by the time Kiriyenko's Government collapsed in 1998 the figure had risen further. In the financial crash of that year the Government defaulted on $20 billion worth of rouble bonds and by early 1999, with IMF negotiations still in train, there seemed little prospect of Russia meeting its scheduled repayment of $17.5 billion due to overseas lenders that year.

Trade and investment

Trade expansion had been an important element in British policy towards the Soviet Union, but there was, especially at times of international tension, a continuing inclination – backed by specific measures in relation to strategic items – to avoid action which would contribute to the Soviet military potential. Earlier chapters have referred to the succession of British–Soviet agreements on bilateral trade, on economic, scientific and technical cooperation and on the settlement of old debts and the grant of new credits. Their conclusion and abrogation over the years provided a convenient symbolic demonstration of the state of relations. They were not without effect, but the vision of vastly increased trade which swam intermittently before the eyes of British businessmen was never realised. There were times in the 1930s and again in the 1950s when Western leaders saw the Soviet economy as capable of posing a real challenge to the West. Their concern was as unfounded as were the hopes of exporters. Events showed that a centrally controlled command economy giving priority to the defence sector and based on an inert society could not in fact match the efficiency or create the market potential of a market-based system operating in a democratic society.

In the final years of the Soviet Union, despite the easing of confrontation and the dramatic opening of Russia to direct contact with Western business, the uncertain legal basis and deteriorating economy still made for poor results. In 1987 British imports from the Soviet Union were £875 million, but exports had fallen off to £432 million, barely more than the level they had attained in the late 1970s. The two governments then set themselves a target of a 40 per cent increase, but by the time the Soviet Union was dissolved in 1991 British imports had risen only to £901 million, while exports had fallen further to £354 million. Matters improved after 1991. Demand was stimulated by the injection of foreign finance and the improvement in British exports was striking. To Russia alone (which accounted for about half the population and rather more than half the trading potential of the former USSR) they had risen by 1997 to £1232 million, while British imports had reached £1476 million. At this level, however, British exports to Russia were only one fifth those of Germany and accounted for substantially less than 1 per cent of British overseas trade, a poor figure if account is taken of Russia's economic potential. There was a long way to go and 1998 brought a further setback.

In terms of investment, Britain was, by 1996, on a cumulative basis, the second largest foreign source, with almost 10 per cent of the total. 350 British firms had offices in Moscow. Another 100 were in St Petersburg and there were in total 1200 joint ventures between British and Russian firms. The oil industry recognised the long term potential and in the services sector there was very substantial activity in legal and accountancy work and in financial management, all directed in one way or another towards the restructuring of the Russian economy. The figures give an over-optimistic impression of the depth of British involvement, but at least a base had been established and the liberalisation of the economy following the dissolution of the Soviet Union had created a potential for expansion very much more significant than had existed at any time since the early years of the century. The 1998 financial collapse was, however, a major setback to investor confidence. It was clear that Russia's potential would not be realised until a sound legal and financial infrastructure and a reliable tax system could be established and criminality brought under control. Until that could be done the prudent investor would be reluctant to undertake long-term commitments. In 1999 all this seemed a very distant prospect but much would turn on the outcome of the elections.

The orientation of the new Russia

After eight crowded years of the new Russia, is there any basis for confidence in her future? The trauma which Russian society suffered through the dissolution of the Soviet Union was as profound as, arguably more profound than, that experienced by Russia in 1917, or by Germany in 1918 and 1945. In seeking to assess the future policies of any country which has first subjected itself to and then emerged from a period of totalitarian rule, it is right to ask how far that phenomenon reflected continuing national characteristics, and how far it stemmed from a temporary conjunction of circumstances and personalities. In the case of the Soviet regime the circumstances and the personalities are well documented. But what of the underlying national characteristics? It is easy enough to identify aspects of the Soviet system which reflected the distinguishing characteristics of earlier Russian regimes, characteristics which flowed from a combination of historical and geographical factors, embedded traditions and that indefinable thing called national temperament. The Marxist–Leninist ideology was indeed new, but autocratic rule from the centre was something to which the Russian masses had become accustomed over the centuries. So, too, were the tradition of secrecy, the xenophobia, the suppression of individual opinion, the whole secret police system, the subordination of the individual to the collective. It is easy, too, to list the customary generalisations about the Russian character – an ability to endure extreme hardship, a strange combination of a wild and sometimes violent irrationality and a search for security within a stable community, a tendency to take emotions to excess, to love more deeply, hate more bitterly, mourn more tragically, drink more deeply, to toil harder and idle longer than other nations. Clichés they may be, but they are none the less valid. Oblomov, Lopakhin, Raskolnikov, Bezukhov all survived into and beyond the Soviet era. If there is, however, one feature which we can see as a Russian characteristic, enduring from the Tsarist to the Soviet era and perhaps recognisable in post-Soviet Russia, it is the way in which a continuing readiness to subordinate the individual to the community, whether in theological *sobornost*, the village *mir* or the Party structure, has been broken by the occasional violent eruption. In seeking to encourage individualism without destroying that sense of community, Herzen took nineteenth-century England and Tsarist Russia as opposite poles:

> Two extreme one sided developments have led to two absurdities: to the Englishman, proud of his rights and independent, whose independence is founded on a form of polite cannibalism, and to the poor Russian peasant, impersonally swallowed up in the village commune, given over into serfdom without rights and in virtue of this, become the 'victuals' of the landowner. How are these two developments to be reconciled, how is the contradiction between them to be resolved? How is the independence of the Englishman to be kept without the cannibalism, how is the individuality of the [Russian] peasant to be developed without the loss of the principle of the commune? Precisely in this lies the whole agonizing problem of our century, precisely in this consists the whole problem of socialism.[8]

Having now lurched from the peasant commune to the Soviet state and then to a free market oligarchy, it is arguable that Russia now faces the obverse of the Herzen dilemma, the task of creating a new sense of community. A characteristic, arguably the primary characteristic, of the Soviet state was the way in which the interwoven machinery of party and government created a tight structure regulating every aspect of the life of the citizen and every external relationship of the state. A primary characteristic of the new Russia at the end of the twentieth century was that its governmental and party structures were largely superficial and irrelevant to the life of the citizen. The Russian people, their individual rights restored, are no longer 'swallowed up' in the state, no longer its serfs, but the economic cannibals abound and the masses have yet to find in society a new community in which they can feel at ease. Seeking it, they may find themselves drawn into the classic conflict between the Europhiles and the Russian nationalists, a clash which is in essence a clash between two concepts of Russia's destiny, and which finds its expression in both domestic and foreign policy.

It is one of the clichés of history to see Russia, straddling Europe and Asia, as uncertain whether its primary orientation is to the East or to the West, whether it is the most Eastern of European powers or the most Western of Asiatic powers. For all that the Russians themselves have seen this dichotomy, it has been a false choice. With most of its land mass in Asia and most of its population in Europe, with Europe and Asia mingled in its genes, threatened over the centuries from both directions, Russia has had to look both ways. The effective policy debate has been not between an Asian and a European destiny, but between those who saw Russia within a European context and those who saw her shaping a very distinct, essentially Russian destiny. Was she to shape herself in a Western European image or was she to remain true to a romantic notion of Russia's own distinctive character? This was the essence of the nineteenth-century debate and it is still the essence of the debate. Is she to return to her own faith – ill-defined though that may be – or, having tasted the burger bun, the holy communion wafer of the West, is she to pursue the search for a Western type of society? Is she now to persevere, albeit hesitantly and erratically, with the democratic experiment or, in frustration, to go back to Solzhenitsyn's advice 'that the evolution of our country from one form of authoritarianism to another would be the most natural, the smoothest, the least painful path of development for it to follow'.[9]

It might be said that first Gorbachev, by starting on the road towards a free society based on the rule of law, and then Yeltsin, by defeating the first counter-revolution, made Russia's choice for it. The doctrine which had dictated the development of the Soviet state, shaped the pattern of international relations into a contest of ideology and power and poisoned the British–Russian relationship throughout seven decades has been abandoned. Yeltsin's Constitution gave him over-riding Presidential power. He used that power to create a well-intentioned, but inefficient apparatus of government and a grossly corrupt plutocracy. The Duma has not yet bred democratic leaders of obvious stature.

In domestic terms the reform process may well be largely irreversible, but power and wealth have not been diffused widely outside the major cities and the financial and industrial boyars of the new Russia have not yet had their beards shorn. With the old Russia swept away in 1917, seven decades of Communism ended in the dissolution of Soviet Russia. A first decade of democracy finds the social structure of the new

Russia fragile and unstable. With the dissolution of the Soviet state, Russia was the political equivalent of that primeval soup which contained all the elements necessary for life on earth, the raw material from which men or monsters might come. The shape of new life forms is discernible but their future development is still uncertain. In the first edition of this book, written as the Soviet empire was close to collapse, it was assumed wrongly that, although old-style Soviet socialism would wither and its empire collapse, the Communist Party would probably retain its grip on the Soviet Union itself. It is not unreasonable today to hope that the post-Soviet reform process will be continued and democratic institutions consolidated in the new century. But Russia has a remarkable capacity for proving the reasonable assumption false.

With the resignation of Boris Yeltsin on 31 December 1999, the shaping of a post-Soviet society will be the primary task of the new Russian Duma and the new President. It is early yet to foresee the outcome. The basic issues are, however, reasonably clear. Any policy based on imitation of Western systems, unless demonstrably successful, is inherently vulnerable. The weakness of the reformers was that the great achievements of the ending of Communism, the increase in individual liberty, freedom of expression and freedom of economic activity had, in political terms, been cashed in, while the benefits of a market economy had yet to be conclusively demonstrated. Faced with the old cry, 'We asked for bread and you gave us chatter', the reformers had to rely on swift fulfilment of the promise that their policies would gradually increase the prosperity of the masses, curb the extremes of corruption and bring the long-deferred, but slowly emerging, improvement in living standards. In Moscow and St Petersburg some successes could be claimed, but throughout much of the country economic reform had brought personal deprivation and a reversion to a primitive subsistence economy as the only means of avoiding starvation.

Russia and the West may now reasonably hope that the initial response to Vladimir Putin and his Unity grouping represents solid support for the growing body of pragmatists whose aim is a stable and effective government, asserting Russian interests, while maintaining the essentials of a free society and a good relationship with the West. In the Duma the nostalgic Communists, still the largest single party, hanker after the grey cocoon of the Soviet state, while others pursue special interests and a dwindling band of nationalists and demagogues seek, as every agitator in a broken state has always done, to exploit humiliation with dreams of new glory. Soviet Communism inherited something from Great Russian messianism and did its best to implant

Russian patriotism into Soviet man. Those who cherish similar ambitions today have one failed counter-revolution behind them. Their irrelevance to the living conditions of the ordinary Russian must surely limit their appeal. Yet there has long been a yearning for a strong leader – even a new Stalin. The hope must be that in responding to the patriotic impulse Putin will not take it to excess. It will not be an easy path for him to tread or for the West to accommodate.

Ideology or interest in foreign policy?

For many years analysts debated the respective roles of ideology and national interest in Soviet foreign policy and, as Ambassador in Moscow, Sir Duncan Wilson was not alone in arguing that the West should not under-estimate the extent to which, even during the Soviet years, national interest was, in practice, the primary consideration. Be that as it may, it was Marxist–Leninist dogma which dictated the terms of the underlying confrontation. Now, with a non-Communist government, the absence of a formal dogma should make for a more complex, multi-faceted relationship. To the extent that interests do not conflict and frustrated national pride does not obscure them, there is the potential for a substantial and productive relationship with the West.

The points where British and Russian interests coincide and those where they conflict should, in theory, be easy to perceive. The resultant policies should be easy to determine, if not to execute. National interests have, however, something in common with subatomic physical phenomena, in terms of the interaction between the subject and the observer. To state it in terms of the obvious, the nature of the Soviet system was such that the perception of national interest by the Government of the Soviet Union led it for many years to pursue policies which in many respects were different from and contrary to its own national interest as perceived by a British observer. As Brimelow put it in 1964, the ideological horse was pulling the cartload of Russian interests in the wrong direction. Many factors, chance among them, led to the downfall of the Soviet Union, but among them was the false perception of national interest which led the Soviet Government to give excessive priority to its strategic nuclear force and, in doing so, to create a gross and unsustainable distortion of its economy. The national interests perceived by Britain and Russia in the twenty-first century may to a certain extent be a matter of objective determination, but they will again depend upon the nature of the parties and the environment in which they operate. The relationship which flows from those perceived interests will in turn be varied by the parties' perceptions. Thus, even without the constraint of a governing Marxist–Leninist ideology, Russia's policies will depend upon the way in which, more loosely defined, her people and her rulers see themselves and see us.

For the greater part of 70 years – and for much of a century before that – Britain and Russia saw one another as opponents and defined their interests accordingly. In some – but only some – respects they now see themselves as partners in a wider international community and to the extent that they do so their common interest in European security and economic development will come to the fore, over-riding differing special interests. If, however, policies formed on this basis fail to bear fruit – as Gorbachev discovered – Russia may redefine her national interest and on this occasion may do so in terms of some kind of Slavophile fundamentalism.

Gorbachev was clear in his desire for the Soviet Union to find its place within a 'common European home'. With his downfall and with the dissolution of the Soviet Union, there was an understandable feeling that the balance of advantage had been tilted too far towards the West. The pressure of nationalist opinion and Yeltsin's own temperament then, as has been indicated above, brought a greater emphasis on the assertion of Russia's distinctive national interests. There has been no turning away from Europe, but rather a 'new Realism', an assertion of Russia's distinctive role, as a power with her own interests in Europe and beyond it. At a conference of Intelligence Service staffs in 1994 Yeltsin put that assertion in clear terms: 'Ideological confrontation has been replaced by a struggle for spheres of influence in geopolitics.' In 1997, when Russia was accepted as a member of the Council of Europe, he claimed that 'Europe without Russia is not Europe' and called on other European leaders to establish 'a greater Europe without dividing lines'.[10] He organised tripartite Franco–German–Russian summits. In his annual message to the Federal Assembly in February 1998, however, the message was blunt. On the one hand, the emphasis was on the 'near abroad', the former Republics of the Soviet Union, and on the other it was on Russia's world-wide role: 'Russia's foreign policy initiatives and steps, as befits a great power, encompass all important international problems and virtually the entire world in terms of geography … without Russia it is impossible to resolve acute international issues productively – be it the Bosnian problem, an Arab–Israeli settlement or the situation in the Middle East'.

The formulation was one not of confrontation, but of the exercise of influence in a multi-polar world. In relation to Europe the role of the OSCE was stressed. On one issue Russia remained firm: 'The concept of NATO-centrism and its manifestation in the shape of the expansion of the North Atlantic alliance' was rejected as 'unacceptable to Russia. We shall oppose these plans firmly but without sliding towards confrontation'. NATO membership for the Baltic Republics would be 'interpreted in Russia as a threat to national security' and would 'entail a review of the entire set of relations with NATO'. But, significantly, the primary task in foreign policy was that of 'ensuring favourable external conditions for economic growth and the transition to the country's revival'. In this last respect there could be little doubt that foreign policy correctly reflected Russia's over-riding national interest.[11]

A speech by former Prime Minister Primakov to the regional leaders gathered in the Fatherland/All Russia bloc had much the same flavour. 'Our bloc ... is a union of supporters of a strong state ... every one a professional ... common aim of doing as much as possible for our Russia, our fatherland ... preserve Russia within its current borders ... use the influence of the state to control economic processes in the country in the interests of taxpayers, not for the enrichment of a small group of rascals ... preservation of the traditions of the unique Russian civilisation ... rigorous control over law enforcement ... not allow our country be ignored ... Russia has been and still is a superpower because of its might, its potential and its history ... an equal partner to other states'.

At the time of taking office as Acting President Vladimir Putin left his policy options open, but bis first remarks suggest that a similar line may emerge. It will be that of a Russia which will be determined to make its voice heard in Europe, using both bilateral and multilateral relations to that end and pursuing both economic and defence considerations. On the wider front it will seek to demonstrate that it has inherited the superpower status of the Soviet Union. It will develop its relationship with the IMF, the IBRD and the WTO, make what it can of the Joint Council with NATO and extract maximum value from its agreement with the EU. But there is no question of it submerging its Russian identity in a European identity. As a world power it will do its best to re-establish a bilateral strategic relationship with the United States. Yeltsin had already declared his intention of working for a START 3 Treaty which would establish complete parity in strategic arms between Russia and the United States.[12] As it gains strength Russia will increasingly be prepared to act independently, seeking, as it is already doing in relation to Iraq and Yugoslavia, to establish itself as the dominant power in the arc of actual or potential trouble ranging from Bosnia through to Afghanistan. More narrowly, it will pursue its special interest in relations with the other Republics of the former Soviet Union, rebuilding as far as possible the economic links which were broken by the dissolution of the Union, protecting the interests of the 25 million Russian nationals living in those Republics and asserting a primary role in the resolution of inter-Republican disputes, several of which have already demonstrated an ability to escalate into violence. It will not wish to be drawn into violence elsewhere, but it may well calculate that if, in the last resort, it has again to have recourse to armed force in the 'near abroad' it will be able to do so with impunity, judging, probably correctly, that NATO will shrink from a direct armed response. It must be in the Russian national interest to seek advantage from stability in its relationship with both China and Japan. Some success has been achieved in removing long-standing sources of border friction with China. In relation to Japan Yeltsin has shown no greater readiness than his predecessors to sacrifice territory for the sake of good relations. But already, under the pressure of economic deprivation in the disputed islands, there are the first signs of a search for compromise. With the ending of the dream of leadership of a world-wide Communist movement, Russia will have little incentive to meddle in Third World disputes and few direct interests to safeguard. But old instincts die hard. The great power syndrome will still be potent. Active hostility towards the West may be constrained by the need for economic assistance, but gratitude may give way to resentment and cooperation will not come easily.

A policy on these lines, representing a hardening of the Yeltsin policy rather than a radical departure from it, would seem to be the most likely choice of the new Russian Government. It would have the triple aim of holding together the Federation, enhancing its internal standing and providing a solid base for economic recovery. Independent in character, it would have within it the potential for mutually useful cooperation. It could well on occasion conflict with the interests of Britain and her Western partners, but need not carry an inherent risk of major confrontation. Nevertheless, the range of options is wide and so are their implications for relations with the West. The Chechnyan war, with its demonstration of indifference to Western humanitarian protests, has given a bad start. Russia could at the one extreme drift back to external confrontation and internal intolerence or, if new failures were to follow those of the Yeltsin years, to disillusion, a restless search for alternatives and a risk of the poverty, disorder and disintegration which would flow from a failure of central policy. A calculation of national interest may indicate the unprofitability of the former and the maturing of civil society make the latter less probable, but the tussle for Russia's soul may not yet be over and Western policy may yet exercise a significant influence on it.

British–Russian relations

The original theme of this book was the oscillating British–Soviet relationship, each swing reflecting a change in the balance between the search for a basis of mutual interest, be it only the basic interest of self-preservation, and the profound conflict of ideology and power. Geography and history combined to ensure that some of the focal points of conflict between Britain and Tsarist Russia were carried over into the Soviet period. But in that period the relationship was conditioned primarily by the ideology adopted by Russia after the 1917 Revolution, an ideology claiming world-wide validity and having at its core a continuing confrontation with the Western democracies. Not only did Marxist–Leninist ideology postulate confrontation, it also had the effect of ensuring that at times when the element of confrontation in the relationship might be reduced, the conduct of that relationship became a matter of political controversy in Britain. It constituted a unique problem in the conduct of British foreign policy. The dissolution of the Soviet Union at the end of 1991 and the rejection of Marxist–Leninist doctrine brought that theme to an end. The Soviet Union is gone. So, too, is the Imperial Britain of 1917. In place of the Soviet Union is the new Russian Federation, a state no longer defined by ideology, but by geo–political realities, a state with a resource base matching that of the United States, a state with the potential to be one of the world's major powers, wishing to realise that potential but, as yet, impotent and uncertain both as to the means of doing so and the ends to be attained. In place of the Britain of 1917 is a leading medium-sized power, still playing a world-wide role, but rarely in a position to do so independently. Looking back, how should we evaluate British policy over the years in its response first to the overthrow of Imperial Russia in 1917; then in its conduct of relations with the Soviet Union prior to 1939, during the 1939–45 war and between 1945 and 1985; in its response to the Gorbachev reforms; and in its conduct of relations with the Russian Federation after 1991? How should we assess the prospect for the twenty-first century?

In Chapter 11 we briefly examined the course of British relations with the former Soviet Union in terms of the Soviet assessment of the 'correlation of forces'. But this can provide only a partial basis for a judgement of the effectiveness of British policy since, if there is one more or less constant feature, it is that British governments have rarely considered the relationship with Russia in its own right. They have rarely needed to do so. In so far as Russia has mattered to Britain, it has largely been as a factor in some wider calculation. Prior to 1917 Imperial Russia had been a potentially dangerous element in British imperial policy, threatening to straddle the line of communications to India and, even perhaps, India itself. From this had stemmed an underlying hostility, suppressed only by Russia's potential as a counter to the domination of the Continent by France or Germany. When the October Revolution came, Russia mattered as a critical factor in the war with Germany and the British Government was ready to support any regime which would keep Russia in the war. With the war over, the continued intervention was motivated not so much by any desire to see a restoration of the Tsarist regime, but rather by fear of the disruptive effect of international Bolshevism. Ill-conceived, ill-planned and muddled in its execution, it did little more than to establish mutual hostility as the basis for the initial relationship with the new regime. Yet such was the nature of that regime that it is hard to believe that a warmer welcome from Britain – even if that had been politically conceivable – would, in the long run, have proved fruitful. Certainly Lloyd George's efforts bore little fruit.

A mixture of contempt and suspicion motivated much of British policy in the inter-war years, mixed with bursts of rather uncritical left-wing admiration which grew in proportion as Russia seemed to grow in significance as a counter to the growing threat of Nazi Germany. The net effect of a mixture of half-thought-out and conflicting policies by Conservative and Labour Governments in the 1920s and 1930s must have been to convince Stalin of the underlying antipathy and feebleness of will of the British establishment. It was scarcely surprising that, on a harsh judgement of power, he decided to reject the belated and half-hearted offer of an alliance with Britain and France and throw in his lot with Hitler, a leader who shared only too many of his own instincts. Criticism of British policy in those years is easy enough. To judge whether other policies would have been feasible and, if pursued with vigour, successful is more difficult. Given that Britain and the Soviet Union were to be driven into alliance in 1941, it must at least be the case that, awful though Stalin was as a potential ally, British interests might have been better served had the attempt to forge that alliance been made earlier and pursued with more determination. But it cannot be more than 'might have been'. The political price exacted by Stalin in respect of the states on his Western borders, a price which Hitler was prepared to pay and then repudiate, could not have been honourably accepted by a British Government.

During the war, when Britain and the Soviet Union were allies, it is hard to fault the broad conduct of British policy. Given Britain's own desperate position, the provision of supplies and the sacrifice made to carry them to Russia were generous. The response, even taking account of the extent of Soviet losses, was grudging to the point of being hostile. In the controversy over the opening of a Second Front the mistake made by Britain was not in the substance of policy, but in the failure to understand the danger of raising false expectations, a basic error of diplomacy, but not of policy. It was through no fault of British policy that the alliance did not survive into the post-war years. The Soviet Union effectively killed it.

In those post-war years British policy, despite changes of government, remained remarkably consistent. The Soviet grip on Eastern and much of Central Europe had been won by force of arms and was maintained by a combination of military and political power, deployed in ways which any earlier imperial power would have well understood. Behind it lay an expansionist and confrontational ideology with world-wide objectives. There could be no serious question but that the right response was to build up the military capability and political will of Western Europe and the United States, while avoiding the risk of direct hostilities and taking such opportunities as were open to promote the maturing of Soviet society. The principal question which arises in relation to those years is whether, in this last respect, a more open policy could have brought faster results. There were indeed times when both France and Germany were more forthcoming, the former in tone and the latter, eventually, in substance. It was argued, not least by Churchill and Macmillan, that Britain should do likewise, but French policy cannot be said to have had any positive effect and may on occasion have played into Soviet hands. The German case was very different. Germany opened the door to the collapse of the Soviet empire and the reconstruction of Central and Eastern Europe. But although Britain shared the quadripartite responsibility for a German settlement, the key to that door was in German, not British hands. It is to the credit of Brandt and his successors that it was turned. As Germany took the lead in European–Soviet relations so, on the global scale, the United States was already doing, first in the contest for nuclear supremacy and then with the initiation of direct bilateral bargaining from the time of the Cuban missile crisis. This did not mean that there was no room for British influence. Where it was exercised it was usually well judged, for example when Macmillan took the lead in defusing the Berlin crisis with his visit to Khrushchev and worked for the Test Ban Treaty; when British delegates fought stubbornly against Soviet blandishments to ensure that the CSCE Final Act contained solid, bankable commitments; when Thatcher joined Reagan in a hawkish response to the invasion of Afghanistan; when successive British governments got the arms control balance broadly right; and when Thatcher finally took the lead in welcoming Gorbachev. Year by year the honest reporting of the BBC World Service was heard with respect throughout the Soviet Union and achieved as much or more than all the conventional diplomacy.

In relation to later periods, judgement must be suspended. As first the Soviet empire and then the Soviet Union disintegrated, the British desire was that this process should be carried through peaceably; that the separate republics should be helped to begin the long task of achieving peace and prosperity under stable democratic institutions; and, externally, that they should take their rightful place in the international community. In all this Britain's role was, at best, limited. In retrospect it may be seen that there was a failure to understand the depth of the problem of creating a wholly new political, economic and social structure in Russia; that the criticism of Gorbachev was too severe and the support for Yeltsin too uncritical; and that the headlong economic reform, urged on by the IMF, precipitated the collapse of the economy. Yet Britain supported Gorbachev long after he had lost the support of his own people and without Yeltsin the new Russia would have reverted to the political repression and economic stagnation of the Brezhnev years. It is as hard today to judge the long-term effect of the Gorbachev–Yeltsin Revolution as it was 80 years ago to judge the effect of the October Revolution. It is, as it was, for the Russians to make their own future. British governments can be content that they have tried where they could to lend a helping hand. The British people have intermittently over the centuries been fascinated by Russia. There has been much to fascinate them in the decade and a half since Gorbachev first began the dismantlement of the Soviet system. But in the past that fascination has never led to a deep and lasting engagement with Russia. As disillusion grows in Russia, so the West grows weary of the sheer intractability of Russia's problems. The danger now is that Russian disillusion will meet a Western lack of interest.

The prospect

Even during the Soviet period there were, as we have noted, relatively few occasions when it made sense to consider the British–Soviet relationship other than in the wider context of relations between the Soviet Union and the Western democracies. This was not simply a reflection of the imbalance in military power which made it necessary for Britain to formulate its policy in conjunction with allies. Much less powerful countries, especially those such as Finland which were situated close to the border of the Soviet Union, had necessarily to develop a bilateral relationship with their dominant neighbour. In Britain's case, however, the tone of the relationship was set not by issues peculiar to Britain, of which there were very few, but by the nature of the wider challenge of Soviet policy, a challenge which could only be effectively met by a collective response.

In the formulation and execution of that response Britain could, on occasion, play a leading part, but it did so normally in the pursuit of a broad Western interest and only to a lesser extent in furthering a uniquely British interest. If, as we expect, the new Russia pursues a foreign policy based on national interest and lacking the base of a confrontational ideology, the whole character of relations will change.

Individual issues can be considered on their merits rather than as mere facets of a global struggle. To a certain extent this is already happening. If it continues – and it must be an objective of British policy to ensure that there is no reversion to the policies of confrontation – there will be a greater scope for the development of bilateral policies reflecting both the convergence and divergence of the respective interests of Russia and her partners. The British Government will, however, still find it necessary in many cases to negotiate and implement those policies within wider structures. British membership of the EU largely excludes the bilateral negotiation of inter-governmental trade policy and provides a mechanism for the coordination of foreign policy. British defence and security policy in relation to Russia fall effectively into a NATO context. Other issues of international peace and security require UN consideration. In a whole range of technical issues the bilateral relationship falls within the ambit of specialised international bodies. If the conduct of an independent British policy towards Russia in the twenty-first century is unrealistic, the active participation by Britain in the formulation of a wider policy is correspondingly enhanced. Fortunately there is at present between Britain, her European partners and the United States, no serious difference of view as to the elements of that policy. There is, however, the potential for future divergence.

A feature of British–Russian relations during the pre-Soviet and early Soviet eras was the primary interest of both governments in preventing the domination of continental Europe by a hostile power. It was not until the post-1945 years that, with Soviet power projected into Central Europe, the Soviet Union was itself perceived in specifically military terms as a direct threat to the security of the United Kingdom. Now, with that power withdrawn, Russia does not constitute such a threat and is unlikely to do so in the immediate future. The European dimension of British security rests firmly upon the political and military basis of the EU and NATO, plus the OSCE. From a British perspective these constitute no threat to Russia's national interest, but the Russian perspective is different and there is an inherent tension in a situation where the eastern boundary of NATO has been brought into an area of political instability close to the Western frontier of Russia. So long as Russia has no more than a fringe relationship with both EU and NATO there may well be conflicts of interest, especially if there is any question of further NATO enlargement. The conflict of interest may be more apparent than real but, as has been argued above, perceptions matter. Russia, like Germany in the 1920s, may now be at the nadir of her power. It must be assumed that in the coming century she will continue to be a substantial military power with conventional and nuclear forces probably in excess of those held by the European members of NATO. It will be important for Britain, within NATO, to pursue the objective of a genuine peace rather than an armed stalemate and to do so while Russia remains ready to share this objective.

Outside Europe, the classic area of British–Russian conflict has been the arc of instability on Russia's southern and south western borders. Within that arc Britain shares the broad interest of the Western powers in maintaining stability, an interest which need not conflict with Russia's interest, although a resurgent Russia will expect to exercise a degree of influence which the West may resent. The potential for a conflict of interest in relation to this area was demonstrated shortly before this book was going to press by the action of the Russian Government in withdrawing its Ambassador from London 'for consultations' as a strong gesture of disapproval of the British and American military action against Iraq. The last time on which such action was taken was in 1971, in response to the British expulsion of Soviet agents and it had then been followed by a virtual freezing of bilateral relations for the next two years. In 1998, there was a chill rather than a freeze and it lasted for a matter of months.

The Russian action was motivated primarily by resentment that the British and American Governments had intervened in an area which Russia regarded in rather the same light as the United States regarded the Caribbean. The British–Russian 'partnership' of 1992 already seemed, at best, rather thin and the tensions which developed over the NATO action in Kosovo showed how, in that area, there might be no real conflict of national interest, but there was a potentially serious clash of influence and power.

The contraction from the Soviet Union to Russia has meant that for the Russian Government there is now, as we have noted, an inner ring of primary concern, namely the relationship with the independent Republics, each raising different concerns, whether Ukraine, Belarus, the arc from Kazakhstan to Moldova or, again different in character, the Baltic States of Latvia, Lithuania and Estonia. Within that inner ring Russia's direct interests are strong and Russia will expect to exercise primacy. There need be no challenge to any direct British interest, but Russian involvement in the conflicts in Abkhazia, in Nagorny-Karabakh, in Georgia, in Tadjikistan and in Moldova showed the potential for future trouble. The ferocious operation against Chechnya, carried out with warm popular support and continued in the face of widespread external condemnation, showed the temper of the Russian people and the paucity of Western constraints. These factors will not quickly change. Within the outer ring of former Soviet Republics the implications of Russian military action would be graver and the irrelevance of external military constraint no less. The avoidance, the containment and the peaceful resolution of future conflicts can best be facilitated and the constraints enhanced if by various means, including the use of NATO and the EU, Russia can work out a cooperative relationship with the Western community. This should be an objective of British policy.

So far as the economy is concerned, for the first time since the brief dawn a century ago, there is, even in the present chaos, the prospect of Russia's economic potential being developed within a free market system. If that prospect can be realised, Russia, for so long no more than on the periphery, could within the next twenty or thirty years move into the first rank of the world's trading nations and, as she does, bilateral relationships may well develop significantly. For Russia, Britain may remain no more than a useful, by no means essential, trading partner but, from the British perspective Russia may be relatively more important and the mirage of a major increase in the level of British exports of goods and services could at last become a reality.

This study began with the question: what is meant by a 'normal' relationship with Russia? The normality we have sought is a relationship which combines three main factors: the removal of doctrinal confrontation at the governmental level; cooperative participation in international bodies; and such a thickening of personal and professional contacts as will create throughout Russia a genuine sense of integration into the international community. A characteristic feature of the Soviet years was the extent to which the whole area of bilateral relations was dominated to a quite abnormal extent by the inter-governmental relationship. On the Soviet side virtually all international transactions were conducted by governmental or quasi-governmental bodies. Commercial, financial, technical and cultural relationships with private British organisations and individuals were minimal in scope, controlled through a structure of inter-governmental agreements and fully exploited by the KGB. Very few Russians other than official delegations were permitted by the Soviet authorities to visit Britain. An important element in British policy was the encouragement of private contact and the exchange of information through a whole range of Government-sponsored bodies, prominent among them the Great Britain–USSR Association, the British Council and the BBC World Service. All this activity was much facilitated by the conclusion of the CSCE Final Act and in turn helped to create the conditions in which the new Russia was born. But it was an uphill task. Potentially the most important feature of the international orientation of the new Russia is the extent to which private contacts are now able to proceed independently of government. The governmental role should be confined to those areas which, in a free society, fall necessarily to governmental bodies and, beyond this area, to the establishment of a framework within which the level and content of relations will be determined by individual rather than governmental interests. All this is much easier now that, for a time at least, the relationship with Russia is no longer a matter of political controversy in Britain. The nineteenth century had its Russophobes and Russophiles, the 1920s had the Diehards. The nomenclature of the Cold War years was different. The policy clash was more sophisticated and there was a far greater range of views between the two extremes of the out-and-out cold warriors and the fellow travellers, but a degree of political polarisation remained. Now, with thinking about the future of Russia polarised not between love and hate but between pessimism and optimism it is at least possible to make a dispassionate judgement, even if an accurate one is more difficult than ever. The best evidence of the development of private contacts is the fact that in 1997 alone there were about 100 000 private visits to Britain by individual Russians. It is reasonable to ask whether the flow might not become even greater. Would British or Russian security be gravely threatened if the visa regime were abolished?

The enhancement of private contacts should help to broaden the base of internationally aware Russians in all areas of public life from whom the new leadership is emerging. Yeltsin and many of the leading figures of his era were drawn from the old Soviet nomenklatura and potential new leaders were slow to emerge from the inchoate mass of the old Duma. Now Vladimir Putin, born in 1952, schooled in the KGB, Prime Minister in September 1999 and Acting President on 31 December represents a new generation. Virtually unknown to the West, he has been quick to exploit Russia's yearning for firm leadership and national greatness. If he secures a mandate as President, he, his appointees and his party will shape the new Russia and determine her course in world affairs. Much will turn on the choices they make. It is customary to argue – and with some truth – that the better the British and the Russians know one another and develop common interests the easier it will be to reduce, if not to eliminate, national confrontation. With Russia in flux and a new generation in power, the argument has special force.

Throughout the Soviet era, British Prime Ministers made intermittent efforts to establish a direct relationship with the Soviet leaders. Churchill believed he had some success with Stalin, Macmillan with Khrushchev and Wilson with Kosygin, but the evidence is scanty. Not until the Thatcher–Gorbachev relationship did top-level contact begin to acquire solid content. In the final years of Yeltsin, the obstacle was not so much the Russian system, as the incapacity of its leader. Ambassadors and their staffs, except for a brief period under Khrushchev, had no more than formal contact with the Soviet Foreign Minister and virtually none with other Politburo members. The day-to-day working relationship was conducted, as indeed it would be in most countries, with middle-ranking and senior officials, but at this level, despite constant effort, the opportunities to move from formal contact to a relationship of mutual confidence were rare. The beginning of a qualitative change can be dated from 1985 and now, after fourteen years, the working relationship can be regarded as approaching normality as between two substantial powers. The temporary withdrawal of the Soviet Ambassador at the end of 1998 in response to the British and American action against Iraq was symptomatic of the difficulty which Russia will experience in keeping a balance between the assertion of a role as heir to a hostile superpower and the construction of a stable relationship with the Western powers. It represented a residue of mutual irritability which only the most optimistic could expect to disappear from the 'normality' of future British–Russian relations. The task of diplomacy is to contain it within sensible limits.

The conduct of relations with the Soviet Union merited treatment as a unique exercise in diplomacy. For many years it consisted, in Kennan's words, of policies which would 'give the hand of time a chance to work' – occasionally giving a nudge, but basically holding firm while Russia sought her own salvation. Now, however much it is in the interests of Russia herself, of Britain and of the whole international community, that she should pursue the search for salvation in the construction of a durable, free, democratic society, it is the Russian people who must make their choice. Just as, in the decades of confrontation, British policy helped to give them the opportunity to make a free choice, so in the decades to come, there will be opportunities to influence the outcome. The conduct of relations will provide problems enough of delicate diplomatic adjustment if points of friction are to be reduced and mutual advantage maximised. The relationship will be complex. It may on occasion be stormy. It will have considerable potential to shape the world for better or for worse. But it will no longer have that unique character which was given by the subordination of Russia to Marxist–Leninist dogma. The world may be content that in the end, for all the contradictions and inconsistencies of public opinion and government policy, Britain played a worthy part in the conduct of relations with the Soviet Union. The job is still only half done. In the conduct of relations with the new Russia all is still open.

Appendix 1 Chronology of Relations

This chronology contains the dates of the principal events in the relationship between Britain and the Soviet Union during the period 1917–91, and between Britain and the Russian Federation in the period 1991–9 together with a somewhat arbitrary selection of lesser events and the dates of a very few key international events establishing the wider framework within which the bilateral relationship was set. Visits by British, Soviet and Russian Heads of Government and Foreign Ministers have been included, but most other ministerial and parliamentary visits have not. Dates of agreements are those of signature and dates of meetings are opening dates unless otherwise specified. For dates of changes of Government, see Appendix 2.

1917
15 Mar	Abdication of Tsar Nicholas II
7 Nov	Bolshevik seizure of power (October Revolution; the date according to the calender at that time in use in Russia was 25 October)
15 Dec	Armistice between Russia and Germany
23 Dec	Anglo–French Convention on 'activity in Southern Russia'

1918
Jan	M. M. Litvinov appointed Soviet representative in London and R. B. Lockhart British representative in Petrograd
7 Jan	HM Ambassador leaves Petrograd
Feb	Petrograd Embassy closed
3 Mar	Treaty of Brest-Litovsk signed
Mar	Final German offensive on Western front
6 Mar	First British landing at Murmansk
5 Apr	British–Japanese landing at Vladivostok
24 May	General Poole 'British Military Representative in Russia' at Murmansk
22 Jul	British economic mission in Moscow
2–4 Aug	Major Allied operations begun in Russia
9 Aug	British Consulate-General, Moscow, closed
30 Aug	Assassination attempt on Lenin
31 Aug	Murder of British Naval Attaché, Petrograd
Sep	Litvinov expelled
19 Oct	Lockhart returns to Britain
11 Nov	End of hostilities Britain and Germany
13 Nov	Brest-Litovsk Treaty denounced
23–7 Nov	British forces at Novorossisk, Sebastopol and Odessa

1919

4–6 Mar	British Government decides to withdraw from Russia
15 Mar	Comintern founded
12 Jun	Declaration of Allied support for Kolchak
4 Jul	State of war with Bolsheviks
8 Nov	Lloyd George Speech on peace in Russia
8 Dec	'Curzon Line' proposed for Soviet–Polish frontier

1920

10 Jan	*De facto* recognition of Georgia and Azerbaidjan
6 Feb	Kolchak executed
11 Feb	Anglo–Soviet agreement on exchange of prisoners of war
7 May	Poles capture Kiev
31 May	Soviet negotiators arrive in London
9 Jun	Soviet company Arcos established in London
1 Aug	Formation of National Communist Party in Britain
Aug	Soviet forces outside Warsaw
10 Sep	Soviet negotiator Kamenev expelled

1921

| 16 Mar | Anglo–Soviet Trade Agreement |

1922

| 10 Apr | Genoa Conference opens |
| 16 Apr | Treaty of Rapallo |

1923

| 8 May | Curzon ultimatum |

1924

21 Jan	Death of Lenin
1 Feb	British *de jure* recognition of Soviet Union. Chargés d'Affaires appointed London and Moscow
14 Apr	Anglo–Soviet Conference London
8 Aug	Anglo–Soviet General and Commercial Treaties signed
25 Oct	Zinoviev Letter published
21 Nov	Anglo–Soviet Treaties repudiated

1925

6 Apr	Anglo–Soviet trade union conference London. Joint Advisory Council established
12 Oct	Leadership of British Communist Party arrested
16 Oct	Treaty of Locarno

1926

| 24 Apr | Soviet–German Treaty of Neutrality and Friendship |
| 1 May | General Strike in Britain |

Chronology of Relations

1927
12 May   Police raid on London office of Arcos
27 May   Diplomatic relations and trade agreement suspended (Note dated 26 May)

1929
3 Oct   Protocol on re-establishment of relations
Dec   Ambassadors appointed London and Moscow

1930
1 Jan   *Daily Worker* founded
16 Apr   Temporary Anglo–Soviet Trade Agreement
2 Oct   Anglo–Soviet Debts and Claims Committee set up

1932
Feb   Debt talks break down
Sep   Macmillan in Soviet Union
17 Oct   Notice of termination of Trade Agreement
29 Nov   Franco–Soviet Treaty

1933
30 Jan   Hitler Chancellor of Germany
12–18 Apr   Trial of British engineers in Moscow
19–20 Apr   British and Soviet trade embargoes
1 Jul   Embargoes removed

1934
16 Feb   Temporary Anglo–Soviet Trade Agreement
Jul   Vansittart–Maisky discussions
18 Sep   Soviet membership of League of Nations

1935
28 Mar   Eden, Lord Privy Seal, in Moscow
2 May   Franco–Soviet Treaty
16 May   Czech–Soviet Treaty

1936
Jan   Litvinov in London
7 Mar   German reoccupation of Rhineland
19 Jul   Spanish Civil War begins
30 Jul   Anglo–Soviet Export Credit Agreement
25 Nov   Anti-Comintern Pact

1937
17 Jul   Anglo–Soviet Naval Agreement

1938
13 Mar	Austrian *Anschluss* with Germany
29 Sep	Munich agreement on Czechoslovakia

1939
12 Mar	German occupation of Czechoslovakia
31 Mar	British guarantee to Poland
13 Apr	British guarantee to Romania and Greece
14 Jun	Strang arrives Moscow for tripartite negotiations
22 Jul	Soviet–German trade talks
13 Aug	British military delegation arrives Moscow
23 Aug	Soviet–German Non-Aggression Treaty and secret Protocol
25 Aug	Tripartite talks broken off
1 Sep	German attack on Poland
3 Sep	British declaration of war on Germany, Anglo–Soviet Naval Agreement suspended
30 Nov	Soviet attack on Finland

1940
12 Mar	Soviet–Finnish peace treaty
1, 5, 8 Aug	Incorporation of Lithuania, Latvia and Estonia into Soviet Union

1941
22 Jun	German attack on Soviet Union
12 Jul	Anglo–Soviet declaration on mutual assistance
4 Oct	Anglo–Soviet agreement on military supplies
7 Dec	Japanese attack on Pearl Harbor
8 Dec	United States and United Kingdom at war with Japan
15–18 Dec	Eden in Moscow

1942
29 Jan	Treaty of Alliance USSR, United Kingdom, Iran
26 May	Anglo–Soviet Treaty of Alliance
27 Jun	Anglo–Soviet agreement on military supplies
12 Aug	Churchill in Moscow

1943
15 May	Dissolution of Comintern
31 Jan	German surrender at Stalingrad
18–30 Oct	Foreign Ministers' Conference, Moscow
19 Oct	Anglo–Soviet agreement on military supplies
28 Nov–1 Dec	Teheran Conference of Heads of Government

1944
1 Jun	Allied landings in northern France
9–18 Oct	Churchill in Moscow

Chronology of Relations 353

1945
4–12 Feb	Yalta Conference of Heads of Government
Feb–Mar	British Parliamentary Delegation to USSR
2 Apr–10 May	Mrs Churchill in USSR
8 May	Surrender of Germany
17 Jul–2 Aug	Potsdam Conference of Heads of Government
6 Aug	Atomic bomb on Hiroshima
15 Aug	Surrender of Japan
11 Sep–2 Oct	Council of Foreign Ministers, London
16–26 Dec	Council of Foreign Ministers, Moscow

1946
5 Mar	Churchill's Fulton speech
25 Apr–16 May	Council of Foreign Ministers, Paris
15 Jun–12 Jul	Council of Foreign Ministers, Paris
4 Nov–12 Dec	Council of Foreign Ministers, New York

1947
5 Oct	Foundation of Cominform
10 Mar–24 Apr	Council of Foreign Ministers, Moscow
12 Mar	Truman Doctrine
2 Jul	Soviet withdrawal from Marshall Aid talks
25 Nov–15 Dec	Council of Foreign Ministers, London
27 Dec	Anglo–Soviet Trade and Payments Agreement

1948
25 Feb	Communist coup in Czechoslovakia
17 Mar	Brussels Treaty
24 Jun	Berlin Blockade
Jul–Dec	Talks on long-term trade agreement

1949
4 Apr	North Atlantic Treaty
23 May	Council of Foreign Ministers, Paris

1950
26 Apr	War in Korea

1951
25 May	Defection of Burgess and Maclean

1953
5 Mar	Death of Stalin
11 May	Churchill calls for summit conference
Jun	Cruiser *Sverdlov* visits for Coronation
17 Jun	Riots in East Germany
27 Jul	Korean Armistice

1954

25 Jan–18 Feb	Foreign Ministers' Conference, Berlin
26 Apr–21 Jul	Foreign Ministers' Conference, Geneva
10 Aug	Attlee and Labour Party delegation to Moscow
23 Oct	Paris agreements. German membership of NATO and Western European Union

1955

7 May	USSR annuls Anglo–Soviet Treaty of Alliance
15 May	Austrian State Treaty
18–23 Jul	Heads of Government Conference, Geneva
27 Oct–16 Nov	Foreign Ministers' Conference, Geneva

1956

Feb	Twentieth CPSU Congress denunciation of Stalin
18 Apr	Dissolution of Cominform
18–27 Apr	Bulganin and Khrushchev visit UK
Oct	Riots in Poland
4 Nov	Soviet forces attack Budapest
5 Nov	Anglo–French attack on Port Said

1957

| 4 Oct | First Soviet earth satellite |

1958

| 31 Oct | UK–US–Soviet talks on Nuclear Test Ban Treaty |
| 10 Nov | Soviet ultimatum on Berlin |

1959

21 Feb–3 Mar	Macmillan in Moscow
11 May–30 Jun	Foreign Ministers' meeting on Germany
24 May	Anglo–Soviet Trade Agreement. Great Britain–USSR Association formed
13 Jul–5 Aug	Foreign Ministers' meeting on Germany
1 Dec	Anglo–Soviet Cultural Agreement

1960

3 Jan	UK–US–USSR talks on Nuclear Test Ban open in Geneva
4 Feb	Anglo–Soviet Parliamentary group formed
15 May	Abortive Paris summit

1961

22 Mar	Sentences in British naval secrets case
17 Apr	Bay of Pigs invasion of Cuba
3 May	George Blake sentenced
May–Jul	British and Soviet Trade Fairs in Moscow and London
2–4 Jun	Kennedy and Khrushchev in Vienna
9 Aug	British application for membership of EEC

Chronology of Relations 355

13 Aug	Berlin Wall
10 Oct	Gromyko in London

1962
15–28 Oct	Cuban missile crisis

1963
23 Jan	Philby defects to USSR from Beirut
7–11 May	Wynne–Penkovsky trial in Moscow
3–8 Aug	Earl of Home in Moscow
5 Aug	Partial Test Ban Treaty

1964
23 Apr	Anglo–Soviet Trade Agreement extended
27 Jul–1 Aug	Butler in Moscow
15 Oct	Chinese nuclear device exploded

1965
16–20 Mar	Gromyko in London
22–3 Jul	Trial of Gerald Brooke in Moscow
29 Nov–4 Dec	Stewart in Moscow
2 Dec	Anglo–Soviet Consular Convention

1966
21–4 Feb	Wilson in Moscow
16–19 Jul	Wilson in Moscow for British industrial fair
22–5 Nov	Brown in Moscow

1967
6–13 Feb	Kosygin in UK
24–6 May	Brown in Moscow
5 Jun	Arab–Israeli War
25 Aug	London–Moscow hot line set up

1968
5 Jan	Anglo–Soviet Agreement on Financial and Property Claims
19 Jan	Anglo–Soviet Agreement on Technological Cooperation
22–4 Jan	Wilson in Moscow
26 Mar	Anglo–Soviet Technology Agreement
3 Apr	Anglo–Soviet Navigation Treaty
22–4 May	Stewart in Moscow
1 Jul	Nuclear Non-Proliferation Treaty
20 Aug	Soviet invasion of Czechoslovakia

1969
3 Jun	Long-term Anglo–Soviet Trade Agreement
22 Jul	Gerald Brooke released in exchange for Krögers

1970
12 Aug   FRG–Soviet Treaty

1971
Jan   Anglo–Soviet Joint Commission set up
3 Sep   Quadripartite Agreement on Berlin
24 Sep   105 Soviet officials expelled from London

1972
22–30 May   Nixon in Moscow. Anti-Ballistic Missile Treaty and SALT I
21 Dec   Basic Treaty between FRG and GDR

1973
1 Jan   British entry into EEC
18–22 May   Brezhnev in Bonn
18–25 Jun   Brezhnev in United States
3–7 Jul   European Security Conference, Helsinki
2–10 Sep   Duke of Edinburgh in Soviet Union
Oct   Negotiations on reduction of forces in Central Europe (MBFR), Vienna
6 Oct   Arab–Israeli War
2–5 Dec   Sir A. Douglas-Home in Moscow

1974
6 May   Anglo–Soviet Agreement on Economic, Scientific and Technological Cooperation
27 Jun–3 Jul   Nixon in Moscow
23–4 Nov   Ford in Vladivostok

1975
13–17 Feb   Wilson and Callaghan in Moscow. UK–Soviet Protocol on Consultations. Economic and Commercial Agreements.
30 Apr   Fall of Saigon
1 Aug   CSCE Final Act
Oct   Cuban troops in Angola
24–5 Oct   First meeting Anglo–Soviet Round Table

1976
22–5 Mar   Gromyko in London
28 Mar–1 Jun   Exchange of naval visits

1977
9–11 Oct   Owen in Moscow
10 Oct   Anglo–Soviet Agreement on Prevention of Accidental Nuclear War

1979
Mar   Duke of Edinburgh in Moscow
16–18 Jun   Carter and Brezhnev in Geneva

18 Jun	SALT II Agreement
26 Jun	Mrs Thatcher meets Kosygin in Moscow
27 Dec	Soviet invasion of Afghanistan

1980
Jul	Olympic Games in Moscow

1981
30 Jul	Carrington in Moscow
23–5 Nov	Brezhnev in Bonn
13 Dec	Martial Law in Poland

1982
5 Feb	UK sanctions against Poland and Soviet Union
10 Nov	Death of Brezhnev

1984
9 Feb	Death of Andropov
15–21 Dec	Gorbachev in United Kingdom

1985
10 Mar	Death of Chernenko. Thatcher in Moscow
18–21 Nov	Reagan–Gorbachev in Geneva

1986
Jan	Yeltsin Moscow Party Secretary
25 Feb–6 Mar	27th Party Congress CPSU
26 Apr	Chernobyl disaster
13–16 Jul	Shevardnadze in London
15 Jul	Anglo–Soviet Agreement on Mutual Waiver of Claims
10–13 Oct	Reagan–Gorbachev in Reykjavik

1987
28 Mar–1 Apr	Thatcher in Soviet Union
7 Dec	Gorbachev stopover in UK
7–10 Dec	Gorbachev in Washington
8 Dec	INF Treaty signed

1988
15 Feb	Howe in Moscow
29 May–2 Jun	Reagan in Moscow
1 Jun	INF Treaty ratified

1989
14–16 Feb	Howe in Moscow
15 Feb	Soviet withdrawal from Afghanistan
6 Mar	CSE talks open
5–7 Apr	Gorbachev in UK

23 Sep	Thatcher–Gorbachev meeting
9 Nov	Berlin Wall opened
20 Dec	Shevardnadze in London

1990
15 Mar	Gorbachev elected President of USSR by Congress of People's Deputies
1–12 Apr	Hurd in Moscow
29 May	Yeltsin elected Chairman RSFSR Supreme Soviet
May–Jun	Gorbachev to US
2–13 Jul	28th CPSU Congress Gorbachev General Secretary, Yeltsin resigns
12 Sep	Treaty on Final Settlement for Germany
3 Oct	Unification of Germany
19 Nov	CFE Treaty signed
17–25 Dec	Fourth Congress of People's Deputies

1991
13 Jan	Russian attack on Vilnius TV
16 Jan–28 Feb	Gulf War
4–6 Mar	Major in Moscow
23 Apr	Novo–Ogarevo agreement on new Union Treaty
12 Jun	Yeltsin elected President of RSFSR
Jul	Warsaw Pact dissolved
31 Jul	START Treaty signed
19–21 Aug	Attempted coup against Gorbachev
24 Aug	Gorbachev resigns as General Secretary CPSU
9–11 Sep	Hurd in Moscow
6 Nov	Yeltsin decrees end of activity of CPSU and RCP on Russian territory
7–8 Dec	Belovezhskaya Pushcha meeting
25 Dec	RSRSR becomes Russian Federation
	Gorbachev resigns as President of USSR
31 Dec	USSR dissolved

1992
20 Jan	Hurd in Moscow
30 Jan	Yeltsin in UK
12 Jun	Kozyrev in London
17 Jun	Yeltsin–Bush meeting
25–28 Aug	Kozyrev in London
12–14 Oct	Kozyrev in London
9–10 Nov	Yeltsin in UK
	Treaty on Principles of Relations between UK and Russian Federation

1993
3 Jan	Yeltsin and Bush sign Start II in Moscow
1 Apr	Hurd in Moscow

Chronology of Relations 359

5 Apr	Yeltsin–Clinton summit in Vancouver
21 Sep	Decree dissolving Russian Parliament
25–28 Oct	Kozyrev in UK
4 Oct	White House stormed
12 Dec	Elections in Russia

1994
22–24 May	Hurd in Moscow
24–25 Sep	Yeltsin in UK
16–19 Oct	British Royal visit to Moscow
11 Dec	Russian forces in Chechnya

1995
9 May	Major in Moscow
6–7 Jun	Kozyrev in London
21 Jul	Kozyrev in London (Bosnia Contact Group)
5 Sep	Rifkind in Moscow
17 Dec	Duma elections

1996
18 Apr	Major in Moscow
24–25 Jun	Primakov in London
3 Jul	Yeltsin re-elected President
3–5 Dec	Primakov in London

1997
27 Feb	Primakov in London
27 May	NATO–Russia Permanent Joint Council established
13–15 Jul	Cook in Moscow
Jul	British hostages taken in Chechnya
5–6 Oct	Blair in Moscow
17 Dec	Protocol extending NATO to Poland Hungary and Czech Republic

1998
15–17 May	Yeltsin in Birmingham (G8)
24–25 Jun	Primakov in London (EU–Troika)
8 Oct	Ivanov in London (Kosovo)
18 Dec	Russian Ambassador withdrawn temporarily from London for consultations

1999
March	Cook in Moscow
21–22 Jul	Ivanov in London
Dec	Russian attack a Chechnya
19 Dec	Duma elections
31 Dec	Yeltsin resigns. Putin Acting President

Appendix 2 The British, Soviet and Russian Leadership, 1917–99

The relationship between Britain and Russia has been so heavily influenced by the personality of the leaders of the two countries that the reader may find it helpful to see them listed. This Appendix therefore contains the names of British Prime Ministers and Foreign Secretaries from 1917 to the present day, with the year of their accession to office given in brackets. In the case of the Soviet Union the names shown are those of the General Secretary of the Communist Party and the Foreign Minister. M. S. Gorbachev was elected President of the Soviet Union by the Congress of People's Deputies on 15 March 1990. On 23 August 1991 he resigned as General Secretary of the CPSU, but remained as President of the Soviet Union until 25 December 1991, immediately before the dissolution of the state on 31 December.

UNITED KINGDOM		SOVIET UNION	
Prime Minister	**Foreign Secretary**	**First Secretary or General Secretary**	**People's Commissar for Foreign Affairs/Foreign Minister**
D. Lloyd George (1916)	A. J. Balfour (1916)	V. I. Lenin (1917)	L. Trotsky (1917)
			G. V. Chicherin (1918)
	Earl Curzon (1919)		
A. Bonar Law (1922)			
S. Baldwin (1923)			
J. R. MacDonald (1924)	J. R. MacDonald (1924)	J. V. Stalin (1924)	
S. Baldwin (1924)	A. Chamberlain (1924)		
J. R. MacDonald (1929)	A. Henderson (1929)		M. M. Litvinov (1930)
	Marquess of Reading (1931)		
	Sir J. Simon (1931)		

360

UNITED KINGDOM		SOVIET UNION	
Prime Minister	Foreign Secretary	First Secretary or General Secretary	People's Commissar for Foreign Affairs/Foreign Minister
S. Baldwin (1935)	Sir S. Hoare (1935) A. Eden (1935)		
N. Chamberlain (1937)	Lord Halifax (1938)		V. M. Molotov (1939)
W. S. Churchill (1940)	A. Eden (1940)		
C. Attlee (1945)	E. Bevin (1945) H. Morrison (1951)		A. Y. Vyshinsky (1949)
W. S. Churchill (1951)	A. Eden (1951)	G. M. Malenkov (1953) N. S. Khrushchev (1953)	
A. Eden (1955)	H. Macmillan (1955) J. Selwyn Lloyd (1955)		V. M. Molotov (1953) D. Shepilov (1956) A. A. Gromyko (1957)
H. Macmillan (1957) Sir A. Douglas-Home (1963)	Earl of Home (1960) R. A. Butler (1963)		
H. Wilson (1964)	P. Gordon-Walker (1964) M. Stewart (1965) G. Brown (1966) M. Stewart (1968)	L. I. Brezhnev (1964)	
E. Heath (1970)	Sir A. Douglas-Home (1970)		
H. Wilson (1974) J. Callaghan (1975)	J. Callaghan (1974) A. Crosland (1976) D. Owen (1977)		

UNITED KINGDOM		SOVIET UNION	
Prime Minister	Foreign Secretary	First Secretary or General Secretary	People's Commissar for Foreign Affairs/Foreign Minister
M. Thatcher (1979)	Lord Carrington (1979)		
	F. Pym (1982)	Y. Andropov (1982)	
	Sir G. Howe (1983)	K. Chernenko (1984)	
		M. S. Gorbachev (1985)	E. Shevardnadze (1985)
	J. Major (1989)		
	D. Hurd (1989)		
J. Major (1990)	M. Rifkind (1995)		A. Bessmertnykh (1990)
A. Blair (1997)	R. Cook (1997)		B. Pankin (1991)

The Soviet Union was dissolved on 31 December 1991. From 1 January 1992 the names shown are those of the President, the Chairman of the Government and the Foreign Minister.

President	Chairman	Foreign Minister
B. Yeltsin		A. Kozyrev (1992)
	Y. Gaidar (Acting) (1992)	
	V. Chernomyrdin (1992)	
		E. Primakov (1996)
	S. Kiriyenko (Apr 1998)	
	E. Primakov (Nov 1998)	I. Ivanov (1998)
	S. Stepashin (Jun 1999)	
	V. Putin (Sep 1999)	
V. Putin (Acting Dec 1999)		

Appendix 3   British, Soviet and Russian Diplomatic Representatives, 1917–99

British diplomatic representatives in Moscow

After the abdication of the Emperor Nicholas in March 1917, Sir George Buchanan remained in Petrograd until 15 January 1918. After his departure Mr. F. Lindley remained as Chargé d'Affaires until 8 March 1918 and Mr R. B. Lockhart conducted informal relations with the Soviet authorities as Consul-General first in Petrograd and then in Moscow between January and October 1918. Mr R. M. (later Sir Robert) Hodgson took up his duties as Official Agent in charge of the British Commercial Mission in Moscow in July 1921 and was appointed Chargé d'Affaires on the establishment of diplomatic relations with the Soviet Union on 1 February 1924. He continued in that appointment until the suspension of relations by the British Government on 27 May 1927.

Relations were resumed in accordance with the Protocol of 3 October 1929 and the United Kingdom was subsequently represented by the following Ambassadors Extraordinary and Plenipotentiary.

HM Representatives are shown with date of appointment, but with subsequent style where appropriate:

7 Dec 1929	Sir Esmond Ovey
24 Oct 1933	Viscount Chilston
19 Jan 1939	Sir William Seeds
12 Jun 1940	Sir Stafford Cripps
4 Feb 1942	Sir Archibald Clark Kerr (later Lord Inverchapel)
14 May 1946	Sir Maurice Peterson
22 Jun 1949	Sir David Kelly
18 Oct 1951	Sir Alvary Gascoigne
1 Oct 1953	Sir William Hayter
19 Feb 1957	Sir Patrick Reilly
13 Oct 1960	Sir Frank Roberts
27 Nov 1962	Sir Humphrey (later Lord) Trevelyan
27 Aug 1965	Sir Geoffrey Harrison
3 Oct 1968	Sir Duncan Wilson
9 Sep 1971	Sir John Killick
12 Nov 1973	Sir Terence Garvey
9 Jan 1976	Sir Howard Smith
28 Mar 1978	Sir Curtis Keeble
16 Sep 1982	Sir Iain Sutherland
18 Jul 1985	Sir Bryan Cartledge
20 Sep 1988	Sir Rodric Braithwaite

'The Soviet Union was dissolved on 31 December 1991 and diplomatic relations were established between the United Kingdom and the Russian Federation. HM Representatives in Moscow were:

31 Dec 1991	Sir Rodric Braithwaite
3 Jun 1992	Sir Brian Fall
12 Jul 1995	Sir Andrew Wood

Soviet diplomatic representatives in London

The Government of the Russian Soviet Federative Socialist Republic (later the Union of Soviet Socialist Republics) was represented in the United Kingdom informally by L. B. Krasin during the period from 15 May 1921 to 23 July 1923. Mr Krasin was succeeded on that date by C. G. Rakovsky and on the establishment of diplomatic relations on 8 February 1924, Mr Rakovsky was appointed Chargé d'Affaires, an appointment which he held until 14 November 1925. On 30 October 1925 L. B. Krasin was appointed to London, but did not take up the appointment until 11 October 1926 and, although holding the rank of Ambassador, was received in the capacity of Chargé d'Affaires. During the period between 15 November 1925 and 10 October 1926 and again from 25 November 1926 until the suspension of diplomatic relations by the British Government on 27 May 1927 A. P. Rosengolz acted as Chargé d'Affaires.

Relations were resumed in accordance with the Protocol of 3 October 1929 and the Soviet Union was subsequently represented by the following Ambassadors Extraordinary and Plenipotentiary:

20 Dec 1929	G. Y. Sokolnikov
8 Nov 1932	I. M. Maisky
15 Oct 1943	F. T. Gusev
23 Jan 1947	G. N. Zarubin
7 Aug 1952	A. A. Gromyko
28 May 1953	Y. A. Malik
25 Mar 1960	A. A. Soldatov
10 Feb 1966	M. N. Smirnovsky
5 Jul 1973	N. M. Lunkov
10 Dec 1980	V. I. Popov
11 Jun 1986	L. M. Zamyatin
27 Nov 1991	B. Pankin

After the dissolution of the Soviet Union on 31 December 1991, the Representatives of the Russian Federation in London were:

31 Dec 1991	B. Pankin
19 Sep 1994	A. Adamishin
7 Jul 1997	Y. Fokine

Notes

The purpose of these notes is primarily to aid those whose who wish to go back to the original sources of quotations and references. The Governmental documents cited are held in the Public Record Office and in most cases are identified in the notes by standard PRO references. References to Cabinet and War Cabinet minutes are identified by PRO Class numbers, Piece numbers and meeting numbers in the CAB 23 series to September 1939; the CAB 65 series from 1939 to 1945; and the CAB 128 series thereafter. Cabinet memoranda are similarly identified in the CAB 24, CAB 66 and CAB 129 series, together with the memorandum number. Sir Winston Churchill's papers are identified by numbers in the PREM 3 Class. Foreign Office documents are almost exclusively in the FO 371 Class and in most cases are identified by the Class and Piece number only. In some cases, however the Foreign Office file number and document number have been added. References to Embassy telegrams are normally shown under the name of the originating post and are from the Ambassador or Chargé d'Affaires unless otherwise noted. Telegrams from the Foreign Office issue on the authority of the Secretary of State. Only a study of the jackets will distinguish those which bear his personal imprint from those sent in his name by officials of varying degrees of seniority.

In those cases where documents are reproduced in the collected volumes of *Documents on British Foreign Policy* (DBFP), I have used references from that volume, rather than from the PRO. For the reader who wishes to refer to the full texts, particularly in respect of the exchanges between the Foreign Secretary and HM Representatives, without the need for reference to the Public Record Office, I commend these volumes. They do not, however, indicate the full process of policy formulation. Since the first edition of this book, the Foreign and Commonwealth Office has published two exceptionally useful volumes of documents: *Documents of British Policy Overseas*, Series III, Vols 1 and 2. The first of these deals with the conduct of relations between Britain and the Soviet Union between 1968 and 1973 and the second with the Conference on Security and Cooperation in Europe.

Those who are not familiar with the Foreign Office filing system as it operated until a few years ago may find it mystifying and frustrating. It had its merits, but the swift identification and location of documents was not, in my experience, high among them. Each document, on receipt, was placed in its own paper jacket, identified by a green band and the letter G if it was of particular sensitivity, numbered in a single consecutive series and also assigned to a file, before being passed to the most junior officer in the responsible Department. He would write on the jacket his observations and recommendations for action, sign his name and pass it on up the chain. A signature alone would send it on its way into the higher reaches and if necessary to the Secretary of State, but, in this variant of snakes and ladders, an initial would return it to the registry, unseen – except in the case of multiple copy telegrams – by those senior to the initialler. The junior reaches of the service tended to divide between the firm-minded initialler, the prudent signer and the loquacious minuter, setting out at length and on occasion with an apparent authority which did not wholly match his standing in the Office, the course of action required of the British Government. Multiple copies of telegrams were made, of which one only was placed in a jacket. The more important documents were, at the discretion of the Department, printed for the information of the Monarch, of Ministers and in many cases of Commonwealth Governments. The volumes of printed documents are a convenient record, but, unfortunately, few telegrams were printed and from the Second World War onwards the print volumes have not been transferred to the Public Record Office.

The original jackets with their minutes are preserved in the PRO Pieces. They can provide a remarkably valuable indication of the process by which policy was formulated and modified between the most junior reaches of the Office and the Secretary of State. The main files of which the jackets formed part were often very generalised. Several subjects would be contained within one file and one topic could span several files. Related jackets on individual topics were tied in bundles until action was complete. The bundles were then split up and the jackets returned to one or more main files in the numerical sequence in which they had been entered. It is in this dispersed form that the jackets appear in the main at the PRO. It was a system which, well operated, could make for the efficient conduct of business, by bringing together only directly relevant papers, but it tended to frustrate the discovery of relevant documents after a lapse of one year, let alone thirty or more. I gratefully acknowledge the work of earlier researchers and the help of the PRO staff in tracing the sequence of events, but I am only too conscious of the gaps which remain in the record of these eighty years of diplomacy. The reader will not, I hope, seek total consistency in the naming of those who feature in it. I have in general, used the names by which British statesman were known during the period when they were most closely concerned with British–Soviet relations.

In this study of British policy, I have made only limited use of the Soviet documents. In relation to the Soviet period the reader's attention is, however, drawn to the bibliography annexed to *Soviet Foreign Policy*, eds A. Gromyko and B. Ponomarev (Moscow: Nauka, 1980) (to which should be added the two volumes of documents on Soviet– British relations 1941-5 published in Moscow in 1983); to J. Degras (ed.) *Soviet Documents on Foreign Policy 1917–1941*, 3 vols (Oxford University Press, RIIA, 1951–3); and to V. A Ryzhikov, *Soviet–English Relations* (Moscow: Mezhdunarodnye Otnosheniia, 1987). The official volumes of Soviet diplomatic documents, where referred to in the text are noted as DSFP. The German Documents published by HMSO are referred to as DGFP and the United States diplomatic documents as FRUS.

It is important to note that in preparing this revised edition I have been able to make only very limited use of the Soviet documents which have became available following the dissolution of the Soviet Union.

The field of Russian and Soviet studies is wide and the range of other works indirectly relevant to the British–Russian relationship even wider. I have not therefore, attempted a bibliography, but have indicated in the notes, where appropriate, a very few specialised works examining the conduct of relations during certain periods. For a general view of British–Soviet relations, F. S Northedge and A. Wells, *Britain and Soviet Communism* (Macmillan, 1982) can be recommended, particularly in respect of economic and cultural relations; W. P. and Z. K. Coates, *A History of Anglo–Soviet Relations* (London: Lawrence & Wishart, 1943–58) contains some information on the early years, but is heavily coloured by the authors' political views. On the nineteenth-century British view of Russia I would commend J. H. Gleason, *The Genesis of Russophobia in Great Britain* (Oxford: Oxford University Press, 1950). On the British-Russian relationship in the years between 1894 and 1914 there is Keith Neilson *Britain and the Last Tsar* (Oxford: Clarendon Press, 1995), although some may think that Neilson goes rather far in his emphasis on the importance of Russia in the formulation of British foreign policy at that time. On the Second World War period a recent study is James Reynolds, *Allies at War: The Soviet, American and British Experience 1939–45* (New York: Martin's Press, 1994). Among the recent works on the Cold War period it may be helpful to draw attention to the documents published by the Cold War International History Project at the Woodrow Wilson Center, Washington DC. There has been a spate of books on the collapse of the Soviet Union and the early post-Soviet period, but the British–Soviet relationship during these years has not attracted much attention. I would, however, commend Neil Malcolm *Russia and Europe: An End to Confrontation* (London: Pinter for RIIA, 1994).

Introduction: Britain and Imperial Russia

1. J. A. R. Marriott, *Anglo–Russian Relations 1689–1943* (London: Methuen, 1944).
2. Quoted by Sir W. Hayter in his valedictory despatch from Moscow, 22 Dec 1956 FO371/129139.
3. 39 HC Deb 14 December 1837 Col 1111.
4. 138 HC Deb 24 May 1855 Col 1006.
5. Marriott, *Anglo–Russian Relations*.
6. G. N. Curzon, *Persia*, II (London: Longmans 1892) p. 465
7. G. N. Curzon *Russia in Central Asia* (London: Longmans 1899).
8. Letter of 29 March 1853, *The Letters of Queen Victoria 1837–61*, eds A. C. Benson and Viscount Esher (London, 1907).
9. *Ibid*.
10. See Keith Neilson, *Britain and the Last Tsar* (Oxford: Clarendon Press 1995).
11. *The Times*, 26 December 1900.
12. *The Times*, 14 February 1899.
13. *Novoe Vremya*, quoted in a Petrograd despatch of 3 February 1912.
14. Sir George Buchanan *My Mission to Russia*, I (London: Cassell,1923), p. 89.
15. Buchanan, *My Mission*, I, p. 91.
16. *Novoe Vremya*, quoted in a Petrograd despatch of 3 February 1912.
17. Buchanan, *My Mission*, I, p. 138.
18. Buchanan, *My Mission*, I, p. 139.
19. Lecture by G.Paish Royal Statistical Society December 1910, quoted by B. Ischchanian, *Die ausländischen Elemente in der russischen Volkswirtschaft*, (Berlin, 1913).
20. *Ibid*.
21. I. Maisky, *Journey into the Past* (London: Hutchinson, 1962).

368 Notes

22. Parliamentary Questions answered by Chancellor of the Exchequer, 19 April 1921, quoted in FO 371/9363 (N3530/2407/38). An attempt to convert this and other figures into a 1998 equivalent cannot be very meaningful, but as a proportion of budget revenue a figure of £30 000 million would give an indication of the order of magnitude of the British wartime loans in today's terms.
23. Buchanan, *My Mission*, II, p. 28.
24. *Ibid.*, p. 49.
25. D. Lloyd George, *War Memoirs*, II (London: Odhams, 1933–6), p. 1892.
26. Buchanan, *My Mission*, II, pp. 92–100.
27. CAB 23/2 W.C.100
28. H. Nicolson, *King George the Fifth*, (London: Constable, 1952).
29. CAB 23/2 W.C. 139.
30. CAB 23/2 W.C. 144.
31. Meriel Buchanan, *Petrograd, the City of Trouble 1914–1918* (London, 1918).
32. Telegram, Petrograd to Foreign Office no. 1771, 8 November 1917.

1 Response to revolution

1. CAB 23/4 W.C. 269.
2. Lloyd George, *War Memoirs*, II, p. 1544.
3. Quoted by D. Lloyd George, *War Memoirs*, II, p. 1610. Lloyd George says that Haig had under-estimated the effect, but later in Cabinet he remarked at one point that he was 'unable to understand the rather alarmist tone' about the transfer of German forces from the East.
4. CAB 23/4 W.C. 286.
5. Articles by H. N. Brailsford and M. S. Farbman in *The Herald*, 17 November 1917 and 5 January 1918.
6. Lloyd George, *War Memoirs*, II, p. 1643.
7. CAB 24/35 Memorandum GT 2932 and CAB 23/4 W.C. 295.
8. CAB 23/4 W. C. 289.
9. Telegram, FO to Petrograd, 3 December 1917, quoted in R. H. Ullman, *Anglo–Soviet Relations 1917–1921* (Princeton University Press, 1961) vol. I, p. 46.
10. The text of the Convention is at DBFP, series I, III, pp. 369–70.
11. CAB 23/4 W.C. 306.
12. R. H. Bruce Lockhart, *Memoirs of a British Agent* (London: Putnam, 1932) p. 1.
13. *Ibid.*, p. 206.
14. *Ibid.*, p. 204.
15. CAB 23/4 W.C. 308.
16. CAB 23/4 W.C. 290.

2 Intervention

1. The steps by which the British Government was led into the policy of intervention and then extricated itself are described and analysed in great detail in Richard Ullman's masterly work *Anglo–Soviet Relations 1917–1921*. In the

present chapter, which is based largely on the War Cabinet minutes, space does not permit more than an analysis of the main thrust of events. Although the official documents in the Public Record Office had not been opened at the time Ullman was writing his first volume, they do not significantly change the assessment which he formed, and for those who wish to study in detail this important period of diplomatic history his book must be regarded as the definitive work. Among the various works dealing with the intervention and the civil war a lively account of the operations conducted by the British forces in Russia is contained in Christopher Dobson and John Miller, *The Day We Almost Bombed Moscow* (London: Hodder & Stoughton, 1986).
2. Buchanan, *My Mission*, II, p. 247.
3. This letter from Captain Garstin, who joined Lockhart's staff, is on FO 371/3318. Garstin was later transferred to General Poole's forces in Archangel, where he won the MC and was killed in August 1918.
4. FO 371/3283 (Petrograd Telegram 179 of 20 January 1918).
5. FO Telegram to Petrograd, no. 129.
6. FO Telegram to Petrograd, no. 287.
7. Lockhart, *Memoirs*, p. 230.
8. CAB 23/5, W.C. 341.
9. CAB 23/5, W.C. 353.
10. Quoted from Hoffmann's memoirs by J. W. Wheeler-Bennett, *Brest-Litovsk: The Forgotten Peace* (London: Macmillan, 1938), p. 244.
11. 29 HL Debs 9 April 1918 Col. 618.
12. Lloyd George, *War Memoirs*, II, p. 1889.
13. Wheeler-Bennett, *Brest-Litovsk*, p. 227.
14. Despatch of 16 March by A. J. Balfour quoted in Lloyd George, *War Memoirs*, II, p. 1898.
15. CAB 24/46 Memorandum GT 4046. See also FO 371/3285.
16. FO 371/3285/58693.
17. FO 371/3285/64890 FO Telegram 65 to Moscow (Lockhart), 13 April 1918.
18. CAB 23/6 WC 410. CAB 24/51 Memorandum GT 4519.
19. See, for instance, memorandum by General Knox with covering note by CIGS CAB 24/47 GT 4156.
20. CAB 23/7 WC 446.
21. FO 371/3285/58026.
22. CAB 23/6 WC 413.
23. FO 371/3286 Telegram 210 from Moscow to Foreign Office.
24. FO 371/3286 FO Telegram 191 to Moscow.
25. FO 371/3289.
26. FO Telegram 82 to New York, 20 June 1918.
27. CAB 24/54 Memorandum GT 4812. Lindley is referred to as HM Principal Representative in Russia. There must be some doubt as to the extent to which his functions went beyond that of political advice to the northern group of forces.
28. CAB 23/6 WC 432.
29. Lloyd George, *War Memoirs*, II, p. 1871.
30. FO 371/3287.
31. Moscow Telegram 347 of 5 August 1918.

32. A. Gromyko and B. Ponomarev (eds), *Soviet Foreign Policy* (Moscow, 1980), I, p. 75 *et seq*. This work is referred to at various points. Now something of a historical curiosity, it still represents a convenient summary of the conventional Soviet foreign policy doctrines with which Britain policy-makers were confronted as late as the end of the 1970s. V. A. Ryzhikov, *Soviet–English Relations* (Moscow, 1982) contains a carefully researched exposition of the conventional Soviet view, but the pattern which it presents corresponds poorly to the complex evolution of British policy.
33. Gromyko and Ponomarev, *Soviet Foreign Policy*, I, p. 82.
34. See, for example, R. N. B. Lockhart, *Ace of Spies* (London: Hodder & Stoughton, 1967) on Sidney Reilly; Sir Paul Dukes, *The Story of ST25* (London: Cassell, 1938) and G. Hill, *Go Spy the Land* (London: Cassell, 1932). For the description of Cromie's work see telegram dated 6 September 1918 from Lindley in Archangel to Balfour in *Collection of Reports on Russia No 1 1919* (HMSO).
35. CAB 23/7 WC 469.
36. FO 371/3337/185499.
37. Article by D. Young, *The Herald*, 14 September 1918.
38. CAB 24/63, Memorandum GT 5648.
39. CAB 23/8 WC 481.
40. These figures are taken from a map in W. S. Churchill, *The World Crisis: 'The Aftermath* (London: Thornton Butterworth, 1929), with some necessary amendment such as the exclusion of the forces in the Caucasus, which arrived shortly after the end of the war with Germany.
41. FO 371/3319/143998, Telegram from Lindley in Archangel.
42. CAB 23/8 WC 489.
43. CAB 23/8 WC 502.
44. Winston S. Churchill, *The World Crisis*, p. 169.
45. D. Lloyd George, *The Truth About the Peace Treaties* (London: Gollancz, 1938), p. 316.
46. CAB 23/42 Imperial War Cabinet, 31 December 1918.
47. Lloyd George, *The Truth*, p. 367.
48. *Soviet Documents*, I (Moscow, 1957), p. 549, quoted by Ullman, *Anglo–Soviet Relations*, II, p. 87.
49. CAB 23/42 Imperial War Cabinet, 23 December 1918.
50. CAB 23/9 WC 531.
51. Lloyd George, *The Truth*, p. 370, and Churchill, *The World Crisis*, p. 173.
52. CAB 23/9 WC 541.
53. Interdepartmental Conference on Eastern Affairs and CAB 25/9 WC 542.
54. 114 HC Deb, 16 April 1919, Col. 2939–2943.
55. Lloyd George, *The Truth*, p. 568.
56. Churchill, *The World Crisis*, p. 183.
57. CAB 23/15 WC 588A.
58. DBFP Minutes of Supreme Allied Council, 25 July 1919, p. 202, Appendix D.
59. FO 371/4096/110398/11/57.
60. CAB 24/96 CP 469.
61. DBFP, series I, vol. I, Meeting of Heads of Delegations, 20 August 1919.
62. 116 HC Deb, 29 May 1919, Col. 1522.

63. FO 371/3961/145297/38.
64. Lloyd George, *The Truth*, p. 370.
65. *The Times*, 12 April 1919.
66. CAB 24/89 Memorandum GT 8207.
67. DBFP, series I, vol. I, Minutes Heads of Delegations, 15 September 1919.

3 Facing the facts

1. It has been convenient to refer, up to this point, to the Bolshevik and anti-Bolshevik forces in Russia, since it was largely in these terms that policy was discussed in London during the period of the intervention. The Soviet Government was not recognised *de facto* by Britain until March 1921. The change in terminology was gradual, but with the ending of the intervention and the opening of negotiations for a trade agreement the British Government were in practice dealing with the Soviet Government and, making a somewhat arbitrary choice, I have from the beginning of this chapter referred to the Soviet Government as such.
2. *The Times*, 10 November 1919.
3. For those who wish to follow these negotiations in detail there is a very full account and analysis in Richard H. Ullman, *The Anglo–Soviet Accord* (Princeton University Press, 1972). Stephen White, *Britain and the Bolshevik Revolution* (London: Macmillan, 1979) deals with the conduct of relations from 1917 to 1924 especially from the point of view of the influence of the labour and financial and industrial interests on the British side.
4. Labour Party Report of the Nineteenth Annual Conference (London, 1919), p. 156 (see S. R. Graubard, *British Labour and the Russian Revolution*, Harvard University Press, 1956, pp. 73–4).
5. CAB 23/11 WC 599.
6. K. Jefferey (ed.), *The Military Correspondence of Field Marshal Sir Henry Wilson 1918–1922* (London: Bodley Head for Army Records Society, 1985).
7. DBFP, series I, vol. III, no. 342.
8. *Ibid.*, vol. II, pp. 867–70.
9. *Ibid.*, vol. III, no. 664.
10. DBFP, series I, vol. VII, no. 24.
11. In April 1919 the Government published a *Collection of Reports on Bolshevism in Russia* (HMSO Cmd. 8, 1919) with descriptions of the early stages of the terror. For the Reverend North's views, see *The Times*, 24 May 1920. For the memorial to the Prime Minister, see *The Times*, 23 February 1920 and for the comment by the CIGS see Jeffery, *Military Correspondence*, Doc. 84.
12. For Churchill's speech at Sunderland on 3 January 1920, see *Manchester Guardian*, 5 January 1920. For his Cabinet Memorandum of 17 January 1920, see file 18/OJ/2 on CAB 21/177.
13. Cmd. 587: *Agreement Between His Majesty's Government and the Soviet Government of Russia for the Exchange of Prisoners, 1920.*
14. FO 371/195172/1089/38.
15. CAB 24/106 CP 1350. Also DBFP, series I, vol. XII, no. 708.
16. *The Times*, 28 May 1920.

372 Notes

17. 131 HC Deb, 14 July 1920, Col. 2369–71 has text.
18. 131 HC Deb, 14 July 1920, Col. 2371-4.
19. Sir C. E. Calwell, *Field Marshal Sir Henry Wilson* (London: Cassell, 1927), II, p. 255.
20. 132 HC Deb, 21 July 1920, Col. 485.
21. DBFP, series I, vol. VIII, no. 79.
22. For a description of the interception of these telegrams, see R. H. Ullman, *The Anglo–Soviet Accord*, III, ch. 7.
23. 133 HC Deb, 10 August 1920, Col. 272.
24. International Labour Office, *The Congress of the Labour and Socialist International*, Geneva, 31 July–5 August 1920 (Geneva, 1920) cited by Graubard, *British Labour*.
25. *The Times* 19 August 1920 contains the texts of this exchange of messages.
26. CAB 23/22 C 49 (20).
27. Telegram, Lenin to Kamenev, cited by Ullman, *Anglo–Soviet Accord*, III, p. 296.
28. CAB 23/22 p. 237, Conclusions of Ministerial Conference, 2 September 1920.
29. CAB 23/22 C 61 (20).
30. CAB 24/114 Memorandum CP 2099, 14 November 1920.
31. CAB 23/23 C 64 (20).
32. Cmd. 1207: *Trade Agreement between His Britannic Majesty's Government and the Government of the Russian Socialist Federal Soviet Republic.*
33. 164 HC Deb, 15 May 1923, Col. 282.
34. 139 HC Deb, 22 March 1921, Cols 2511–12.
35. *The Times*, 17 March 1921.

4 Working relations

1. 139 HC Deb, 22 March 1921, Col. 2506.
2. DBFP, series I, vol. XX, no. 389, N9386/9924/4/38.
3. DBFP, series I, vol. XX, no. 414.
4. Documents on FO 371/6916 contain the report of a Foreign Office examination of the evidence and a detailed note from the Secret Intelligence Service of the means by which an agent had secured documents from the Berlin Office. It was known to the SIS that Berlin was a centre for the circulation of forged Soviet documents, but the circumstances in which this evidence was obtained satisfied them of its accuracy.
5. DBFP, series I, vol. XX, no. 424, Report by Hodgson citing an article by Radek.
6. DBFP, series I, vol. XIX, no. 1.
7. *The Times*, 13 April 1922.
8. DBFP, series I, vol. XIX, no. 6.
9. A very full study of the Conference is contained in Carole Fink, *The Genoa Conference* (University of North Carolina Press, 1984).
10. DBFP, series I, vol. XX no. 438.
11. Gromyko and Ponomarev, *Soviet Foreign Policy*, p. 165.

12. 154 HC Deb, 25 May 1922, Cols 1449–1468.
13. FO 371/9363 N2524/2524/38.
14. CAB 23/46 C30 (23).
15. DBFP series I, vol. XXV, no. 222, N1670/10/38.
16. 176 HC Deb, 7 August 1924, Col. 3183.
17. Crowe to MacDonald, 26 October 1924, on FO 371/10478 N7838/G.
18. The whole incident has continued to baffle and intrigue politicians and historians. In 1999, on the instructions of the Foreign Secretary, the Chief Historian of the Foreign and Commonwealth Office published the result of a thorough investigation of all the available evidence including not only the FCO files but also those of the SIS, the Security Service and other British Government Departments, as well as certain Russian and American archives. Her conclusion, which appeared in the series of FCO History Notes under the title *'A most extraordinary and mysterious business': The Zinoviev Letter of 1924*, was that the evidence permitted no definitive conclusion as to the authorship of the letter. Nevertheless, a 'best guess' was that it was a forgery created at the behest of White Russians determined to derail the Treaties and that individuals connected with the Intelligence Services in Britain would have been well placed to encourage its dissemination. The FCO publication contains a comprehensive bibliography.

5 Relations broken and resumed

1. CAB 23/48 C 49 (24) and CAB 23/49 C 59, C 60 (24).
2. 179 HC Deb, 15 December 1924, Cols 673–679.
3. FO 371/11015/N1314/102/38.
4. DBFP, series I, vol. XXV, p. 677, N3432/102/38.
5. CAB 23/50 C 36 (50). Chicherin's comment is on FO 371/11786 N387/387/38.
6. J. Degras (ed.), *Soviet Documents on Foreign Policy, 1917–1941* (Oxford University Press for RIIA, 1952–3), II, p. 1.
7. *Ibid.*, p. 39.
8. FO 371/11786 N2241/387/38.
9. The development of British–Soviet relations between 1924 and 1926 is described in G. Gorodetsky, *The Precarious Truce* (Cambridge University Press, 1977) and this covers the trade union aspect in particular detail.
10. CAB 23/53 C 40 (26).
11. DBFP, series I, vol. XXV, no. 323, N4187/114/38.
12. CAB 24/180 Memorandum CP 250.
13. 197 HC Deb, 25 June 1926, Col. 776.
14. Cmd. 2862, 1926.
15. *The Times*, 13 July 1926.
16. CAB 23/54 C 12(27) and CAB 24/184 Memoranda CP 25 (27) and 27 (27).
17. DBFP, series 1A, vol. III, no. 3.
18. DBFP, series 1A, vol. III, no. 21.
19. 203 HC Deb, 3 March 1927, Cols 610–626.
20. CAB 23/55 C 33 (27).

21. 206 HC Deb, 26 May 1927, Col. 2217. Cmd. 2874 of 1927: *Documents Illustrating the Hostile Activities of The Soviet Government and the Third International against Great Britain.*
22. *Manchester Guardian,* 25 July 1927, quoted by W. P. and Z. K. Coates, *A History of Anglo–Soviet Relations* (London: Lawrence & Wishart, 1943) 1.
23. DBFP, series 1A, vol. III, Report from Mr Preston in Leningrad on conditions immediately prior to his departure.
24. DBFP, series II, vol. VII, no. 1.
25. Degras, *Soviet Documents,* II, p. 236.
26. *The Times,* 4 September 1928.
27. Low cartoon, reproduced in R. K. Middlemas and A. J. L. Barnes, *Baldwin* (London: Weidenfeld & Nicolson, 1969), p. 525.
28. Note on Anglo–Soviet Relations (1929–1931), reproduced as Appendix 1 to DBFP, series II, vol. VII.
29. DBFP, series II, vol. VII, no. 24. For Sir E. Ovey's impressions on arrival, see FO 371/14052.
30. DBFP, series II, vol. VII. No. 135.
31. 269 HC Deb, 20 October 1932, Col. 449.
32. W. Strang, *Home and Abroad* (London: Deutsch, 1956).
33. The diplomatic exchanges are reproduced at length in DBFP, series II, vol. VII, and will not be individually annotated.
34. 275 HC Deb, 15 March 1933, Col. 1945.
35. 276 HC Deb, 20 March 1933, Col. 19.
36. DBFP, series II, vol. VII, no. 529.
37. DBFP, series II, vol. VII, no. 500.

6 The approach to war

1. Harold Macmillan, *Winds of Change,* 5 vols (London: Macmillan 1966–72), vol. 1.
2. Middlemas and Barnes, *Baldwin,* p. 1038.
3. Meeting at 10 Downing Street, 28–9 July 1936, quoted in *ibid.,* p. 947.
4. Strang, *Home and Abroad.*
5. DBFP, series II, vol. VII, no. 487.
6. *Ibid.,* no. 396.
7. I. M. Maisky, *Who Helped Hitler?* (London: Hutchinson, 1964), p. 44.
8. R. G. Vansittart, *The Mist Procession* (London: Hutchinson, 1958).
9. DBFP, series II, vol. VII, no. 545. (For Sir P. Loraine's remark, see no. 575.)
10. DBFP, series II, vol. VII, no. 582.
11. 292 HC Deb, 13 July 1934, Col. 697 *et seq.*
12. Maisky, *Who Helped Hitler?*
13. DBFP, series II, vol. VII, no. 608.
14. *Ibid.,* no. 570.
15. *Ibid.,* vol. XII, no. 121.
16. *Ibid.,* no. 199.
17. *Ibid.,* no. 484.
18. CAB 24/247 Memorandum COS 326 Committee of Imperial Defence February 1934.

19. CAB 24/253 Memorandum CP 41 (35).
20. DBFP, series II, vol. XII, no. 515.
21. A. Eden, *Facing the Dictators* (London: Cassell, 1962), II, p. 141.
22. DBFP, series II, vol. VII, no. 656.
23. Eden, *Facing the Dictators*, II, p. 144 *et seq*.
24. DBFP, series II, vol. XII, nos 669, 670, 673.
25. Quoted by Gromyko and Ponomarev, *Soviet Foreign Policy*, I, p. 283.
26. DBFP, series II, vol. XV, Appendix IV.
27. CAB 23/85 C 56 (36).
28. 310 HC Deb, 26 March 1926, Col. 1541.
29. A. Blunt, *Picasso's Guernica* (Oxford University Press, 1969), quoted by A. Boyle, *The Climate of Treason* (London: Hutchinson, 1979). This is one of those phases in the British–Soviet relationship which merit a more detailed examination, particularly in the light of the Spanish archives, than is feasible within the compass of this chapter. Its relevance to my theme lies in the contemporary perception of those involved and the consequences which flowed therefrom.
30. DBFP, series II, vol. XVII, no. 311.
31. *Ibid.*, vol. XVIII, Appendix I.
32. *Ibid.*, no. 366. Memorandum by N. Chamberlain, 2 April 1937.
33. DBFP, series III, vol. I, no. 148.
34. See J. Haslam, *The Soviet Union and the Struggle for Collective Security in Europe 1933–39* (London: Macmillan, 1984).
35. See, for instance, letter from Viscount Chilston of 24 January 1938. DBFP, series II, vol. XIX, no. 467.
36. DBFP, series III, vol. I, nos 90 and 116.
37. Soviet Foreign Policy Documents (DSFP), vol. XXI, no. 172.
38. DSFP, series II, vol. XXI, nos 348–9.
39. DBFP series III, vol. II, nos 1043, 1071.
40. Lord Butler, *The Art of the Possible* (London: Hamish Hamilton, 1971).
41. DSFP, series II, vol. XXI, no. 270.
42. *Ibid.*, no. 406.
43. CAB 23/95 C 41 (38). For the Pravda reference, see Ryzhikov, *Soviet–English Relations*, p. 66.
44. CAB 23/96 C 57 (38).
45. DBFP, series III, vol. III, no. 325.
46. *Ibid.*, vol. IV, nos 24, 103, 121.
47. *Ibid.*, vol. IV, no. 446.
48. 345 HC Deb, 31 March 1939, Cols 2415–6.
49. Sir K. G. Feiling, *Neville Chamberlain* (London: Macmillan, 1970), p. 403.
50. CAB 23/98 C 18 (39).
51. DBFP, series III, vol. IV, no. 597.
52. *Ibid.*, vol. V, no. 279.
53. *Ibid.*, no. 304.
54. CAB 23/99 C 24 (39).
55. CAB 23/99 C 26 (39).
56. DBFP, series III, vol. V, no. 282.
57. *Ibid.*, nos 520, 530.
58. *Ibid.*, no. 509.

59. *Ibid.*, no. 576.
60. *Ibid.*, no. 589.
61. 347 HC Deb, 19 May 1939, Cols 1809–62.
62. CAB 23/99 C 27 (39).
63. CAB 23/99 C 30 (39).
64. 348 HC Deb, 7 June 1939, Cols 400–402.
65. DBFP, series III, vol. VI, no. 55.
66. Strang describes the course of the negotiations in some detail in *Home and Abroad*.
67. DBFP, series III, vol. VI, no. 272.
68. *Ibid.*, no. 376.
69. *Ibid.*, no. 474.
70. A useful analysis of the German–Soviet negotiations is contained in G. H. Weinberg, *Germany and the Soviet Union 1939–41* (Leiden: E. J. Brill, 1954).
71. DBFP, series III, vol. VI, no. 453.
72. Documents on German Foreign Policy (DGFP), series D, vol. VI, no. 761.
73. DGFP, series D, vol. VI, no. 766.
74. *Ibid.*, vol. VII, nos. 229–30.
75. *Ibid.*, no. 213.
76. DBFP, series III, vol. VI, Appendix V.
77. The full records of the military talks are at Appendix II of DBFP, series III, vol. VII.
78. Gromyko and Ponomarev, *Soviet Foreign Policy*, I, p. 376, claimed that the Soviet Government agreed to the Treaty with Germany 'only after it had finally become apparent that Britain and France were unwilling to cooperate with the USSR in resisting Nazi aggression'. Ryzhikov (see Chapter 2, n 32) disposed of the negotiations with Britain and France as the failure of an attempt to entrap the Soviet Union in a one-to-one war with Germany. Yakovlev's conclusion that the existence of the secret protocol was not in doubt was published in *Pravda* on 18 August 1989.
79. CAB 23/101 C 41 (39).

7 Alliance

1. The course of British–Soviet diplomatic exchanges during the war is set out in Sir Llewellyn Woodward, *British Foreign Policy in the Second World War* (London: HMSO, 1970) and the military aspect of the relationship may be followed in the official *History of the Second World War*, 7 vols, (London: HMSO, 1956–76) as well as in various specialised works. Churchill's *History of the Second World War* sets out the principal top-level governmental exchanges which constituted the essence of the British–Soviet relationship during the war years.

    The British official documents for the period between the declaration of war on Germany in September 1939 and the German attack on the Soviet Union in June 1941 are also dealt with in G. Gorodetsky, *Stafford Cripps' Mission to Moscow 1940–42* (Cambridge University Press, 1984). A Soviet view of the wartime relationship may be found in I. Maisky, *Memoirs of a Soviet Ambassador* (London: Hutchinson, 1967). The Soviet official docu-

ments include Stalin's correspondence with Churchill, Attlee, Roosevelt and Truman (2 vols, Moscow, 1976); two further volumes of wartime documents (Moscow, 1983); and records of the wartime conferences (6 vols, Moscow, 1978–80).
2. W. S. Churchill, *History of the Second World War* (London: Cassell, 1950), I, p. 360.
3. CAB 65/2, W. M. 101 (39).
4. COS (40) 252.
5. For this minuting, see FO 371/24845 and FO 371/24846/N2779/40/384.
6. FO 371/24844 N5808/30/38.
7. FO 371/24844 N5937/30/38.
8. W. Warlimont, *Im Hauptquartier der deutschen Wehrmacht 1939–45* Frankfurt: Bernard & Graebe, 1962).
9. Weinberg, *Germany and the Soviet Union*, p. 116.
10. FO 371/24845 N 6875 N7047/30/38.
11. CAB 65/10 288 C (40) 3.
12. Cadogan diaries, p. 362, quoted in Gorodetsky, *Stafford Cripps' Mission*.
13. PREM 3 403/7 T18.
14. Gorodetsky analyses the incident in some detail, but confuses the picture in one minor respect by failing to understand that Eden's follow-up telegram expressing 'hope' that Cripps would deliver the message constituted, in Foreign office language, an instruction to do so.
15. FO 371/29465 N1658 N1667 and N1828/30/38.
16. Gromyko and Ponomarev, *Soviet Foreign Policy*, I, p. 410.
17. Churchill, *The Second World War*, III, p. 58.
18. See F. H. Hinsley, *British Intelligence in the Second World War* (London: HMSO, 1981).
19. JIC (41) 234.
20. CAB 79/12 COS(41)218.
21. Churchill, *The Second World War*, IV, p. 388.
22. Telegram to Cripps, 5 September 1941, quoted in *ibid.*, III, p. 365.
23. *Ibid.*, p. 312.
24. Cmd. 6304.
25. PREM 3 403/3 T 417.
26. PREM 3 403/3 T 418.
27. Churchill, *The Second World War*, III, p. 354.
28. WP(41)238 on PREM 3 393/1.
29. Cmd. 6376.
30. PREM 3 403/3 T 802.
31. CAB 65/24 WM (41) 111.
32. PREM 3 395/6.
33. CAB 66/20 Memorandum WP (41) 288 Revise.
34. Hinsley, *British Intelligence*, pp. 58–67.
35. The references to the Washington discussions are based on FRUS, 1942, vol. III, pp. 566–83. For the British *aide-memoire*, see PREM 3 333/8.
36. PREM 3 403/405 T 1031/2.
37. Churchill, *The Second World War*, IV, p. 415.
38. Michael Howard, *Grand Strategy* (London: HMSO, 1972), IV, pp. 34–40.
39. PREM 3 333/3 T 125/2.

40. PREM 3 333/5 T 792/3.
41. Gromyko and Ponomarev, *Soviet Foreign Policy*, I, p. 432.
42. PREM 3 333 T 922/3.
43. PREM 3 393/9.
44. PREM 3 393/3 T 1031/2.
45. PREM 3 393/10 T1464/3 N5746/4013/38.
46. PREM 3 393/10 T1625/3.
47. 421 HC Deb, 16 Apr 1946, Cols 2513–2519.
48. Figures taken from B. B. Schofield, *The Russian Convoys* (London: Batsford, 1964) and HC Deb (see n. 47).
49. PREM 3 402 Tel 1049 to Moscow.
50. FO 371/6957 N 6353 and 7386/66/38.
51. PREM 3 402 CP (44) 8 and Churchill, *The Second World War*, V, pp. 309–12.
52. *Ibid.*, p. 318.
53. FO 371/40741 U/6254, 7618, 6793, 7841. See V. Rothwell, *Britain and the Cold War* (London: Cape, 1982).
54. FO 371/40702, WP (44) 409, U6594/180/70.
55. Churchill, *The Second World War*, VI, p. 180.
56. PREM 3 352 (C 11228/1077/55).
57. CAB 66/47 WM (44) 122, 123.
58. PREM 3 396/5.
59. Under continued Polish pressure, Gorbachev admitted the truth and described the murders as one of the gravest crimes of Stalinism. In 1992 the relevant Politburo minute dated 5 March 1940 was disclosed. Signed by Stalin, it ordered trial, without the accused being present, followed by death by shooting.
60. For the record of the conference, see FO 800/414.
61. This date taken from Woodward, *British Foreign Policy*, V, p. 262, differs from that of 5 January given by Churchill.
62. Woodward, *British Foreign Policy*, V, p. 264.
63. For the text of the Declaration, see FO 800/416/140.
64. The existing works on this episode should not be relied on. There is, however, an analysis of one of the more controversial issues in Anthony Cowgill, Lord Brimelow and Christopher Booker, *The Repatriations from Austria in 1945* (London: Sinclair Stevenson, 1990).
65. 408 HC Deb, 27 February 1945, Col. 1284.
66. Churchill to Roosevelt 13 and 27 March 1945, Churchill, *The Second World War*, VI, p. 349.
67. *Ibid.*, p. 397.
68. *Ibid.*, p. 458.
69. Washington telegram of 7 July 1945 quoted in Churchill, *The Second World War*, V, p. 487.
70. Memorandum given to US Ambassador, dated 27 May 1945, quoted in Churchill, *The Second World War*, VI, p. 461.
71. FO 371/50912/5471.
72. Woodward, *British Foreign Policy*, V, p. 353, gives a reference PM/45/322 FO 800/416/63/37 which does not appear to be correct.
73. FO 371/50866 PM/45/324 U6125/3628/70.
74. For the full record of the conference see FO 371/50867 U6197.

75. Eden and Cadogan diaries quoted by Robert Rhodes James, in *Anthony Eden* (London: Weidenfeld & Nicolson, 1986).
76. CAB 128/1 CM 18(45).
77. FO 800/415 FO Telegram, 4 February 1945.
78. FO 371/36954.
79. FO 371/43304.
80. FO 371/3695/5158.
81. FO 371/43304.
82. Strang, *Home and Abroad*.
83. The PREM 3 Series of files in the Public Record Office contains Churchill's papers. CAB 120/858 and 120/859 contain the messages exchanged between Churchill and Stalin from November 1942 onwards.
84. D. Dilks, *The Diaries of Sir Alexander Cadogan 1939–45* (London: Cassell, 1971), p. 586.
85. R. A. Eden, *The Reckoning* (London: Cassell, 1960), p. 514.
86. Churchill, *The Second World War*, V, p. 408.
87. FO 371/43304.
88. CAB 120/158.
89. On the mood in Britain see A. Calder, *The People's War: Britain 1939–45* (London: Cape, 1969) and W. James, *The Russia Complex: The British Labour Party and the Soviet Union* (Manchester University Press, 1977).

8 Post-war confrontation

1. FO 371/86761 Russia Committee minute, 7 February 1950.
2. See 'The Sources of Soviet Conduct', in *American Diplomacy 1900–1950* (University of Chicago, 1951), pp. 107, 121, and also G. F. Kennan, *Memoirs 1925–50* (Boston: Little, Brown, 1967).
3. Among the many works of this topic, one may note, in addition to Kennan's own works, studies such as Adam B. Ulam, *The Rivals* (New York: Viking Press, 1971).
4. The course of British policy during the critical years from 1945 to 1951 has been analysed in detail in Lord Bullock's authoritative work, *Ernest Bevin: Foreign Secretary 1945–51* (London: Heinemann, 1983).
5. FO 371/47856.
6. 414 HC Deb, 9 October 1945, Col. 40.
7. FO 371/47883.
8. FO 371/56763/4065; CAB 133/82; FO 800/507/SU/45/7.
9. FO 371/56763/4065 and 4157.
10. *The Times*, 6 March 1946.
11. *Pravda*, 13 March 1946.
12. CAB 129/9 CP (46) 186.
13. Quoted by Rothwell, *Britain and the Cold War, 1941–47*, p. 264.
14. 423 HC Deb, 24 June 1946, Col. 1850.
15. 423 HC Deb, 5 June 1946, Col. 2038.
16. FO 371/66546/76. In this context, see also Raymond Smith, 'A climate of opinion: British officials and the development of British Soviet Policy 1945–7', *International Affairs*, 64, (4) (Autumn 1988).

380 Notes

17. FO 371/66279 and 66370/7458.
18. See *inter alia* PREM 9/702 and related documents quoted by Anne Deighton, in *International Affairs*, 63 (3), p. 460.
19. CAB 129/9 CP (46) 186.
20. FO 371/66467/1038.
21. FO 800/475, ME/64/22 quoted by R. Smith and J. Zametica, in *International Affairs*, 61 (2) (Spring 1985).
22. FO 800/476 ME 47/1.
23. *The Times*, 5 January 1948.
24. CAB 129/23 CP (48) 5, 6, 7, 8.
25. CAB 129/27 CP (48) 134.
26. FRUS 1948, vol. II, pp. 895–6.
27. CAB 128/13 CM 43 (48).
28. See also G. F. Kennan, *Memoirs* and record of British–US Chiefs of Staff meeting 30 June in W. Condit, *The History of the Joint Chiefs of Staff, vol. II: 1947–49*, pp. 136–7, quoted in Avi Shlaim, 'Britain, the Berlin Blockade and the Cold War', *International Affairs*, 60 (1) (1983–4).
29. 452 HC Deb, 30 June 1948, Col. 2233.
30. CAB 128/13 CM 57 (48).
31. CAB 128/13 CM 61 (48).
32. 456 HC Deb, 22 September 1948, Col. 911.
33. CAB 128/13 CM 54 (48).
34. FO 371/86766 Minute by Rae and paper by Harrison dated 11 April.
35. FO 371/86761.
36. 481 HC Deb, 30 November 1950, Col. 1336.
37. CAB 128/18 CM 47 (50).
38. CAB 128/18 CM 60 (50).
39. FO 371/86766.
40. CAB 129/43 CP (50) 294.
41. CAB 129/47 CP (51) 239.
42. FO 371/94850 NS 1073/10G.
43. On Burgess and Maclean, see Cmd 9577 of 1955. On the wider field, the many revealing works include Andrew Boyle, *The Climate of Treason* (London: Hutchinson, 1979) and Chapman Pincher, *Their Trade is Treachery* (London: Sidgwick & Jackson, 1981). A survey of covert Soviet operations in Britain appears in P. Shipley, *Hostile Action* (London: Pinter, 1989). See also Nigel West and Oleg Tsarev, *The Crown Jewels: The British Secrets Exposed by the KGB Archives* (Yale, 1999) and Nigel West, *Venona: The Greatest Secret of the Cold War* (HarperCollins, 1999).

9 The Khrushchev years

1. 515 HC Deb, 11 May 1953, Col. 897.
2. CAB 129/61 C (53) 187.
3. CAB 129/61 C (53) 194.
4. Eden diary, 27 September 1953, quoted by Robert Rhodes James in *Anthony Eden*.
5. R. A. Eden, *The Reckoning*, pp. 58–9.

6. Gromyko and Ponomarev, *Soviet Foreign Policy*, II, p. 174.
7. FO 371-111690, Letter F. Roberts, 29 January 1954.
8. FO 371/111691.
9. CAB 129/67 C (54) 136.
10. Eden, *The Reckoning*.
11. Rhodes James, *Anthony Eden*, p. 382.
12. FO 371/111706 NS 1073/35.
13. 529 HC Deb, 23 June 1954, Col. 548.
14. FO 371/111691.
15. 189 HL Deb, 28 July 1954, Cols 233-240.
16. CAB 128/27 CC (54) 48, 52 and FO Telegram 873 to Moscow.
17. Soviet note of 24 July 1954 and CAB 128/27 CC (54) 53.
18. Macmillan, *Tides of Fortune* (London: Macmillan, 1969), p. 559.
19. Eden, *The Reckoning*, p. 171.
20. FO 371/116652, NS 1021/38 and FO 371/116654 NS 1021/69.
21. Stalin to Zilliacus, 14 October 1947, FO 371/111670 NS 1051/31G 'Short History of the Anglo–Soviet Treaty'. For the formal annulment of the Treaty, see Cmd. 9385 of 1955.
22. Gromyko and Ponomarev, *Soviet Foreign Policy*, II, p. 206.
23. CAB 128/29 CM 23 (55).
24. 549 HC Deb, 27 February 1956, Cols 837–963.
25. FO 371/122770 NS 1015/6.
26. CAB 128/29 CM 45 (55).
27. White Paper SU no. 1, 1956.
28. Eden, *The Reckoning*, p. 361.
29. CAB 128/30 CM 31 (56).
30. Eden, *Full Circle* (London: Cassell, 1960–5), p. 363.
31. For a full record of the visit see FO 371/122836 NS 1052/656G.
32. CAB 128/29 CM 34 (55).
33. The Foreign Office and Cabinet archives for the years after 1957 were, at the time of writing, still closed and the account of the diplomatic exchanges during the period 1958–63 consequently drew heavily on Macmillan's memoirs to supplement the published documents. Later archives are now available and some use was made of them in a section entitled 'Macmillan and the Soviet Union', in Keeble, *Harold Macmillan: Aspects of a Political Life*, ed. R Aldous & S. Lee (London: Macmillan, 1999), but these did not change the main thrust of the present chapter.
34. Macmillan, *Riding the Storm* (London: Macmillan, 1971), p. 252.
35. See Cmd. 380 of 1957 and 423 of 1958 for this exchange and later correspondence with the Soviet Union on summit talks.
36. CAB 128/31 CC 74 (57).
37. CAB 128/31 CC 74, 76 (57).
38. C (58) 9, 21 January 1958.
39. 582, HC Deb, February 1958, Col 1224.
40. Macmillan, *Pointing the Way* (London: Macmillan, 1972) p. 73.
41. Diary entry, 26 July 1959, quoted in Macmillan, *Pointing the Way*, p. 80.
42. Macmillan diary, 25 June, 1961, quoted by Horne, *Macmillan*, II.
43. Macmillan, *At the End of the Day* (London: Macmillan, 1973) p. 178.

44. *The Road to Communism* (Moscow, 1962) p. 497, quoted by Gromyko and Ponomarev, *Soviet Foreign Policy*, II, p. 262.
45. Macmillan diary, 4 November 1962, quoted by Horne, *op. cit.*

10 Between the Europeans and the superpowers

1. H. Kissinger, *The White House Years* (London: Weidenfeld & Nicolson, 1979).
2. Gromyko and Ponomarev (eds), *Soviet Foreign Policy*, II, p. 245.
3. CAB(63) 3, 31 October 1963.
4. FO 371/177670, Minute by Howard Smith, 17 March 1964.
5. FO 371/177680, Despatch from Sir H. Trevelyan, 6 August 1964.
6. FO 371/177681.
7. FO 371/177671.
8. FO 371/177672 and 177681, December 1964.
9. FO 371/188922 FO Tel 2237 to Washington, 28 February 1966 and FO 371/188924.
10. FCO 28/380, 1968.
11. DBPO, series III, vol. 1, pp. 14–22.
12. *Sunday Telegraph*, 2 July 1967.
13. DBPO, series III, vol. I. 48 OPD (68) 45.
14. DBPO, series III, vol. I, p. 69 CC(68)38 CAB 128/43.
15. H. Wilson, *The Labour Government 1964–1970* (London: Weidenfeld & Nicolson, 1971).
16. 592 HC Deb, 26 August 1958, Col. 1283.
17. Gromyko and Ponomarev, *Soviet Foreign Policy*, II, p. 426.
18. DBPO, series III, Vol. I, pp. 138–158 OPD(69)8, and pp. 200–205 JIC(A)69)41.
19. DBPO, series III, vol. I, p. 287.
20. DBPO, series III, vol. I, p. 474.
21. DBPO, series III, vol. I, p. 477.
22. DBPO, series III, vol. 1, pp. 513–530.
23. DBPO, series III, vol. I, p. 510.
24. CC (67)7, 9 February 1967.
25. FCO Minute, 18 April 1972, DBPO, series III, vol. I, Doc. 2, p. 18.
26. DBPO, Doc. 104, p. 354.
27. Cmd. 5924, 1975.
28. DBPO, series III, vol. II, p. 462.
29. For a discussion of the complex issues involved in the use of economic instruments in the context of East–West relations see P. Hanson, *Western Economic Statecraft in East–West Relations* ((London: Routledge for the RIIA, 1988).
30. NATO Council statement, 31 May 1984.

11 The end of confrontation

1. Cm 207 Treaty Series, no. 42 (1987).
2. 180 HC Deb, Cols 180 and 392, 14–15 November 1989.
3. Thatcher, *The Downing Street Years*, p. 789

4. See *Russia and Europe, an End to Confrontation*, ed. Neil Malcolm (London: Pinter for RIIA, 1994).
5. Thatcher, *The Downing Street Years*, pp. 792 and 795.
6. *Ibid*, p. 800–1.
7. 176 HC Deb. 176, Col. 454.
8. Thatcher, *The Downing Street Years*, p. 803.
9. *Ibid*. p. 804.
10. 183 HC Deb Col. 851, 16 January 1991.
11. 186 HC Deb Col. 323, 21 October 1991 Col 323.
12. Gromyko and Ponomarev, *Soviet Foreign Policy*, I, p. 9.
13. N. I. Lebedev, *Great October* (Moscow: Nauka, 1978) pp. 3, 12.
14. L. I. Brezhnev, *Following Lenin's Course* (Moscow: Progress, 1975), pp. 94–5.
15. BBC Summary of World Broadcasts, 5 November 1987; Tass 25 July 1988.

12 A New Russia

1. Cm 2160 and 2347, 1993.
2. *Izvestiya*, 30 June 1992.
3. *The Times*, 11 November 1992.
4. 250 HC Deb Col. 28, 18 October 1993.
5. 253 HC Deb Col. 1071, 1 February 1995.
6. 252 HC Deb Col. 686, 17 January 1995.
7. BBC Monitoring Service, 8 May 1996.
8. Herzen, *Sochineniia VII*, p. 279–80.
9. Alexander Solzhenitsyn *et al.*, *From under the Rubble* (London: Collins, 1974).
10. Itar Tass, 10 October 1997.
11. Centre TV Moscow, 28 August 1999, reported in BBC Summary of World Broadcasts.
12. Itar Tass, 17 May 1998, reported in BBC Summary of World Broadcasts.

Index

Abyssinia, *see* Ethiopia
Afghanistan
  Soviet occupation, 292, 296–8
  Soviet threat, 128
  Soviet withdrawal, 305
  threat to India, 5–6
  1921 guarantees, 83
agreements, *see* treaties
Aitmatov, Chingiz, 294
Aldermaston marches, 254
Alexeyev, General, M. V., 50, 52, 53
Andropov, Yuri, 303
Anglo–Soviet Round Table, 286
Angola, 287
appeasement, 132–42
Archangel
  intervention at, 37, 38, 39, 42, 46, 53
  withdrawal from, 64–5
Arcos Raid, 108–9
Armenia, independence, 60, 65, 70, 322
arms control
  future Russian policy, 337
  Lloyd George's policy, 90
  nuclear testing, 254–5, 258–9, 269–70
  Rapacki plan, 254
  see also treaties
Asquith, H. H., 9
Astakhov, 154
Attlee, Rt. Hon. C. R. (Earl Attlee)
  extension of Anglo–Soviet alliance, 215
  Korean War, 230
  policy towards Soviet Union, 215, 219, 220–1
  Potsdam, 199–200
  UK defence strategy, 219
Austria
  Anschluss, 138
  State Treaty, 227, 249–50
Azerbaidjan, independence, 60, 65, 70, 322

Baku
  commissars shot, 54
  intervention, 46, 54
  oil supplies, 168
  proposed bombing, 161
Baldwin, F. L., 96
Baldwin, Rt. Hon. Stanley (Earl Baldwin), 96–7, 102, 107, 122–3
  meets Litvinov, 134
  Metro-Vickers trial, 117
  National Government, 114
  1929 election, 111
Balfour, A. J. (Earl of Balfour)
  blockade of Russia, 63
  defines Lockhart's role, 42–3
  policy towards Russia, 24
  reaction to October Revolution, 19
Baltic States,
  British policy, 153, 163, 165, 173
  entry of Soviet forces, 163
  German–Soviet treaty, 155
  guarantees proposed in 1939, 150–1
  incorporation into USSR, 165
  and NATO membership, 337
  recognition, 60
  UN membership, 314, 322
  see also Estonia, Latvia, Lithuania
Barbarossa operation, attack on USSR, 164–8
BBC, 255, 313, 342
Beaverbrook, Lord
  meets Maisky, 140
  supplies for USSR, 171
Beck, Colonel, 145
Belarus, 90
  formation of CIS, 314
  UN membership, 322
Benes, E., 140
Berlin
  blockade, 222–5
  quadripartite responsibility, 268
  Wall, 261–2, 306
  1953 disturbances, 240

1954 conference, 242–3
1958 crisis, 256–8
Bessarabia, Soviet seizure, 155, 163
Bevin, Rt Hon. E.
  Anglo–Soviet alliance, 212, 215
  Berlin blockade, 222–5
  Council of Foreign Ministers, 211–12
  death, 234
  friction with United States, 212
  Marshall Plan, 217
  meets Stalin, 212
  policy towards Germany, 215, 217, 233–4
  policy towards Soviet Union, 233–4
  at Potsdam, 199–200
  Soviet–Polish war, 72, 80
  TUC victory, 105
Blair, A, 325
  policy towards Russia, 326
blockade of Russia, 62–3, 79
Blunt, A., 135
Bosnia, 326
Bolsheviks
  armistice proposals, 58
  British policy towards, 20–1, 37
  dissolution of Assembly, 32
  relations with, 28–9, 32, 42, 50–2
  state of war with, 48–63
  see also civil war, intervention, revolution
Brandt, W., Ostpolitik, 281–2
Brest-Litovsk, *see* treaties
Brezhnev, L. I.
  appointed First Secretary, 271–2
  death, 300
  invitation to UK, 273
  meets Callaghan, 287
  meets Wilson, 273
  policy stagnation, 266, 288, 291, 294
  policy towards Afghanistan, 296
  Following Lenin's Course, 315
Briand, A., 88–9
Brimelow, Sir T. (Lord Brimelow), 272
Brown, George, Rt Hon., row with Khrushchev, 252
Brzezinski, Z., 297
Buchanan, Sir G.
  aid to Cossacks, 26
  alliance with Russia, 10

  appointment and early reports, 9, 10
  ill health, 26
  interview with Tsar, 14
  leaves Petrograd, 23
  prospects for Lenin's government, 17
  reports October revolution, 19
  possible replacement, 16
  communication from Trotsky, 23
Bulganin, Marshal N. A.
  in Britain, 251–3
  relations with Eden, 251, 253
Bullitt W., 61
Burgess G., 135, 235–6
Butler R. A. (Lord Butler)
  Czech crisis, 140
  policy towards Soviet Union, 161
  1939 negotiations, 153–4
Byrnes J., 211

Cadogan, Sir A.
  Soviet neutrality, 165
  talks with Maisky, 139
  views on Churchill, 199
  work of Military Mission, 203
Callaghan, Rt. Hon. L. J. (Lord Callaghan)
  communism in Portugal, 287
  policy towards Soviet Union, 288
Campbell J. R., 99
Carrington, Lord, talks on Afghanistan, 298
Carter J., President, 295, 297
Catherine the Great, 4
Caucasus
  British support, 60, 69
  British withdrawal, 59, 65
  conflicts, 324, 345
  entry of Red Army, 72
  intervention, 40, 46, 60
  proposed UK–US air force, 178
  recognition of republics, 60
  see also Chechnya
Cecil, Lord Robert (Viscount Cecil)
  intervention, 37, 44, 51, 54–5
  Russia Committee, 28
  support for anti-Bolsheviks, 25, 26
  'zones of influence' convention, 26

Chamberlain, Rt Hon. Sir A.
  breach of relations, 108–9
  Foreign Secretary, 102
  policy towards Soviet Union,
    102–103, 134
Chamberlain, Rt Hon. A. N.
  European policy, 137
  Maisky's report on, 140
  policy towards Soviet Union, 145,
    150
  Prime Minister, 123
  replaced by Churchill, 162
Chancellor, R., 3
Chechnya,
  Russian attack, 324, 325, 338, 345,
    347
Chernenko, K., 300, 303
Chernomyrdin, V., 327
Chicherin, G. V.
  at Genoa conference, 89
  in London, 12, 15
  opinion of Locarno Treaty, 104
  on state of war with Britain, 48
  succeeded by Litvinov, 115
  1921 Trade Agreement, 75
Chilston, Viscount, reports on Soviet
    Union, 125, 138
China
  future Russian policy, 328
  Korean War, 229–30
  nuclear weapons, 270
  proposed sale of Harrier aircraft, 296
  Sino–Soviet dispute, 268
  United Nations, 230
  1927 disturbances, 107–8
Churchill, W. S. (Sir Winston)
  aid to Soviet Union, 168
  alliance with Soviet Union, 147, 149
  Berlin: blockade, 222–3;
    disturbances (1953), 240
  change in Soviet Union, 246–7
  coexistence, 244
  contest with Lloyd George, 19
  convoys to Soviet Union, 181–2
  Eastern Europe, spheres of interest
    in, 190–1
  Fulton speech, 214
  German–Soviet agreement of 1939,
    160

hydrogen bomb, 244
Iron Curtain, 196, 214
Korean War, 230
Maisky reports on, 140
Malenkov, proposed meeting with,
    240, 246–7
  in Malta, 191
  in Moscow, 176–7, 191
  messages to Stalin, 162, 166, 181,
    203
  policy on Poland, 185–6, 187,
    195–6, 240
  policy after Stalin, 239–40, 241–3
  post-1918 policy, 56–7, 59, 71
  post-1945 frontiers, 173
  at Potsdam, 198–9
  proposed use of German troops in
    intervention, 66
  'Red menace', 103, 106, 108–9
  Second Front, 174–9
  Soviet threat, 189, 195–6
  Soviet Union and League of
    Nations, 127
  strategic exports, 244
  summits, 203–4, 228
  at Teheran, 185–6
  and Truman, 196–7
  at Yalta, 192–5
Civil War, 60–1, 63–6
  see also intervention
Clark Kerr, Sir A. (Lord Inverchapel)
  post-war planning, 183
  Second Front, 179
  Stalin, 201–2
Clemenceau, G.
  Bolsheviks, 26
  Polish intervention, 66
  trade with Russia, 70
Cocom, see trade
Cold War
  defined, 206
  Labour restiveness, 251
Cominform, 218
Comintern, 99, 113, 115, 132
  Anti-Comintern Pact, 136
commerce, see trade
Commonwealth of Independent
    States, 314
Communist Party (British)

arrest of leaders, 105, 106
Czechoslovakia, 278
formation, 79
conferences
  Anglo–Soviet (1924), 98
  Anglo–Soviet trade unionists, 105
  see also under individual locations
containment, doctrine, 206–7, 234–5
convoys, *see* supplies
correlation of forces, 221, 316, 340
Council of Foreign Ministers
  formation, 200
  meetings, 211–12, 217, 219, 224, 227
  role, 208
Crabb, Commander, 252
Crimean War, 5
Cripps, Sir S.
  ambassador, 162
  delays Churchill's message to Stalin, 166
  interview with Stalin, 162, 165
  memorandum to Molotov, 166
  return to London, 166
  visits Moscow, 161
  and Vyshinsky, 164, 166
Cromie, Captain F. N. A., murder, 50, 51
Crowe, Sir E., 99
Cuba, 263–4
Curzon of Kedleston, Marquess
  Afghanistan, 6, 86, 95
  Caucasus, 65, 69
  Foreign Secretary, 58
  intervention, 37, 64, 65
  Lausanne conference, 93
  Lord President, 102
  Poland, 72–3; Curzon line, 77, 186, 193
  prisoners of war, 72
  Soviet subversion, 86–7
  trade negotiations, 73–4
  1923 ultimatum, 95–6
Czechoslovakia
  Czech–Soviet Treaty, 133
  German occupation, 143
  Marshall Plan, 217
  troops in Russia, 31, 37, 39, 45, 49, 53, 62

1938–9 crises, 138–43
1948 *coup*, 222
1968 crisis, 277–8

Daily Worker, 113
Daladier, E., 148
Davison, S., 95
Declaration of Common Purpose, UK–US (1957), 256
Declaration on Liberated Europe, 193, 195
Denikin, General A. I., 55, 57, 61–2, 69, 71–2
  threatens Moscow, 64–5
detente, 285–6, 295, 301
Diehards, 85, 107–8
  see also Joynson-Hicks
disarmament, *see* arms control
Disraeli, B. (Lord Beaconsfield), 5
Drummond, Air Marshal Sir P. R. M., 178
Dubcek, A., 277
Duff Cooper, 188
Dulles, John F., 239
  rollback policy, 241
Dumbarton Oaks conference, 188
Dunsterville, Major-General L. C., 46, 54

Eastern Europe
  peace treaties, 216
  political evolution, 306–7
  UK policy, 191, 198, 208–9
  see also Declaration on Liberated Europe and *individual countries*
Eastern Locarno, 127
Eden, Sir A. (Earl of Avon)
  Berlin conference, 244
  coexistence, 246
  comments on Churchill, 199
  convoys, 182
  exchanges with Bulganin, 248, 251, 253
  Geneva conferences, 245–6, 250–1
  German attack on USSR, 167
  Germany and NATO, 248
  Korean War, 238
  Khrushchev visit, 251–3
  in Moscow, 129–32, 173, 183–4

Eden, Sir A. (Earl of Avon) (*cont.*)
  opinion of Stalin, 203
  at Potsdam, 198
  Prime Minister, 250
  resignation, 139, 254
  Suez, 253
  summits, 242, 247
  1939 negotiations, 149
Edinburgh, Duke of, visits Moscow, 296
Edward VII, King, 8
Eisenhower, Dwight D., President,
  and Churchill, 244, 247
  Hungarian crisis, 254
  invites Khrushchev, 259
  and Macmillan, 255
  Paris summit, 260
Eliot, Sir Charles, 53, 62
Elizabeth I, Queen, and Ivan IV, 3
Elizabeth II, Queen, in Moscow, 323-4
Enigma, 174
espionage, 95, 109, 235-6, 258, 279-80, 325
Estonia, 62, 312
  see also Baltic States
Ethiopia
  Italian invasion, 135
  Soviet intervention, 287
European Advisory Commission, 184, 187-8, 197, 202
  Berlin, 224
European Defence Community, 233, 239, 247
European integration, 239, 256, 267
European security, 247-8, 277
  see also Helsinki

Falklands War, Soviet reaction, 299
Finland,
  British aid, 160
  independence, 60-1
  Russian Civil War, 64
  Soviet attack, 160-1
  Soviet policy, 216, 220
  UK declaration of war, 172
fisheries, 95, 112
Foch, Marshal F., Civil War, 66
France
  European Defence Community, 248
  fall of Paris, 162
  German entry into NATO, 248
  relations with Soviet Union, 26, 58, 68-9, 90, 93, 104, 126, 268, 287
  Soviet-Finnish war, 160-1
  Vietnam, 245
  1939 negotiations, 156
Fuchs, V., 235

Garstin, Captain, 30
gas, use against Bolsheviks, 65
Gascoigne, Sir A., Korean War, 231
Gaulle, C. de, President, 256, 268, 276
GB-USSR Association, 258
General Strike, 105
Geneva
  Foreign Ministers' Conference (1954), 245
  Laos Conference, 262
  Summit Conference (1957), 250-1
Genoa Conference (1922), 88-91
George V, King, 15, 97
Georgia
  conflict, 345
  recognition, 31, 65, 72
  support, 71
Germany
  attacks Greece, Yugoslavia, 165
  attacks Holland, Belgium, 161
  attacks Poland, 156, 159
  attacks Soviet Union, 164, 168
  conscription, 128
  and Czechoslovakia, 138-41
  declaration of war, 159
  Federal Republic of Germany, 224-5, 238
  German Democratic Republic, 225, 282
  NATO, 218, 249
  Ostpolitik, 281-2,
  policy towards Bolsheviks, 33, 41
  post-1945 settlement, 184, 187, 198-9, 209, 214-5, 217, 221-2, 227, 233-4
  quadripartite responsibility, 268
  rearmament, 232-3
  relations with Soviet Union, 90-1, 130, 154-5, 164, 281-2, 287, 295, 309

reunification, 165, 233–4, 238, 243, 308–9
Rhineland, 134
surrender in Italy, 195
trade with Soviet Union, 165, 295
see also Berlin, World War I, World War II
Gladstone, W. E., 6
Gorbachev, M. S.
  arms control, 305
  career, 302–3
  foreign policy, 319
  leaves CPSU, 314
  reforms, 303–8, 310
  resigns, 314
  Thatcher relationship, 304, 307, 310
  visits Britain, 303, 305
  1991 *coup*, 313
Gough, Lt. Gen. Sir H., 62, 64
Greece
  German attack, 165
  Soviet policy, 216, 218, 220
  US aid, 217
Gregory, J. D., 65, 107
Grey, Sir E., 10
Gromyko, A. A., 276, 290, 298
Group of Seven, 328

Hague Conference (1922), 92
Hailsham, Viscount, Test-Ban Treaty, 269
Halifax, Viscount
  ambassador to United States, 197
  Baku bombing, 160
  Foreign Secretary, 139
  Maisky talks with, 140
  1939 negotiations, 141, 146–7, 148–52
Harding, Mrs. S., 95
Harvey, Sir O., 69
Hayter, Sir W.
  coexistence, 246
  Soviet policy, 248, 251
Heath, Rt. Hon. E. R. G.
  Prime Minister, 278
  Test-Ban Treaty, 269
Helsinki Conference, 284, 286
Henderson, A.
  Foreign Secretary, 111
  in Petrograd, 16
Herriot, E., 126
Hess, R., 166
Hewlett Johnson, 122
Hill, G., 50
Hinsley, Cardinal A., 147
Hitler, A.
  attack on Soviet Union, 163–8
  Chancellor, 116
  meeting with Simon, 130
Hoare, Sir S. (Viscount Templewood), 149
Hodges, F., 80
Hodgson, R. M. (Sir Robert), 86, 97, 103, 106, 110
Holman, Maj-Gen. H. C., 62
Home, Earl of (Sir A. Douglas-Home, Lord Home of the Hirsel), 262, 269
  expulsion of Soviet agents, 280
  in Moscow, 280
Hopkins, Harry, 196
Horne, Sir R.
  breach of relations, 108
  1921 agreement, 82–3
Howe, Rt. Hon. Sir G., 305
Hudson, R., 143, 145
Hull, Cordell, 175
Hungary
  British aid, 307
  Soviet occupation, 253
  UK declaration of war, 172–3
Hurd, D., 312, 323

IMF, funding for Russia, 323
India
  Khrushchev visit, 251
  Soviet influence, 228–9
Indo-China, Geneva Conference, 246
intervention in Russia
  landings, 43, 45–7
  operations, 52–4, 62–6
  preparations, 36–43
investment
  pre-1914, 11, 90
  in Russian Federation, 330–1
Iran
  Anglo–Soviet campaign, 172
  Soviet withdrawal, 218

Iraq, 344
Ironside, Maj. Gen. E., 62
Ivan IV, Tsar, 3

Jackling, Sir R., 283
Japan
  Manchuria, 115
  and Russia, 338
  Soviet entry into war, 191, 197
  1939 hostilities with Soviet Union, 153
  see also intervention
Jaruzelski, Gen., 298
Johnson, Lyndon, 276, 277
Joint Advisory Council, 105
Joynson-Hicks, W. (Viscount Brentford), 103, 105, 106, 108–9, 114
Jupiter, operation, 176, 178

Kamenev, L.
  trial, 136
  1921 negotiations, 78, 81
Kaplan, Fanny, 49
Katyn, 190
Kelly, Sir D., 234
Kemp, Rear-Admiral T. W., 28
Kennan, George, 206–7, 216, 308, 348
Kennedy, John F.
  Cuba, 264
  and Khrushchev, 261
  and Macmillan, 265
Kerensky, A. F., 16–17
Keynes, J. M. (Lord Keynes), 122
KGB, 2, 289, 315, 346
  see also espionage
Khasbulatov, R., 323
Khrushchev, N. S.
  Berlin crisis, 257–8, 261
  British visit, 252–3
  denounces Stalin, 251
  and Eisenhower, 260
  at Geneva, 250–1
  in India, 251
  Paris summit, 260
  Soviet power, 255–6
Kiev, capture by Poles, 72
Kiriyenko, S., 327
Kissinger, Henry, 265

Knox, Maj. Gen. A. W. F., 16, 31, 40, 62
Know How Fund, 307
Kolchak, Admiral A. V., 57, 62, 65
Korean War, 229–31, 239
Kornilov, General, 16
Kosovo, 345
Kosygin, A.
  in London, 274
  meets Thatcher, 296
  relations with Wilson, 272–6
Kozyrev, A., 323
Krasin, L
  Chargé d'Affaires, 107
  1921 negotiations, 73–5, 77, 81
Kroger, P. and H., 258
Kuibyshev, evacuation of Embassies, 173

Labour movement
  attitude to Bolsheviks, 51
  policy towards Soviet Russia, 68, 79–80
Landsbergis, President, 312
Lansbury, G., 79
Laos, Geneva Conference, 262
Latvia, 31, 62, 312
  see also Baltic States
Lausanne Conference, 93
Law, Rt. Hon. A. Bonar, 19, 69, 96
League of Nations
  Soviet expulsion, 160
  Soviet membership, 125, 127
Leahy, Admiral, 208
Lebedev, N. I., 315
Lenin, V. I.
  attack on, 49
  doctrine, 87, 218, 303, 315; *see also* USSR ideology
  Genoa Conference, 90
  NEP, 97
  peace proposals, 22
  reprisals against, 50
  on state of war with Britain, 48
Lindley, F. (Sir Francis), 31–2, 41, 44
Lindsay, Sir R., 107
Lithuania, 62
  admission to U. N., 314
  attack on TV station, 312

declaration of sovereignty, 312
see also Baltic States
Litvinov, M. M.
  arrest, 50
  British–Soviet relations, 127
  Commissar for Foreign Affairs, 115, 125
  collective security, 125, 131, 139
  dismissal, 147
  in London, 12, 15, 28, 134
  meets Eden in Moscow, 131
  Metro–Vickers trial, 117
  Poland, 143
  policy of peace, 119
  Urquhart agreement, 93
  1921 negotiations, 73
  1939 negotiations, 143, 145
Lloyd George, D. (Earl Lloyd George)
  Bolshevism, 60–61
  Bullitt, 62
  clash with Churchill, 19, 56–7
  fall, 93
  Genoa Conference, 88–91
  Guildhall speech, 67
  Maisky, talks with, 140
  October Revolution, 20
  Polish policy, 72–3, 75–7
  Prinkipo, 58
  post-1918 policy towards Soviet Union, 54–62, 67–72
  Rapallo, 317
  Spa Conference, 76
  World War I policy, 13–14, 16, 46
  1918 election, 56
  1921–4 treaties, 3, 99
  1939 negotiations, 149
Lockhart, R. H. B., 27–8, 32–3, 37
  reports, 42, 51
  support for anti-Bolsheviks, 42, 50–51
Lonsdale G., 258
Loraine, Sir P., 126
Lvov, Prince, 16
Lvov, 186

McCarthy, J., 235
MacDonald, Rt Hon. J. R.
  Metro-Vickers trial, 118
  National Government, 114, 122
  and Nicholas II, 8
  opinion of Bolsheviks, 97
  Soviet Union and Germany, 130
  United Socialist Council, 15
  Zinoviev Letter, 99–101
  1923–4 Government, 97–101
  1929 Government, 111, 113–14
MacDonald, W., 117
Macdonogh, Maj. Gen. Sir G. M. W., 26, 41, 43, 55
MacKillop, D., 136
Maclean, D., 122, 135, 235–6
Maclean, Sir F., 142, 161
Macmillan, H. (Earl of Stockton)
  Berlin, 257–8, 261–2
  BBC, 255
  Communism, 121, 256
  and Eisenhower, 255
  exchanges with Bulganin, 255
  and Kennedy, 264
  and Khrushchev, 258–60
  Paris summit, 260
  Prime Minister, 254
  Test-Ban Treaty, 258, 262, 269
  visits Finland, 160
  visits to Soviet Union, 121, 257–8
McNeil, H., 235
Maisky, I.
  ambassador, 12, 114, 117, 161, 201, 292
  British trade, 161
  with Eden in Moscow, 131
  on guarantee to Poland, 144
  refugee, 10
  talks with British politicians, 139–40
Major, J.
  and Gorbachev, 313
  and Yeltsin, 313, 324
Malenkov, G. M.
  Chairman, Council of Ministers, 239
  Churchill proposal, 246–7
Malik, Y., 231, 243
Malleson, Maj. Gen. W., 54
Malta, UK–US meeting, 191
Marsh, Brig. Gen. F. G., 64
Marshall, G.
  European recovery, 217
  US policy, 216
Marxism, *see* USSR, ideology

Mason Macfarlane, Lt. Gen. Sir N., 170
May, A. Nunn, 235
Metropolitan–Vickers, trial of employees, 116–8
Middle East
  Khrushchev policy, 252
  UK policy, 218–9
Mikolajcik, 196
military missions, 170, 174, 201
Milner, Viscount, 14, 26–7, 39, 55
Mirbach, Count von, 41, 49
Molotov, V. M.
  Berlin Conference, 244
  Berlin visit, 164
  Council of Foreign Ministers, 211
  Cripps comment on, 161
  meets Eden, 131
  Geneva Conference, 245
  Marshall Plan, 217
  Poland, 195
  replaces Litvinov, 147
  second front, 175–6, 179
  1939 negotiations, 148–54
Montgomery, B., Field Marshal (Viscount Montgomery), 216
Montreux Conference, 135
Morrison, Rt Hon. H., 234
Moscow
  British Embassy, 288–300
  British threat to bomb, 64
  Churchill visits, 176–7, 190–1
  Denikin threat, 64
  Eden visits, 131, 173
  Foreign Ministers' wartime meetings, 179, 183–4
  German threat, 173
  Government moves from Petrograd, 41
Munich agreement, 141, 159
Murmansk
  Hurricanes, 171
  intercept station, 175
  intervention, 28, 37–8, 46, 53–4
  supply base, 14
Muscovy Company, 3

Nagy, Imre, 253
NATO
  extension to Eastern Europe, 326
  formation, 227
  German membership, 248
  NATO–Russia Joint Council, 327
  policy towards Soviet Union, 301
  see also treaties
Neurath, von, and Simon, 130
New Economic Policy, 84, 97
New Political Thinking, 308
Nicholas II, Tsar
  deposition and murder, 14, 49, 51
  meets Edward VII, 8
  relations with Britain, 10, 14, 15
Nixon, President R., 280
Non-Intervention Committee, 135
nuclear weapons, *see* arms control

O'Grady, J. M. P., 72
Olympic Games, boycott, 297–8
O'Malley, O. S. (Sir O.), 94
Orel, 64
Ottawa Conference, 114
Ovey, Sir E., 112, 117, 123
Owen, Rt Hon. D., 287

Paderewski, I. J., 66
Palmerston, Viscount, 4–5
Paris Summit (1960), 260
Peace Conference (1919), 55–6, 58
peaceful coexistence, 246, 251, 316
Pearl Harbor, 173
Penkovsky, O., 258
perestroika, see Gorbachev
Persia, *see* Iran
Peter the Great, Tsar, 3, 4
Peterson, Sir M., 215
Philby, K., 235
Pirie-Gordon, H., 64
planning, post-1945, 183–91
Poland
  British aid, 307
  British guarantee, 143
  frontier, 173–4, 186, 199
  independence, 60, 62
  partition, 159
  post-1945 settlement, 183, 185–6, 190–1, 193, 195–6, 199
  relations with Russia, 6
  Warsaw uprising, 189–90
  war with Russia, 66, 72–3, 77–9

1939 negotiations, 143–5, 151, 155–8
1941 agreement with Soviet Union, 170
1980 crisis, 292, 298–9
Poole, Maj. Gen. F. C., 37, 39, 46, 54
Portugal, 287
Post-Hostilities Planning Committee, 188
Potsdam Conference (1945), 197–200
Primakov, Y., 327
Prinkipo, proposed conference, 58–9, 69
propaganda, 74, 86, 112, 131, 167, 175, 216
Putin, V., 328
   Acting President, 334, 338, 345, 347

Quebec Conference, 179, 183

Rakovsky, C., 98
Rapacki, atom-free zone, 254
Rawlinson, General Sir H., 62
Reagan, R., President, 299
Reilly, Sir P., 256
Reilly, S., 50
religion, 95
repatriation of Soviet prisoners, 193–4
revolution
   March 1917, 14
   November 1917, 16–17; British reaction, 19–26
   1905, 8
Reynaud, P., 136
Rhineland, reoccupation, 134
Ribbentrop, J. von, 130, 154–5, 164
Roberts, Sir F.
   Berlin blockade, 223–4
   Soviet policy, 210, 212–3
Robertson, G.
   Berlin, 224
Romania
   cooperation with Germany, 165
   UK declaration of war, 172
   1939 negotiations, 143, 155–6
Roosevelt, F. D., President
   aid to Soviet Union, 167
   with Churchill in Washington, 178
   at Malta, 191
   and Second Front, 175, 178
   at Teheran, 185
   withdrawal of US forces, 194
   at Yalta, 191–4
Russell, B. (Earl Russell), 79, 210
Russia (pre-1917)
   British relations with, 1–17
   Russo-Japanese War, 8
   wartime loans, 13
Russia Committee, 28, 43, 214, 229
Russian Federation
   British trade and investment, 330–1
   British policy towards, 343–8
   declaration of sovereignty, 312
   economic crisis, 327–8, 329
   financial aid, 329
   foreign policy, 326, 336–9
   political orientation, 332–5
   Security Council, 312
   successor to USSR, 322
   visas, 347
   withdrawal of ambassador, 347
Russophobia, 6–7, 346
Russophilia, 6–7, 9
Rutskoi, A. Vice President, 323

Salisbury, Marquess of, 241, 247
San Francisco Conference, 188
Sargent, Sir O., 129, 161, 197
Sazonov, S. D., 10
Scapa Flow, proposed conference, 179, 183
Schnurre, 154
Schulenburg, Count W., 154
Sealion, Operation, 163
Second Front, 170–1, 174–9, 185, 187
Secret Intelligence Service, 50, 117
Seeds, Sir W., 142, 146, 147, 150, 154, 161
Shevardnadze, E., warns of coup, 312
Shinwell, E. (Lord Shinwell), 80
Siberia, *see* intervention
Simon, Sir J., 114–15, 122–3, 126, 130
   Metro–Vickers trial, 116–8
Sledgehammer, operation, 175
Sokolnikov. G., 34, 112
Soviet Union, *see* USSR
Spa, conference (1920), 76
Spain, Civil War, 135–6
Sputnik, 255

Stalin, J. V.
  and Churchill, 161–2, 171, 176–8, 190–1, 214
  convoys, 181
  death, 239
  denunciation by Khrushchev, 251
  German–Soviet agreement, 155
  Hess incident, 167
  League of Nations, 127
  meets Bevin, 212
  meets Eden, 131
  Poland, 190
  post-1945 planning, 183
  purges, 136, 138
  relations with Britain, 86, 104, 110, 118, 165–6, 215
  relations with United States, 210
  revival of support for, 294
  Second Front, 176, 178–9
  summits, 203
  at Teheran, 186
  1939 speech, 142, 145, 155
Stalingrad, 186
Stepashin, S., 328
Strang, W. (Lord Strang)
  coexistence, 246
  with Eden in Moscow, 131
  European Advisory Commission, 202
  Metro–Vickers trial, 117–18, 124
  1939 negotiations, 151–2
strategy
  British military, 21–2, 33, 43, 129–30, 134, 167, 170 188, 198, 218–9, 221, 226–7, 233
  coordination with Soviet, 174–6, 178, 185, 187
Stresemann, G., 110
submarine L55, 110
subversion, *see* propaganda
Suez crisis, 253
summit diplomacy, 203–4
  see also individual conferences
supplies, 171–2, 177, 180–3

Teheran
  Conference, 183–6
  US hostages, 297
Thatcher, M.
  German reunification, 308–9
  and Gorbachev, 304, 307, 310, 313
  in Moscow, 296, 304, 312
  policy towards Soviet Union, 296, 301, 308
  and Yeltsin, 311
Thomson, Maj.-Gen. W. H., 62
Thornton, L. C., 117
trade
  agreements: of 1921, 73–5, 82, 86–7, 96, 109; of 1930, 113–5; of 1934, 126, 143; of 1947, 219; of 1975, 285
  British–Russian, 3, 10–11, 330
  British–Soviet, 44, 85, 110, 114, 231, 252, 274–5, 295
  Defence League, 114
  embargoes, 117–18, 232, 298
  imperial preference, 115
  strategic controls, 244
Trades Union Congress,
  and Czechoslovakia, 278
  General Strike, 105
treaties and agreements (*note: Only those referred to in the text*)
  Anglo–French (1917), 26, 55
  Anglo–Russian (1907), 8; with Ivan IV, 3
  Anglo–Soviet (1924), 98, 103; alliance (1942), 172–4, 189, 212, 215, 216, 249; construction of Embassies (1987), 304; declaration (1941), 170; exchange of prisoners (1920), 72; protocol on consultations (1975), 285; science and culture (1987), 304; supply protocol (1941–3), 172, 180
  Anglo–Soviet–Iranian (1942), 172
  Anti-Ballistic Missile, 283
  Anti-Comintern, 136
  Austrian State (1955), 249
  Belovezhskaya Puschcha (1991), 314
  Brest-Litovsk (1918), 34
  Brussels (1948), 222
  Conventional Forces in Europe (1990), 327

CSCE (Helsinki) Final Act, 286–7
Dunkirk (1947), 219
EU–Russia, Partnership and Cooperation (1997), 328
Final Settlement for Germany (1990), 309
Franco–Czech (1926), 104
Franco–Polish (1926), 104
Franco–Soviet (1932), 116; (1935)133–4, 136
FRG–Czech (1973), 282
FRG–GDR (1972), 282
FRG–Poland (1970), 282
FRG–Soviet (1970), 282
German–Soviet (1926), 104; (Aug 1939), 91, 154, 156, 158; (Sept 1939), 159
INF, 305
Locarno (1925), 104, 133–4
London (1915), 13, 23
North Atlantic (1949), 224
Nuclear Non-Proliferation (1968), 281
Quadripartite on Berlin (1971), 282
Rapallo, 90–1
SALT I and II, 283, 295
Soviet–Czech (1935), 133
Soviet–Polish (1932), 116; (1941) 170
UK–Russia Principles of Relations (1992), 322
Versailles, 88
Trevelyan, H. (Lord Trevelyan), 271
Tripolitania, Soviet policy, 216
Trotsky, L., 16, 28, 30, 33
Truman, H. President
  aid to Greece and Turkey, 217
  Korean War, 230
  Potsdam, 197
  proposal to meet Stalin, 196–7
Turkey
  relations with Soviet Union, 165, 185, 220
  US aid, 217
  US missiles removed, 264

U2 aircraft, 260
Ukraine, 2, 26, 31, 34, 60
  formation of CIS, 314
  separatism, 142
  UN membership, 322
United Nations
  conception, 188, 193
  Hungary, 254
  Korea, 230
  role, 208
United States
  1918 policy, 45
  post-1945 policy, 197–8, 206–12, 216–17, 247–8
  see also under subjects and individuals
USSR
  armed forces, 126
  arms control, 304–5
  arms for Egypt, 248
  British policy towards: *this is the theme running through much of the book – some specific references which may be noted are on pages,* 102, 106–8, 159–60, 226, 233, 241, 276, 279, 284, 315, 317–8, 340–2 (*others are indexed under relevant events and individuals*)
  claims against, 90, 92, 98, 112
  collapse of empire, 306–7
  Communist Party, 303
  conduct of relations, 283–301; *see also* diplomatic relations
  credits, 98, 131, 135, 286
  diplomatic relations, 86, 98, 107–9, 111–2
  disarmament, 127; *see also* arms control
  dissolution, 314
  economy, 255, 294–5
  enters Czechoslovakia, 277–8
  European Community, relations with, 337, 344
  famine, 88
  foreign policy, 234, 284, 288, 315–9
  ideology, 219, 272, 303, 335, 339
  immunity of trade representatives, 109, 113
  Korean War, 229–31
  Marshall Plan, 217
  Middle East, 218
  national interest, 272, 335–9
  nuclear weapons, 228, 321

USSR (*cont.*)
  peaceful coexistence, 316, 318
  post-1945 role, 206–10, 212–15, 216, 220
  purges, 136, 138
  recognition, 83, 97
  Suez, 255
  and third world, 226, 229, 263, 338
  under Brezhnev, 291, 293–5, 300; Khrushchev, 241, 255; *see also* Gorbachev reforms
  relationship with United States, 225–6, 276
  World War II alliance, 200–5
  1920–1 negotiations, 73–5, 81–3
  1939 negotiations, 142–58
  see also under subjects and individuals
Urquhart, L., 92–3

Vansittart, R. (Lord Vansittart)
  discussions with Maisky, 124, 127, 140
  Metro–Vickers trial, 117
  Soviet policy, 115, 128, 129–30, 133–4, 136, 161
Victoria, Queen, 6, 7
Vietnam War, 275–6
Vladivostok, Allied landing, 38–9
Voroshilov, Marshal K. E., 130, 155
Vyshinsky, A., 166, 184, 218, 227

Wardrop, O., 49
Wavell, Field Marshal Sir A. (Earl Wavell), 134, 172

Webb, S. (Lord Passfield), 122
Wells, H. G., 122
Wilson, Rt Hon. H. (Lord Wilson), 3, 219, 270–6, 285–6
Wilson, Sir Horace, 140
Wilson, Woodrow, President, 38, 45, 60, 63
Wise, E. F., 69, 108
World Economic Conference, 118
World Trade Organisation, 328
World War I, 13–16, 22, 33–6, 44, 47
World War II, *see under subjects and individuals*
Wrangel, General Baron P. N., 61, 72, 75
Wynne, G., 258

Yalta Conference, 191–5
Yeltsin, B., President,
  foreign policy, 324
  and Gorbachev, 311
  health, 325, 327
  in London, 311, 322
  resigns, 334
  shelling White House, 323
  1991 coup, 313
Young, D., 51
Yudenich, General N. N., 57, 61–2, 64, 66
Yugoslavia, 165–6

Zinoviev
  alleged letter, 99–101, 102–3
  trial, 136